ARCTIC EXPLORATIONS

IN THE YEARS 1853, '54, '55

BY

ELISHA KENT KANE, M. D., U. S. N.

VOL. II.

PHILADELPHIA
CHILDS AND PETERSON,
124 ARCH STREET.
1856.

J.Warr.

HENRY GRINNELL.

Henry Grinnell

Arctic Explorations

in

1853, 1854, 1855

Elisha Kent Kane

In two volumes

Volume II

Arno Press & The New York Times
New York * 1971

PHYSICIAN TRAVELERS

Editor
ROBERT M. GOLDWYN, M.D.

This book is reprinted from a copy in the
Francis A. Countway Library of Medicine

Library of Congress Catalog Card No. 74-115615
ISBN 0-405-01735-9
ISBN for complete set 0-405-01710-3

Manufactured in the United States of America, 1971

Physician Travelers

ARCTIC EXPLORATIONS:

The Second Grinnell Expedition

IN SEARCH OF

SIR JOHN FRANKLIN,

1853, '54, '55.

BY

ELISHA KENT KANE, M.D., U. S. N.

ILLUSTRATED BY UPWARDS OF THREE HUNDRED ENGRAVINGS,

From Sketches by the Author.

THE STEEL PLATES EXECUTED UNDER THE SUPERINTENDENCE OF J. M. BUTLER,
THE WOOD ENGRAVINGS BY VAN INGEN & SNYDER.

VOL. II.

PHILADELPHIA:
CHILDS & PETERSON, 124 ARCH STREET.
J. B. LIPPINCOTT & CO., 20 N. FOURTH ST.
BOSTON: PHILLIPS, SAMPSON & CO., 13 WINTER STREET.
NEW YORK: G. P. PUTNAM & CO., 321 BROADWAY.
CINCINNATI: APPLEGATE & CO., 48 MAIN STREET.
1856.

STEREOTYPED BY L. JOHNSON & CO.
PHILADELPHIA.
PRINTED BY J. B. LIPPINCOTT & CO.

CONTENTS.

CHAPTER VI.

CHAPTER VII.

CHAPTER VIII.

CHAPTER IX.

CHAPTER X.

CHAPTER XI.

CHAPTER XII.

CHAPTER XXVII.

CHAPTER XXVIII.

CHAPTER XXIX.

APPENDIX.

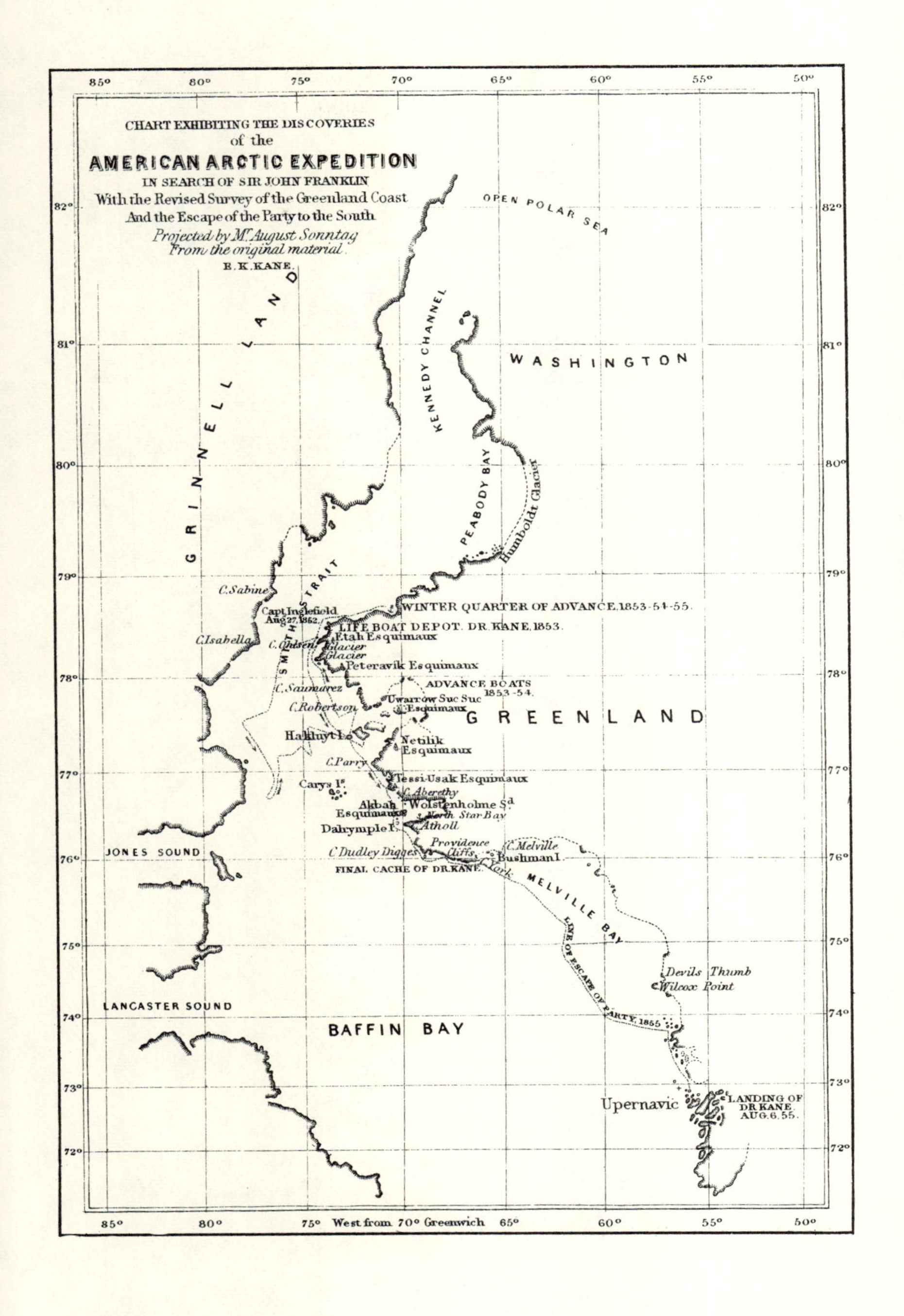
CHART EXHIBITING THE DISCOVERIES
of the
AMERICAN ARCTIC EXPEDITION
IN SEARCH OF SIR JOHN FRANKLIN
With the Revised Survey of the Greenland Coast
And the Escape of the Party to the South
Projected by Mr. August Sonntag
From the original material.
E. K. KANE.
OPEN POLAR SEA
GRINNELL LAND
KENNEDY CHANNEL
WASHINGTON
PEABODY BAY
Humboldt Glacier
SMITH STRAIT
C. Sabine
WINTER QUARTER OF ADVANCE, 1853-54-55.
Capt Inglefield Aug 27. 1852.
LIFE BOAT DEPOT. DR. KANE. 1853.
C. Isabella
Etah Esquimaux
Glacier
Glacier
Peteravik Esquimaux
ADVANCE BOATS 1853-54.
C. Saumarez
Uwarrow Suc Suc Esquimaux
C. Robertson
GREENLAND
Hakluyt I.
Netilik Esquimaux
C. Parry
Tessi-Usak Esquimaux
Carys Is.
C. Aberethy
Akbah Esquimaux
Wolstenholme Sd.
North Star Bay
Dalrymple I.
Atholl
Providence Cliffs
C. Melville
C. Dudley Digges
Bushman I.
JONES SOUND
FINAL CACHE OF DR. KANE.
C. York
MELVILLE BAY
LINE OF ESCAPE OF PARTY, 1855
Devils Thumb
Wilcox Point
LANCASTER SOUND
BAFFIN BAY
Upernavic
LANDING OF DR. KANE. AUG. 6. 55.
West from Greenwich

ARCTIC EXPLORATIONS.

CHAPTER I.

MODES OF LIFE — THE INSIDE DOG — PROJECTED JOURNEY — DOG-HABITS—THE DARKNESS—RAW MEAT—PLANS FOR SLEDGING—THE SOUTHEAST WINDS — PLAN OF JOURNEY — A RELISHING LUNCH—ITINERARY—OUTFIT—CARGO AND CLOTHING—KAPETAH AND NESSAK—FOOT-GEAR—THE FOX TAIL—CARPET-KNIGHTS—BURNING CABLES.

"JANUARY 6, 1855, Saturday.—If this journal ever gets to be inspected by other eyes, the color of its pages will tell of the atmosphere it is written in. We have been emulating the Esquimaux for some time in every thing else; and now, last of all, this intolerable temperature and our want of fuel have driven us to rely on our lamps for heat. Counting those which I have added since the wanderers came back, we have twelve constantly going, with the grease and soot everywhere in proportion.

"I can hardly keep my charts and registers in any thing like decent trim. Our beds and bedding are absolutely black, and our faces begrimed with fatty carbon like the Esquimaux of South Greenland. Nearer to us, our Smith's Straits Esquimaux are much more cleanly in this branch of domestic arrangements. They attend their lamps with assiduous care, using the long radicles of a spongy moss for wick, and preparing the blubber for its office by breaking up the cells between their teeth. The condensed blubber, or more properly fat, of the walrus, is said to give the best flame.

"Our party, guided by the experience of the natives, use nearly the same form of wick, but of cotton. Pork-fat, boiled to lessen its salt, is our substitute for blubber; and, guided by a suggestion of Professor Olmstead, I mix a portion of resin with the lard to increase its fluidity. Sundry devices in the way of metal reverberators conduct and diffuse the heat, and so successfully that a single wick will keep liquid ten ounces of lard with the air around at minus 30°.

"The heat given out by these burners is astonishing. One four-wicked lamp not very well attended gives us six gallons of water in twelve hours from snow and ice of a temperature of minus 40°, raising the heat of the cabin to a corresponding extent, the lamp being entirely open. With a line-wick, another Esquimaux plan, we could bake bread or do other cookery. But the crust of the salt and the deposit from the resin are constantly fouling the flame; and the consequence is that we have been more than half the time in an atmosphere of smoke.

"Fearing the effect of this on the health of every one, crowded as we are, and inhaling so much insoluble foreign matter without intermission, I have to-day reduced the number of lights to four; two of them stationary, and communicating by tin funnels with our chimney, so as to carry away their soot.

"Mr. Wilson has relapsed. I gave him a potash (saleratus) warm bath to-day, and took his place at watch. I have now seven hours' continuous watch at one beat.

"January 12, Friday.—In reviewing our temperatures, the monthly and annual means startle me. Whatever views we may have theoretically as to the distribution of heat, it was to have been expected that so large a water-area but thirty-five miles to the S.W. by W. of our position would tell upon our records; and this supposition was strengthened by the increased fall of snow, which was clearly due to the neighborhood of this water.

"January 13, Saturday.—I am feeding up my few remaining dogs very carefully; but I have no meat for them except the carcasses of their late companions. These have to be boiled; for in their frozen state they act as caustics, and, to dogs famishing as ours have been, frozen food often proves fatal, abrading the stomach and œsophagus. One of these poor creatures had been a child's pet among the Esquimaux. Last night I found her in nearly a dying state at the mouth of our *tossut*, wistfully eyeing the crevices of the door as they emitted their forbidden treasures of light and heat. She could not move, but, completely subdued, licked my hand,—the first time I ever had such a civilized greeting from an Esquimaux dog. I carried her in among the glories of the moderate paradise she aspired to, and cooked her a dead-puppy soup. She is now slowly gaining strength, but can barely stand.

"I want all my scanty dog-force for another attempt to communicate with the bay settlements. I am confident we will find Esquimaux there alive, and they *shall* help us. I am not satisfied with Petersen, the companion of my last journey: he is too cautious for the emergency. The occasion is one that calls for every risk short of the final one that man can encounter. My mind is made up, should wind and ice at all point to its successful accomplishment, to try the thing with Hans. Hans is completely subject to my will, careful and attached to me, and by temperament daring and adventurous.

"Counting my greatest possible number of dogs, we have but five at all to be depended on, and these far from being in condition for the journey. Toodla, Jenny,—at this moment officiating as wet-nurse,—and Rhina, are the relics of my South Greenland teams; little Whitey is the solitary Newfoundlander; one big yellow and one feeble little black, all that are left of the powerful recruits we obtained from our Esquimaux brethren.

"It is a fearful thing to attempt a dog-trot of near one hundred miles, where your dogs may drop at any moment, and leave you without protection from fifty degrees below zero. As to riding, I do not look to it: we must run alongside of the sledge, as we do on shorter journeys. Our dogs cannot carry more than our scanty provisions, our sleeping-bags and guns.

"At home one would fear to encounter such hoop-spined, spitting, snarling beasts as the Esquimaux dogs of Peabody Bay. But, wolves as they are, they are far from dangerous: the slightest appearance of a missile or cudgel subdues them at once. Indispensable to the very life of their masters, they are treated, of course, with studied care and kindness; but they are taught from the earliest days of puppy-life a savory fear that makes them altogether safe companions even for the children. But they are absolutely ravenous of every thing below the human grade. Old Yellow, who goes about with arched back, gliding through the darkness more like a hyena than a dog, made a pounce the other day as I was feeding Jenny, and, almost before I could turn, had gobbled down one of her pups. As none of the litter will ever be of sledging use, I have taken the hint, and refreshed Old Yellow with a daily morning puppy. The two last of the family, who will then, I hope, be tolerably milk-fed, I shall reserve for my own eating.

"January 14, Sunday.—Our sick are about the same; Wilson, Brooks, Morton, McGary, and Riley unserviceable, Dr. Hayes getting better rapidly. How grateful I ought to be that I, the weakling of a year ago, am a well and helping man!

"At noonday, in spite of the mist, I can see the horizon gap of Charlotte Wood Fiord, between Bessie Mountain and the other hills to the southeast, growing lighter; its twilight is decidedly less doubtful. In four or five days we will have our noonday sun not more than eight degrees below the horizon. This depression, which was Parry's lowest, enabled him by turning the paper toward the south to read diamond type. We are looking forward to this more penumbral darkness as an era. It has now been fifty-two days since we could read such type, even after climbing the dreary hills. One hundred and twenty-four days with the sun below the

A SKETCH.

horizon! One hundred and forty before he reaches the rocky shadowing of our brig!

"I found an overlooked godsend this morning,—a bear's head, put away for a specimen, but completely frozen. There is no inconsiderable quantity of meat adhering to it, and I serve it out raw to Brooks, Wilson, and Riley.

"I do not know that my journal anywhere mentions

our habituation to raw meats, nor does it dwell upon their strange adaptation to scorbutic disease. Our journeys have taught us the wisdom of the Esquimaux appetite, and there are few among us who do not relish a slice of raw blubber or a chunk of frozen walrus-beef. The liver of a walrus (awuktanuk) eaten with little slices of his fat,—of a verity it is a delicious morsel. Fire would ruin the curt, pithy expression of vitality which belongs to its uncooked juices. Charles Lamb's roast-pig was nothing to awuktanuk. I wonder that raw beef is not eaten at home. Deprived of extraneous fibre, it is neither indigestible nor difficult to masticate. With acids and condiments, it makes a salad which an educated palate cannot help relishing; and as a powerful and condensed heat-making and anti-scorbutic food it has no rival.

"I make this last broad assertion after carefully testing its truth. The natives of South Greenland prepare themselves for a long journey in the cold by a course of frozen seal. At Upernavik they do the same with the narwhal, which is thought more heat-making than the seal; while the bear, to use their own expression, is 'stronger travel than all.'

"In Smith's Sound, where the use of raw meat seems almost inevitable from the modes of living of the people, walrus holds the first rank. Certainly this pachyderm, whose finely-condensed tissue and delicately-permeating fat—oh! call it not blubber—assimilate it to the ox, is beyond all others, and is the very best fuel a man can swallow. It became our constant companion whenever we could get it; and a frozen liver upon our sledge was valued far above the same weight of pemmican. Now as I write, short of all meat, without an ounce of walrus for sick or sound, my thoughts recal the frost-tempered junks of this pachydermoid amphibion as the highest of longed-for luxuries.

"My plans for sledging, simple as I once thought them, and simple certainly as compared with those of the English parties, have completely changed. Give me an eight-pound reindeer-fur bag to sleep in, an Esquimaux lamp with a lump of moss, a sheet-iron snow-melter or a copper soup-pot, with a tin cylinder to slip over it and defend it from the wind, a good *pièce de résistance* of raw walrus-beef; and I want nothing more for a long journey, if the thermometer will keep itself as high as minus 30°. Give me a bear-skin bag and coffee to boot; and with the clothes on my back I am ready for minus 60°,—but no wind.

"The programme runs after this fashion. Keep the blood in motion, without loitering on the march: and for the halt, raise a snow-house; or, if the snow lie scant or impracticable, ensconce yourself in a burrow or under the hospitable lee of an inclined hummock-slab. The outside fat of your walrus sustains your little moss fire: its frozen slices give you bread, its frozen blubber gives you butter, its scrag ends make the soup. The snow supplies you with water; and when you are ambitious of coffee there is a bagful stowed away in your boot. Spread out your bear bag, your only heavy movable; stuff your reindeer bag inside, hang your boots up outside, take a blade of bone, and scrape off all the ice from your furs. Now crawl in, the whole party of you, feet foremost; draw the top of your dormitory close, heading to leeward. Fancy yourself in Sybaris; and, if you are only tired enough, you may sleep——like St. Lawrence on his gridiron, or even a trifle better.

"January 16, Tuesday.—Again the strange phenomena of the southeast winds. The late changes of the barometer ushered them in, and all hands are astir with their novel influences. With minus 16° outside, our cabin ceiling distils dirty drops of water, our beds become doubly damp, and our stove oppressive. We are vastly more comfortable, and therefore more healthy, below hatches, when it is at —60° on deck than when it rises above —30°. The mean heat of our room since the return of the party is, as nearly as can be determined, +48°.

"The sick generally are about the same; but Wilson has symptoms showing themselves, that fill me with distress. The state of things on board begins to press upon me personally; but by sleeping day-hours I manage well enough. Hans, Ohlsen, and myself are the only three sound men of the organized company.

"January 17, Wednesday.—There is no evading it any longer: it has been evident for the past ten days that the 'present state of things cannot last.' We require meat, and cannot get along without it. Our sick have finished the bear's head, and are now eating the condemned abscessed liver of the animal, including some intestines that were not given to the dogs. We have about three days' allowance; thin chips of raw frozen meat, not exceeding four ounces in weight for each man per diem. Our poor fellows eat it with zest; but it is lamentably little.

"Although I was unsuccessful in my last attempt to reach the huts with the dogs, I am far from sure that with a proper equipment it could not be managed by walking. The thought weighs upon me. A foot-travel does not seem to have occurred to my comrades; and at first sight the idea of making for a point seventy-five miles by the shortest line from our brig, with this awfully cold darkness on, is gloomy enough.

"But I propose walking at first only as far as the broken hut at Anoatok, (the 'wind-loved spot,') and giving our poor dogs a chance of refreshing there. After this, Hans and myself will force them forward as far as we can, with nothing but our sleeping-gear, and spend the second night wherever they happen to break down. After that, we can manage the rest of the journey without any luggage but our personal clothing.

"It seems hard to sacrifice the dogs, not to speak of the rest of the party; but the necessity is too palpable and urgent. As we are now, a very few deaths would break us up entirely. Still, the emergency would not move me if I did not feel, after careful, painful thought, that the thing can be accomplished. If by the blessing of the Great Ruler it should prove successful, the result will secure the safety of all hands. No one knows as yet of my intention except Hans himself. I am quietly preparing a special outfit, and will leave with the first return of moonlight.

"McGary, my relief, calls me: he has foraged out some raw cabbage and spiced it up with curry-powder, our only remaining pepper. This, with a piece of corn-bread,—no bad article either,—he wants me to share with him. True to my old-times habitude, I hasten to the cabbage,—cold roast-beef, Worcester sauce, a head of endive, and a bottle—not one drop less—of Preston ale, (I never drink any other.) McGary, 'bring on de beans!'

"January 18, Thursday, midnight.—Wind howling on deck,—a number nine gale, a warm southeaster directly from the land. The mean temperature of this wind is —20°. Warm as this may seem, our experience has taught us to prefer —40° with a calm to —10° with a gale in the face.

"If we only had daylight, I should start as soon as the present wind subsides, counting on a three days' intermission of atmospheric disturbance. But we have no moon, and it is too dark to go tumbling about over the squeezed ice. I must wait.

"I alluded yesterday to my special equipment. Let me imagine myself explaining to the tea-table this evening's outfit, promise and purposes.

I. *Itinerary.*—From brig Advance, Rensselaer Harbor, to the Esquimaux huts of Etah Bay, following the line of ice-travel close along the coast:—

1.	From brig to Ten-mile Ravine	10	miles.
2.	From Ten-mile Ravine to Basalt Camp	6	"
3.	From Basalt Camp to Helen River	10	"
4.	Helen's River to Devil's Jaws (off Godsend Island)	9	"
5.	Godsend Island to Anoatok and Hummock Pass	7	"
6.	Hummock Pass to Refuge Inlet	7	"
7.	Refuge Inlet to Cape Hatherton	8	"
8.	Cape Hatherton to Second Hummock Pass	12	"
9.	Across Second Pass to south end of Littleton Island	8	"
10.	South end of Littleton Island to Point Salvation	2	"
11.	Point Salvation to Esquimaux huts	12	"
	Total travel in miles	91	miles.

II. *Temperature.*—Mean, about —45°. Range —40° to —60°.

III. *Resources.*—Five half-starved dogs; Hans Cristian, Dr. Kane, a light sledge, and outfit.

IV. *Outfit.*—To encounter broken ice in the midst of darkness and at a temperature destructive to life, every thing depends upon your sledge. Should it break down, you might as well break your own leg: there is no hope for you. Our sledge then is made of well-tried oak, dovetailed into a runner shod with iron. No metal is used besides, except the screws and rivets which confine the sledge to its runners. In this intense cold, iron snaps like glass, and no immovable or rigidly-fastened wood-work would stand for a moment the fierce concussions of the drive. Every thing is put together with lashings of seal-skin, and the whole fabric is the skeleton framework of a sledge as flexible as a lady's work-basket, and weighing only forty pounds. On this we fasten a sacking-bottom of canvas, tightly stretched, like its namesake of the four-post bedstead, around the margin. We call this ticking the apron and cover; the apron being a flap of sixteen inches high, surrounding the cover, and either hanging loose at its sides like a valance, or laced up down the middle. Into this apron and cover you pack your cargo, the less of it the better; and then lace and lash the whole securely together.

V. *The cargo* may consist of:—1, a blanket-bag of fur, if you can get it; but on our present sleigh-ride, buffalo being too heavy and our reindeer-skins all destroyed by wet, I take an eider-down coverlet, adding—2, a pillow stuffed with straw or shavings, to be placed under the small of the back while sleeping; 3, an extra pair of boots; and, 4, a snow-saw.

"Superadd to these the ancient soup-pot, our soap-stone kollopsut, one Esquimaux lamp, one lump of moss, one cup, and a tinder-box; all these for the kitchen;—a roll of frozen meat-biscuit, some frozen lady-fingers of raw hashed fox, a small bag of coffee, and twenty-four pieces of hard tack, (ship's bread,) for the larder;—our fire-arms, and no less essential ice-poles:—all these, no more nor less, and you have the entirety of our outfit,—the means wherewith we are to track this icy labyrinth, under a frozen sky, for an uncertain asylum some ninety-three miles off.

"In general, eight powerful wolf-like dogs will draw such a cargo like the wind:—I have but four wretched animals, who can hardly drag themselves.

"The clothing or personal outfit demands the nicest

study of experience. Except a spare pair of boots, it is all upon the back. It requires the energies of tyrant custom to discipline a traveller into comfort under these Smith Sound temperatures; and, let him dress as he may, his drill will avail but little unless he has a windless atmosphere without and a heat-creating body within.

"Rightly clad, he is a lump of deformity waddling

KAPETAH.

NESSAK.

over the ice, unpicturesque, uncouth, and seemingly helpless. It is only when you meet him covered with rime, his face peering from an icy halo, his beard glued with frozen respiration, that you look with intelligent appreciation on his many-coated panoply against King Death.

"The Smith's Straits fox-skin jumper, or *kapetah*, is a closed shirt, fitting very loosely to the person, but adapted to the head and neck by an almost air-tight hood, the *nessak*. The kapetah is put on from below;

the arms of the man pass through the arms of the garment, and the head rises through a slit at the top: around this slit comes up the hood. It is passed over the head from behind and made to embrace the face and forehead. Underneath the kapetah is a similar garment, but destitute of the hood, which is put on as we do an inner shirt. It is made of bird-skins chewed in the mouth by the women till they are perfectly soft, and it is worn with this unequalled down next the body. More than five hundred auks have been known to contribute to a garment of this description.

"So far the bust and upper limbs. The lower extremities are guarded by a pair of bear-skin breeches, the *nannooke*,—the characteristic and national vestiture of this strange people. They are literal copies, and in one sense fac-similes, of the courtly knee-buckled ones of our grandfathers, but not rising above the crests of the pelvis, thus leaving exposed those parts which in civilized countries are shielded most carefully.

"I regard these strange and apparently-inconvenient articles of dress as unique. They compressed the muscles, which they affected to cover, in a manner so ungrandisonian that I leave a special description of their structure to my note-book.

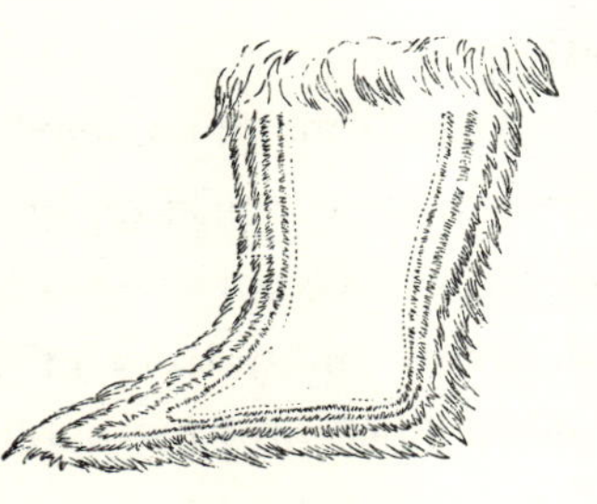

BOOT AND SOCKS.

"The foot-gear consists of a bird-skin short sock, with a padding of grass nicely distributed over the sole. Outside of this comes a bear-skin leg, sewed with great skill to the natural sole of the plantigrade, and abundantly wadded about the foot with dry non-conducting straw.

"When this simple wardrobe is fully adjusted to the person, we understand something of the wonderful endurance of these Arctic primates. Wrangell called the Jacuti iron men, because they slept at —50° opposite the fire, with their backs exposed. Now, they of Smith's Sound have always an uncovered space between the waistband of the nannooke and the kapetah. To bend forward exposes the back to partial nudity; and, no matter what the attitude, the entire chest is open to the atmosphere from below. Yet in this well-ventilated costume the man will sleep upon his sledge with the atmosphere 93° below our freezing-point.

"The only additional articles of dress are a fox's tail, held between the teeth to protect the nose in a wind, and mitts of seal-skin well wadded with sledge-straw.

"When I saw Kalutunah, who guided the return-party to the brig from Tesseusak, the temperature was below —50°. He was standing in the open air, comfortably scratching his naked skin, ready for a second journey; which, in effect, he made eight hours afterward.

"We—I mean our party of American hyperboreans—are mere carpet-knights aside of these indomitable savages. Experience has taught us to follow their guidance in matters of Arctic craft; but we have to add a host of European appendages to their out-door clothing.

"Imagine me, then, externally clad as I have described, but with furs and woollens layer upon layer inside, like the shards of an artichoke, till I am rounded into absolute obesity. Without all this, I cannot keep up my circulation on a sledge; nor indeed

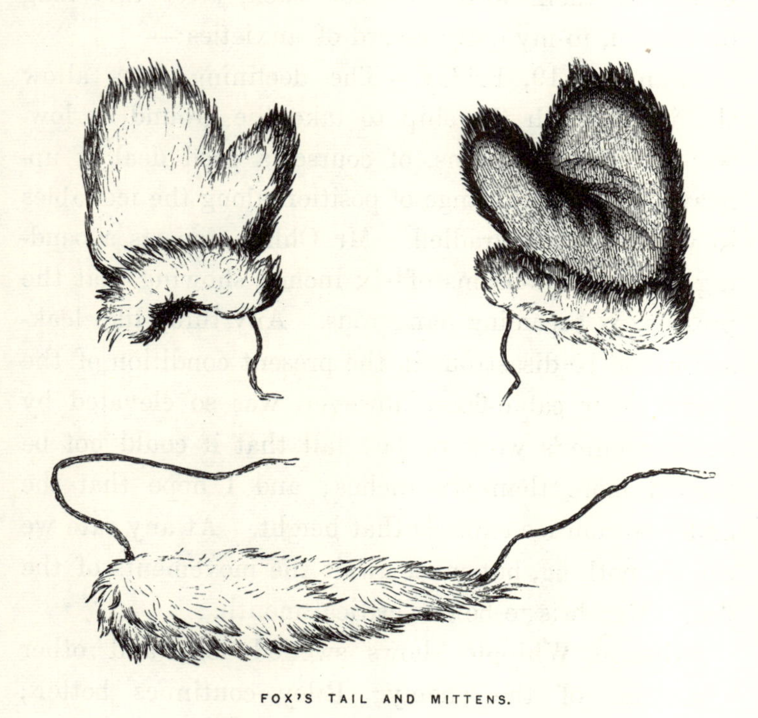

FOX'S TAIL AND MITTENS.

without active exercise, if the thermometer is below —54°, the lowest at which I have taken the floes. I have to run occasionally, or I should succumb to the cold."

So much for my resources of travel, as I have thrown them together from different pages of my journal. **The** apparent levity with which I have detailed them seems out of keeping with the date under which they stand. In truth, I was in no mirthful humor at any time during the month of January. I had a grave office to perform, and under grave responsibilities; and I had measured them well. I come back, after this long digression, to my daily record of anxieties:—

"January 19, Friday.—The declining tides allow the ice beneath the ship to take the ground at low-water. This occasions, of course, a good deal of up-heaval and some change of position along the ice-tables in which we are cradled. Mr. Ohlsen reports a bending of our cross-beams of six inches, showing that the pressure is becoming dangerous. Any thing like leakage would be disastrous in the present condition of the party. Our cabin-floor, however, was so elevated by our carpenter's work of last fall that it could not be flooded more than six inches; and I hope that the under-bottom ice exceeds that height. At any rate we can do nothing, but must await the movements of the floe. March is to be our critical month.

"George Whipple shows swelled legs and other symptoms of the enemy; Riley continues better; Brooks weak, but holding his ground; Wilson no better; if any thing, worse. I am myself so disabled in the joints as to be entirely unfit to attend to the traps or do any work. I shall try the vapor-bath and sweat, Indian fashion.

"January 21, Sunday.—We have been using up our tar-laid hemp hawsers for nearly a week, by way of eking out our firewood, and have reduced our consumption of pitch-pine to thirty-nine pounds a day. But the fine particles of soot throughout the room have affected the lungs of the sick so much that I shall be obliged to give it up. I am now trying the Manilla; but it consumes too rapidly: with care we may make something of it.

"January 22, Monday.—Busy preparing for my trip to the lower Esquimaux settlement. The barometer remains at the extraordinary height of 30·85,—a bad prelude to a journey!

"Petersen caught another providential fox. We divided him into nine portions, three for each of our scurvied patients.——I am off."

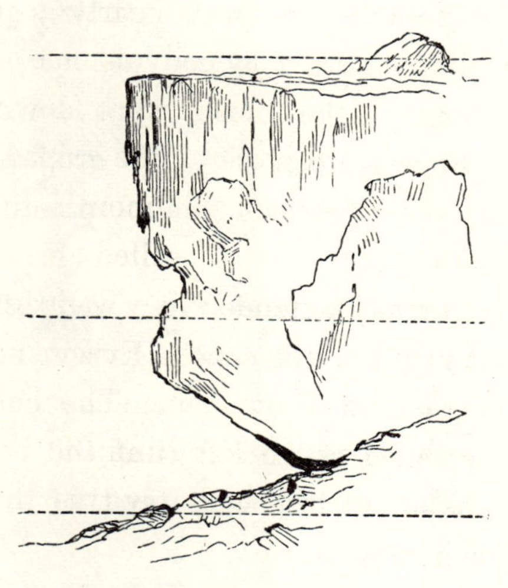

SECTION OF ICE-FOOT

CHAPTER II.

A BREAK DOWN — THE HUT IN A STORM — TWO NIGHTS IN THE HUT—FROST AGAIN—THE BACK TRACK—HEALTH ROLL—MEDICAL TREATMENT—HEALTH FAILING—UNSUCCESSFUL HUNT—THE LAST BOTTLES.

"JANUARY 29, Monday.—The dogs carried us to the lower curve of the reach before breaking down. I was just beginning to hope for an easy voyage, when Toodla and the Big Yellow gave way nearly together; the latter frightfully contorted by convulsions. There was no remedy for it: the moon went down, and the wretched night was upon us. We groped along the ice-foot, and, after fourteen hours' painful walking, reached the old hut.

"A dark water-sky extended in a wedge from Littleton to a point north of the cape. Everywhere else the firmament was obscured by mist. The height of the barometer continued as we left it at the brig, and our own sensations of warmth convinced us that we were about to have a snow-storm.

"We hardly expected to meet the Esquimaux here, and were not disappointed. Hans set to work at once to cut out blocks of snow to close up the entrance to the hut. I carried in our blubber-lamp, food, and bedding, unharnessed the dogs, and took them into the same shelter. We were barely housed before the storm broke upon us.

NEARING THE HUT

"Here, completely excluded from the knowledge of things without, we spent many miserable hours. We could keep no note of time, and, except by the whirring of the drift against the roof of our kennel, had no information of the state of the weather. We slept, and cooked coffee, and drank coffee, and slept, and cooked coffee, and drank again; and when by our tired instincts we thought that twelve hours must have passed, we treated ourselves to a meal,—that is to say, we divided impartial bites out of the raw hind-leg of a fox, to give zest to our biscuits spread with frozen tallow.

"We then turned in to sleep again, no longer heedful of the storm, for it had now buried us deep in with the snow.

"But in the mean time, although the storm continued, the temperatures underwent an extraordinary change. I was awakened by the dropping of water from the roof above me; and, upon turning back my sleeping-bag, found it saturated by the melting of its previously-condensed hoar-frost. My eider-down was like a wet swab. I found afterward that the phenomenon of the warm southeast had come unexpectedly upon us. The thermometers at the brig indicated +26°; and, closer as we were to the water, the weather was probably above the freezing-point.

"When we left the brig—how long before it was we did not know—the temperature was —44°. It had risen at least seventy degrees. I defy the strongest man not to suffer from such a change. A close, oppressive sensation attacked both Hans and myself. We both suffered from cardiac symptoms, and are up to this moment under anxious treatment by our comrades. Mr. Wilson, I find, has had spasmodic asthma from it here, and Brooks has a renewal of his old dyspnœa.

"In the morning—that is to say, when the combined light of the noonday dawn and the circumpolar moon permitted our escape—I found, by comparing the time as indicated by the Great Bear with the present increased altitude of the moon, that we had been pent up nearly two days. Under these circumstances we made directly for the hummocks, *en route* for the bay. But here was a disastrous change. The snow had accumulated under the windward sides of the inclined tables to a height so excessive that we buried sledge, dogs, and drivers, in the effort to work through. It was all in vain that Hans and I harnessed ourselves to, or lifted, levered, twisted, and pulled. Utterly exhausted and sick, I was obliged to give it up. The darkness closed in again, and with difficulty we regained the igloë.

"The ensuing night brought a return to hard freezing temperatures. Our luxurious and downy coverlet was a stiff, clotted lump of ice. In spite of our double lamp, it was a miserable halt. Our provisions grew short; the snow kept on falling, and we had still forty-six miles between us and the Esquimaux.

"I determined to try the land-ice (ice-foot) by Fog Inlet; and we worked four hours upon this without a breathing-spell,—utterly in vain. My poor Esquimaux, Hans, adventurous and buoyant as he was, began to cry like a child. Sick, worn out, strength gone, dogs fast and floundering, I am not ashamed to admit that, as I thought of the sick men on board, my own equanimity also was at fault.

"We had not been able to get the dogs out, when the big moon appeared above the water-smoke. A familiar hill, 'Old Beacon Knob,' was near. I scrambled to its top and reconnoitred the coast around it. The ridge about Cape Hatherton seemed to jut out of a perfect chaos of broken ice. The water—that inexplicable North Water—was there, a long black wedge,

THE WATER.

overhung by crapy wreaths of smoke, running to the northward and eastward. Better than all yet,—could I be deceived?—a trough through the hummock-ridges, and level plains of ice stretching to the south!

"Hans heard my halloo, and came up to confirm me. But for our disabled dogs and the waning moonlight, we could easily have made our journey. It was with a rejoiced heart that I made my way back to our miserable little cavern, and restuffed its gaping entrance with the snow. We had no blubber, and of course no fire; but I knew that we could gain the brig, and that, after refreshing the dogs and ourselves, we could now assuredly reach the settlements.

"We took the back track next morning over Bedevilled Reach upon the mid-ice floes, and reached the brig by 4 P. M. on Friday; since when I have been so stiff and scorbutic, so utterly used up, that to-day gives me a first return to my journal.

"January 30, Tuesday.—My companions on board felt all my disappointment at bringing back no meat; but infinite gladness took the place of regret when they heard the great news of a passage through the hummocks. Petersen began at once to busy himself with his wardrobe; and an eight-day party was organized almost before we turned in, to start as soon as the tempestuous weather subsides and the drifts settle down. It is four days since, but as yet we dare not venture out.

"That there is no time for delay, this health-table will show:—

"Henry Brooks: Unable any longer to go on deck: we carry him with difficulty from his berth to a cushioned locker.

"McGary: Less helpless; but off duty, and saturated with articular scurvy.

"Mr. Wilson: In bed. Severe purpuric blotches, and nodes in limbs. Cannot move.

"George Riley: Abed; limbs less stiff, gums better, unable to do duty.

"Thomas Hickey, (our cook:) Cannot keep his legs many days more; already swelled and blistered.

"William Morton: Down with a frozen heel; the bone exfoliating.

"Henry Goodfellow: Scurvied gums, but generally well.

"Dr. Hayes is prostrate with his amputated toes:—Sontag just able to hobble. In a word, our effective force is reduced to five,—Mr. Ohlsen, Mr. Bonsall, Petersen, Hans, and the Commander; and even of these some might, perhaps, be rightfully transferred to the other list. We have the whole burden of the hourly observations and the routine of our domestic life, even to the cooking, which we take in rotation.

" . . . . Still this remarkable temperature; the barometer slowly librating between 29·20 and the old 30·40. Snow falling: wind from the southwest, hauling by the west to north: yet the thermometer at —10° and +3°. We long anxiously for weather to enable our meat-party to start. The past two days our sick have been entirely out of meat: the foxes seem to avoid our traps. I gave Wilson one raw meal from the masseter muscle which adhered to another old bear's head I was keeping for a specimen. But otherwise we have had no anti-scorbutic for three days.

"Among other remedies which I oppose to the distemper, I have commenced making sundry salts of iron; among them the citrate and a chlorohydrated tincture. We have but one bottle of brandy left: my applying a half-pint of it to the tincture shows the high value I set upon this noble chalybeate. My nose bled to-day, and I was struck with the fluid brickdusty poverty of the blood. I use iron much among my people: as a single remedy it exceeds all others, except only the specific of raw meat: potash for its own action is well enough to meet some conditions of the disease, and we were in the habit of using freely an ex-

FOX-TRAPS.

temporaneous citrate prepared from our lime-juice; but, as our cases became more reduced and complicated with hemorrhages, iron was our one great remedy.

"January 31, Wednesday.—The weather still most extraordinary. The wind has hauled around, and is now blowing from the north and northeast, usually our coldest and clearest quarter. Yet the diffused mist continues, the snow falls, and the thermometer never records below —20°.

"Our sick are worse; for our traps yield nothing, and we are still without fresh food. The absence of raw fox-meat for a single day shows itself in our scurvy. Hemorrhages are becoming common. My crew,—I have no crew any longer,—the tenants of my bunks cannot bear me to leave them a single watch. Yet I cannot make Petersen try the new path which I discovered and found practicable. Well; the wretched month is over. It is something to be living, able to write. No one has yet made the dark voyage, and January the thirty-first is upon us.

"February 2, Friday.—The weather clears, the full moon shows herself, the sledge is packed, and Petersen will start to-morrow.

"February 3, Saturday.—He is gone with Hans. A bad time with Brooks, in a swoon from exhaustion!

"February 4, Sunday.—Mr. Ohlsen breaks down: the scurvy is in his knee, and he cannot walk. This day, too, Thomas Hickey, our acting cook, gives way completely. I can hardly realize that among these strong men I alone should be the borne-up man,—the only one, except Mr. Bonsall, on his legs. It sometimes makes me tremble when I think how necessary I am to sustain this state of things. It is a Sunday thought, that it must be for some wise and good end I am thus supported.

"Made an unsuccessful hunt out toward Mary River: but, although the daylight was more than ample, tracked nothing. Our sick have been on short commons for the last five days; and we have given up the traps for want of fresh meat to bait them with. The fiord looked frightfully desolate. Where once was a torrent fighting among ice and rocks, is now a tunnel of drifted snow. Mary Leiper River is a sinuous ravine, swept dry by the gales which issue from the hills, and its rocky bed patched with the frozen relics of its waters.

"I made a dish of freshened codfish-skin for Brooks and Wilson; they were hungry enough to relish it. Besides this, I had kept back six bottles of our Scotch ale to meet emergencies, and I am dealing these out to them by the wine-glass. It is too cold for brewing in our apartment: the water freezes two feet above the floor. I have given up my writing-table arrangements, and my unfortunate study-lamp is now fixed under a barrel to see if it cannot raise a fermenting temperature. I shall turn brewer to-morrow if it succeeds."

FOX-TRAP.

CHAPTER III.

THE FIRE-CLOTHED BAG — THE WRAITH — COOKERY—A RESPITE — THE COMING DAWN — THE TRUST — PROSPECTS — ARGUMENT — COLORED SKIES—STOVE-FITTING.

"FEBRUARY 6, Tuesday.—At ten, last evening, not long after my journal-record, I heard voices outside. Petersen and Hans had returned. I met them silently on deck, and heard from poor Petersen how he had broken down. The snows had been increasing since my own last trial,—his strength had left him; the scurvy had entered his chest; in a word, he had failed, and Hans could not do the errand alone. Bad enough!

"But to-day our fortunes are on the mend. It has been beautifully clear; and for the first time a shade of bronzed yellow has warmed our noonday horizon, with a gentle violet running into rich brown clouds, totally unlike our night skies. Hans and I started for a hunt,—one to explore new grounds, the other to follow tracks in the recent snow. The result was two rabbits, the first-fruits of the coming light, and the promise of more in the numerous feeding-traces among the rocks of Charlotte Wood Fiord. The meat, our first for ten days, was distributed raw. By keeping the rabbits carefully covered up, they reached the ship sufficiently unfrozen to give us about a pint of raw blood. It was a grateful cordial to Brooks, Wilson, and Riley.

"February 7, Wednesday.—The weather was misty when I went out this morning, and the twinkling of the stars confirmed Petersen's prognostic of a warm southeaster before evening. Mist, stars, and Petersen were right. The gale is upon us, darkening the air with snow, and singing in wild discords through the rigging.

"It is enough to solemnize men of more joyous temperament than ours has been for some months. We are contending at odds with angry forces close around us, without one agent or influence within eighteen hundred miles whose sympathy is on our side.

"My poor fellows, most of them bred in the superstitions of the sea, are full of evil bodings. We have a large old seal-skin bag on deck, that holds our remnant of furs. It hangs from the main-stay, and we have all of us jested in the times of ordinary darkness about its grotesque physiognomy. To-night it has worn a new character. One of the crew, crawling outside, saw it swinging in the storm with furious energy, and pounding against the mast like a giant boxing-glove. It glowed too with supernatural light; and he is sure it spoke some dreadful message, though he was too much perturbed to give it audience. There is no reasoning with him about it, and his messmates' laugh, as they attempt to ridicule his fear, is like the ghost-story merriment of a nursery circle."

It was an ugly and withal an anxious night. Mr. Goodfellow, the youngest of our party, had left the cabin soon after dinner for an inland stroll with his gun, and he had not returned when the scanty twilight closed before its time. The wind blew off the coast, piling the snow in great hills and changing the whole face of the floe. As the darkness wore on we became uneasy, and at last alarmed, at his absence. We burnt bluelights and Roman candles to guide him through the night; but it was six o'clock in the morning before he came in, happily none the worse for his adventure.

Honest Tom Hickey had been on the deck reconnoitring for him while the gale was at its height. He came down to the mess just before the alarm of the thumping fur-bag, declaring he had seen Mr. Goodfellow moving cautiously along the land-ice and jumping down on the field below. He hurried his tea-things to give him a warm supper, but no one came. In the result, though Tom volunteered to make search at the spot where he had seen his messmate, and Riley offered to accompany him, and I myself looked diligently afterward with a lantern for some hundreds of yards around, we found nothing but fresh drifted snow, without the trace of a human foot. Tom had seen a *wraith;* he believes it religiously, and associates its mysterious advent with the luminous fur-bag.

"There must be some warm southern area over

which this wind comes, some open water it may be, that is drawing nearer to us, to minister after a time to our escape. But we must go alone. I have given up all hope of rescuing our little vessel. She has been safeguard and home for us through many lengthened trials; but her time has come. She can never float above the waves again. How many of us are to be more fortunate?

"February 9, Friday.—Still no supplies. Three of us have been out all day, without getting a shot. Hans thinks he saw a couple of reindeer at a distance; and his eyes rarely deceive him. He will try for them to-morrow. I have fitted out for him a tent and a sleeping-bag on the second table-land; and the thermometer is now so little below zero that he will be able to keep the field for a steady hunt. Our sick are sinking for want of fresh food. It is the only specific:—I dislike to use the unphilosophical term; but in our case it is the true one. In large quantities it dissipates the disease; in ordinary rations it prevents its occurrence; in small doses it checks it while sustaining the patient. We have learned its value too well to waste it; every part of every animal has its use. The skin makes the basis of a soup, and the claws can be boiled to a jelly. Lungs, larynx, stomach, and entrails, all are available. I have not permitted myself to taste more than an occasional entrail of our last half-dozen rabbits. Not that I am free from symptoms of the universal pest. I am conscious of a stiffness in the tendons, and a shortness of breath, and a weariness of the bones, that should naturally attend the eruption which covers my body. But I have none of the more fearful signs. I can walk with energy after I get warmed up, I have no bleeding of the gums, and, better than all, thank God, I am without that horrible despondency which the disease nourishes and feeds on. I sleep sound and dream pleasantly,—generally about successes in the hunt, or a double ration of reindeer or ptarmigan.

"It has been a true warm southeaster. The housing-sails have been blown off by the storm, and we are buried up in a snow-drift. But one such feathery quilt is worth all the canvas covering in the world.

"My brewing apparatus has worked well, thanks to stove and storm; and I have on hand now as unsavory a dose of flax-seed and quinine as was ever honored by the name of beer.

"February 10, Saturday.—Three days' respite! Petersen and myself have made a fruitless hunt; but Hans comes in with three rabbits. Distribution:—the blood to Ohlsen and Thomas; and to the other eight of the sick men full rations; consuming a rabbit and a half. I cannot risk the depression that a single death would bring upon the whole party, and have to deal unfairly with those who can still keep about, to save the rest from sinking. Brooks and Ohlsen are in a precarious condition: they have lost the entire mucous membrane of the alveoli; and Mr. Wilson requires special attendance every hour to carry him through.

"The day is beginning to glow with the approaching sun. The south at noon has almost an orange tinge. In ten days his direct rays will reach our hill-tops; and in a week after he will be dispensing his blessed medicine among our sufferers.

"February 12, Monday.—Hans is off for his hunting-lodge, 'over the hills and far away,' beyond Charlotte Wood Fiord. I have sent Godfrey with him; for I fear the boy has got the taint like the rest of us, and may suffer from the exposure. He thinks he can bring back a deer, and the chances are worth the trial. We can manage the small hunt, Petersen and I, till he comes back, unless we break down too. But I do not like these symptoms of mine, and Petersen is very far from the man he was. We had a tramp to-day, both of us, after an imaginary deer,—a *bennisoak* that has been supposed for the last three days to be hunting the neighborhood of the waterpools of the big fiord, and have come back jaded and sad. If Hans gives way, God help us!"

It is hardly worth while to inflict on the reader a succession of journal-records like these. They tell of nothing but the varying symptoms of sick men, dreary, profitless hunts, relieved now and then by the signalized incident of a killed rabbit or a deer seen, and the longed-for advent of the solar light.

We worked on board—those of us who could work at all—at arranging a new gangway with a more gentle slope, to let some of the party crawl up from their hospital into the air. We were six, all told, out of eighteen, who could affect to hunt, cook, or nurse.

Meanwhile we tried to dream of commerce with the Esquimaux, and open water, and home. For myself, my thoughts had occupation enough in the question of our closing labors. I never lost my hope. I looked to the coming spring as full of responsibilities; but I had

DETACHED ICE-BELT.

bodily strength and moral tone enough to look through them to the end. A trust, based on experience as well as on promises, buoyed me up at the worst of times. Call it fatalism, as you ignorantly may, there is that in the story of every eventful life which teaches the inefficiency of human means and the present control of a Supreme Agency. See how often relief has come at the moment of extremity, in forms strangely unsought, almost at the time unwelcome; see, still more, how the back has been strengthened to its increasing burden, and the heart cheered by some conscious influence of an unseen Power.

Thinking quietly over our condition, I spread out in my diary the results which it seemed to point to. After reviewing our sick-list and remarking how little efficiency there was in the other members of the party, my memorandum went on:—

"We have three months before us of intense cold. We have a large and laborious outfit to arrange, boats, sledges, provisions, and accoutrements for a journey of alternating ice and water of more than thirteen hundred miles. Our carpenter is among the worst of our invalids. Supposing all our men able to move, four at least of them must be carried by the rest, three in consequence of amputation, and one from frost-wounds; and our boats must be sledged over some sixty or perhaps ninety miles of terrible ice before launching and loading them. Finally, a part of our force, whatever it may be, must be detailed to guard our property from the Esquimaux while the other detachments are making their successive trips to the open water. So much for the shadow of the picture!

"But it has two sides; and, whether from constitutional temperament or well-reasoned argument, I find our state far from desperate. I cheer my comrades after this fashion:—

"1. I am convinced, from a careful analysis of our disease, that under its present aspects it is not beyond control. If with the aid of our present hunting-resources or by any providential accession to them I can keep the cases from rapid depression, next month ought to give us a bear, and in the mean time Hans may find a deer; and, with a good stock of fresh meat even for a few days, I can venture away from the vessel to draw supplies from the Esquimaux at Etah. I should have been there before this, if I could have been spared for forty-eight hours. We want nothing but meat.

"2. The coming of the sun will open appliances of moral help to the sick, and give energy to the hygienic resorts which I am arranging at this moment. Our miserable little kennel, where eighteen are crowded into the space of ten, is thoroughly begrimed with lampblack from the inevitable smoke of our fuel. The weather has prevented our drying and airing the sleeping-gear. The floor is damp from the conducted warmth of the sea-water under us, melting the ice that has condensed everywhere below. Sunshine and dry weather will cure all this. I have window-sash ready to fix over the roof and southern side of the galley-house; and our useless daguerreotype plates, tacked over wooden screens, make admirable mirrors to transfer the sun-rays into the cabin. I have manufactured a full-draught pipe for our smoky stove. Chloride of sodium must do the rest.

"3. While we live we will stick together: one fate shall belong to us all, be it what it may.

"There is comfort in this review; and, please God in his beneficent providence to spare us for the work, I will yet give one more manly tug to search the shores of Kennedy Channel for memorials of the lost; and then, our duties over here, and the brig still prison-bound, enter trustingly upon the task of our escape.

"February 21, Wednesday.—To-day the crests of the northeast headland were gilded by true sunshine, and all who were able assembled on deck to greet it. The sun rose above the horizon, though still screened from our eyes by intervening hills. Although the powerful refraction of Polar latitudes heralds his direct appearance by brilliant light, this is as far removed from the glorious tints of day as it is from the mere twilight. Nevertheless, for the past ten days we have been watching the growing warmth of our landscape, as it emerged from buried shadow, through all the stages of distinctness of an India-ink washing, step by step, into the sharp, bold definition of our desolate harbor scene. We have marked every dash of color which the great Painter in his benevolence vouchsafed to us; and now the empurpled blues, clear, unmistakable, the spreading lake, the flickering yellow: peering at all these, poor wretches! every thing seemed superlative lustre and unsurpassable glory. We had so grovelled in darkness that we oversaw the light.

"Mr. Wilson has caught cold and relapsed. Mr. Ohlsen, after a suspicious day, startles me by an attack of partial epilepsy; one of those strange indescribable spells, fits, seizures, whatever name the jargon gives them, which indicate deep disturbance. I conceal his case as far as I can; but it adds to my heavy pack of troubles to anticipate the gloomy scenes of epileptic transport introduced into our one apartment. McGary holds his own.

"The work of stove-fitting is completed, and a new era marks its success. The increased draught which the prospective termination of our winter allows me to afford to our fuel brings an unhoped-for piece of good fortune. We can burn hemp cable and cast-off running-gear. By the aid of a high chimney and a good regulating valve, the smoke passes directly into the open air, and tarred junk is as good as oak itself. This will save our trebling, and, what is more, the labor of cutting it. In truth, very little of it has been used up, scarcely more than a single streak. We have been too weak to cut it off. All our disposable force was inadequate last Saturday to cut enough for a day's fuel in advance.

"The sickness of a single additional man would have left us without fire."

SCRATCHED GNEISS.

CHAPTER IV.

THE BENNESOAK—A DILEMMA—THE SUN—END OF FEBRUARY—OUR CONDITION—THE WARM SOUTHEASTER—MOONLIGHT—THE LANDSCAPE.

"February 22, Thursday.—Washington's birthday: all our colors flying in the new sunlight. A day of good omen, even to the sojourners among the ice. Hans comes in with great news. He has had a shot at our bennesoak, a long shot; but it reached him. The animal made off at a slow run, but we are sure of him now. This same deer has been hanging round the lake at the fiord through all the dim returning twilight; and so many stories were told of his appearance and movements that he had almost grown into a myth. To-morrow we shall desire his better acquaintance.

"The Esquimaux call the deer when he is without antlers a bennesoak. The greater number of these animals retain their antlers till the early spring, beginning to drop them about the return of sunshine; but some of the strongest lose them before the winter sets in. They are gregarious in their habits, and fond of particular localities. Where they have been gathered together year after year, the accumulation of discarded antlers is immense. They tell me at Holsteinberg, where more than four thousand reindeer-skins find a market annually, that on the favorite hunting-grounds these horns are found in vast piles. They bring little or nothing at Copenhagen, but I suppose would find a ready sale among the button-workers of England.

"February 23, Friday.—Hans was out early this morning on the trail of the wounded deer. Rhina, the least barbarous of our sledge-dogs, assisted him. He was back by noon, with the joyful news, 'The tukkuk dead only two miles up big fiord!' The cry found its way through the hatch, and came back in a broken huzza from the sick men.

"We are so badly off for strong arms that our reindeer threatened to be as great an embarrassment to us as the auction drawn-elephant was to his lucky master. We had hard work with our dogs carrying him to the brig, and still harder, worn down as we were, in getting him over the ship's side. But we succeeded, and were tumbling him down the hold, when we found ourselves in a dilemma like the Vicar of Wakefield with his family picture. It was impossible to drag the prize into our little moss-lined dormitory; the *tossut* was not half big enough to let him pass: and it was equally impossible to skin him anywhere else without freezing our fingers in the operation. It was a happy escape from the embarrassments of our hungry little council to determine that the animal might be carved before skinning as well as he could be afterward; and in a very few minutes we proved our united wisdom by a feast on his quartered remains.

"It was a glorious meal, such as the compensations of Providence reserve for starving men alone. We ate, forgetful of the past, and almost heedless of the morrow; cleared away the offal wearily: and now, at 10 P. M., all hands have turned in to sleep, leaving to their commanding officer the solitary honor of an eight hours' vigil.

"This deer was among the largest of all the northern specimens I have seen. He measured five feet one inch in girth, and six feet two inches in length, and stood as large as a two years' heifer. We estimated his weight at three hundred pounds gross, or one hundred and eighty net. The head had a more than usually cumbrous character, and a long waving tuft of white hair, that depended from the throat, gave an appearance of excessive weight to the front view.

"The reindeer is in no respect a graceful animal. There is an apparent want of proportion between his cumbrous shoulders and light haunch, which is ungainly even in his rapid movements. But he makes up for all his defects of form when he presents himself as an article of diet.

"February 24, Saturday.—A bitter disappointment met us at our evening meal. The flesh of our deer was nearly uneatable from putrefaction; the liver and intestines, from which I had expected so much, utterly so. The rapidity of such a change, in a temperature so low as minus 35°, seems curious; but the Green landers say that extreme cold is rather a promoter than otherwise of the putrefactive process. All the graminivorous animals have the same tendency, as is well known to the butchers. Our buffalo-hunters, when they condescend to clean a carcass, do it at once; they have told me that the musk-ox is sometimes tainted after five minutes' exposure. The Esquimaux, with whom there is no fastidious sensibility of palate, are in the practice at Yotlik and Horses' Head, in latitude 73° 40′, even in the severest weather, of withdrawing the viscera immediately after death and filling the cavity with stones.

"February 25, Sunday.—The day of rest for those to whom rest can be; the day of grateful recognition for all! John, our volunteer cook of yesterday, is down: Morton, who could crawl out of bed to play baker for the party, and stood to it manfully yesterday, is down too. I have just one man left to help me in caring for the sick. Hans and Petersen, thank God! have vitality enough left to bear the toils of the hunt. One is out with his rifle, the other searching the traps.

"To-day, blessed be the Great Author of Light! I have once more looked upon the sun. I was standing on deck, thinking over our prospects, when a familiar berg, which had long been hid in shadow, flashed out in sun-birth. I knew this berg right well: it stood between Charlotte Wood Fiord and Little Willie's Monument. One year and one day ago I travelled toward it from Fern Rock to catch the sunshine. Then I had to climb the hills beyond, to get the luxury of basking in its brightness; but now, though the sun was but a single degree above the true horizon, it was so much elevated by refraction that the sheen stretched across the trough of the fiord like a flaming tongue. I could not or would not resist the influence. It was a Sunday act of worship: I started off at an even run, and caught him as he rolled slowly along the horizon, and before he sank. I was again the first of my party to rejoice and meditate in sunshine. It is the third sun I have seen rise for a moment above the long night of an Arctic winter.

"February 26, Monday.—William Godfrey undertook to act as cook to day, but fainted before completing the experiment. The rest of us are little better; and now it looks as if we were to lose our best caterer, for Hans too shows signs of giving way to the scurvy.

"I have been at work for an hour, cutting up the large Manilla hawser for fuel. I do not know that I have any very remarkable or valuable quality; but I do know that, however multiform may be my virtues, I am a singularly awkward hand in chopping up frozen cables.

"February 28, Wednesday.—February closes: thank God for the lapse of its twenty-eight days! Should the thirty-one of the coming March not drag us further downward, we may hope for a successful close to this dreary drama. By the tenth of April we should have seal; and when they come, if we remain to welcome them, we can call ourselves saved.

"But a fair review of our prospects tells me that I

must look the lion in the face. The scurvy is steadily gaining on us. I do my best to sustain the more desperate cases; but as fast as I partially build up one, another is stricken down. The disease is perhaps less malignant than it was, but it is more diffused throughout our party. Except William Morton, who is disabled by a frozen heel, not one of our eighteen is exempt. Of the six workers of our party, as I counted them a month ago, two are unable to do out-door work, and the remaining four divide the duties of the ship among them. Hans musters his remaining energies to conduct the hunt. Petersen is his disheartened moping assistant. The other two, Bonsall and myself, have all the daily offices of household and hospital. We chop five large sacks of ice, cut six fathoms of eight-inch hawser into junks of a foot each, serve out the meat when we have it, hack at the molasses, and hew out with crowbar and axe the pork and dried apples, pass up the foul slop and cleansings of our dormitory; and, in a word, cook, *scullionize*, and attend the sick. Added to this, for five nights running I have kept watch from 8 P.M. to 4 A.M., catching cat-naps as I could in the day without changing my clothes, but carefully waking every hour to note thermometers.

"Such is the condition in which February leaves us, with forty-one days more ahead of just the same character in prospect as the twenty-eight which, thank God! are numbered now with the past. It is saddening to think how much those twenty-eight days have impaired our capacities of endurance. Yet there are resources—accidental perhaps, mercifully providential let me rather term them, contingent certainly, so far as our prescience goes—which may avail to save us: another reindeer of sound carcass, a constant succession of small game, supplies of walrus from the fugitive Esquimaux, or that which I most expect and hope for—a bear. We have already seen some tracks of these animals; and last March there were many of them off Coffee Gorge and the Labyrinth. If Hans and myself can only hold on, we may work our way through. All rests upon destiny, or the Power which controls it.

"It will yet be many days before the sun overrides the shadow of Bessie Mountain and reaches our brig. The sick pine for him, and I have devised a clever system of mirrors to hasten his visit to their bunks. He will do more for them than all medicine besides.

"That strange phenomenon, the warm south and southeast winds which came upon us in January, did not pass away till the middle of this month. And, even after it had gone, the weather continued for some days to reflect its influence. The thermometer seldom fell below —40°, and stood sometimes as high as —30°. It has been growing colder for the last three days, ranging from —46° to —51°; and the abundant snows of the warm spell are now compacted hard enough to be traversable, or else dissipated by the heavy winds. There is much to be studied in these atmospheric changes. There is a seeming connection between the increasing cold and the increasing moonlight, which has sometimes forced itself on my notice; but I have barely strength enough to carry on our routine observations, and have no time to discuss phenomena.

"Two attempts have been made by my orders, since the month began, to communicate with the Esquimaux at their huts. Both were failures. Petersen, Hans, and Godfrey came back to denounce the journey as impracticable. I know better: the experience of my two attempts in the midst of the darkness satisfies me that at this period of the year the thing can be done; and, if I might venture to leave our sick-bay for a week, I would prove it. But there are dispositions and influences here around me, scarcely latent, yet repressed by my presence, which make it my duty at all hazards to stay where I am.

"March 1, Thursday.—A grander scene than our bay by moonlight can hardly be conceived. It is more dream-like and supernatural than a combination of earthly features.

"The moon is nearly full, and the dawning sunlight, mingling with hers, invests every thing with an atmosphere of ashy gray. It clothes the gnarled hills that make the horizon of our bay, shadows out the terraces in dull definition, grows darker and colder as it sinks into the fiords, and broods sad and dreary upon the ridges and measureless plains of ice that make up the rest of our field of view. Rising above all this, and shading down into it in strange combination, is the intense moonlight, glittering on every crag and spire, tracing the outline of the background with

J. Hamilton — Engraved at J.M. Butler's establishment 84 Chestnut St. — J.Mc Goffin.

ICE BERGS NEAR KOSOAK,

LIFE BOAT COVE.

(From a sketch by Dr Kane.)

contrasted brightness, and printing its fantastic profiles on the snow-field. It is a landscape such as Milton or Dante might imagine,—inorganic, desolate, mysterious. I have come down from deck with the feelings of a man who has looked upon a world unfinished by the hand of its Creator "

THE GRAVES BY MOONLIGHT.

CHAPTER V.

OUR CONDITION — THE RESORTS — THE SICK — THE RAT IN THE INSECT-BOX — ANTICIPATIONS — HANS'S RETURN — FAMINE AT ETAH — MYOUK ON BOARD — WALRUS-TACKLE — THE MEAT DIET.

My journal for the beginning of March is little else than a chronicle of sufferings. Our little party was quite broken down. Every man on board was tainted with scurvy, and it was not common to find more than three who could assist in caring for the rest. The greater number were in their bunks, absolutely unable to stir.

The circumstances were well fitted to bring out the character of individuals. Some were intensely grateful for every little act of kindness from their more fortunate messmates; some querulous; others desponding; others again wanted only strength to become mutinous. Brooks, my first officer, as stalwart a man-o'-war's man as ever faced an enemy, burst into tears when he first saw himself in the glass. On Sunday, the 4th, our last remnant of fresh meat had been doled out. Our invalids began to sink rapidly. The wounds of our amputated men opened afresh. The region about our harbor ceased to furnish its scanty contingent of game. One of our huntsmen, Petersen, never very reliable in any thing, declared himself unfit for further duty. Hans was unsuccessful: he made several wide circuits, and saw deer twice; but once they were beyond range, and the next time his rifle missed fire.

I tried the hunt for a long morning myself, without meeting a single thing of life, and was convinced, by the appearance of things on my return to the brig, that I should peril the *morale*, and with it the only hope, of my command by repeating the experiment.

I labored, of course, with all the ingenuity of a well-taxed mind, to keep up the spirits of my comrades. I cooked for them all imaginable compounds of our unvaried diet-list, and brewed up flax-seed and lime-juice and quinine and willow-stems into an abomination which was dignified as beer, and which some were persuaded for the time to believe such. But it was becoming more and more certain every hour, that unless we could renew our supplies of fresh meat, the days of the party were numbered.

I spare myself, as well as the readers of this hastily-compiled volume, when I pass summarily over the details of our condition at this time.

I look back at it with recollections like those of a nightmare. Yet I was borne up wonderfully. I never doubted for an instant that the same Providence which had guarded us through the long darkness of winter was still watching over us for good, and that it was yet in reserve for us—for some; I dared not hope for all—to bear back the tidings of our rescue to a Christian land. But how I did not see.

On the 6th of the month I made the desperate venture of sending off my only trusted and effective huntsman on a sledge-journey to find the Esquimaux of Etah. He took with him our two surviving dogs in our lightest sledge. The Arctic day had begun to set in; the ice-track had improved with the advance of the season; and the cold, though still intense, had moderated to about eighty degrees below the freezing-point. He was to make his first night-halt at Anoatok; and, if no misadventure thwarted his progress, we hoped that he might reach the settlement before the end of the second night. In three or at furthest four days more, I counted on his return. No language can express the anxiety with which our poor suffering crew awaited it.

"March 8, Thursday.—Hans must now be at the huts. If the natives have not gone south, if the walrus and bear have not failed them, and if they do not refuse to send us supplies, we may have fresh food in three days. God grant it may come in time!

"Stephenson and Riley are dangerously ill. We have moved Riley from his bunk, which, though lighter than most of the others, was dampened by the accumulations of ice. He is now upon a dry and heated platform close to the stove. Dr. Hayes's foot shows some ugly symptoms, which a change of his lodging-place may perhaps mitigate; and I have determined, therefore, to remove him to the berth Riley has vacated as soon as we can purify and dry it for him.

"In clearing out Riley's bunk, we found that a rat had built his nest in my insect-box, destroying all our specimens. This is a grave loss; for, besides that they were light of carriage, and might therefore have accompanied us in the retreat which now seems inevitable, they comprised our entire collection, and, though few in numbers, were rich for this stinted region. I had many spiders and bees. He is welcome to the whole of them, however, if I only catch him the fatter for the ration.

"March 9, Friday.—Strength going. It was with a feeling almost of dismay that I found how difficult it was to get through the day's labors,—Bonsall and myself the sole workers. After cleansing below, dressing and performing the loathsome duties of a nurse to the sick, cutting ice, cooking and serving messes, we could hardly go further.

"I realize fully the moral effects of an unbroken routine: systematic order once broken in upon, discomfort, despondency, and increase of disease must follow of course. It weighed heavily on my spirit to-day when I found my one comrade and myself were barely able to cut the necessary fuel. The hour of routine-nightfall finds us both stiff and ill at ease. Having to keep the night-watch until 6 A.M., I have plenty of time to revolve my most uncomfortable thoughts.

"Be it understood by any who may peradventure read of these things in my journal, that I express them nowhere else. What secret thoughts my companions may have are concealed from me and from each other; but none of them can see as I do the alternative future now so close at hand: bright and comforting it may be; but, if not, black and hopeless altogether.

"Should Hans come back with a good supply of walrus, and himself unsmitten by the enemy, our sick would rise under the genial specific of meat, and our strength probably increase enough to convey our boats to the North Water. The Refuge Inlet Polynia will hardly be more than forty miles from our brig, and, step by step, we can sledge our boats and their cargoes down to it. Once at Cape Alexander, we can support our sick by our guns, and make a regular Capua of the bird-colonies of Northumberland Island. This, in honest truth my yet unswerving and unshaken hope and expectation, is what I preach to my people; and often in the silent hours of night I chat to some sleepless patient of cochlearia salads and glorious feasts of loons and eider-ducks.

"On the other side, suppose Hans fails: the thought is horrible. The Spitzbergen victims were, at about this date, in better condition than we are: it was not until the middle of April that they began to die off. We have yet forty days to run before we can count upon the renovating blessings of animal life and restoring warmth. Neither Riley nor Wilson can last half that time without a supply of antiscorbutic food.

Indeed, there is not a man on board who can hope to linger on till the spring comes unless we have relief.

"I put all this down in no desponding spirit, but as a record to look back upon hereafter, when the immediate danger has passed away, and some new emergency has brought its own array of cares and trials. My mind is hopeful and reliant: there is something even cheering in the constant rally of its energies to meet the calls of the hour.

"March 10, Saturday.—Hans has not yet returned; so that he must have reached the settlement. His orders were, if no meat be obtained of the Esquimaux, to borrow their dogs and try for bears along the open water. In this resource I have confidence. The days are magnificent.

". . . . I had hardly written the above, when '*Bim, bim, bim!*' sounded from the deck, mixed with the chorus of our returning dogs. The next minute Hans and myself were shaking hands.

"He had much to tell us; to men in our condition Hans was as a man from cities. We of the wilderness flocked around him to hear the news. Sugar-teats of raw meat are passed around. 'Speak loud, Hans, that they may hear in the bunks.'

"The 'wind-loved' Anoatok he had reached on the first night after leaving the brig: no Esquimaux there of course; and he slept not warmly at a temperature of 53° below zero. On the evening of the next day he reached Etah Bay, and was hailed with joyous welcome. But a new phase of Esquimaux life had come upon its indolent, happy, blubber-fed denizens. Instead of plump, greasy children, and round-cheeked matrons, Hans saw around him lean figures of misery: the men looked hard and bony, and the children shrivelled in the hoods which cradled them at their mothers' backs. Famine had been among them; and the skin of a young sea-unicorn, lately caught, was all that remained to them of food. It was the old story of improvidence and its miserable train. They had even eaten their reserve of blubber, and were seated in darkness and cold, waiting gloomily for the sun. Even their dogs, their main reliance for the hunt and for an escape to some more favored camping-ground, had fallen a sacrifice to hunger. Only four remained out of thirty: the rest had been eaten.

"Hans behaved well, and carried out my orders in their full spirit. He proposed to aid them in the walrus-hunt. They smiled at first with true Indian contempt: but when they saw my Marston rifle, which he had with him, they changed their tone. When the sea is completely frozen, as it is now, the walrus can only be caught by harpooning them at their holes or in temporary cracks. This mode of hunting them is called *utok*. It requires great skill to enter the harpoon, and often fails from the line giving way in the struggles of the animal. They had lost a harpoon and line in this manner the very day before Hans's arrival. It required very little argument to persuade them to accept his offered company and try the effect of his cone-ball on the harpooned animal before he made good his retreat.

"I have not time to detail Hans's adventurous hunt, equally important to the scurvied sick of Rensselaer and the starving residents of Etah Bay. Metek (the eider-duck) speared a medium-sized walrus, and Hans gave him no less than five Marston balls before he gave up his struggles. The beast was carried back in triumph, and all hands fed as if they could never know famine again. It was a regular feast, and the kablunah interest was exalted to the skies.

"Miserable, yet happy wretches, without one thought for the future, fighting against care when it comes unbidden, and enjoying to the full their scanty measure of present good! As a beast, the Esquimaux is a most sensible beast, worth a thousand Calibans, and certainly ahead of his cousin the Polar bear, from whom he borrows his pantaloons.

"I had directed Hans to endeavor to engage Myouk, if he could, to assist him in hunting. A most timely thought: for the morning's work made them receive the invitation as a great favor. Hans got his share of the meat, and returned to the brig accompanied by the boy, who is now under my care on board. This imp—for he is full of the devil—has always had a relishing fancy for the kicks and cuffs with which I recall the forks and teaspoons when they get astray; and, to tell the truth, he always takes care to earn them. He is very happy, but so wasted by hunger that the work of fattening him will be a costly one. Poor little fellow!

born to toil and necessity and peril; stern hunter as he already is, the lines of his face are still soft and child-like. I think we understand one another better than our incongruities would imply. He has fallen asleep in a deer-skin at my feet.

"March 11, Sunday.—The sick are not as bright as this relief ought to make them. The truth is, they are fearfully down. Neither poor Wilson nor Riley could bear the meat, and they both suffered excessive pain with fever from a meal that was very limited in quantity. Even the stoutest could hardly bear their once solicited allowance of raw meat. I dispensed it cautiously, for I knew the hazards; but I am sure it is to be the salvation of all of us. It gives a respite at any rate, and we could not in reason ask for more.

"Hans is making a walrus-harpoon and line; and, as soon as he and Myouk have freshened a little, I shall send them back to Anoatok in search of water-cracks. I am hard-worked, getting little rest, yet gratefully employed, for my people seem to thank me. My cookery unfortunately shows itself on the smeared pages of my journal.

"March 12, Monday.—The new tackle is finished. Myouk had lost his ussuk-line upon the iceberg, but we supplied its place with a light Manilla cord. Hans made the bonework of his naligeit from the reindeer-antlers which are abundant about the hills. They both rest to-night, and make an early start in the morning for their working-ground.

"The less severe cases on our sick-list are beginning

to feel the influence of their new diet; but Wilson and Brooks do not react. Their inclination for food, or rather their toleration of it, is so much impaired that they reject meat in its raw state, and when cooked it is much less prompt and efficient in its action. My mode of serving it out is this:—Each man has his saucer of thinly-sliced frozen walrus-heart, with lime-juice or vinegar, before breakfast; at breakfast, blood-gravy with wheaten bread; at dinner, steaks slightly stewed or fried, without limit of quantity; none at tea proper; but at 8 P.M. a renewed allowance of raw slices and vinegar. It shows how broken down the party is, that under the appetizing stimulations of an Arctic sky all our convalescents and well men together are content with some seven pounds of meat. Their prostrate comrades are sustained by broth."

ICE-RAFT.

CHAPTER VI.

LINE OF OPEN WATER—AWAHTOK—HIS FIRST-BORN—INSUBORDINATION—THE PLOT—THE DEVELOPMENT—THE DESERTION.

"MARCH 13, Tuesday.—I walked out with Hans and Myouk to give them God-speed. Myouk had made me dress his frosted feet with rabbit-fur, swaddled with alternate folds of flannel and warm skins. The little scamp had not been so comfortable since his accident. The dogs were only four in number, for 'Young Whitey' had been used up at Etah; but the load was light, and Myouk managed to get a fair share of riding. Hans, with the consequential air of 'big Injin,' walked ahead.

"I enjoined on them extreme caution as to their proceedings. They are to stretch over to the Bergy ground, of dismal associations, and to look for ice-cracks in the level channel-way. Here, where I so nearly lost my life, they will seek bears and walrus, and, if they fail, work their way downward to the south. They sleep to-night in a snow-burrow, but hope to-morrow to reach Anoatok.

"March 15, Thursday.—Hans and Myouk returned at eight o'clock last night without game. Their sleep, in a snow-drift about twenty miles to the northward, in a temperature of —54°, was not comfortable, as might be expected. The marvel is how life sustains itself in such circumstances of cold. I have myself slept in an ordinary canvas tent without discomfort, yet without fire, at a temperature of —52°.

"Myouk was very glad to get back to my warm quarters; but Hans was chop-fallen at the dearth of game. They found no open water, but ice, ice, ice, as far to the north and east as the eye could range from an iceberg-elevation of eighty feet. It is the same opposite Anoatok; and, according to the Esquimaux, as far south of Cape Alexander as a point opposite Akotloowick, the first Baffin Bay huts. Beyond this, in spite of the severity of the winter, there is an open sea. It is in the month of March, if at all during the year, that the polynias are frozen up. Those of Refuge Bay and Littleton were open during the whole of last winter; and, considering how very severe the weather is now and has been for months past, I question very much if such extensive areas as the so-called North Water ever close completely.

"Hans saw numerous tracks of bears; and I have no doubt now but that we can secure some of these animals before the seal-season opens. One large beast passed in the night close by the snow-burrow in which our would-be hunters were ensconced. They followed his tracks in the morning; but the dogs were exhausted and the cold was excessive, and they wisely returned to the brig.

" . . . . To-day we have finished burning our last Manilla hawser for fuel, the temperature remaining at the extraordinary mean of —52°. Our next resort must be to the trebling of the brig: Petersen—what remains of him, for the man's energies are gone—is now at work cutting it off. It is a hard trial for me. I have spared neither exertion, thought, nor suffering, to save the sea-worthiness of our little vessel, but all to no end: she can never bear us to the sea. Want of provisions alone, if nothing else, will drive us from her; for this solid case of nine-foot ice cannot possibly give way until the late changes of fall, nor then unless a hot summer and a retarded winter afterward allow the winds to break up its iron casing.

"March 16, Friday.—We have just a scant two day's allowance of meat for the sick. Hans has done his best; but there is nothing to be found on the hills: and I fear that a long hunting-journey to the south is our only resource.

"Awahtok: I have often mentioned him as a plump, good-natured fellow. He was one of my attachés; by which I mean one of the many who stick to me like a plaster, in order to draw or withdraw a share of the iron nails, hoops, buttons, and other treasures which I represent. Awahtok always struck me as a lazy, pleasant sort of fellow, a man who would be glad to bask in sunshine if he could find any. He has a young wife of eighteen, and he himself is but twenty-two. His hut is quite cleanly, and we become his guests there with more satisfaction than at any other hostel in the village of Etah. Awahtok is evidently happy with his wife, and, the last time I saw him, was exulting over the first pledge of their union, a fine little girl. Well, all this about Awahtok is a prelude to the fact that he has just buried his daughter alive under a pile of stones.

"Myouk, who gave us the news to-day, when delicately questioned as to the cause of this little family arrangement, answered, with all simplicity of phrase, that the child had certain habits, common I believe to all the varieties of infancy.

"The month is gliding on, but without any contributions to science, though there are many things about me to suggest investigation.

"It is as much as I can do to complete the routine of the days and enable them to roll into each other. What a dreary death in life must be that of a maid or man of all work!

"March 17, Saturday.—I have been getting Hans ready for the settlement, with a five-sinnet line of Maury's sounding-twine. The natives to the south have lost nearly all their *allunaks* or walrus-lines by the accidents of December or January, and will be unable to replace them till the return of the seal. A good or even serviceable allunak requires a whole ussuk to cut it from. It is almost the only article whose manufacture seems to be conducted by the Esquimaux with any care and nicety of process. Our sounding-line will be a valuable contribution to them, and may perchance, like some more ostentatious charities, include the liberal givers among those whom it principally blesses.

"March 18, Sunday.—I have a couple of men on board whose former history I would give something to know,—bad fellows both of them, but daring, energetic, and strong. They gave me trouble before we reached the coast of Greenland; and they keep me constantly on the watch at this moment, for it is evident to me that they have some secret object in view, involving probably a desertion and escape to the Esquimaux settlements. They are both feigning sickness this morning; and, from what I have overheard, it is with the view of getting thoroughly rested before a start. Hans's departure with the sledge and dogs would give them a fine chance, if they could only waylay him, of securing all our facilities for travel; and I should not be surprised if they tried to compel him to go along with them. They cannot succeed in this except by force.

"I am acting very guardedly with them. I cannot punish till I have the evidence of an overt act. Nor can I trust the matter to other hands. It would not do to depress my sick party by disclosing a scheme which, if it could be carried out fully, might be fatal to the whole of us. All this adds to my other duties those of a detective policeman. I do not find them agreeable.

"March 19, Monday.—Hans got off at eleven. I have been all right in my suspicions about John and

Bill. They were intensely anxious to get together this morning, and I was equally resolved to prevent any communication between them. I did this so ingeniously that they did not suspect my motive, by devising some outside duty for one or the other of them and keeping his comrade in the plot at work under my own eye. Their impatience and cunning little resorts to procure the chance of a word in private were quite amusing. It might be very far otherwise if they could manage to rob us of our dogs and gain the Netlik settlements.

"I hope the danger is over now. I shall keep the whole thing to myself; for, situated as we are, even the frustration of a mutinous purpose had best be concealed from the party.

"Petersen brought in to-day five ptarmigan, a cheering day's work, promising for the future, and allowing me to give an abundant meal to the sickest, and something to the sick. This is enough to keep up the health-working impression of the fresh-meat diet.

"March 20, Tuesday.—This morning I received information from Stephenson that Bill had declared his intention of leaving the brig to-day at some time unknown. John, being now really lame, could not accompany him. This Stephenson overheard in whispers during the night; and, in faithful execution of his duty, conveyed it to me.

"I kept the news to myself; but there was no time to be lost. William, therefore, was awakened at 6 A.M. —after my own night-watch—and ordered to cook breakfast. Meantime I watched him. At first he appeared troubled, and had several stealthily-whispered interviews with John: finally his manner became more easy, and he cooked and served our breakfast-meal. I now felt convinced that he would meet John outside as soon as he could leave the room, and that one or both would then desert. I therefore threw on my furs and armed myself, made Bonsall and Morton acquainted with my plans, and then, crawling out of our dark passage, concealed myself near its entrance. I had hardly waited half an hour,—pretty cold work too,—when John crawled out, limping and grunting. Once fairly out, he looked furtively round, and then with a sigh of satisfaction mounted our ricketty steps entirely cured of his lameness. Within ten minutes after he had gained the deck the door opened again, and William made his appearance, booted for travel and clad in buffalo. As he emerged into the hold, I confronted him. He was ordered at once to the cabin; and Morton was despatched on deck to compel the presence of the third party; while Mr. Bonsall took his station at the door, allowing no one to pass out.

"In a very few minutes John crawled back again, as lame and exhausted as when he was last below, yet growing lamer rapidly as, recovering from the glare of the light, he saw the tableau. I then explained the state of things to the little company, and detailed step by step to the principals in the scene every one of their plans.

"Bill was the first to confess. I had prepared myself for the emergency, and punished him on the spot. As he rose with some difficulty, I detailed from the log-book the offences he had committed, and adduced the proofs.

"The short-handed condition of the brig made me unable to confine him; therefore I deemed it best to remove his handcuffs, to accept his protestations of reform, and put him again to work. He accepted my lenity with abundant thanks, went to duty, and in less than an hour deserted. I was hunting at the time, but the watch reported his having first been discovered on the ice-foot, and out of presenting-distance. His intention undoubtedly is to reach Etah Bay, and, robbing Hans of sledge and dogs, proceed south to Netlik.

"Should he succeed, the result will be a heavy loss to us. The dogs are indispensable in the hunt and in transporting us to Anoatok. The step however is not likely to be successful. At all events, he is off, and I regret that duty prevents my rejoicing at his departure, John remains with us, closely watched, but apparently sincere in his protestations of absolute reform."

SEAL-SKIN CUP.

CHAPTER VII.

COLLOQUY IN THE BUNKS — WINTER TRAVEL — PREPARATIONS — REINDEER FEEDING-GROUNDS — TERRACED BEACHES — A WALK — OCCUPATIONS.

"MARCH 21, Wednesday.—On this day one year ago Mr. Brooks and his party were frozen up in the hummocks. The habit of comparing the condition of two periods, of balancing the thoughts and hopes of one with the realized experience of the other, seems to me a very unprofitable one. It interferes with the practical executive spirit of a man, to mix a bright and happy past with a dim and doubtful present. It's a maudlin piece of work at best, and I'll none of it.

"But listen to poor Brooks there, talking. He is sitting up, congratulating himself that he can nearly straighten his worst leg. 'Well, Mr. Ohlsen, I thought we would never get through them hummocks. You know we unloaded three times; now, I would not say it then, but seeing I am down I'll tell you. When we laid down the last pemmican-case, I went behind the ice, and don't remember nothing till Petersen called me into the tent. I think I must have strained something, and gone off like in a kind of fit.'

"Ohlsen, who is as self-absorbed a man as I ever knew, replies by stating that his boots pinched him; to which poor Brooks, never dwelling long on his own troubles, says in a quiet, soliloquizing way, 'Yes, and Baker's boots pinched him too; but it wasn't the boots, but the killing cold outside of them. There was Pierre: his boots were moccasins, with deer-skin foot-rags, but he died of cold for all that; and there's Mr. Wilson and me, both hanging on in neither one way nor t'other: it's a question which of us lasts the longest.' McGary, another bedridden, but convalescent, I hope, here raises himself on his elbows and checks Brooks for being so down in the mouth; and Brooks, after a growling rejoinder, improves his merry reminiscences by turning to me.

"'Captain Kane, five nights to come one year, you came in upon four of us down as flat as flounders. I didn't look at your boots, but I know you wore Esquimaux ones. It was a hard walk for you, the greatest thing I ever heard tell off; but'—here he begins to soliloquize—'Baker's dead, Pierre's dead, and Wilson and I——'. 'Shut up, Brooks! shut up!' I broke in, whispering across the boards that separated our blankets; 'you will make the patients uncomfortable.' But no: the old times were strong upon him; he did not speak loud, but he caught me by both hands, and said, in his low bass, quiet tones, 'Doctor, you cried when you saw us, and didn't pull up till we jabbed the stopper down the whiskey-tin and gave you a tot of it.'

"The general tone of the conversation around is like this specimen. I am glad to hear my shipmates talking together again, for we have of late been silent. The last year's battle commenced at this time a year ago, and it is natural the men should recall it. Had I succeeded in pushing my party across the bay, our success would have been unequalled; it was the true plan, the best-conceived, and in fact the only one by which, after the death of my dogs, I could hope to carry on the search. The temperatures were frightful, —40° to —56°; but my experience of last year on the rescue-party, where we travelled eighty miles in sixty odd hours, almost without a halt, yet without a frost-bite, shows that such temperatures are no obstacle to travel, provided you have the necessary practical knowledge of the equipment and conduct of your party. I firmly believe that no natural cold as yet known can arrest travel. The whole story of this winter illustrates it. I have both sledged and walked sixty and seventy miles over the roughest ice, in repeated journeys, at fifty degrees below zero, and the two parties from the south reached our brig in the dead of winter, after being exposed for three hundred miles to the same horrible cold.

"The day has been beautifully clear, and so mild that our mid-day thermometers gave but 7°. This bears badly upon the desertion of Godfrey, for the probabilities are that he will find Hans's buffalo-robe at the hut, and thus sleep and be refreshed. In that case, he can easily reach the Esquimaux of Etah Bay, and may as easily seize upon the sledge-dogs, rifle, and trading-articles. The consequences of such an act would be very disastrous; nearly all my hopes of lifting the sick, and therefore of escaping in boats to the south, rest upon these dogs. By them only can we hunt bear and early seal, or rapidly transport ourselves to the tide-holes (*polynia*) of the spring, where we can add water-fowl to our game-list. I am entirely without a remedy. We cannot pursue him, nor could we have well prevented his escape; it is the most culpable desertion I ever knew or heard of. Bonsall, Petersen, and myself are the only men now on board who can work for the rest. Save the warnings of a secret trouble, the fox gnawing under the jacket, I do better than the rest; but I bear my fox. Bonsall is evidently more disabled.

"March 22, Thursday.—Petersen's ptarmigan are all gone, (five of them,) and of the rabbit but two rations of eight ounces each remain. We three, Bonsall, Petersen, and myself, have made up our minds to walk up Mary River Ravine until we reach the deer-plains, and there separate and close in upon them. To-day is therefore a busy one, for we must prepare beforehand the entire daily requirements of the sick: the ice for melting water must be cut in blocks and laid near the stove; the wood, of which it requires one entire day to tear enough out for two days, must be chopped and piled within arm-reach; the bread must be cooked and the provisions arranged, before we can leave our comrades. When we three leave the brig, there will not be a single able man on board. McGary is able to leave his bed and stump about a little; but this is all. Need the dear home-folks, who may some day read this, wonder that I am a little careworn, and that I leave the brig with reluctance? Of we three God-supported men, each has his own heavy load of scurvy.

"March 23, Friday.—We started this morning, overworked and limping, rather as men ending a journey than beginning one. After four hours of forced walking, we reached the reindeer feeding-grounds, but were too late: the animals had left at least two hours before our arrival. An extensive rolling country, rather a lacustrine plain than a true plateau, was covered with traces of life. The snow had been turned up in patches of four or five yards in diameter, by the hoofs of the reindeer, over areas of twenty or fifty acres. The extensive levels were studded with them; and wherever we examined the ground-surface it was covered with grasses and destitute of lichens. We scouted it over the protruding syenites, and found a couple of ptarmigan and three hares: these we secured.

"Our little party reached the brig in the evening, after a walk over a heavy snow-lined country of thirty miles. Nevertheless, I had a walk full of instructive material. The frozen channel of Mary River abounds in noble sections and scenes of splendid wildness and desolation. I am too tired to epitomize here my notebook's record; but I may say that the opportunity which I had to-day of comparing the terrace and boulder lines of Mary River and Charlotte Wood Fiord enables me to assert positively the interesting fact of a secular elevation of the crust, commencing at some as yet undetermined point north of 76°, and continuing to the Great Glacier and the high northern latitudes of Grinnell Land. This elevation, as connected with the equally well-sustained depression of the Greenland coast south of Kingatok, is in interesting keeping with the same undulating alternation on the Scandinavian side. Certainly there seems to be in the localities of these elevated and depressed areas a systematic compensation.

"I counted to-day forty-one distinct ledges or shelves of terrace embraced between our water-line and the syenitic ridges through which Mary River forces itself. These shelves, though sometimes merged into each other, presented distinct and recognisable embankments or escarps of elevation. Their surfaces were at a nearly uniform inclination of descent of 5°, and their breadth either twelve, twenty-four, thirty-six, or some other multiple of twelve paces. This imposing series of ledges carried you in forty-one gigantic steps to an elevation of four hundred and eighty feet; and, as the first rudiments of these ancient beaches left the granites which had once formed the barrier sea-coast, you could trace them passing from drift-strewn rocky barricades to cleanly-defined and gracefully-curved shelves of shingle and pebbles. I have studies of these terraced beaches at various points on the northern coast of Greenland. They are more imposing and on a larger scale than those of Wellington Channel, which are now regarded by geologists as indicative of secular uplift of coast. As these strange structures wound in long spirals around the headlands of the fiords,

THE TERRACED FIORDS.

they reminded me of the parallel roads of Glen Roy,—a comparison which I make rather from general resemblance than ascertained analogies of causes.

"There is a boulder ten miles from our brig, say seven from the coast,—a mass of rounded syenite,—at an altitude of eleven hundred feet, resting, entirely isolated, upon coarse sandstone: its cubical contents cannot be less than sixty tons. Tired as I am by this hard walk, I feel that it has rewarded me well. It was too cold for the pocket-sextant; but I managed to sketch in such features of the opposite coast as were not marked in our charts of last August. I had a full view of the inland glacier throughout a linear trend of twenty miles. I can measure the profitless non-observing routine of the past winter by my joy at this first break-in upon its drudgery. God knows I had laid down for myself much experimental observation, and some lines of what I hoped would be valuable travel and search; but I am thankful that I am here, able to empty a slop-bucket or rub a scurvied leg.

"My people had done well during my absence, and welcomed me back impressively.

"March 24, Saturday.—Our yesterday's ptarmigan gave the most sick a raw ration, and to-day we killed a second pair, which will serve them for to-morrow. To my great joy, they seem on that limited allowance to hold their ground. I am the only man now who scents the fresh meat without tasting it. I actually long for it, but am obliged to give way to the sick.

"Yesterday's walk makes my scorbutized muscles very stiff. I went through my routine of labor, and, as usual in this strange disease, worked off my stiffness and my pain.

"Bonsall and Petersen are now woodmen, preparing

our daily fuel. My own pleasant duty consists in chopping from an iceberg six half-bushel bagfuls of frozen water, carrying it to the brig and passing it through the scuttle into our den; in emptying by three several jobs some twelve to fifteen bucketfuls from the slop-barrel; in administering both as nurse and physician to fourteen sick men; in helping to pick eider-down from its soil as material for boat-bedding; in writing this wretched daily record, eating my meals, sleeping my broken sleeps, and feeling that the days pass without congenial occupation or improving pursuit.

"Hans has not returned. I give him two days more before I fall in with the opinion which some seem to entertain, that Godfrey has waylaid or seized upon his sledge. This wretched man has been the very bane of the cruise. My conscience tells me that almost any measure against him would be justifiable as a relief to the rest; but an instinctive aversion to extreme measures binds my hands."

WOMEN'S SKIN KNIVES, FROM GRAVES AT DISCO.

CHAPTER VIII.

THE DELECTABLE MOUNTAINS—REVIEW OF MARCH—THE DESERTER AGAIN—HIS ESCAPE—GODFREY'S MEAT—CONVALESCENT.

"March 25, Sunday.—A hard-working, busy Sunday it has been,—a cheerless, scurvy-breeding day; and now by the midnight, which is as it were the evening of its continued light, I read the thermometers unaided except by the crimson fires of the northern horizon. It is, moreover, cold again, —37°, and the enemy has a harder grip on my grasshopper. Bonsall and Kane took the entire home-work on themselves to-day, that Petersen might have a chance of following rabbit-tracks up Mary River. He succeeded in shooting one large hare and a couple of ptarmigan,—thus giving our sick a good allowance for one day more.

"Refraction with all its magic is back upon us; the 'Delectable Mountains' appear again; and, as the sun has now worked his way to the margin of the north-western horizon, we can see the blaze stealing out from the black portals of these uplifted hills, as if there was truly beyond it a celestial gate.

"I do not know what preposterous working of brain

led me to compare this northwestern ridge to Bunyan's Delectable Mountains; but there was a time, only one year ago, when I used to gaze upon them with an eye of real longing. Very often, when they rose phantom-like into the sky, I would plan schemes by which to reach them, work over mentally my hard pilgrimage across the ice, and my escape from Doubting Castle to this scene of triumph and reward. Once upon your coasts, O inaccessible mountains, I would reach the Northern Ocean and gather together the remnants of poor Franklin's company. These would be to me the orchards and vineyards and running fountains. The 'Lord of the Hill would see in me a pilgrim.' 'Leaning upon our staves, as is common with weary pilgrims when they stand to talk with any by the way,' we would look down upon an open Polar sea, refulgent with northern sunshine.

"I did try to gain these summits; and when I think of poor Baker's and Pierre's death, of my own almost fatalistic anxiety to cross the frozen sea, and of the terrible physical trial by which we saved our advance party, I cannot help dwelling, as something curious in its likeness, on another scene which Bunyan's explorers witnessed among the Delectable Mountains. 'They hied them first to the top of a hill called Error, which was very steep on the farthest side. So Christian and Hopeful looked down, and saw at the bottom several men dashed all to pieces by a fall which they had from the top.

"'Then said the shepherds, "More than you see lie

dashed to pieces at the bottom of this mountain—and *have continued to this day unburied*, for an example to others to take heed how they clamber too high, or how they come too near to the brink of this mountain."'

"March 31, Saturday.—This month, badly as its daily record reads, is upon review a cheering one. We have managed to get enough game to revive the worst of our scurvy patients, and have kept in regular movement the domestic wheel of shipboard. Our troubles have been greater than at any time before; perhaps I ought to say they are greatest as the month closes: but, whatever of misery Bonsall and Petersen and myself may have endured, it seems nearly certain now that at least four men will soon be able to relieve us. Brooks, McGary, Riley, and Thomas, have seen the crisis of their malady, and, if secured from relapse, will recover rapidly. Ohlsen also is better, but slow to regain his powers. But the rest of the crew are still down.

"The game-season besides is drawing nearer; and, once able to shoot seal upon the ice, I have little fears for the recovery of the larger portion of our party. Perhaps I am too sanguine; for it is clear that those of us who have till now sustained the others are beginning to sink. Bonsall can barely walk in the morning, and his legs become stiffer daily; Petersen gives way at the ankles; and I suffer much from the eruption, a tormenting and anomalous symptom, which affects eight of our sick. It has many of the characteristics of exanthemata; but is singularly persistent, varied in its phases, and possibly in its result dangerous.

"The moral value of this toilsome month to myself has been the lesson of sympathy it has taught me with the laboring man. The fatigue and disgust and secret trials of the overworked brain are bad enough, but not to me more severe than those which follow the sick and jaded body to a sleepless bed. I have realized the sweat of the brow, and can feel how painful his earnings must be to whom the grasshopper has become a burden.

"April 2, Monday.—At eleven o'clock this morning Mr. Bonsall reported a man about a mile from the brig, apparently lurking on the ice-foot. I thought it was Hans, and we both went forward to meet him. As we drew closer we discovered our sledge and dog-team near where he stood; but the man turned and ran to the south.

"I pursued him, leaving Mr. Bonsall, who carried a Sharpe rifle, behind; and the man, whom I now recognised to be Godfrey, seeing me advance alone, stopped and met me. He told me that he had been to the south as far as Northumberland Island; that Hans was lying sick at Etah, in consequence of exposure; that he himself had made up his mind to go back and spend the rest of his life with Kalutunah and the Esquimaux; and that neither persuasion nor force should divert him from this purpose.

"Upon my presenting a pistol, I succeeded in forcing him back to the gangway of the brig; but he refused to go farther; and, being loath to injure him, I left him under the guardianship of Mr. Bonsall's weapon while

I went on board for irons; for both Bonsall and myself were barely able to walk, and utterly incapable of controlling him by manual force, and Petersen was out hunting: the rest, thirteen in all, are down with scurvy. I had just reached the deck, when he turned to run. Mr. Bonsall's pistol failed at the cap. I jumped at once to the gun-stand; but my first rifle, affected by the cold, went off in the act of cocking, and a second, aimed in haste at long but practicable distance, missed the fugitive. He made good his escape before we could lay hold of another weapon.

"I am now more anxious than ever about Hans. The past conduct of Godfrey on board, and his mutinous desertion, make me aware that he is capable of daring wrong as well as deception. Hans has been gone more than a fortnight: he has been used to making the same journey in less than a week. His sledge and dogs came back in the possession of the very man whom I suspected of an intention to waylay him; and this man, after being driven by menaces to the ship's side, perils his life rather than place himself in my power on board of her.

"Yet he came back to our neighborhood voluntarily, with sledge and dogs and walrus-meat! Can it have been that John, his former partner in the plot, was on the look-out for him, and had engaged his aid to consummate their joint desertion?

"One thing is plain. This man at large and his comrade still on board, the safety of the whole company exacts the sternest observance of discipline. I have called all hands, and announced it as a standing order of the ship, and one to be observed inflexibly, that desertion, or the attempt to desert, shall be met at once by the sternest penalty. I have no alternative. By the body of my crew, sick, dependent, unable to move, and with every thing to lose by the withdrawal of any portion of our efficient force, this announcement was received as a guarantee of their personal safety. But it was called for by other grave considerations. There is at this time on the part of all, men as well as officers, a warm feeling toward myself, and a strict, stanch fidelity to the expedition. But, for moral reasons which would control me, even if my impulse were different, I am constrained for the time to mingle among them without reserve, to act as a servant to their wants, to encourage colloquial equality and good-humor; and, looking only a little way ahead to the juncture when a perfectly-regulated subordination will become essential, I know that my present stand will be of value.

"This sledge-load of Godfrey's meat, coming as it does, may well be called a Godsend: one may forgive the man in consideration of the good which it has done us all. We have had a regular feed all round, and exult to think we need no catering for the morrow. It has cheered our downhearted sick men wonderfully. Our brew of beer, too,—the 'Arctic Linseed Mucilage Adaptation,'—turns out excellent. Our grunts and growls are really beginning to have a good-natured twang. Our faces lessen as our shadows promise to increase. I think I see a change which points to the happier future.

"Our sick, however, are still non-operatives, and our one room is like the convalescent ward of a hospital, with Bonsall and myself for the only nurses."

NESSARK—JUMPER-HOOD

CHAPTER IX.

ROUTINE—GETTING UP—BREAKFAST—WORK—TURNING IN—HANS STILL MISSING—THE DETERMINATION.

"April 3, Tuesday.—To-day I detained Petersen from his hunt, and took a holiday rest myself,—that is to say, went to bed and——sweated: to-morrow I promise as much for Bonsall.

"While here in bed I will give the routine of a day in this spring-time of year:—

"At 7.30 call 'all hands;' which means that one of the well trio wakes the other two. This order is obeyed slowly. The commander confesses for himself that the breakfast is wellnigh upon table before he gets his stiff ankles to the floor. Looking around, he sees the usual mosaic of sleepers as ingeniously dovetailed and crowded together as the campers-out in a buffalo-bag. He winds his way through them, and, as he does so, some stereotyped remarks are interchanged. 'Thomas!'—our ex-cook, now side by side with the first officer of the expedition,—'Thomas, turn out!' Eugh-ng, sir.' 'Turn out; get up.' 'Ys-sir;' (sits bolt upright, and rubs his eyes.) 'How d'you feel, Mr.

Ohlsen?' 'Better, sir.' 'How 've you passed the night, Mr. Brooks?' 'Middlin', sir.' And, after a diversified series of spavined efforts, the mystical number forms its triangle at the table.

"It still stands in its simple dignity, an unclothed platform of boards, with a pile of plates in the centre. Near these is a virtuoso collection of cups grouped in a tumulus or cairn, commencing philosophically at the base with heavy stoneware, and ending with battered tin: the absolute pinnacle a debased dredging-box, which makes a bad goblet, being unpleasantly sharp at its rim. At one end of this table, partly hid by the beer-barrel, stands Petersen; at the side, Bonsall; and a lime-juice cask opposite marks my seat. We are all standing: a momentary hush is made among the sick; and the daily prayer comes with one heart:—'Accept our gratitude, and restore us to our homes.'

"The act of devotion over, we sit down, and look—not at the breakfast, but at each other.

"It may sound absurd to those who cannot understand the narrowing interest which we three availables feel in our continued mutual ability, for me to say that we spend the first five minutes in a detail of symptoms. The state of each man's gums and shins and ankles, his elbows, loins, and kidneys, is canvassed minutely and compared with his yesterday's report: the recital might edify a specialist who was anxious to register the Protean indications of scurvy. It is sometimes ludicrous, but always sad.

"Now for the bill of fare. 'Who cooked?'—I am describing a gala-day.—'It was Morton: he felt so much better that he got up at six; but he caved in soon after:'—

"First, coffee, great comforter to hard-worked men; one part of the genuine berry to three of navy-beans; next, sugar: what complex memories the word brings back!—the veritable sugar has been long ago defunct; but we have its representative molasses twice a week in our tea. Third, butter; there it is in a mutilated vegetable-dish; my own invention, melted from salt beef and washed in many waters: the unskilled might call it tallow. Fourth, a real delicacy, not to be surpassed in court or camp, for Morton was up to see to it:—a pile of hot rolls of fine Virginia flour. What else? Nothing else: the breakfast resolves itself into bean-coffee, tallow, and hot bread. Yet a cordial meal it is. I am sorry to hurry over it so uncourteously, for I could dwell with Charles Lamb's pensive enthusiasm upon the fleshpots; but I have been longer in describing the feast than it takes us to dispose of it. I hurry on with the interesting detail. Dinner is breakfast, with the beans converted into soup instead of coffee; and supper boasts of stewed apples.

"Work commences at nine. Petersen is off with his gun, and the two remaining dearly-beloved Rogers arrange their carte: one makes the round of the sick and deals out their daily allowance of raw meat; the other goes to cutting ice. Those who can sit in bed and work, pick eider-down or cotton, for coverlets to our boat-bedding on the escape; others sew canvas bags for the same purpose; and Brooks balls off twine in order to lay up 'small stuff.'

"At times when the sun comes out very brightly, Brooks and Wilson get permission to go on deck. One of us assists them, and, by the aid of creeping and crawling, these poor cripples manage to sit upon the combings of the hatch and look around in the glorious daylight. The sight seldom fails to affect them. There are emotions among rude, roughly-nurtured men which vent themselves in true poetry. Brooks has about him sensibilities that shame me.

"The afternoon, save to the cook, is a season of rest; a real lazy, lounging interval, arrested by the call to supper. The coming night-watch obliges me to take an evening cat-nap. I state this by way of implying that I never sleep o' daytimes.

"After supper, we have a better state of things than two weeks ago. Then the few tired outworkers were regaled by the groans and tossings of the sick. There was little conversation, and the physiognomy of our smoke-blackened little den was truly dismal. Now daylight pours in from the scuttle, the tea-kettle sings upon the stove, the convalescents rise up on their elbows and spin merry yarns. We are not yet sufficiently jolly for cards; but we are sufficiently thankful to do without them. At nine, silence almost unbroken prevails throughout our dormitory, and the watch-officer slips on his bear-skin, and, full of thoughts of to-morrow, resigns himself to a round of little routine observances, the most worthless of which is this unbroken record of the changing days.

"April 6, Friday.—Our little family is growing more and more uneasy about Hans. William reported him sick at Etah; but we had no faith in this story, and looked on his absence as merely the result of fatigue from exposure. But there really seems ground for serious apprehension now. My own fear is that William may have conveyed to him some false message, or some threat or reproof, using my name, and in this way deterred him from returning. Hans is very faithful; but he is entirely unaware of William's desertion, and he is besides both credulous and sensitive. I am attached to Hans: he has always been a sort of henchman, a body-guard, the companion of my walks. He is a devout Moravian; and when the party withdrew from the brig last fall he refused to accompany them on grounds of religious obligation. The boy has fixed, honorable principles. Petersen thinks that he ought to be sent for, but he has not thought out the question who is to be sent. Bonsall is too lame to travel; Petersen himself is infinitely the best fitted, but he shirks the duty, and to-day he takes to his bed: I alone am left.

"Clearly duty to this poor boy calls me to seek him, and clearly duty to these dependent men calls upon me to stay. Long and uncomfortably have I pondered over these opposing calls, but at last have come to a determination. Hans was faithful to me: the danger to him is imminent; the danger to those left behind only contingent upon my failure to return. With earnest trust in that same supervising Agency which has so often before in graver straits interfered to protect and carry me through, I have resolved to go after Hans.

"The orders are given. In three hours I will be equipped and ready to take advantage of the first practicable moment for the start. It makes me write gravely; for I am far from well, very far from strong, and am obliged to drive our reduced team twice seventy miles. The latter half of the journey I shall have to do entirely on foot, and our lowest night-temperatures are under —40°.

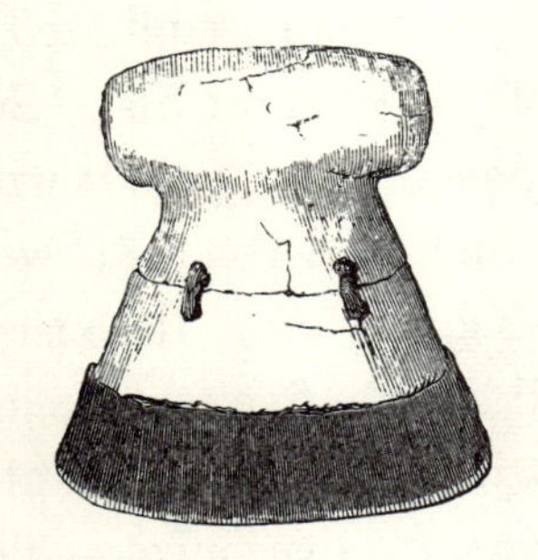

ESQUIMAUX WOMAN'S KNIFE.

CHAPTER X.

JOURNEY AFTER HANS—ESQUIMAUX SLEDGING—HANS FOUND—RECEPTO AMICO—EXPLANATION—FURTHER SEARCH—MATURING PLANS—CHANCES OF ESCAPE—FOOD PLENTY—PAULIK—FAMINE AMONG THE ESQUIMAUX—EXTINCTION—LIGHT HEARTS—DESERTER RECOVERED.

"APRIL 10, Tuesday.—I left the brig at 10½ A.M., with but five dogs and a load so light as to be hardly felt.

"It requires some suggestive incident to show us how we have gradually become assimilated in our habits to the necessities of our peculiar life. Such an incident I find in my equipment. Compare it with similar sledge-outfits of last winter, and you will see that we are now more than half Esquimaux. It consists of—

"1. One small sledge, five feet six by two.

"2. An extra jumper and sack-pants for sleeping.

"3. A ball of raw walrus-meat.—This is all.

"The sledge is portable, and adapted to jump over the chasms of the land-ice, and to overturn with impunity, save to the luckless driver. It has two standards, or, as we call them, "up-standers," which spring like elbows from its hinder extremity.

"They serve as handles, by which, running or walking behind, you guide the sledge, lift it over rugged places, or rest yourself and your dogs while in progress together.

"The extra jumper is a bear-skin jacket, or rather shirt, which after being put on is overlapped at the waist by a large pair of footed trowsers. No winter traveller should be without these:—at temperatures below —25° or —30° they are invaluable. Blanket-

CAPE INGLEFIELD, (REFUGE HARBOR.)

bags are nearly useless below —30°, in a gale of wind; it riddles through them.

"The ball of raw meat is made by chopping into inch-pieces walrus or other meat, and pouring among it hot tallow, by which the pieces are prevented from freezing too hard, so that you can readily cut out your meal as it is required. A little butter, if you have some, will contribute to soften it: olive-oil perhaps would be better; but without some such luxurious additions a man in too great a hurry for dinner might be apt to risk his teeth. In the present journey, having nothing but tallow, I made my meat-ball like a twist-loaf, and broke it with a stone.

"I have no incidents to record in the shape of disaster. My dogs were in excellent condition, and the ice good for travel. The real incident of the journey was its early success. My dogs, in spite of low feeding, carried me sixty-four miles in eleven hours.

"Faithful Hans! Dear good follower and friend! I was out on the floes just beyond the headlands of our old 'Refuge Harbor,' when I made out a black speck far in to shoreward. Refraction will deceive a novice on the ice; but we have learned to baffle refraction. By sighting the suspected object with your rifle at rest, you soon detect motion. It was a living animal—a man. Shoreward went the sledge; off sprang the dogs ten miles an hour, their driver yelling the familiar provocative to speed, 'Nannook! nannook!' 'A bear! a bear!' at the top of his lungs.

"There was no room for mistaking the methodical seal-stalking gait of Hans. He hardly varied from it as we came near; but in about fifteen minutes we were shaking hands and jabbering, in a patois of Esquimaux and English, our mutual news. The poor fellow had been really ill: five days down with severe pains of limbs have left him still a 'little veek;' which means with Hans well used up. I stuck him on the sledge and carried him to Anoatok.

"Fortunately Anoatok for once belied its name: there was no wind, and the sun broke down upon us with a genial +14°, although the shade gave —25°.

I had brought with me, expecting the boy might need it, a small mustard-bottle of our treasured molasses, and a little tea. We keep a camp-kettle at this hut, and both of us wore in our belts the inseparable tin-cup. How the boy enjoyed his hot tea! Metek had given him a few lumps of frozen walrus-liver, the very best provision for cold travel: our appetites were good; and, the two thus fitly harmonizing, we crunched away right merrily.

"Hans reached Etah with Myouk two days after leaving us, and at once commenced his hunt. In the course of five days of most hazardous ice-range, he killed two fine young animals; his three companions in the hunt killing only three. He had the great advantage of my powerful Marston rifle, but his tackle was very inferior. Our sinnet-laid twine would not stand the powerful struggles of the beast, and on one occasion parted while fast in a large female. Still his success must have acquired for him the good-will of these people, for in the 'flens' or hunting-division of spoil they gained by his companionship.

"In the sickness that followed his long exposure, he tells me, he was waited on most carefully at the settlement. A young daughter of Shunghu elected herself his nurse, and her sympathies and smiles have, I fear, made an impression on his heart which a certain damsel near Upernavik might be sorry to hear of.

"Hans cached part of his meat at Littleton Island, after sending a load by William to the brig. He had no difficulty, I find, in penetrating this man's designs. He was indeed urged by him to agree that they should drive off together to the south and so leave us sledgeless. Upon Hans's refusal, he tried to obtain his rifle; but this of course was easily prevented. He consented at last to take up the meat, with a view of making

WALRUS CACHE.

terms with me and securing probably a companion. Baffled in this, as I have mentioned, he made his escape a second time to Etah. There I might be content to leave him, an unwelcome guest, and dependent upon the Esquimaux. Strong and healthy as he is, our daily work goes on better for his absence, and the ship seems better when purged by his desertion; but the example is disastrous; and, cost what it may, I must have him back.

"April 11, Wednesday.—Hans started again to bring back the meat from Littleton Island cache. If he feels strengthened, I have given him a commission to which I attach the greatest importance.

"My hopes of again undertaking a spring journey to Kennedy Channel were strong in the early months of the winter; but, as our dogs died away a second time, and the scurvy crept in upon us, I became sad and distrustful as to the chance of our ever living to gain the open water. The return of the withdrawing party absorbed all my thoughts. They brought news of disaster, starvation, and loss of dogs, among the natives. Our prospects seemed at the lowest ebb. Still, I cherished a secret hope of making another journey, and had determined to undertake it alone with our poor remnant of four dogs, trusting to my rifle for provision. In fact, this continuation of my one great duty has been constantly before me, and I now think that I can manage it. Thus:—The Esquimaux have left Northumberland Island, and are now near Cape Alexander, as a better hunting-ground. Kalutunah, the best and most provident man among them, has managed to save seven dogs. I have authorized Hans to negotiate *carte-blanche*, if necessary, for four of these, even as a loan; promising as a final bait the contingent possession of my whole team when I reach the open water on my return. On this mission I send my '*fides Achates*,' and await his return with anxious hope.

"I have seen, almost from the first day of our imprisonment by the ice, the probability, if nothing more, that we might never be able to liberate the ship. Elsewhere in this journal I have explained by what construction of my duty I urged the brig to the north, and why I deemed it impossible honorably to abandon her after a single season. The same train of reasoning now leads me to mature and organize every thing for an early departure without her in case she cannot be released. My hopes of this release are very feeble; and I know that when it does occur, if ever, the season will, like the last, be too far advanced for me to carry my people home. All my experience, carefully reviewed from my note-books and confirmed by consultation with Petersen, convinces me that I must start early, and govern my boat and sledges by the condition of the ice and hunting-grounds.

"Whatever of executive ability I have picked up during this brain and body-wearing cruise warns me against immature preparation or vacillating purposes. I must have an exact discipline, a rigid routine, and a perfectly-thought-out organization. For the past six weeks I have, in the intervals between my duty to the sick and the ship, arranged the schedule of our future course. Much of it is already under way. My journal shows what I have done, but what there is to do is appalling.

"I state all this to show how much I hazard and possibly sacrifice by my intended journey to the north, and to explain why I have so little time and mood for scientific observation or research. My feelings may be understood when I say that my carpenter and all the working men, save Bonsall, are still on their backs; and that a month's preliminary labor is needed before I can commence the heavy work of transporting my three boats over the ice to the anticipated water. At the moment of my writing this, the water is over eighty miles in a straight line from our brig.

"April 12, Thursday.—The wind still blowing as yesterday, from the southward and eastward. This is certainly favorable to the advance of open water. The long swell from the open spaces in Baffin's Bay has such a powerful effect upon the ice, that I should not wonder if the floes about Lifeboat Cove, off McGary Island, were broken up by the first of May.

"Our sick have been without fresh food since the 5th; but such is the stimulus imparted by our late supply that they as yet show no backward symptoms. McGary and Ohlsen and Brooks and Riley sun themselves daily, and are able to do much useful jobbing. Thomas begins to relieve me in cooking, Riley to take a spell at the slops, Morton cooks breakfast, and, aided by McGary and Ohlsen, has already finished one worsted quilted camp-blanket, with which I intend to cover our last remaining buffalo-skins. Wilson comes on slowly; Dr. Hayes's toe begins to heal; Sontag is more cheery. With the exception of Goodfellow, John, and Whipple, I can feel that those of my little household are fast becoming men again.

"April 13, Friday.—Our sick—which still means all hands except the cook, which means the captain—

entered this morning on their eighth day of fasting from flesh. One or two have been softening about the gums again for some days past, and all feel weak with involuntary abstinence. The evening comes, and 'Bim! bim! bim!' sounds upon the deck: Hans is back with his dogs. Rabbit-stew and walrus-liver!—a supper for a king!

"This life of ours—for we have been living much in this way for nine months past—makes me more charitable than I used to be with our Esquimaux neighbors. The day provides for itself; or, if it does not, we trust in the morrow, and are happy till to-morrow disappoints us. Our smoke-dried cabin is a scene worth looking at: no man with his heart in the right place but would enjoy it. Every man is elbowed up on his platform, with a bowl of rich gravy-soup between his knees and a stick of frozen liver at his side, gorging himself with the antiscorbutic luxuries, and laughing as if neither ice nor water was before him to traverse.

"Hans has brought Metek with him, and Metek's young nephew, a fine-looking boy of fourteen.

"I do not know whether I have mentioned that some little time before our treaty of alliance and mutual honesty Metek stole the gunwale of the Red Eric. He has been, of course, in something of uncertainty as to his political and personal relations, and his present visit to the nalegak with a noble sledge-load of walrus-meat is evidently intended as a propitiation for his wrong.

"They are welcome, the meat and Metek, abundantly. He is the chieftain of Etah, and, as such, a vassal of him of Aūnatok, the 'Open Place,' which we have named Rensselaer Harbor. He speaks sadly, and so does Hans, of the fortunes of the winter.

PAULIK, METEK'S NEPHEW.

"The Netelik settlement on Northumberland Island was already, when we heard of it last, the refuge of the natives from the farther South, even beyond Wostenholme. It has always been a hunting stronghold; but, as the winter darkness advanced, the pressure of numbers combined with their habitual improvidence to dissipate their supplies.

"It seems that the poor wretches suffered terribly,—even more than our neighbors of Etah Bay. Their laws exact an equal division; and the success of the best hunters was dissipated by the crowds of feeble claimants upon their spoils. At last the broken nature of the ice-margin and the freezing-up of a large zone of ice prevented them from seeking walrus. The water was inaccessible, and the last resource pressed itself upon them. They killed their dogs. Fearful as it sounds when we think how indispensable the services of these animals are to their daily existence, they cannot now number more than twenty in the entire ownership of the tribe. From Glacier South to Glacier North, from Glacier East to the rude icebound coast which completes the circuit of their little world, this nation have but twenty dogs. What can they hope for without them?

"I can already count eight settlements, including about one hundred and forty souls. There are more, perhaps, but certainly not many. Out of these I can number five deaths since our arrival; and I am aware of hardships and disasters encountered by the survivors, which, repeated as they must be in the future, cannot fail to involve a larger mortality. Crime combines with disease and exposure to thin their numbers: I know of three murders within the past two years; and one infanticide occurred only a few months ago. These facts, which are open to my limited sources of information, cannot, of course, indicate the number of deaths correctly. They confirm, however, a fearful conclusion which these poor wretches have themselves communicated to us,—that they are dying out; not lingeringly, like the American tribes, but so rapidly as to be able to mark within a generation their progress toward extinction. Nothing can be more saddening, measured by our own sensibilities, than such a conviction; but it seems to have no effect upon this remarkable people. Surrounded by the graves of their dead, by huts untenanted yet still recent in their memory as homesteads, even by caches of meat which, frozen under the snow by the dead of one year, are eaten by the living of the next, they show neither apprehension nor regret. Even Kalutunah—a man of fine instincts, and, I think, of heart—will retain his apathy of face as, by the aid of Petersen, our interpreter, I point out to him the certainty of their speedy extinction. He will smile in his efforts to count the years which must obliterate his nation, and break in with a laugh as his children shout out their 'Amna Ayah' and dance to the tap of his drum.

"How wonderful is all this! Rude as are their ideas of numbers, there are those among this merry-hearted people who can reckon up to the fate of their last man.

"After Netelik, the receptacle of these half-starved fugitives, had been obliged itself to capitulate with famine, the body corporate determined, as on like occasions it had often done before, to migrate to the seats of the more northern hunt.

"The movements of the walrus and the condition of

the ice seem to be known to them by a kind of in stinct; so, when the light came, they harnessed in their reserve of dogs and started for Cape Alexander.

"It could not, one might suppose, have been a very cheerful migration,—women, children, and young babies thrusting themselves into a frozen wilderness at temperatures below —30°, and sometimes verging on —60°. But Hans, with a laugh that seemed to indicate some exquisite point of concealed appreciation of the ludicrous, said they travelled generally in squads, singing 'Amna Ayah,' and, when they reached any of the halting-huts, ate the blubber and liver of the owners and danced all night. So at last they came to Utak-soak, the 'great caldron,' which we call Cape Alexander, and settled down at Peteravik, or the 'Welcome Halt.'

"At first game was scarce here also; but the season came soon when the female walrus is tending her calf on the ice, and then, but for the protracted exposure of the hunt, there was no drawback to its success. They are desperately merry now, and seem to have forgotten that a second winter is ahead of them. Hans said, with one of his quiet laughs, 'One-half of them are sick and cannot hunt: these do nothing but eat, and sing "Amna Ayah."'

"April 18, Wednesday.—I am just off a two hundred miles' journey, bringing back my deserter, and, what is perhaps quite as important, a sledge-load of choice walrus-cuts.

"I found from Hans that his negotiation for the dogs

had failed, and that unless I could do something by individual persuasion I must give up my scheme of a closing exploration to the north. I learned too that Godfrey was playing the great man at Etah, defying recapture; and I was not willing to trust the influence he might exert on my relations with the tribe. I determined that he should return to the brig.

"I began by stratagem. I placed a pair of foot-cuffs on Metek's sledge, and, after looking carefully to my body-companion six-shooter, invited myself to ride back with him to Etah. His nephew remained on board in charge of Hans, and I disguised myself so well in my nessak that, as we moved off, I could easily have passed for the boy Paulik, whose place I had taken.

"As our eighty miles drew to an end, and that which we call the settlement came close in view, its population streamed out to welcome their chief's return. Among the first and most prominent was the individual whom I desired to meet, waving his hand and shouting 'Tima!' as loudly as the choicest savage of them all. An instant later and I was at his ear, with a short phrase of salutation and its appropriate gesture. He yielded unconditionally at once, and, after walking and running by turns for some eighty miles before the sledge, with a short respite at Anoatok, is now a prisoner on board.

"My remaining errand was almost as successful."

CHAPTER XI.

HARTSTENE BAY—ESQUIMAUX DWELLINGS—A CROWDED INTERIOR —THE NIGHT'S LODGING—A MORNING REPAST—MOURNING FOR THE DEAD—FUNERAL RITES—PENANCE.

ETAH is on the northeastern curve of Hartstene Bay, facing to the south and west. As you stretch over from the south point of Littleton Island to the main, the broken character of the ice subsides into a traversable plain, and the shore-scenery assumes a singular wildness. The bottom series of plutonics rises to grand and mountainous proportions, and in the background, soaring above these, are the escaladed greenstones of the more northern coast. At the very bottom of the bay are two perforations, one a fortress-mantled fiord, the other a sloping ravine: both are occupied by extensions of the same glacier.

The fiord points to Peteravik, where Kalutunah and his hungry southern corps have now taken up their quarters; the other is the oft-mentioned settlement of Etah. A snow-drift, rising at an angle of forty-five degrees till it mingles with the steep sides of a moun tain, is dotted by two dark blemishes upon its pure

C. Schuessele. Engraved at J.M Butler's establishment 84 Chestnut St. J.C.Mc Rae

LIFE IN THE ESQUIMAUX IGLÖE

ETAH

white. Coming nearer, you see that the dirt-spots are perforations of the snow: nearer still, you see above each opening a smaller one, and a covered roof connecting them. These are the doors and windows of the settlement; two huts and four families, but for these vent-holes entirely buried in the snow.

The inmates of the burrows swarmed around me as I arrived. "Nalegak! nalegak! tima!" was yelled in chorus: never seemed people more anxious to propitiate, or more pleased with an unexpected visit. But they were airily clad, and it blew a northwester; and they soon crowded back into their ant-hill. Meantime preparations were making for my in-door reception, and after a little while Metek and myself crawled in on hands and knees, through an extraordinary tossut thirty paces long. As I emerged on the inside, the salute of "nalegak" was repeated with an increase of energy that was any thing but pleasant.

There were guests before me,—six sturdy denizens of the neighboring settlement. They had been overtaken by the storm while hunting, and were already crowded upon the central dais of honor. They united in the yell of welcome, and I soon found myself gasping the ammoniacal steam of some fourteen vigorous, amply-fed, unwashed, unclothed fellow-lodgers. I had come somewhat exhausted by an eighty miles' journey through the atmosphere of the floes: the thermometer inside was at +90°, and the vault measured fifteen feet by six. Such an amorphous mass of compounded humanity one could see nowhere else: men, women, children, with nothing but their native dirt to cover them, twined and dovetailed together like the worms in a fishing-basket.

No hyperbole could exaggerate that which in serious

PORTRAIT OF ANINGNAH.

earnest I give as the truth. The platform measured but seven feet in breadth by six in depth, the shape being semi-elliptical. Upon this, including children and excluding myself, were bestowed thirteen persons.

The kotluk of each matron was glowing with a flame sixteen inches long. A flipper-quarter of walrus, which lay frozen on the floor of the netek, was cut into steaks; and the kolopsuts began to smoke with a burden of ten or fifteen pounds apiece. Metek, with a little amateur aid from some of the sleepers, emptied these without my assistance. I had the most cordial invitation to precede them; but I had seen enough of the culinary régime to render it impossible. I broke my fast on a handful of frozen liver-nuts that Bill brought me, and, bursting out into a profuse perspiration, I stripped like the rest, threw my well-tired carcass across Mrs. Eider-duck's extremities, put her left-hand baby under my armpit, pillowed my head on Myouk's somewhat warm stomach, and thus, an honored guest and in the place of honor, fell asleep.

Next morning, the sun nearly at noonday height, I awoke: Mrs. Eider-duck had my breakfast very temptingly ready. It was forked on the end of a curved piece of bone,—a lump of boiled blubber and a choice cut of meat. The preliminary cookery I had not seen: I am an old traveller, and do not care to intrude into the mysteries of the kitchen. My appetite was in its usual blessed redundance, and I was about to grasp the smiling proffer, when I saw the matron, who was manipulating as chief intendant of the other kotluk, performing an operation that arrested me. She had in her hand a counterpart of the curved bone that supported my *déjeuner*,—indeed, it is the universal implement of an Esquimaux cuisine; and, as I turned my head, I saw her quietly withdrawing it from beneath her dress, and then plunging it into the soup-pot before her, to bring out the counterpart of my own smoking morsel. I learned afterward that the utensil has its two recognised uses; and that, when not immediately wanted for the purposes of pot or table, it ministers to the "royal luxury" of the Scottish king. I dare not amplify this description.

Dirt or filth in our sense is not a conceived quality with these Esquimaux. Incidentally it may be an annoyance or obstruction; but their nearest word, "Eberk," expresses no more than this.

It is an ethnological trait of these ultra-northern nomads,—so far as I know, a unique one; and must be attributed not alone to their predatory diet and peculiar domestic system, but to the extreme cold, which by rapid freezing resists putrefaction and prevents the joint accumulation of the dogs and the household from being intolerable. Their senses seem to take no cognizance of what all instinct and association make revolting to the sight and touch and smell of civilized man.

My note-book proves this by exact and disgusting details, the very mildest of which I cannot transfer to these pages.

I spent some time at Etah in examining the glacier and in making sketches of things about me. I met several old friends. Among the rest was Awahtok, only now recovering from his severe frost-bite, the effect of his fearful adventure with Myouk among the drifting ice. I gave him a piece of red flannel and powwowed him. He resides with Ootuniah in the second hut, a smaller one than Metek's, with his pretty wife, a sister of Kalutunah's. I could hardly believe the infanticide story which Hans had told me of this young couple; and, pretending ignorance of the matter, I asked after the child's health. Their manner satisfied me that the story was true; they turned their hands downward, but without any sign of confusion. They did not even pay its memory the cheap compliment of tears, which among these people are always at hand.

There is a singular custom which I have often noticed here as well as among some of the Asiatics, and which has its analogies in more cultivated centres. I allude to the regulated formalities of mourning for the dead. They weep according to system; when one begins all are expected to join, and it is the office of courtesy for the most distinguished of the company to wipe the eyes of the chief mourner. They often assemble by concert for a general weeping-match; but it happens sometimes that one will break out into tears and others courteously follow, without knowing at first what is the particular subject of grief.

It is not, however, the dead alone who are sorrowed for by such a ceremony. Any other calamity may call for it as well: the failure of a hunt, the snapping of a walrus-line, or the death of a dog. Mrs. Eider-duck, *née* Small Belly, (Egurk,) once looked up at me from her kolupsut and burst into a gentle gush of wo. I was not informed of her immediate topic of thought, but with remarkable presence of mind I took out my handkerchief,—made by Morton out of the body of an unused shirt,—and, after wiping her eyes politely, wept a few tears myself. This little passage was soon over; Mrs. Eider-duck returned to her kolupsut, and Nalegak to his note-book.

The ceremonial mourning, however, is attended sometimes, if not always, by observances of a more serious character. So far as my information goes, the religious notions of the Esquimaux extend only to the recognition of supernatural agencies, and to certain usages by which they may be conciliated. The angekok of the tribe—the prophet, as he is called among our Indians of the West—is the general counsellor. He prescribes or powwows in sickness and over wounds, directs the policy and movements of the little state, and, though not the titular chief, is really the power behind the throne. It is among the prerogatives and duties of his office to declare the appropriate oblations and penances of grief. These are sometimes quite oppressive. The bereaved husband may be required even to abstain from the seal- or walrus-hunt for the whole year, from *Okiakut* to *Okiakut*—winter to winter. More generally he is denied the luxury of some article of food, as the rabbit or a favorite part of the walrus; or he may be forbidden to throw back his nessak, and forced to go with uncovered head.

A sister of Kalutunah died suddenly at Peteravik. Her body was sewed up in skins, not in a sitting posture, like the remains which we found in the graves at the South, but with the limbs extended at full length; and her husband bore her unattended to her resting-place, and covered her, stone by stone, with a rude monumental cairn. The blubber-lamp was kept burning outside the hut while the solitary funeral was in progress; and when it was over the mourners came together to weep and howl, while the widower recited his sorrows and her praise. His penance was severe, and combined most of the inflictions which I have described above.

It is almost as difficult to trace back the customs of the Smith's Sound Esquimaux as it is to describe their religious faith. They are a declining—almost an obsolete—people, "*toto orbe divisos*," and too much engaged with the necessities of the present to cherish memorials of the past. It was otherwise with those whom we met in the more southern settlements. These are now for the most part concentrated about the Danish posts, in very different circumstances, physical as well as moral, from their brethren of the North.

CHAPTER XII.

THE ESQUIMAUX OF GREENLAND — CHANGE OF CHARACTER — LABORS OF THE MISSIONARIES—NÖLUK—THE OMINAKS—PINGEIAK AND JENS — THE ANGEKOKS — HUSUTOKS — THE IMNAPOK — THE DECREE.

SOME thirty years ago the small-pox found its way among the natives of the upper coast, and most of those who escaped or survived its ravages sought the protection of the colony. Others followed from the more inland regions; and now there is not an Esquimaux, from the Great Glaciers of Melville Bay down to Upernavik, who does not claim fellowship in that community.

We found traces of their former haunts much farther north than they appear to have been noticed by others; some of such a character as to indicate for them a tolerably recent date. I have already mentioned the deserted huts which we came upon in Shoal-Water Cove, in lat. 78° 27′, and the stone fox-traps upon the rocks near them. Other huts, evidently of Esquimaux construction, but very ancient, were found on the in-shore side of Littleton Island; and among the cairns around them that had served to conceal provisions or that now covered the remains of the dead, were numerous implements of the chase.

The huts which I saw near Refuge Harbor, in lat. 78° 33′, were much more perfect, and had been inhabited very recently. From some of the marks which I have referred to in my journal, there was reason to suppose that the inmates might return before the opening of another season.

It was still otherwise with those that we met at Karsuk and elsewhere farther to the south. These, though retaining signs of comparatively modern habitation, were plainly deserted homes. I met at Upernavik an ancient woman, the latest survivor of the few who escaped from these settlements during the general pestilence.

The labors of the Lutheran and Moravian missionaries have been so far successful among these people that but few of them are now without the pale of professed Christianity, and its reforming influences have affected the moral tone of all. Before the arrival of these self-sacrificing evangelists, murder, incest, burial of the living, and infanticide, were not numbered among crimes. It was unsafe for vessels to touch upon the coast; treachery was as common and as much honored as among the Polynesians of the Eastern seas. Crantz tells us of a Dutch brig that was seized by the natives at the port of Disco, in 1740, and the whole crew murdered; and two years later the same fate befell the seamen of another vessel that had accidentally stranded.

But for the last hundred years Greenland has been safer for the wrecked mariner than many parts of our own coast. Hospitality is the universal characteristic, enjoined upon the converted as a Christian duty, but everywhere a virtue of savage life. From Upernavik to Cape Farewell, the Esquimaux does not hesitate to devote his own meal to the necessities of a guest.

The benefits of the missionary school are not confined to the Christianized natives; and it is observable that the virtues of truth, self-reliance, and generous bearing, have been inculcated successfully with men who still cherish the wild traditionary superstitions of their fathers. Some of these are persons of strongly-marked character, and are trusted largely by the Danish officials. One of them, the nalegak-soak, or great chief, Nöluk, claims to have been the king or "head-man" of his people.

But among the native Greenlanders, as among other nomads, there seems to be no recognition of mastership except such as may be claimed by superiority of prowess. They have definite traditions of the organized games and exercises by which this superiority used to be authenticated. Indeed, the custom obtained until within the two last generations, and is traceable still in many of the periodical sports. Wrestling, jumping, tracking by the fingers or with hooked arms, pushing heel to heel in a sitting posture, dealing and receiving alternate blows on the left shoulder, shooting farther and with the stronger bow, carrying the heavier stone the greater distance, were among their trials of strength. I have seen some of these stones at Fortuna Bay and Disco Fiord, which remain as they were left at the end of the contest, memorials of the athlete who sustained their weight.

Nöluk is a remarkably powerful man, and as straight and graceful as an Iroquois. He is now a grandfather by his second wife; but he is still the best hunter of the settlement, and disdains to comply with the usage which would transfer his dog-teams and apparatus of the hunt to his grown-up son. During the pestilence of 1820 he resided fifty-six miles north of Upernavik, at Tessiusak, in lat. 73° 36′: I have seen the ruins of his hut there. When all the families fled from the sick, Nöluk still drove his sledge homeward and deposited food regularly for his dying wife. On his last visit he saw her through the window a corpse, and his infant son sucking at her frozen breast. Parental instinct was mastered by panic: he made his way to the south without crossing the threshold.

Among the regal perquisites of the Nalegak-soak was the questionable privilege of having as many wives as he could support. Besides this, he had little except an imperfectly-defined claim to certain proceeds of the hunt. In old times, the subordinate Nalegaks, chieftains of minor settlements, held their office by a similar title of personal might among their immediate fellows; thus constituting something like a system of feudal sovereignties without hereditary descent.

It is related, however, much as it is in histories with which we are more familiar, that the supremacy of the "Great Master" sometimes encountered rebuke from his barons. The Upernavik reindeer-hunters used to ascend the Salmon River, near Svartehuk, to a point from which by a single day's journey they could reach Okossisak, a hunting-station of the Ominaks. It so happened upon one occasion, when the Ominaks had been more than ordinarily successful in the chase, that a band of Upernaviks, with whom fortune had been less propitious, determined to pay them a predatory visit, attended by their great chief, the liege lord of both tribes. They found the Ominaks with their chief in company, a short chunky fellow, who proffered the accustomed hospitalities of his tent in true knightly style. But, in reply to the salutation "Be seated and eat," the Great Upernavik, whose companions were watching for their cue, gave a scowl, the reverse of the uniform formula of acceptance, which is simply to sit down and be filled. Hereupon old Ominak strung silently a heavy bow, and, drawing his arrow to the head, buried it in the narrow cleft of a distant rock, soliloquizing, as it struck, "He who is better than I am is my master." I give his words in the original for an exercise in phonetics: "Kinajougenerua," who is better, "Ovanöt," than I am; the rest of the sentence—"is my master"—being understood: an elliptical form of expression very common among these people, and often aided by accompanying gestures. Thus euphoniously solicited, the Upernaviks sat down and ate, and, pronouncing the brief acknowledgment, "Thanks," which always ends a stranger's meal, went their way in peace.

The old practice which is found among some of the Asiatic and North American tribes, of carrying off the bride by force, is common among the Esquimaux, and reluctantly abandoned even by the converted. The ceremonial rite follows at the convenience of the parties. Jens, the son of my old friend Cristiansen at Pröven, came very nigh being left a bachelor by an exercise of this custom. He was not quite ready to perform the gallant function himself toward his lady-love, when a lusty rival, one Pingeiak, carried her off bodily in dead of night. The damsel made good fight, however, and, though the abduction was repeated three times over, she managed to keep her troth. In the result, Jens, as phlegmatic and stupid a half-breed as I ever met with, got the prettiest woman in all North Greenland. Pingeiak was the best hunter and had the largest tent, but Jens was the son of the head-man. I believe such things may come about in other parts of the world.

I remember other instances among parties whom I knew. A young aspirant for the favors of an unbaptized daughter of the settlement at Sever-nik got a companion to assist him, and succeeded in carrying her to his sledge. But the ruthless father had the quicker dog-team, and pursued with such ferocious alacrity that the unlucky devotee of ancient custom had to clamber up a rocky gorge to escape his wrath, leaving the chosen one behind him. The report—for scandal is not frozen out of Greenland—makes the lady a willing eloper, and more courageous than her runaway lover.

The mysteries of the angekok, still so marked in their influence farther to the north, are not openly recognised near the Danish settlements. The last regular professor of them, Kenguit, was baptized at Pröven in 1844, changing his name to Jonathan Jeremias. But as you recede from the missionary influence the dark art is still practised in all its power.

A fact of psychological interest, as it shows that civilized or savage wonder-workers form a single family, is that the angekoks believe firmly in their own powers. I have known several of them personally, after my skill in pow-wow had given me a sort of correlative rank among them, and can speak with confidence on this point. I could not detect them in any resort to jugglery or natural magic: their deceptions are simply vocal, a change of voice, and perhaps a limited profession of ventriloquism, made more imposing by the darkness. They have, however, like the members of the learned professions everywhere else, a certain language or jargon of their own, in which they communicate with each other. Lieutenant-Governor Steffenson, who had charge of the Northern District up to 1829, and was an admirable student of every thing that regards these people, says that their artificial language is nothing but the ordinary dialect of the country, modified in the pronunciation, with some change in the import of the words and the introduction of a few cabalistic terms.

Besides the angekoks, who are looked up to as the hierophants or dispensers of good, they have the *issiutok*, or evil men, who work injurious spells, enchantments, metamorphoses. Like the witches of both Englands, the Old and the New, these malignants are rarely submitted to trial till they have been subjected to punishment—"castigat auditque." The finder of the Runic stone, old Pelemut, was one of them, and dealt with accordingly. Two others, only as far back as 1828, suffered the penalty of their crime on the same day, one at Karmenak, the other at Upernavik. This last was laudably killed after the "old customs," custom being the apology of the rude everywhere for things revolting to modern sense. He was first harpooned, then eviscerated, a flap let down from his forehead "to cover his eyes and prevent his seeing again," —he had the "evil eye," it might seem; and then small portions of his heart were eaten, so as to make it secure that he could not come back to earth unchanged. All this in accordance with venerated ritual.

The other, the Karmenak case, was that of an old sick man. He was dealt with more succinctly by his neighbor Kamokah, now old Tobias; who, at the instance of the issiutok family, pushed him into the sea after harpooning him, and then gave his flesh to the dogs. I have seen Tobias at Pröven, a Christianized man now, of very good repute, and, for aught I know, worthy of it.

The capital punishment with them, as with us, seems in general to be reserved for offences of the higher grade. For those of minor dignity, such as form the staple of our civilized forums, and even those which might find their way profitably into a court of honor, the *Imnapok* is the time-honored tribunal of redress. The original meaning of this word, I believe, is a native dance or singsong; but the institution which now bears the name is of much more dignity, and is found, with only circumstantial differences, among many other tribes within and beyond the Arctic circle.

An Esquimaux has inflicted an injury on one of his countrymen: he has cut his seal-lines, or harmed his dogs, or burnt his bladder-float, or perpetrated some enormity equally grievous. A summons comes to him from the angekok to meet the "country-side" at an Imnapok. The friends of the parties and the idlers of many miles around gather about the justice-seat, it may be at some little cluster of huts, or, if the weather permits, in the open air. The accuser rises and preludes a few discords with a seal-rib on a tom-tom or drum. He then passes to the charge, and pours out in long paragraphic words all the abuse and ridicule to which his outrageous vernacular can give expression. The accused meanwhile is silent; but, as the orator pauses after a signal hit or to flourish a cadence on his musical instrument, the whole audience, friends, neutrals, and opponents, signalize their approval by outcries as harmonious as those which we sometimes hear in our town-meetings at home. Stimulated by the applause, and warming with his own fires, the accuser renews the attack; his eloquence becoming more and more licentious and vituperative, until it has exhausted either his strength or his vocabulary of invective. Now comes the accused, with defence and countercharge and retorted abuse; the assembly still listening and applauding through a lengthened session. The Homeric debate at a close, the angekoks hold a powwow, and a penalty is denounced against the accused for his guilt, or the accuser for his unsustained prosecution.

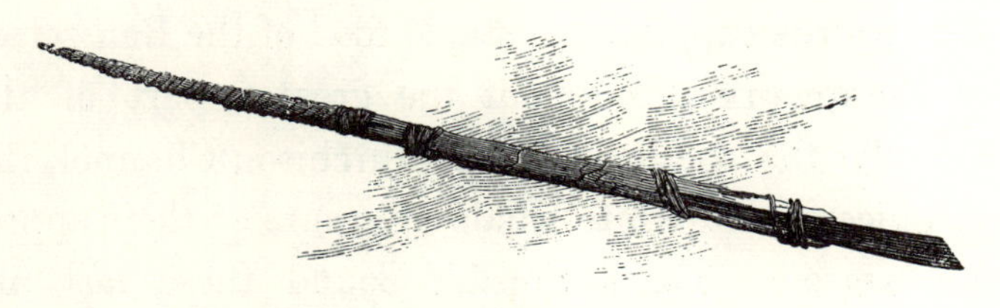

LANCE OF SEA-UNICORN.

CHAPTER XIII.

WALRUS-HUNTING—ESQUIMAUX HABITS—RETURN TO ETAH—PREPARING FOR ESCAPE—MAKING SLEDGES—DR. HAYES.

THE six storm-arrested strangers were off early in the morning: I sent messages of compliment by them to Kalutunah, inviting him to visit the brig; and in the afternoon Myouk and myself followed them to the floes for a walrus-hunt.

The walrus supplies the staple food of the Rensselaer Bay Esquimaux throughout the greater part of the year. To the south as far as Murchison Channel, the seal, unicorn, and white whale alternate at their appropriate seasons; but in Smith's Sound these last are accidental rather than sustained hunts.

The manner of hunting the walrus depends in a considerable degree on the season of the year. In the fall, when the pack is but partially closed, they are found in numbers, hanging around the neutral region of mixed ice and water, and, as this becomes solid with the advance of winter, following it more and more to the south.

The Esquimaux approach them then over the young ice, and assail them in cracks and holes with nalegeit and line. This fishery, as the season grows colder, darker, and more tempestuous, is fearfully hazardous: scarcely a year passes without a catastrophe. It was the theme of happy augury last winter, that no lives had been lost for some months before, and the angekoks even ventured to prophesy from it that the hunt would be auspicious,—a prophecy, like some others, hazarded after the event, for the ice had continued open for the walrus till late in December.

With the earliest spring, or, more strictly, about a month after the reappearance of the sun, the winter famine is generally relieved. January and February are often, in fact nearly always, months of privation; but during the latter part of March the spring fishery commences. Every thing is then life and excitement.

The walrus is now taken in two ways. Sometimes he has risen by the side of an iceberg, where the currents have worn away the floe, or through a tide-crack, and, enjoying the sunshine too long, finds his retreat cut off by the freezing up of the opening; for, like the seal at its attuk, the walrus can only work from below. When thus caught, the Esquimaux, who with keen hunter-craft are scouring the floes, scent him out by their dogs and spear him.

The early spring is the breeding-season, and the walrus then are in their glory. My observations show that they tenant the region throughout the entire year; but at this time the female, with her calf, is accompanied by the grim-visaged father, surging in loving trios from crack to crack, sporting around the berg-water or basking in the sun. While thus on their tours, they invite their vigilant enemies to the second method of capture. This also is by the lance and harpoon; but it often becomes a regular battle, the male gallantly fronting the assault and charging the hunters with furious bravery. Not unfrequently the entire family, mother, calf, and bull, are killed in one of these contests.

The huts—those poor, miserable, snow-covered dens—are now scenes of life and activity. Stacks of jointed meat are piled upon the ice-foot; the women are stretching the hide for sole-leather, and the men cutting out a reserve of harpoon-lines for the winter. Tusky walrus-heads stare at you from the snow-bank, where they are stowed for their ivory; the dogs are tethered to the ice; and the children, each one armed with the curved rib of some big amphibion, are playing ball and bat among the drifts.

On the day of my arrival, four walrus were killed at Etah, and no doubt many more by Kalutak at Peteravik. The quantity of beef which is thus gained during a season of plenty, one might suppose, should put them beyond winter want; but there are other causes besides improvidence which make their supplies scanty. The poor creatures are not idle: they hunt indomitably, without the loss of a day. When the storms prevent the use of the sledge, they still work in stowing away the carcasses of previous hunts. An excavation is made either on the mainland, or, what is preferred, upon an island inaccessible to foxes, and the jointed meat is stacked inside and covered with heavy stones. One such cache, which I met on a small island a short distance from Etah, contained the

CHILDREN PLAYING BALL.

flesh of ten walrus, and I know of several others equally large.

The excessive consumption is the true explanation of the scarcity. By their ancient laws all share with all; and, as they migrate in numbers as their necessities prompt, the tax on each particular settlement is excessive. The quantity which the members of a family consume, exorbitant as it seems to a stranger, is rather a necessity of their peculiar life and organization than the result of inconsiderate gluttony. In active exercise and constant exposure to cold the waste of carbon must be enormous.

When in-doors and at rest, tinkering over their ivory harness-rings, fowl-nets, or other household-gear, they eat as we often do in more civilized lands—for animal enjoyment and to pass away time. But when on the hunt they take but one meal a day, and that after the day's labor is over; they go out upon the ice without breakfast, and, except the "cold cuts," which I confess are numerous, eat nothing until their return. I would average the Esquimaux ration in a season of plenty—it is of course a mere estimate, but I believe a perfectly fair one—at eight or ten pounds a day, with soup and water to the extent of half a gallon.

At the moment of my visit, when returning plenty had just broken in upon their famine, it was not wonderful that they were hunting with avidity. The settlements of the South seek at this season the hunting-ground above, and, until the seals begin to form their basking-holes, some ten days later, the walrus is the single spoil.

I incline to the opinion that these animals frequent the half-broken ice-margin throughout the year; for, after the season has become comparatively open, they are still found in groups, with their young, disporting in the leads and shore-water. They are, of course, secure under such circumstances from the Esquimaux hunters of the Far North, who, not having the kayak of the more southern settlements, can only approach them on the ice.

In the late summer or "ausak," after all ice has melted, the walrus are in the habit of resorting to the rocks. They are then extremely alert and watchful; but the Esquimaux note their haunts carefully, and, concealing themselves in the clefts, await their approach with patient silence, and secure them by the harpoon and line.

My departure from Etah Bay was hastened by news from the brig. Hans brought me a letter from Dr. Hayes, while I was out walrus-hunting near Life-Boat Cove, which apprised me of the dangerous illness of Mr. McGary. I had a load of meat on my sledge, and was therefore unable to make good speed with my four tired dogs; but I rode and ran by turns, and reached the brig, after fifty miles' travel, in seven hours from the time of meeting Hans. I was thoroughly broken down by the effort, but had the satisfaction of finding that my excellent second officer had passed the crisis of his attack.

I left Hans behind me with orders to go to Peteravik and persuade Kalutunah to come to the brig, sending him a capstan-bar as a pledge of future largess,—invaluable for its adaptation to harpoon-shafts.

"April 19, Thursday.—The open water has not advanced from the south more than four miles within the past three weeks. It is still barely within Cape

Alexander. It is a subject of serious anxiety to me. Our experience has taught us that the swell caused by these winds breaks up the ice rapidly. Now, there can be no swell to the southward, or these heavy gales would have done this now. It augurs ill not only for the possible release of the brig, but for the facility of our boat-voyage if we shall be obliged to forsake her, as every thing seems to say we must do soon. Last year, on the 10th of May, the water was free around Littleton Island, and coming up to within two miles of Refuge Inlet. It is now forty miles farther off!

"Petersen and Ohlsen are working by short spells at the boats and sledges.

"I will not leave the brig until it is absolutely certain that she cannot thaw out this season; but every thing shall be matured for our instant departure as soon as her fate is decided. Every detail is arranged; and, if the sick go on as they have done, I do not doubt but that we may carry our boats some thirty or forty miles over the ice before finally deciding whether we must desert the brig.

"April 20, Friday.—A relief-watch, of Riley, Morton, and Bonsall, are preparing to saw out sledge-runners from our cross-beams. It is slow work. They are very weak, and the thermometer sinks at night to —26°. Nearly all our beams have been used up for fuel; but I have saved enough to construct two long sledges of seventeen feet six inches each. I want a sledge sufficiently long to bring the weight of the whaleboat and her stowage within the line of the runner: this will prevent her rocking and pitching when crossing hummocked ice, and enable us to cradle her firmly to the sledge.

"They are at this moment breaking out our cabin bulkhead to extract the beam. Our cabin-dormitory is full of cold vapor. Every thing is comfortless: blankets make a sorry substitute for the moss-padded wall which protected us from —60°.

"April 21, Saturday.—Morton's heel is nearly closed, and there is apparently a sound bone underneath. He has been upon his back since October. I can now set this faithful and valuable man to active duty very soon.

"The beam was too long to be carried through our hatches; we therefore have sawed it as it stands, and will carry up the slabs separately. These slabs are but one and a half inches wide, and must be strengthened by iron bolts and cross-pieces; still, they are all that we have. I made the bolts out of our cabin curtain-rods, long disused. Mr. Petersen aids Ohlsen in grinding his tools. They will complete the job to-morrow,—for we must work on Sunday now,—and by Monday be able to begin at other things. Petersen undertakes to manufacture our cooking and mess-gear. I have a sad-looking assortment of battered rusty tins to offer him; but with stove-pipe much may be done.

"April 22, Sunday.—Gave rest for all but the sawyers, who keep manfully at the beam. Some notion of our weakness may be formed from the fact of these five poor fellows averaging among them but one foot per hour.

"I read our usual prayers; and Dr. Hayes, who feels sadly the loss of his foot, came aft and crawled upon deck to sniff the daylight. He had not seen the sun for five months and three weeks."

BERG-RAFT.

CHAPTER XIV.

KALUTUNAH — THE HUNTING PARTY — SETTING OUT—MY TALLOW-BALL—A WILD CHASE—HUNTING STILL—THE GREAT GLACIER — THE ESCALADED STRUCTURE — FORMATION OF BERGS — THE VISCOUS FLOW—CREVASSES—THE FROZEN WATER-TUNNEL—CAPE FORBES—FACE OF GLACIER.

We continued toiling on with our complicated preparations till the evening of the 24th, when Hans came back well laden with walrus-meat. Three of the Esquimaux accompanied him, each with his sledge and dog-team fully equipped for a hunt. The leader of the party, Kalutunah, was a noble savage, greatly superior in every thing to the others of his race. He greeted me with respectful courtesy, yet as one who might rightfully expect an equal measure of it in return, and, after a short interchange of salutations, seated himself in the post of honor at my side.

I waited of course till the company had fed and slept, for among savages especially haste is indecorous, and then, after distributing a few presents, opened to them my project of a northern exploration. Kalutunah received his knife and needles with a "Kuyanaka," "I thank you:" the first thanks I have heard from a native of this upper region. He called me his friend,—"Asakaoteet," "I love you well,"—and would be happy, he said, to join the "nalegak-soak" in a hunt.

PORTRAIT OF KALUTUNAH.

The project was one that had engaged my thoughts long before daylight had renewed the possibility of carrying it out. I felt that the farther shores beyond Kennedy Channel were still to be searched before our work could be considered finished; but we were without dogs, the indispensable means of travel. We had only four left out of sixty-two. Famine among the Esquimaux had been as disastrous as disease with us: they had killed all but thirty, and of these there were now sixteen picketed on the ice about the brig. The aid and influence of Kalutunah could secure my closing expedition.

I succeeded in making my arrangements with him, provisionally at least, and the morning after we all set

KALUTUNAH'S PARTY.

out. The party consisted of Kalutunah, Shanghu, and Tatterat, with their three sledges. Hans, armed with the Marston rifle, was my only companion from the ship's company. The natives carried no arms but the long knife and their unicorn-ivory lances. Our whole equipment was by no means cumbersome: except the clothes upon our back and raw walrus-meat, we carried nothing. The walrus, both flesh and blubber, was cut into flat slabs half an inch thick and about as long and wide as a folio volume. These when frozen were laid directly upon the cross-bars of the sledge, and served as a sort of floor. The rifle and the noonghak were placed on top, and the whole was covered by a well-rubbed bear-skin, strapped down by a pliant cord of walrus-hide.

Thus stowed, the sledge is wonderfully adapted to its wild travel. It may roll over and over, for it defies an upset; and its runners of the bones of the whale seem to bear with impunity the fierce shocks of the ice. The meat, as hard as a plank, is the driver's seat: it is secure from the dogs; and when it is wanted for a cold cut, which is not seldom, the sledge is turned upside-down, and the layers of flesh are hacked away from between the cross-bars.

We started with a wild yell of dogs and men in chorus, Kalutunah and myself leading. In about two hours we had reached a high berg about fifteen miles north of the brig. Here I reconnoitred the ice ahead. It was not cheering; the outside tide-channel, where I had broken through the fall before, was now full of squeezed ice, and the plain beyond the bergs seemed much distorted. The Esquimaux, nevertheless, acceded to my wish to attempt the passage, and we were soon among the hummocks. We ran beside our sledges, clinging to the upstanders, but making perhaps four miles an hour where, unassisted by the dogs, we could certainly have made but one. Things began to look more auspicious.

We halted about thirty miles north of the brig, after

edging along the coast about thirty miles to the eastward. Here Shanghu burrowed into a snow-bank and slept, the thermometer standing at —30°. The rest of us turned in to lunch; the sledge was turned over, and we were cutting away at the raw meat, each man for himself, when I heard an exclamation from Tatterat, an outlandish Esquimaux, who had his name from the Kittywake gull. He had found a tallow-ball, which had been hid away without my knowledge by my comrades for my private use. Instantly his knife entered the prized recesses of my ball, and, as the lumps of liver and cooked muscle came tossing out in delicate succession, Kalutunah yielded to the temptation, and both of them picked the savory bits as we would the truffles of a "Perigord pâté." Of necessity I joined the group, and took my share; but Hans, poor fellow, too indignant at the liberty taken with my provender, refused to share in the work of demolishing it. My ten-pound ball vanished nevertheless in scarcely as many minutes.

The journey began again as the feast closed, and we should have accomplished my wishes had it not been for the untoward influence of sundry bears. The tracks of these animals were becoming more and more numerous as we rounded one iceberg after another; and we could see the beds they had worn in the snow while watching for seal. These swayed the dogs from their course: yet we kept edging onward; and when in sight of the northern coast, about thirty miles from the central peak of the "Three Brothers," I saw a deep band of stratus lying over the horizon in the direction of Kennedy Channel. This water-sky indicated the continued opening of the channel, and made me more deeply anxious to proceed. But at this moment our dogs encountered a large male bear in the act of devouring a seal. The impulse was irresistible: I lost all control over both dogs and drivers. They seemed dead to every thing but the passion of pursuit. Off they sped with incredible swiftness; the Esquimaux clinging to their sledges and cheering their dogs with loud cries of "Nannook!" A mad, wild chase, wilder than German legend,—the dogs, wolves; the drivers, devils. After a furious run, the animal was brought to bay; the lance and the rifle did their work, and we halted for a general feed. The dogs gorged themselves, the drivers did as much, and we buried the remainder of the carcass in the snow. A second bear had been tracked by the party to a large iceberg north of Cape Russell; for we had now travelled to the neighborhood of the Great Glacier. But the dogs were too much distended by their abundant diet to move: their drivers were scarcely better. Rest was indispensable.

We took a four hours' sleep on the open ice, the most uncomfortable that I remember. Our fatigue had made us dispense with the snow-house; and, though I was heavily clad in a full suit of furs, and squeezed myself in between Kalutunah and Shanghu, I could not bear the intense temperature. I rose in the morning stiff and sore. I mention it as a trait of nobleness on the part of Kalutunah, which I appreciated very sensibly at the time, that, seeing me suffer, he took his kapetah from his back and placed it around my feet.

The next day I tried again to make my friends steer to the northward. But the bears were most numerous upon the Greenland side; and they determined to push on toward the glacier. They were sure, they said, of finding the game among the broken icebergs at the base of it. All my remonstrances and urgent entreaties were unavailing to make them resume their promised route. They said that to cross so high up as we then were was impossible, and I felt the truth of this when I remembered the fate of poor Baker and Schubert at this very passage. Kalutunah added, significantly, that the bear-meat was absolutely necessary for the support of their families, and that Nalegak had no right to prevent him from providing for his household. It was a strong argument, and withal the argument of the strong.

I found now that my projected survey of the northern coast must be abandoned, at least for the time. My next wish was to get back to the brig, and to negotiate with Metek for a purchase or loan of his dogs as my last chance. But even this was not readily gratified. All of Saturday was spent in bear-hunting. The natives, as indomitable as their dogs, made the entire circuit of Dallas Bay, and finally halted again under one of the islands which group themselves between the headlands of Advance Bay and at the base of the glacier.

Anxious as I was to press our return to the brig, I was well paid for my disappointment. I had not realized fully the spectacle of this stupendous monument of frost. I had seen it for some hours hanging over the ice like a white-mist cloud, but now it rose up before me clearly defined and almost precipitous. The whole horizon, so vague and shadowy before, was broken by long lines of icebergs; and as the dogs, cheered by the cries of their wild drivers, went on, losing themselves deeper and deeper in the labyrinth, it seemed like closing around us the walls of an icy world. They stopped at last; and I had time, while my companions rested and fed, to climb one of the highest bergs. The atmosphere favored me: the blue tops of Washington Land were in full view; and, losing itself in a dark water-cloud, the noble headland of John Barrow.

The trend of this glacier is a few degrees to the west of north. We followed its face afterward, edging in for the Greenland coast, about the rocky archipelago which I have named after the Advance. From one of these rugged islets, the nearest to the glacier which could be approached with any thing like safety, I could see another island larger and closer in shore, already half covered by the encroaching face of the glacier, and great masses of ice still detaching themselves and splintering as they fell upon that portion which protruded. Repose was not the characteristic of this seemingly solid mass; every feature indicated activity, energy, movement.

The surface seemed to follow that of the basis-country over which it flowed. It was undulating about the horizon, but as it descended toward the sea it represented a broken plain with a general inclination of some nine degrees, still diminishing toward the foreground. Crevasses, in the distance mere wrinkles, expanded as they came nearer, and were

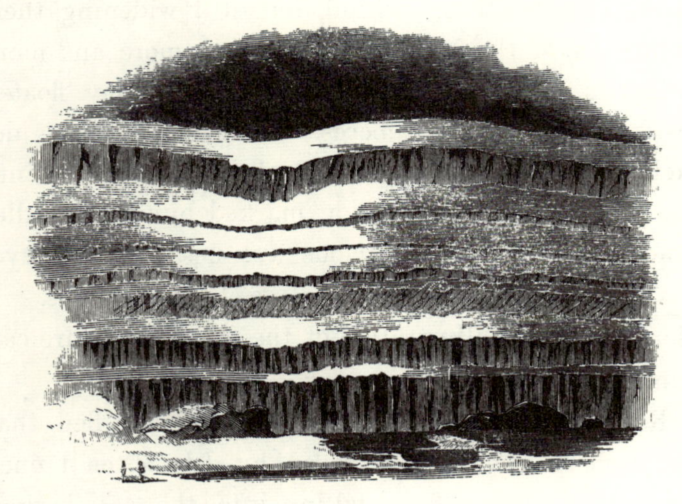

THE ESCALADED STRUCTURE.

crossed almost at right angles by long continuous lines of fracture parallel with the face of the glacier.

These lines too, scarcely traceable in the far distance, widened as they approached the sea until they formed a gigantic stairway. It seemed as though the ice had lost its support below, and that the mass was let down from above in a series of steps. Such an action, owing to the heat derived from the soil, the excessive surface-drainage, and the constant abrasion of the sea, must in reality take place. My note-book may enable me at some future day to develop its details. I have referred to this as the escaladed structure of the Arctic glacier.

The indication of a great propelling agency seemed to be just commencing at the time I was observing it. These split-off lines of ice were evidently in motion, pressed on by those behind, but still widening their fissures, as if the impelling action was more and more energetic nearer the water, till at last they floated away in the form of icebergs. Long files of these detached masses could be traced slowly sailing off into the distance, their separation marked by dark parallel shadows—broad and spacious avenues near the eye, but narrowed in the perspective to mere lines. A more impressive illustration of the forces of nature can hardly be conceived.

Regarded upon a large scale, I am satisfied that the iceberg is not disengaged by *debâcle*, as I once supposed. So far from falling into the sea, broken by its weight from the parent-glacier, it rises from the sea. The process is at once gradual and comparatively quiet. The idea of icebergs being discharged, so universal among systematic writers and so recently admitted by myself, seems to me now at variance with the regulated and progressive actions of nature. Developed by such a process, the thousands of bergs which throng these seas should keep the air and water in perpetual commotion, one fearful succession of explosive detonations and propagated waves. But it is only the lesser masses falling into deep waters which could justify the popular opinion. The enormous masses of the Great Glacier are propelled, step by step and year by year, until, reaching water capable of supporting them, they are floated off to be lost in the temperatures of other regions.

INDICATIONS OF VISCOUS FLOW.

The frozen masses before me were similar in structure to the Alpine and Norwegian ice-growths. It would be foreign to the character of this book to enter upon the discussion which the remark suggests; but it will be seen by the sketch, imperfect as it is, that their face presented nearly all the characteristic features of the Swiss Alps. The *overflow*, as I have called the viscous overlapping of the surface, was more clearly marked than upon any Alpine glacier with which I am acquainted. When close to the island-rocks and looking out upon the upper table of the glacier, I was struck with the homely analogy of the batter-cake spreading itself out under the ladle of the housewife, the upper surface less affected by friction, and rolling forward in consequence.

The crevasses bore the marks of direct fracture and the more gradual action of surface-drainage. The extensive water-shed between their converging planes gave to the icy surface most of the hydrographic features of a river-system. The ice-born rivers which divided them were margined occasionally with spires of discolored ice, and generally lost themselves in the central areas of the glacier before reaching its foreground. Occasionally, too, the face of the glacier was cut by vertical lines, which, as in the Alpine growths, were evidently outlets for the surface-drainage. Every thing was of course bound in solid ice when I looked at it; but the evidences of torrent-action were unequivocal, and Mr. Bonsall and Mr. Morton, at their visits of the preceding year, found both cascades and water-tunnels in abundance.

The height of this ice-wall at the nearest point was about three hundred feet, measured from the water's edge; and the unbroken right line of its diminishing perspective showed that this might be regarded as its constant measurement. It seemed, in fact, a great icy table-land, abutting with a clean precipice against the sea. This is indeed characteristic of all those Arctic glaciers which issue from central reservoirs or *mers de glace* upon the fiords or bays, and is strikingly in contrast with the dependent or hanging glacier of the ravines, where every line and furrow and chasm seems

THE FROZEN WATER-TUNNEL.

to indicate the movement of descent and the mechanical disturbances which have retarded it.

I have named this great glacier after Alexander Von Humboldt, and the cape which flanks it on the Greenland coast after Professor Agassiz.

The point at which this immense body of ice enters

the Land of Washington gives even to a distant view impressive indications of its plastic or semi-solid character. No one could resist the impression of fluidity conveyed by its peculiar markings. I have named it Cape Forbes, after the eminent crystallogist whose views it so abundantly confirms.

CAPE FORBES

As the surface of the glacier receded to the south, its face seemed broken with piles of earth and rock-stained rubbish, till far back in the interior it was hidden from me by the slope of a hill. Still beyond this, however, the white blink or glare of the sky above showed its continued extension.

It was more difficult to trace its outline to the northward, on account of the immense discharges at its base. The talus of its descent from the interior, looking far

J. Hamilton. Engraved at J. M. Butler's establishment 84 Chestnut St. R. Hinshlewood.

GREAT GLACIER OF HUMBOLDT.

(From a sketch by Dr Kane.)

off to the east, ranged from 7° to 15°, so broken by the crevasses, however, as to give the effect of an inclined plane only in the distance. A few black knobs rose from the white snow, like islands from the sea.

The general configuration of its surface showed how it adapted itself to the inequalities of the basis-country beneath. There was every modification of hill and valley, just as upon land. Thus diversified in its aspect, it stretches to the north till it bounds upon the new land of Washington, cementing into one the Greenland of the Scandinavian Vikings and the America of Columbus.

CHAPTER XV.

CAPE JAMES KENT—MARSHALL BAY—ICE-RAFTS—STRIATED BOULDERS—DALLAS BAY—ANTIQUITIES—THE BEAR-CHASE—THE BEAR AT BAY—THE SINGLE HUNT—TEETH-WOUNDS—THE LAST EFFORT—CLOSE OF THE SEARCH.

WHILE the Esquimaux were hunting about the bergs, I sat with my sketch-book, absorbed in the spectacle before me; but, seeing them come to a halt above the island, I gained the nearest sledge, and the whole party gathered together a few miles from the face of the glacier. Here Hans and myself crawled with Tatterat and his dogs into an impromptu snow-hut, and, cheered by our aggregated warmth, slept comfortably. Our little dome, or rather burrow, for it was scooped out of a drift—fell down in the night; but we were so worn out that it did not wake us.

On rising from a sleep in the open air, at a temperature of 12° below zero, the hunt was resumed along the face of the glacier, with just enough of success to wear out the dogs and endanger my chances of return to the brig. In spite of the grandeur of the scenery and the noble displays of force exhibited by the falling bergs, my thoughts wandered back to the party I had left; and I was really glad when Kalutunah yielded to my re-

CAPE JAMES KENT.

newed persuasion and turned his team toward the ice-belt of the southeastern shore.

The spot at which we landed I have called Cape James Kent. It was a lofty headland, and the land-ice which hugged its base was covered with rocks from the cliffs above. As I looked over this ice-belt, losing itself in the far distance, and covered with its millions of tons of rubbish, greenstones, limestones, chlorite slates, rounded and angular, massive and ground to powder, its importance as a geological agent in the transportation of drift struck me with great force. Its whole substance was studded with these varied contributions from the shore: and farther to the south, upon the now

ICE-RAFT.

frozen waters of Marshall Bay, I could recognise raft after raft from the last year's ice-belt, which had been caught by the winter, each one laden with its heavy freight of foreign material.

The water-torrents and thaws of summer unite with the tides in disengaging the ice-belt from the coast; but it is not uncommon for large bergs to drive against it and carry away the growths of many years. I have

RAFT OF BELT-ICE.

found masses that had been detached in this way, floating many miles out to sea,—long, symmetrical tables, two hundred feet long by eighty broad, covered with large angular rocks and boulders, and seemingly impregnated throughout with detrited matter. These rafts in Marshall Bay were so numerous, that, could

RAFT OF SLATES.

they have melted as I saw them, the bottom of the sea would have presented a more curious study for the geologist than the boulder-covered lines of our middle latitudes.

One in particular, a sketch of which I attach, had its origin in a valley where rounded fragments of water-

ROCHE MOUTONNEE, IN ICE-BELT.

washed greenstone had been poured out by the torrents and frozen into the coast-ice of the belt. The attrition of subsequent matter had truncated the great

STRIATED BOULDER FROM MARY LEIPER FIORD

egg-shaped rock, and worn its sides into a striated face, whose scratches still indicated the line of waterflow.

On the southeastern corner of this bay, where some

low islands at the mouth of the fiord formed a sort of protection against the north wind, was a group of Esquimaux remains,—huts, cairns, and graves. Though evidently long deserted, my drivers seemed to know all about them, for they suspended the hunt around the bergs to take a look at these evidences of a bygone generation of their fathers.

There were five huts, with two stone pedestals for the protection of meat, and one of those strange little kennels which serve as dormitories when the igloë is

DALLAS BAY HUTS.

crowded. The graves were farther up the fiord: from them I obtained a knife of bone, but no indications of iron.

These huts stood high up, upon a set of shingle-terraces similar to those of Rensselaer Bay. The belt-ice at their foot was old and undisturbed, and must have been so for years; so too was the heavy ice of the bay. Yet around these old homesteads were bones of the seal and walrus, and the vertebræ of a whale similar to that at the igloë of Anoatok. There must have been both open water and a hunting-ground around them, and the huts had in former days been close upon this water-line. "Una suna nuna?" "What land is this, Kalutunah?" I did not understand his answer, which was long and emphatic; but I found from our

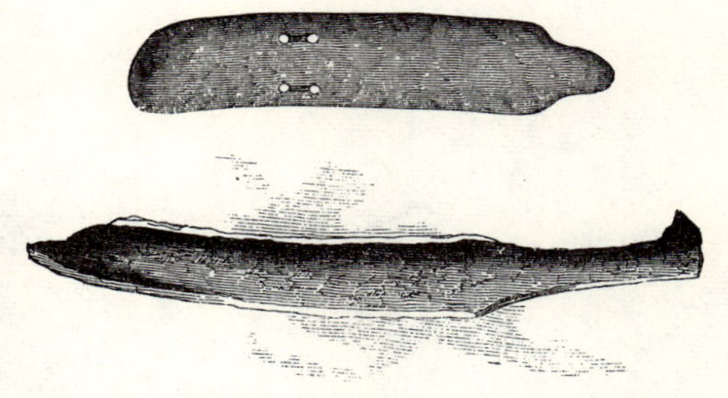

BONE KNIVES FROM PEABODY AND DALLAS BAYS.

interpreter that the place was still called "the inhabited spot;" and that a story was well preserved among them of a time when families were sustained beside its open water and musk-ox inhabited the hills. We followed the belt-ice, crossing only at the headlands of the bays, and arrived at the brig on the afternoon of Wednesday.

Our whole journey had been an almost unbroken and scarcely-varied series of bear-hunts. They had lost for me the attractions of novelty; but, like the contests with the walrus, they were always interesting, because characteristic of this rude people.

The dogs are carefully trained not to engage in contest with the bear, but to retard his flight. While one engrosses his attention ahead, a second attacks him in the rear; and, always alert and each protecting the other, it rarely happens that they are seriously injured, or that they fail to delay the animal until the hunters come up.

Let us suppose a bear scented out at the base of an iceberg. The Esquimaux examines the track with sagacious care, to determine its age and direction, and the speed with which the animal was moving when he passed along. The dogs are set upon the trail, and the hunter courses over the ice at their side in silence. As he turns the angle of the berg his game is in view before him, stalking probably along with quiet march, sometimes snuffing the air suspiciously, but making, nevertheless, for a nest of broken hummocks. The dogs spring forward, opening in a wild wolfish yell, the driver shrieking "Nannook! nannook!" and all straining every nerve in pursuit.

The bear rises on his haunches, inspects his pursuers, and starts off at full speed. The hunter, as he runs, leaning over his sledge, seizes the traces of a couple of his dogs and liberates them from their burden. It is the work of a minute; for the motion is not checked, and the remaining dogs rush on with apparent ease.

Now, pressed more severely, the bear makes for an

iceberg and stands at bay, while his two foremost pursuers halt at a short distance and quietly await the arrival of the hunter. At this moment the whole pack are liberated; the hunter grasps his lance, and, tumbling through the snow and ice, prepares for the encounter.

THE BEAR AT BAY.

If there be two hunters, the bear is killed easily; for one makes a feint of thrusting a spear at the right side, and, as the animal turns with his arms toward the threatened attack, the left is unprotected and receives the death-wound.

But if there be only one hunter, he does not hesitate. Grasping the lance firmly in his hands, he provokes the animal to pursue him by moving rapidly across its path, and then running as if to escape. But hardly is its long unwieldy body extended for the solicited chase, before with a rapid jump the hunter doubles on his track and runs back toward his first position. The bear is in the act of turning after him again when the lance is plunged into the left side below the shoulder. So dexterously has this thrust

THE SINGLE HUNT.

to be made, that an unpractised hunter has often to leave his spear in the side of his prey and run for his life. But even then, if well aided by the dogs, a cool, skilful man seldom fails to kill his adversary.

Many wounds are received by the Etah Bay Esquimaux in these encounters: the bear is looked upon as more fierce in that neighborhood, and about Anoatok and Rensselaer Bay, than around the broken ice to the south. He uses his teeth much more generally than is supposed by systematic writers. The hugging, pawing, and boxing, which characterize the black and grisly bears, are resorted to by him only under peculiar circumstances. While wandering over his icy fields, he will rear himself upon his hind-legs to enlarge his circle of vision; and I have often seen him in this attitude pawing the air, as if practising for an apprehended conflict. But it is only when absolutely beset, or when the female is defending her cub, that the Polar bear shows fight upon its haunches. Among seven hunters who visited the brig last December, no less than five were scarred by direct teeth-wounds of bears. Two of these had been bit in the calves of the legs while running; and one, our friend Metek, had received a like dishonorable wound somewhat higher. Our dogs were seized by the nape of the neck and flung violently many paces to one side.

The bear-hunt ranks foremost among the exhibitions of personal prowess. My intelligent friend Kalutunah excelled in it. Shanghu, his principal associate, was also skilful as well as daring.

They both left the brig after a day's rest, fully laden with wood and other presents, and promising to engage Metek, if they could, to come up with his four dogs. They themselves engaged to loan me one dog from each of their teams. It pleased me to find that I had earned character with these people, at first so suspicious and distrustful. They left on board each man his dog, without a shade of doubt as to my good faith, only begging me to watch the poor animals' feet, as the famine had nearly exterminated their stock.

The month of May had come. Metek, less confiding because less trustworthy than Kalutunah, did not bring his dogs, and my own exhausted team was in almost daily requisition to bring in supplies of food from Etah. Every thing admonished me that the time was at hand when we must leave the brig and trust our fortunes to the floes. Our preparations were well advanced, and the crew so far restored to health that all but three or four could take some part in completing them.

Still, I could not allow myself to pass away from our region of search without a last effort to visit the farther shores of the channel. Our communications with the Esquimaux, and some successful hunts of our own, had given us a stock of provisions for at least a week in advance. I conferred with my officers, made a full distribution of the work to be performed in my absence, and set out once more, with Morton for my only companion. We took with us the light sledge, adding the two borrowed dogs to our team, but travelling ourselves on foot. Our course was to be by the middle ice, and our hope that we might find it free enough from hummocks to permit us to pass.

My journal, written after our return, gives nothing but a series of observations going to verify and complete my charts. We struggled manfully to force our way through,—days and nights of adventurous exposure and recurring disaster,—and at last found our way back to the brig, Morton broken down anew, and my own energies just adequate to the duty of supervising our final departure. I had neither time nor strength to expend on my diary.

The operations of the search were closed.

BEAR-HUNTING ON THE FLOES.

CHAPTER XVI.

PREPARATIONS FOR ESCAPE—PROVISIONS—BOATS—THE SLEDGES—INSTRUMENTS AND ARMS—COOKING APPARATUS—TABLE FURNITURE—CRADLING THE BOATS—THE SLEDGES MOVING—THE RECREATION.

The detailed preparations for our escape would have little interest for the general reader; but they were so arduous and so important that I cannot pass them by without a special notice. They had been begun from an early day of the fall, and had not been entirely intermitted during our severest winter-trials. All who could work, even at picking over eider-down, found every moment of leisure fully appropriated. But since our party had begun to develop the stimulus of more liberal diet, our labors were more systematic and diversified.

The manufacture of clothing had made considerable progress. Canvas moccasins had been made for every one of the party, and three dozen were added as a common stock to meet emergencies. Three pairs of boots were allowed each man. These were generally of carpeting, with soles of walrus and seal hide; and when the supply of these gave out, the leather from the chafing-gear of the brig for a time supplied their place. A much better substitute was found afterward in the gutta percha that had formed the speaking-tube. This was softened by warm water, cut into lengths, and so made available to its new uses. Blankets were served out as the material for body-clothing: every man was his own tailor.

For bedding, the woollen curtains that had formerly decorated our berths supplied us with a couple of large

PROVISION-SACK.

coverlets, which were abundantly quilted with eider-down. Two buffalo-robes of the same size with the coverlets were arranged so as to button on them, forming sleeping-sacks for the occasion, but easily detached for the purpose of drying or airing.

Our provision-bags were of assorted sizes, to fit under the thwarts of the boats. They were of sail-cloth made water-tight by tar and pitch, which we kept from penetrating the canvas by first coating it with flour-paste and plaster of Paris. The bread-bags were double, the inner saturated with paste and plaster by boiling in the mixture, and the space between the two filled with pitch. Every bag was, in sailor-phrase, roped and becketed; in ordinary parlance, well secured by cordage.

These different manufactures had all of them been going on through the winter, and more rapidly as the spring advanced. They had given employment to the thoughts of our sick men, and in this way had exerted a wholesome influence on their moral tone and assisted their convalescence. Other preparations had been begun more recently. The provisions for the descent were to be got ready and packed. The ship-bread was powdered by beating it with a capstan-bar, and pressed down into the bags which were to carry it. Pork-fat and tallow were melted down, and poured into other bags to freeze. A stock of concentrated bean-soup was cooked, and secured for carriage like the pork-fat; and the flour and remaining meat-biscuit were to be protected from moisture in double bags. These were the only provisions we were to carry with us. I knew I should be able to subsist the party for some time after their setting out by the food I could bring from the vessel by occasional trips with my dog-team. For the rest we relied upon our guns.

Besides all this, we had our camp-equipage to get in order, and the vitally-important organization of our system of boats and sledges.

Our boats were three in number, all of them well battered by exposure to ice and storm, almost as destructive of their sea-worthiness as the hot sun of other regions. Two of them were cypress whaleboats, twenty-six feet long, with seven feet beam, and three feet deep. These were strengthened with oak bottom-pieces and a long string-piece bolted to the keel. A washboard of light cedar, about six inches high, served to strengthen

WHALEBOATS AND HOUSING.

the gunwale and give increased depth. A neat housing of light canvas was stretched upon a ridge-line sustained fore and aft by stanchions, and hung down over the boat's sides, where it was fastened (stopped) to a jack-stay. My last year's experience on the attempt to reach Beechy Island determined me to carry but one mast to each boat. It was stepped into an oaken thwart, made especially strong, as it was expected to carry sail over ice as well as water: the mast could be readily unshipped, and carried, with the oars, boat-hooks, and ice-poles, alongside the boat. The third boat was my little Red Eric. We mounted her on the old sledge, the "Faith," hardly relying on her for any purposes of navigation, but with the intention of cut-

RED ERIC—PREPARATIONS FOR ESCAPE.

ting her up for firewood in case our guns should fail to give us a supply of blubber.

Indeed, in spite of all the ingenuity of our carpenter, Mr. Ohlsen, well seconded by the persevering labors of McGary and Bonsall, not one of our boats was positively sea-worthy. The "Hope" would not pass even charitable inspection, and we expected to burn her on reaching water. The planking of all of them was so dried up that it could hardly be made tight by calking.

The three boats were mounted on sledges rigged with rue-raddies; the provisions stowed snugly under the thwarts; the chronometers, carefully boxed and padded, placed in the stern-sheets of the Hope, in charge of Mr. Sontag. With them were such of the instruments as we could venture to transport. They consisted of two Gambey sextants, with artificial horizon, our transit-unifilar, and dip-instruments. Our glasses, with a few of the smaller field-instruments, we carried on our persons. Our fine theodolite we were forced to abandon.

MEAT-BISCUIT CASE.

Our powder and shot, upon which our lives depended, were carefully distributed in bags and tin canisters. The percussion-caps I took into my own possession, as more precious than gold. Mr. Bonsall had a general charge of the arms and ammunition. Places were arranged for the guns, and hunters appointed for each boat. Mr. Petersen took charge of the most important part of our field-equipage, our cooking-gear. Petersen was our best tinker. All the old stove-pipe, now none the better for two winters of Arctic fires, was called into requisition. Each boat was provided with two large iron cylinders, fourteen inches in diameter and eighteen high. Each of them held an iron saucer or lamp, in which we could place our melted pork-fat or blubber, and, with the aid of spun-yarn for a wick, make a roaring fire. I need not say that the fat and oil always froze when not ignited.

Into these cylinders, which were used merely to defend our lamp from the wind and our pots from contact with the cold air, we placed a couple of large tin vessels, suitable either for melting snow or making tea or soup. They were made out of cake-canisters cut

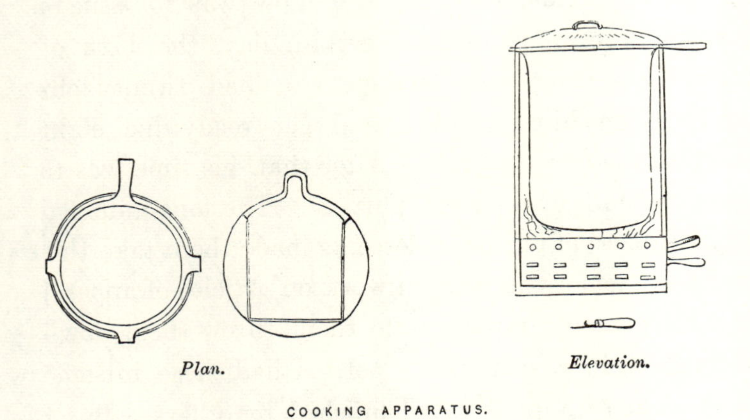

COOKING APPARATUS.

down. How many kindly festival associations hung by these now abused soup-cans! one of them had, before the fire rubbed off its bright gilding, the wedding-inscription of a large fruit-cake.

We carried spare tins in case the others should burn out: it was well we did so. So completely had we exhausted our household furniture, that we had neither cups nor plates, except crockery. This, of course, would not stand the travel, and our spare tin had to be saved for protecting the boats from ice. At this juncture we cut plates out of every imaginable and rejected piece of tinware. Borden's meat-biscuit canisters furnished us with a splendid dinner-service; and some rightly-feared tin jars, with ominous labels of Corrosive Sublimate and Arsenic, which once belonged to our department of Natural History, were emptied, scoured, and cut down into tea-cups.

Recognising the importance of acting directly upon the men's minds, my first step now was to issue a general order appointing a certain day, the 17th of May, for setting out. Every man had twenty-four hours given him to select and get ready his eight pounds of personal effects. After that, his time was to cease to be his own for any purpose. The long-indulged waywardness of our convalescents made them take this hardly. Some who were at work on articles of apparel that were really important to them threw them down unfinished, in a sick man's pet. I had these in some cases picked up quietly and finished by others. But I showed myself inexorable. It was necessary to brace up and concentrate every man's thoughts and energies upon the one great common object,—our departure from the vessel on the 17th, not to return.

I tried my best also to fix and diffuse impressions that we were going home. But in this I was not always successful: I was displeased, indeed, with the moody indifference with which many went about the tasks to which I put them. The completeness of my preparations I know had its influence; but there were many doubters. Some were convinced that my only object was to move farther south, retaining the brig, however, as a home to retreat to. Others whispered that I wanted to transport the sick to the hunting-grounds and other resources of the lower settlements, which I had such difficulty in preventing the mutinous from securing for themselves alone. A few of a more cheerful spirit thought I had resolved to make for some point of look-out, in the hope of a rescue by whalers or English expedition-parties which were supposed still to be within the Arctic circle. The number is unfortunately small of those human beings whom calamity elevates.

There was no sign or affectation of spirit or enthusiasm upon the memorable day when we first adjusted the boats to their cradles on the sledges and moved them off to the ice-foot. But the ice immediately around the vessel was smooth; and, as the boats had not received their lading, the first labor was an easy one. As the runners moved, the gloom of several countenances was perceptibly lightened. The croakers had protested that we could not stir an inch. These cheering remarks always reach a commander's ears, and I took good care of course to make the outset contradict them. By the time we reached the end of our little level, the tone had improved wonderfully, and we were prepared for the effort of crossing the successive lines of the belt-ice and forcing a way through the smashed material which interposed between us and the ice-foot.

This was a work of great difficulty, and sorrowfully exhausting to the poor fellows not yet accustomed to heave together. But in the end I had the satisfaction, before twenty-four hours were over, of seeing our little arks of safety hauled upon the higher plane of the ice-foot, in full trim for ornamental exhibition from the brig; their neat canvas housing rigged tent-fashion over the entire length of each; a jaunty little flag, made out of one of the commander's obsolete linen shirts, decorated in stripes from a disused article of stationery, the red-ink bottle, and with a very little of the blue-bag in the star-spangled corner. All hands after this returned on board: I had ready for them the best supper our supplies afforded, and they turned in with minds prepared for their departure next day.

They were nearly all of them invalids, unused to open air and exercise. It was necessary to train them very gradually. We made but two miles the first day, and with a single boat; and indeed for some time after this I took care that they should not be disheartened by overwork. They came back early to a hearty supper and warm beds, and I had the satisfaction of marching them back each recurring morning refreshed and cheerful. The weather, happily, was superb.

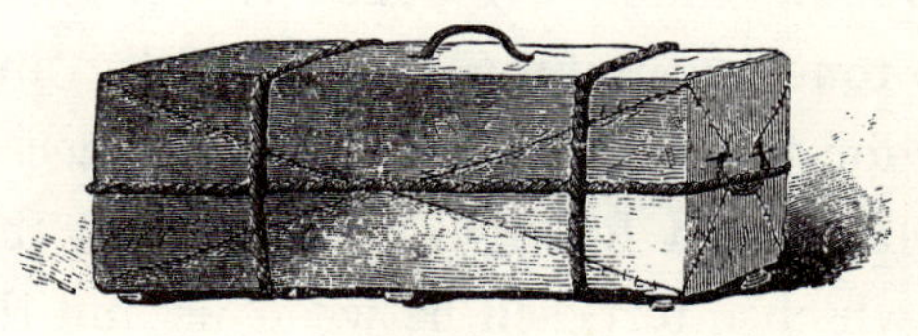

DOCUMENT-BOX.

CHAPTER XVII.

THE PLEDGES — THE ARGUMENT — FAREWELL TO THE BRIG — THE MUSTER — THE ROUTINE — THE MESSES.

OUR last farewell to the brig was made with more solemnity. The entire ship's company was collected in our dismantled winter-chamber to take part in the ceremonial. It was Sunday. Our moss walls had been torn down, and the wood that supported them burned. Our beds were off at the boats. The galley was unfurnished and cold. Every thing about the little den of refuge was desolate.

We read prayers and a chapter of the Bible; and then, all standing silently round, I took Sir John Franklin's portrait from its frame and cased it in an India-rubber scroll. I next read the reports of inspection and survey which had been made by the several commissions organized for the purpose, all of them testifying to the necessities under which I was about to act. I then addressed the party: I did not affect to disguise the difficulties that were before us; but I assured them that they could all be overcome by energy and subordination to command: and that the thirteen hundred miles of ice and water that lay between us and North Greenland could be traversed with safety for most of us, and hope for all. I added, that as men and messmates it was the duty of us all, enjoined by gallantry as well as religion, to postpone every consideration of self to the protection of the wounded and sick; and that this must be regarded by every man and under all circumstances as a paramount order. In conclusion, I told them to think over the trials we had all of us gone through, and to remember each man for himself how often an unseen Power had rescued him in peril, and I admonished them still to place reliance on Him who could not change.

I was met with a right spirit. After a short conference, an engagement was drawn up by one of the officers, and brought to me with the signatures of all the company, without an exception. It read as follows:—

"SECOND GRINNELL EXPEDITION,

"BRIG ADVANCE, May 20, 1855.

"The undersigned, being convinced of the impossibility of the liberation of the brig, and equally convinced of the impossibility of remaining in the ice a third winter, do fervently concur with the commander in his attempt to reach the South by means of boats.

"Knowing the trials and hardships which are before us, and feeling the necessity of union, harmony, and discipline, we have determined to abide faithfully by the expedition and our sick comrades, and to do all that we can, as true men, to advance the objects in view.

HENRY BROOKS,	J. WALL WILSON,
JAMES MCGARY,	AMOS BONSALL,
GEORGE RILEY,	J. J. HAYES,
WILLIAM MORTON,	AUGUST SONTAG,
C. OHLSEN,	&c. &c."

I had prepared a brief memorial of the considerations which justified our abandonment of the vessel, and had read it as part of my address. I now fixed it to a stanchion near the gangway, where it must attract the notice of any who might seek us hereafter, and stand with them as my vindication for the step, in case we should be overtaken by disaster. It closed with these words:—

"I regard the abandonment of the brig as inevitable. We have by actual inspection but thirty-six days' provisions, and a careful survey shows that we cannot cut more firewood without rendering our craft unseaworthy. A third winter would force us, as the only means of escaping starvation, to resort to Esquimaux habits and give up all hope of remaining by the vessel and her resources. It would therefore in no manner advance the search after Sir John Franklin.

"Under any circumstances, to remain longer would be destructive to those of our little party who have already suffered from the extreme severity of the climate and its tendencies to disease. Scurvy has enfeebled more or less every man in the expedition; and an anomalous spasmodic disorder, allied to tetanus, has cost us the life of two of our most prized comrades.

"I hope, speaking on the part of my companions and myself, that we have done all that we ought to do to prove our tenacity of purpose and devotion to the cause which we have undertaken. This attempt to escape by crossing the southern ice on sledges is regarded by me as an imperative duty,—the only means of saving ourselves and preserving the laboriously-earned results of the expedition.

"E. K. KANE,

"*Com. Grinnell Expedition.*

"ADVANCE, RENSSELAER BAY, May 20, 1855."

We then went upon deck: the flags were hoisted and hauled down again, and our party walked once or twice around the brig, looking at her timbers and exchanging comments upon the scars which reminded them of every stage of her dismantling. Our figure-head—the fair Augusta, the little blue girl with pink cheeks, who had lost her breast by an iceberg and her nose by a nip off Bedevilled Reach—was taken from our bows and placed aboard the "Hope." "She is at any rate wood," said the men, when I hesitated about giving them the additional burden; "and if we cannot carry her far we can burn her."

OUR AUGUSTA.

No one thought of the mockery of cheers: we had no festival-liquor to mislead our perception of the real state of things. When all hands were quite ready, we scrambled off over the ice together, much like a gang of stevedores going to work over a quayful of broken cargo.

On reaching the boats, the party were regularly mustered and divided between the two. A rigid inspection was had of every article of personal equipment. Each man had a woollen underdress and an Esquimaux suit of fur clothing,—kapetah, nessak, and nannooke complete, with boots of our own make; that is to say, one pair of canvas faced with walrus-hide, and another inside made of the cabin Brussels carpet. In addition to this, each carried a rue-raddy adjusted to fit him comfortably, a pair of socks next his skin, and a pair of large goggles for snow-blindness, made Esquimaux-fashion by cutting a small slit in a piece of wood. Some of us had gutta percha masks fitting closely to the face, as large as an ordinary domino; but these were still less favorable to personal appearance than the goggles. The provision-bags and other stores were numbered, and each man and officer had his own bag and a place assigned for it, to prevent confusion in rapid stowing and unstowing.

Excluding four sick men, who were unable to move, and myself, who had to drive the dog-team and serve as common carrier and courier, we numbered but twelve men,—which would have given six to a sledge, or too few to move it. It was therefore necessary to concentrate our entire force upon one sledge at a time. On the other hand, however, it was important to the efficiency of our organization that matters of cooking, sleeping, baggage, and rations, should be regulated by separate messes.

The routine I established was the most precise:—Daily prayers both morning and evening, all hands gathering round in a circle and standing uncovered during the short exercise; regulated hours; fixed duties and positions at the track-lines and on the halt; the cooking to be taken by turns, the captains of the boats alone being excused. The charge of the log was confided to Dr. Hayes, and the running survey to Mr. Sontag. Though little could be expected from either of these gentlemen at this time, I deemed it best to keep up the appearance of ordinary voyaging; and after we left the first ices of Smith's Straits I was indebted to them for valuable results. The thermometer was observed every three hours.

To my faithful friend and first officer, boatswain Brooks, I assigned the command of the boats and sledges. I knew how well he was fitted for it; and when forced, as I was afterward during the descent, to be in constant motion between the sick-station, the Esquimaux settlements, and the deserted brig, I felt safe in the assurance of his tried fidelity and indomitable resolution. The party under him was marshalled at the rue-raddies as a single gang; but the messes were arranged with reference to the two whaleboats, and when we came afterward to the open water the crews were distributed in the same way :—

To the Faith.	*To the Hope.*
JAMES MCGARY,	WILLIAM MORTON,
CHRISTIAN OHLSEN,	AUGUSTUS SONTAG,
AMOS BONSALL,	GEORGE RILEY,
CARL J. PETERSEN,	JOHN BLAKE,
THOMAS HICKEY	WILLIAM GODFREY.

With this organization we set out on our march.

CHAPTER XVIII.

THE SICK HUT — TO FIRST RAVINE — MOVING THE SICK — THE HEALTH-STATION — CONVALESCENCE.

I HAD employed myself and the team from an early day in furnishing out accommodations for the sick at Anoatok. I have already described this station as the halting-place of our winter-journeys. The hut was a low dome of heavy stones, more like a cave than a human habitation. It was perched on the very point of the rocky promontory which I have named after Captain Inglefield, of the British Navy. Both to the north and south it commanded a view of the ice-expanse of the straits; and what little sunshine ever broke through the gorges by which it was environed encouraged a perceptible growth of flowering plants and coarse grasses on the level behind it. The ice-belt, now beautifully smooth, brought us almost to the edge of this little plain.

I had made up my mind from an early period that, in the event of our attempting to escape upon the ice, the "wind-loved spot," as the Esquimaux poetically named it, would be well adapted to the purposes of an entrepôt, and had endeavored within the last few weeks to fit it up also as a resting-place for our sick during the turmoil of removing from the brig. I had its broken outlet closed by a practicable door, and the roof perforated to receive a stove-pipe. Still more recently the stone platform or dais had been thoroughly cleansed, and covered with shavings which Ohlsen had saved while working at his boats. Over these again were laid my best cushions; and two blankets, all that we could spare, were employed to tapestry the walls. A small pane of glass, formerly the facing of a daguerreotype, inserted in the door, and a stove, made by combining the copper dog-vane of the galley with some dazzling tin pipes, completed the furniture. It was a gloomy hospital after all for the poor fellows, who, more than sharing all the anxiety of their comrades, could have no relief in the excitement of active toil.

I made many journeys between the brig and Anoatok while the arrangements for our setting out were in progress, and after the sledges were under way. All of our invalids were housed there in safety, one or two of them occupying the dog-sledge for the trip. Most of our provision for the march and voyage of escape had also been stacked in the neighborhood of the huts: eight hundred pounds out of fifteen hundred were already there. The remaining seven hundred I undertook to carry myself, as I had done most of the rest. It would have been folly to encumber my main body with any thing more than their boats and sledges;

they were barely able at first to carry even these. Our effort to escape would indeed have resulted in miserable failure, had we been without our little Esquimaux dog-team to move the sick, and forward the intended lading of the boats, and keep up supplies along the line of march. I find by my notes that these six dogs, well worn by previous travel, carried me with a fully-burdened sledge between seven and eight hundred miles during the first fortnight after leaving the brig,—a mean travel of fifty-seven miles a day.

Up to the evening of the 23d, the progress had been a little more than a mile a day for one sledge: on the 24th, both sledges had reached First Ravine, a distance of seven miles, and the dog-sledge had brought on to this station the buffalo-bags and other sleeping-appliances which we had prepared during the winter. The condition of the party was such that it was essential they should sleep in comfort; and it was a rule therefore during the whole journey, never departed from unless in extreme emergency, never to begin a new day's labor till the party was refreshed from the exertions of the day before. Our halts were regulated by the condition of the men rather than by arbitrary hours, and sleep was meted out in proportion to the trials of the march. The thermometer still ranged below zero; but our housed boats, well crowded, and fully stocked with sleeping-gear, were hardly uncomfortable to weary men; besides which, we slept by day when the sun was warmest, and travelled when we could avoid his greatest glare.

Mr. Morton, Ohlsen, and Petersen, during this time performed a double duty. They took their turn at the sledges with the rest, but they were also engaged in preparing the Red Eric as a comrade boat. She was mounted on our good old sledge, the *Faith*,—a sledge that, like her namesake our most reliable whaleboat, had been our very present help in many times of trouble. I believe every man felt, when he saw her brought out, that stout work was to be done, and under auspices of good.

In the mean time I had carried Mr. Goodfellow to the sick-station with my dog-sledge, and had managed to convey the rest one by one to the same spot. Mr. Wilson, whose stump was still unhealed, and who suffered besides from scurvy, George Whipple, whose tendons were so contracted that he could not extend his legs, and poor Stephenson, just able to keep the lamps burning and warm up food for the rest, were the other invalids, all incapable of moving without assistance. It is just that I should speak of the manly fortitude with which they bore up during this painful imprisonment. Dr. Hayes, though still disabled from his frozen foot, adhered manfully to the sledges.

I have already expressed my belief that this little refuge-hut of Anoatok was the means of saving the lives of these four men. When they were first transported to it, they were all of them so drawn up with scurvy as to be unable to move. There was but one among them able to melt water for the rest. I attended them myself during the first week, at every interval that I could snatch from the duty of transporting our provisions. The temperature in which they lived was at first below zero; but, as the sun rose and the warmth increased, they gradually gained strength, and were able at last to crawl out and breathe in the gladdening air.

Had I attempted to bring them down on our boat-sledges, our progress would have been seriously impeded and their lives jeoparded. I cannot imagine a worse position for a sick and helpless man than some of those which I have described in our transit from the brig.

On the other hand, to have left them for the time behind us would have made it quite possible that they might not at last be reclaimed. Every day was making the ice-travel more difficult and full of hazard till we reached the open water; and they could not fail to know this as soon as they were able to look out on the floes. My occasional visits as I passed Anoatok on my way to Etah, or as I brought supplies for them on the return, gave them assurances of continued interest in their fortunes, and advices of our progress and of their own hopes and ours.

Besides all this, there is something in the insidious disease which was their most dangerous enemy that is best combated by moral excitement. A change of scene, renewed or increased responsibilities, topics of active thought, incitements to physical effort, are among the very best prescriptions for men suffering with the scurvy. I have had reason to feel, while tracing these pages, how reluctantly the system renews its energies under the pressure of a daily unvarying task.

The patients at our sick-station no doubt suffered much, and for a while I never parted from them without anxiety. But their health improved under the stimulus of a new mode of life: and by the time that we called on them to rejoin us their whole tone had undergone a happy change. I congratulate myself, as I write, that all who reached the open water with me are able now to bear a part in society and toil.

THE STOVE AT ANOATOK.

CHAPTER XIX.

TO THE BRIG AGAIN — WELCOME AT THE HUT — LOG OF THE SLEDGES—EDUCATED FAITH—GOOD-BYE TO THE BRIG—METEK'S PRAYER.

As I review my notes of the first few days of our ice-journey, I find them full of incidents interesting and even momentous when they occurred, but which cannot claim a place in this narrative. The sledges were advancing slowly, the men often discouraged, and now and then one giving way under the unaccustomed labor; the sick at Anoatok always dreary in their solitude, and suffering, perhaps, under an exacerbation of disease, or, like the rest of us, from a penury of appropriate food. Things looked gloomy enough at times.

The Red Boat was completed for service in a few days, and joined the sledge-party on the floes,—an additional burden, but a necessary one, for our weary rueraddies; and I set out for the sick-station with Mr. Goodfellow, our last remaining invalid. As my team reached the entrance of Force Bay, I saw that poor

Nessark, the Esquimaux, who had carried Mr. Wilson and some stores to Anoatok, finding his sledge-load too heavy, had thrown out a portion of it upon the ice. He had naturally enough selected the bread for his jettison, an article of diet unknown among the Esquimaux, but precisely that of which our sick were most in need. I lost some time in collecting such parts of his rejected cargo as I could find, and, when I reached the huts after a twelve hours' drive, the condition of our sick men made it imperative that I should return at once to the brig. The dogs gave out while crossing the reach of Force Bay, and I was forced to camp out with them on the ice-belt, but early in the morning I came upon the fires of the sledge-party.

The men were at prayers when I first saw them; but, as they passed to the drag-ropes, I was pained to see how wearily they moved. Poor Brooks's legs were so swollen that he could not brace them in his blanket coverings, and Dr. Hayes could hardly keep his place. The men generally showed symptoms of increasing scurvy. It was plain that they could not hold their own without an increased allowance, if not of meat, at least of fresh bread and hot tea.

Taking with me Morton, my faithful adjutant always, I hurried on to the brig. It was in the full glare of noon that we entered the familiar curve of Rensselaer Bay. The black spars of our deserted vessel cut sharply against the shores; there was the deeply-marked snow-track that led to Observatory Island and the graves of poor Baker and Schubert, with their cairn and its white-cross beacon: every thing looked as when we defiled in funeral procession round the cliffs a year before. But, as we came close upon the brig and drove our dogs up the gangway, along which Bonsall and myself had staggered so often with our daily loads of ice, we heard the rustling of wings, and a large raven sailed away in the air past Sylvia Headland. It was old Magog, one of a pair that had cautiously haunted near our brig during the last two years. He had already appropriated our homestead.

We lighted fires in the galley, melted pork, baked a large batch of bread, gathered together a quantity of beans and dried apples, somewhat damaged but still eatable, and by the time our dogs had fed and rested we were ready for the return. Distributing our supplies as we passed the squads on the floe, I hastened to Anoatok. I had taken Godfrey with us from his party, and, as it was painfully evident that the men could not continue to work without more generous food, I sent him on to Etah with the dogs, in the hope of procuring a stock of walrus-meat.

The little company at the hut welcomed my return. They had exhausted their provisions; their lamp had gone out; the snow-drift had forced its way in at the door so that they could not close it; it was blowing a northeaster; and the thermometer, which hung against the blanketed walls, stood only sixteen degrees above zero. The poor fellows had all the will to protect themselves, but they were lame and weak and hungry and disheartened. We built a fire for them of tarred rope, dried their bedding, cooked them a porridge of meat-biscuit and pea-soup, fastened up their desolate doorway, hung a dripping slab of pork-fat over their lamp-wick, and, first joining in a prayer of thankfulness and then a round of merry gossip, all hands forgot sickness and privation and distance in the contentment of our sleeping-bags. I cannot tell how long we slept, for all our watches ran down before we awoke.

The gale had risen, and it was snowing hard when I replenished the fires of our hearthstone. But we went on burning rope and fat, in a regular tea-drinking frolic, till not an icicle or even a frost-mark was to be seen on the roof. After a time Godfrey rejoined us; Metek came with him; and between their two sledges they brought an ample supply of meat. With part of this I hastened to the sledge-party. They were now off Ten-mile Ravine, struggling through the accumulated snows, and much exhausted, though not out of heart. In spite of their swollen feet, they had worked fourteen hours a day, passing in that time over some twelve miles of surface, and advancing a mile and a half on their way.

A few extracts from their log-book, as kept by Dr. Hayes, may show something of our mode of travel, though it conveys but an imperfect idea of its trials.

Log of Sledge-Party.

"May 23, Wednesday.—Mr. Bonsall, cook, called at 8 P.M. George Riley suffering from snow-blindness, but able to take a place at the drag-ropes. Read prayers, and got under way at 10¼ P.M.

"Took 'Faith' to bluff at head of ravine. Left Dr. Hayes there and returned for 'Hope.' Carried her on to 'Faith's' camp and halted. All hands very much tired. Sledges haul heavy. Snow in drifts on the ice-foot, requiring a standing haul.

"Captain Kane passed us from Esquimaux hut on his way to brig, at 11 A.M., while we were sleeping. Captain Kane overtook and passed us again with his dog-sledge and provision-cargo, on way to sick-station, at two o'clock, Tuesday, while cooking, taking with him William Godfrey.

"May 24, Thursday.—Cook, George Riley, called at 4 P.M. Read prayers and got under way at eight o'clock. Took 'Faith' beyond the headland of yesterday. Melted snow for drink. Left Dr. Hayes here and returned for 'Hope.' Carried her back to 'Faith' camp by 5 A.M. of Friday, and halted. Hayes about the same; Riley's eyes better. Mr. Bonsall and McGary begin to give in. Slush for burning all gone. Party with 'Red Boat' not yet come up.

"May 25, Friday.—Mr. Sontag, cook, called at 6 P.M. Mr. Ohlsen, with the 'Red Boat' and cargo, came up at one o'clock, bringing orders from Captain Kane. Being knocked up, he and his party turned in. After prayers, stowed the spare cargo of the whaleboats into the 'Red Eric,' and all hands, except Mr. Sontag and Dr. Hayes, hauled her down to the ice-foot of the Bedevilled Reach Turn-off station, below Basalt Camp.

"Returned, and reached the whaleboats at five o'clock, Saturday morning. All hands tired, turned in. Riley's eyes well.

"May 26, Saturday.—Strong wind, with snow, during night. Captain Kane came from south at half-past three o'clock with the dog-team, bringing a supply of walrus-beef, with Metek and sledge."

Once more leaving the party on the floe, Morton and myself, with Metek and his sledge in company, revisited the brig, and set ourselves to work baking bread. We had both of us ample experience in this branch of the culinary art, and I could gain some credit, perhaps, with a portion of my readers, by teaching them how bread may be raised in three hours without salt, saleratus, or shortening. But it is not the office of this book to deal in occult mysteries. The thing can be done, and we did it: *sat verbum.* The brig was dreary enough, and Metek was glad to bid it good-bye, with one hundred and fifty pounds on his dog-sledge, consigned to Mr. Brooks. But he carried besides a letter, safely trusted to his inspection, which directed that he should be sent back forthwith for another load. It was something like a breach of faith, perhaps, but his services were indispensable, and his dogs still more so. He returned, of course, for there was no escaping us; his village lay in the opposite direction, and he could not deviate from the track after once setting out. In the mean time we had cooked about a hundred pounds of flour pudding, and tried out a couple of bagfuls of pork-fat;—a good day's work,—and we were quite ready, before the subdued brightness of midnight came, to turn in to our beds. Our beds!—there was not an article of covering left on board. We ripped open the old mattresses, and, all three crawling down among the curled hair, Morton, Metek, and the Nalegak slept as sound as vagrants on a haystack.

On Monday, the 28th, we all set out for the boats and Anoatok. Both Metek and myself had our sledges heavily laden. We carried the last of our provision-bags, completing now our full complement of fifteen hundred pounds, the limit of capacity of our otherwise crowded boats.

It caused me a bitter pang to abandon our collection of objects of Natural History, the cherished fruit of so much exposure and toil; and it was hardly easier to leave some other things behind,—several of my well-tested instruments, for instance, and those silent friends, my books. They had all been packed up, hoping for a chance of saving them; and, to the credit of my comrades, let me say gratefully that they offered to exclude both clothes and food in favor of a full freight of these treasures.

But the thing was not to be thought of. I gave a last look at the desolate galley-stove, the representative of our long winter's fireside, at the still bright coppers now full of frozen water, the theodolite, the chart-box, and poor Wilson's guitar,—one more at the remnant of the old moss walls, the useless daguerreotypes, and the skeletons of dog and deer and bear and musk-ox,—stoppered in the rigging;—and, that done, whipped up my dogs so much after the manner of a sentimentalizing Christian, that our pagan Metek raised a prayer in their behalf.

CHAPTER XX.

NEW STATIONS—THE ICE-MARSHES—POINT SECURITY—OOPEGSOAK—CATCHING AUKS—ANINGNAH—NESSARK.

I FOUND that Mr. Brooks had succeeded in getting his boat and sledges as far as the floe off Bedevilled Reach. I stopped only long enough to point out to him an outside track, where I had found the ice quite smooth and free from snow, and pressed my dogs for the hut. I noticed to my great joy, too, that the health of his party seemed to be improving under our raw-meat specific, and could not find fault with the extravagant use they were making of it.

THE FLOE.

The invalids at the sick-station were not as well as I could have wished: but I had only time to renew their stock of provision and give them a few cheering words. Our walrus-meat was nearly exhausted.

I had fixed upon two new stations farther to the south, as the depôts to which our stores were now to be transported. One was upon the old and heavy floes off Navialik, "the big gull's place,"—a headland opposite Cape Hatherton.—the other on the level ice-plain

ICE-BELT AND CHASM.

near Littleton Island. Having now gathered our stores at Anoatok, I began with a thankful heart to move them onward. I sent on Metek to the farther station with two bags of bread-dust, each weighing ninety pounds, and, having myself secured some three hundred pounds at Navialik, drove on for Etah Bay.

My long succession of journeys on this route had made me thoroughly weary of the endless waste of ice to seaward, and I foolishly sought upon this trip to vary the travel by following the ice-belt. But, upon reaching Refuge Harbor, I found the snow so heavy and the fragments from the cliffs so numerous and threatening, that I was obliged to give it up. A large chasm stopped my advance and drove me out again upon the floes.

Getting beyond a table-land known as Kasarsoak, or "the big promontory," I emerged from the broken ice upon a wide plain. Here I first saw with alarm that the ice had changed its character: the snow which covered it had become lead-colored and sodden by the water from beneath, and ice-fields after ice-fields stretching before me were all covered with stained patches. As I rode along these lonely marshes, for such they were, the increased labor of the dogs admonished me that the floe was no longer to be trusted. It chilled my heart to remember the position of our boats and stores. Nearly nine hundred pounds of food, exclusive of the load now upon my sledge, were still awaiting transportation at Anoatok.

THE ISLAND CAMP.

Two hundred more, including our shot and bullet-bags, were at the Cape Hatherton station; and Metek's load was probably by this time lying on the ice opposite McGary Island. Like Robinson Crusoe with his powder, the reflection came over me:—"Good God! what will become of us if all this is destroyed?"

Only by men experienced in the rapid changes of Arctic ice can the full force of this reflection be appreciated. A single gale might convert the precarious platform, over which we were travelling, into a tumultuous ice-pack. Had the boats their stores on board even, and could they break through without foundering, there was not the remotest prospect of their being liberated in open water; and I knew well what obstacles a wet, sludgy surface would present to our overtasked and almost worn-out party.

I determined, therefore, as soon as I could secure the meat, which was my immediate errand, to make a requisition upon the Esquimaux for two of the four dogs which were still at Etah, and by their aid to place the provisions in safety. The north cape of Littleton Island, afterward called Point Security, was selected for the purpose, and I left orders with the invalids at the sick-station to be in readiness for instant removal. I pursued my journey alone.

It was quite late in the evening when I drew near Etah. I mean that it was verging on to our midnight, the sun being low in the heavens, and the air breathing that solemn stillness which belongs to the sleeping-time of birds and plants. I had not quite reached the little settlement when loud sounds of laughter came to my ear; and, turning the cape, I burst suddenly upon an encampment of the inhabitants.

Some thirty men, women, and children, were gathered

together upon a little face of offal-stained rock. Except a bank of moss, which broke the wind-draught from the fiord, they were entirely without protection from the weather, though the temperature was 5° below zero. The huts were completely deserted, the snow tossut had fallen in, and the window was as free and open as summer to the purifying air. Every living thing about the settlement was out upon the bare rocks.

Rudest of gypsies, how they squalled, and laughed, and snored, and rolled about! Some were sucking bird-skins, others were boiling incredible numbers of auks in huge soapstone pots, and two youngsters, crying, at the top of their voices, "Oopegsoak! Oopegsoak!" were fighting for an owl. It was the only specimen (*Strix nyctea*) that I had seen except on the wing; but, before I could secure it, they had torn it limb from limb, and were eating its warm flesh and blood, their faces buried among its dishevelled feathers.

The fires were of peat-moss greased with the fat of the bird-skins. They were used only for cooking, however, the people depending for comfort on the warmth of close contact. Old Kresut, the blind patriarch of the settlement, was the favored centre, and around him, as a focus, was a coil of men, women, and children, as perplexing to unravel as a skein of eels. The children alone were toddling about and bringing in stores of moss, their faces smeared with blood, and titbits of raw liver between their teeth.

The scene was redolent of plenty and indolence,—

the *dolce far niente* of the short-lived Esquimaux summer. Provision for the dark winter was furthest from their thoughts; for, although the rocks were patched with sun-dried birds, a single hunting-party from

CATCHING AUKS.

Peteravik could have eaten up their entire supplies in a night.

There was enough to make them improvident. The little auks were breeding in the low cones of rubbish under the cliffs in such numbers that it cost them no more to get food than it does a cook to gather vegetables. A boy, ordered to climb the rocks with one of their purse-nets of seal-skin at the end of a narwhal's tusk, would return in a few minutes with as many as he could carry.

The dogs seemed as happy as their masters: they were tethered by seal-skin thongs to prevent robbery, but evidently fed to the full extent of their capacity.

Aningnah, wife of Marsumah, the lady whose likeness beautifies page 114, was one of the presiding deities of the soup-pot, or rather first witch of the caldron. She was a tall, well-made woman, and, next to Mrs. Metek, had a larger influence than any female in the settlement.

During one of my visits to the settlement, I had relieved her from much suffering by opening a furuncle, and the kind creature never lost an opportunity of showing how she remembered it. Poor old Kresut was summarily banished from the central seat of honor, and the nalegak installed in his place. She stripped herself of her bird-skin kapetah to make me a coverlet, and gave me her two-year-old baby for a pillow. There was a little commotion in the tangled mass of humanity as I crawled over them to accept these proffered hospitalities; but it was all of a welcoming sort. I had learned by this time to take kindly and condescendingly the privileges of my rank; and, with my inner man well refreshed with auk-livers, I was soon asleep.

In the morning I left my own tired dogs in charge

of Marsumah, quite confident that his wife would feed them faithfully, and took from them their only team in unequal exchange. Such had become our relations with these poor friends of ours, that such an act of authority would have gone unquestioned if it had cost them a much graver sacrifice. They saw the condition of my own travel-broken animals, and were well aware of the sufferings of our party, so long their neighbors and allies. Old Nessark filled my sledge with walrus-meat; and two of the young men joined me on foot, to assist me through the broken ice between Littleton Island and the mainland.

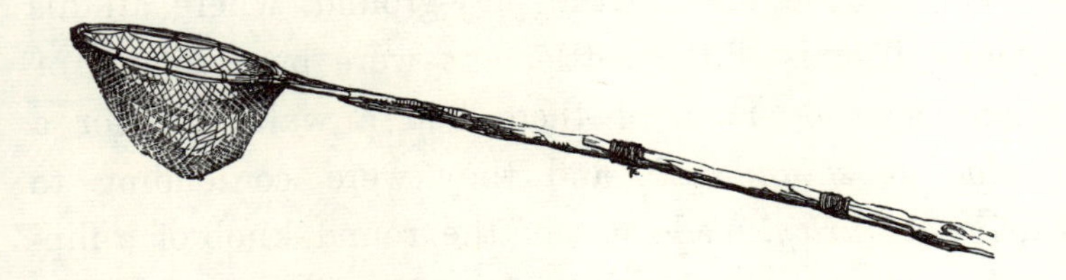

CHAPTER XXI.

THE GAME OF BALL—MY BROTHER'S LAKE—THE POLAR SEASONS—FATE OF THE ESQUIMAUX—THE ESQUIMAUX LIMITS—ESQUIMAUX ENDURANCE—AWAHTOK'S HUNT—HIS ESCAPE—THE GUARDIAN WALRUS.

BEFORE I left Etah on my return, I took an early stroll with Sip-su, "the handsome boy," to the lake back of my old travelling-route, and directly under the face of the glacier.

He led me first to the play-ground, where all his young friends of the settlement were busy in one of their sports. Each of them had a walrus-rib for a *golph* or *shinny-stick*, and they were contending to drive a *hurley*, made out of the round knob of a flipper-joint, up a bank of frozen snow. Roars of laughter greeted the impatient striker as he missed his blow at the shining ball, and eager cries told how close the match was drawing to an end. They were counting on the fingers of both hands, Eight, eight, eight: the game is ten.

Strange,—the thought intruded itself, but there was no wisdom in it,—strange that these famine-pinched wanderers of the ice should rejoice in sports and play-things like the children of our own smiling sky, and that parents should fashion for them toy sledges, and harpoons, and nets, miniature emblems of a life of suffering and peril! how strange this joyous merriment under the monitory shadow of these jagged ice-cliffs! My spirit was oppressed as I imagined the possibility of our tarrying longer in these frozen regions; but it was ordinary life with these other children of the same Creator, and they were playing as unconcerned as the birds that circled above our heads. "Fear not, therefore: ye are of more value than many sparrows."

I do not wonder that the scene at the lake impressed my brother when he visited it on his errand of rescue: Lieutenant Hartstene and he were the only white men, except myself, that have ever seen it.

A body of ice, resplendent in the sunshine, was enclosed between the lofty walls of black basalt; and from its base a great archway or tunnel poured out a dashing stream into the lake, disturbing its quiet surface with a horse-shoe of foam. Birds flew about in myriads, and the green sloping banks were checquered with the purple lychnis and Arctic chickweeds.

I have named this lake after my brother, for it was near its shores that, led by Myouk, he stumbled on the summer tents of the natives and obtained the evidence of our departure south. I built a large cairn here, and placed within it a copper penny, on which was scratched the letter K; but, like many other such deposits, it never met the eyes for which it was intended.

The lake abounds in fish, apparently the salmon-trout; but the natives have not the art of fishing. The stream, which tunnels its way out near the glacier-foot, is about ten feet in diameter; and I was assured that it never completely suspends its flow. Although the tunnel closes with ice, and the surface of the lake freezes for many feet below, the water may still be seen and heard beneath, even in midwinter, wearing its way at the base of the glacier.

This fact is of importance, as it bears upon the temperature of deep ice-beds. It shows that with an atmosphere whose mean is below zero throughout the year, and a mean summer heat but 4° above the freezing-point, these great Polar glaciers retain a high interior temperature not far from 32°, which enables them to resume their great functions of movement and discharge readily, when the cold of winter is at an end, and not improbably to temper to some extent the natural rigor of the climate. Even in the heart of the ice nature has her compensations.

The phases of the Polar year so blend and separate that it is difficult to distribute them into seasons. In the Arctic latitudes a thousand miles to the south, travellers speak of winter and summer as if the climate underwent no intermediate changes. But nature impresses no such contrasts upon any portion of her realm; and, whatever may be the registrations of the meteorologist, the rude Esquimaux of these icy solitudes derives from his own experience and necessities a more accurate and practical system of notation.

He measures his life by winters, as the American Indian does by the summers, and for a like reason. Winter is for him the great dominant period of the year: he calls it "okipok," the season of fast ice.

But when the day has come again, and the first thawing begins to show itself in the sunshine, as winter declines before the promise of spring, he tells you that it is "upernasak," the time of water-drops. It is then the snow-bird comes back and the white ptarmigan takes a few brown feathers. His well-known heath, too, the irsuteet, (*Andromeda tetragona*,) is green again below its dried stems under the snow.

About the end of May, or a little later, comes "upernak," the season of thaws. It is his true summer. Animal and vegetable life are now back again: the floes break upon the sea and drift in ice-rafts about the coasts; snow is disappearing from the hill-tops; and the water-torrents pour down from the long-sealed ravines and valleys.

About the middle of August the upernak has passed into the season of no ice, "aosak," the short interval between complete thaw and reconsolidation. It is never really iceless; but the floes have now drifted to the south, and the sea along the coast is more open than at any other period. It ends with the latter weeks of September, and sees the departure of all migratory life.

The fifth season is a late fall, the "okiakut," when

the water-torrents begin to freeze in the fiords and thawing ceases except at noonday. This terminates when the young ice has formed in a permanent layer on the bays, and winter returns with its long reign of cold and darkness.

It is with a feeling of melancholy that I recall these familiar names. They illustrate the trials and modes of life of a simple-minded people, for whom it seems to be decreed that the year must very soon cease to renew its changes. It pains me when I think of their approaching destiny,—in the region of night and winter, where the earth yields no fruit and the waters are locked,—without the resorts of skill or even the rude materials of art, and walled in from the world by barriers of ice without an outlet.

If you point to the east, inland, where the herds of reindeer run over the barren hills unmolested,—for they have no means of capturing them,—they will cry "Sermik," "glacier;" and, question them as you may about the range of their nation to the north and south, the answer is still the same, with a shake of the head, "Sermik, sermik-soak," "the great ice-wall:" there is no more beyond.

They have no "kresuk," no wood. The drift-timber which blesses their more southern brethren never reaches them. The bow and arrow are therefore unknown; and the kayak, the national implement of the Greenlander, which, like the palm-tree to the natives of the tropics, ministers to almost every want, exists among them only as a legendary word.

The narrow belt subjected to their nomadic range cannot be less than six hundred miles long; and throughout this extent of country every man knows every man. There is not a marriage or a birth or a death that is not talked over and mentally registered by all. I have a census, exactly confirmed by three separate informants, which enables me to count by name about one hundred and forty souls, scattered along from Kosoak, the Great River at the base of a glacier near Cape Melville, to the wind-loved hut of Anoatok.

Destitute as they are, they exist both in love and community of resources as a single family. The sites of their huts—for they are so few in number as not to bear the name of villages—are arranged with reference to the length of the dog-march and the seat of the hunt; and thus, when winter has built her highway and cemented into one the sea, the islands, and the main, they interchange with each other the sympathies and social communion of man, and diffuse through the darkness a knowledge of the resources and condition of all.

The main line of travel is then as beaten as a road at home. The dogs speed from hut to hut, almost unguided by their drivers. They regulate their time by the stars. Every rock has its name, every hill its significance; and a cache of meat deposited anywhere in this harsh wilderness can be recovered by the youngest hunter in the nation.

From Cape York to a settlement at Saunders Island,

called Appah, from the "Appah" or Lumme which colonize here in almost incredible numbers, the drive has been made in a single day; and thence to Netelik. on the main of Murchison Sound, in another. In a third, the long reach has been traversed by Cape Saumarez to the settlement of Karsioot, on a low tongue near Cape Robertson; and the fourth day has closed at Etah, or even Aunatok, the open place,—the resting-place now of our poor deserted Oomiak-soak. This four days' travel cannot be less than six hundred miles; and Amaladok, Metek's half-brother, assured me that he had made it in three,—probably changing his teams.

Their powers of resistance to exposure and fatigue are not greater perhaps than those of a well-trained voyager from other regions. But the necessities of their precarious life familiarize them with dangers from which the bravest among us might shrink without dishonor. To exemplify this, I select a single one from a number of adventures that were familiar in their recent history.

During the famine at Etah last winter, when we ourselves were so much distressed for fresh food, two of my friends, Awahtok and Myouk, determined to seek the walrus on the open ice. It was a performance of the greatest danger; but it was better in their eyes than the sacrifice of their dogs, and they both possessed to the fullest extent that apathetic fatalism which belongs to all lowly-cultivated races. They succeeded in killing a large male, and were in the act of returning joyfully to their village, when a north wind broke up the ice, and they found themselves afloat. The impulse of a European would have been to seek the land; but they knew that the drift was always most dangerous on the coast, and urged their dogs toward the nearest iceberg. They reached it after a struggle, and, by great efforts, made good their landing with their dogs and the half-butchered carcass of the walrus.

Poor Myouk, as he told the story to Petersen, made a frightful picture of their sufferings, the more so from the quiet, stoical manner with which he detailed the facts. It was at the close, he said, of the last moonlight of December, and in the midst of the heavy storm which held Petersen and myself prisoners at Anoatok. A complete darkness settled around them. They tied the dogs down to knobs of ice to prevent their losing their foothold, and prostrated themselves to escape being blown off by the violence of the wind. At first the sea broke over them, but they gained a higher level, and built a sort of screen of ice.

On the fifth night afterward, judging as well as they could, Myouk froze one of his feet, and Awahtok lost his great toe by frost-bite. But they kept heart of grace, and ate their walrus-meat as they floated slowly to the south. The berg came twice into collision with floes, and they thought at one time that they had passed the Utlak-soak, the Great Caldron, and had entered the North Water of Baffin's Bay. It was toward the close of the second moonlight, after a month's imprisonment, living as only these iron men could live, that they found the berg had grounded. They liberated their dogs as soon as the young ice would bear their weight, and, attaching long lines to them, which they cut from the hide of the dead walrus, they succeeded in hauling themselves through the water-space which always surrounds an iceberg, and reaching safe ice. They returned to their village like men raised from the dead, to meet a welcome, but to meet famine along with it.

I believe the explanation was never given to me in detail, or, if it was, I have forgotten it; but the whole misadventure was referred to an infringement of some canonical ritual in their conduct of the hunt. The walrus, and perhaps the seal also, is under the protective guardianship of a special representative or prototype, who takes care that he shall have fair play. They all believe that in the recesses of Force Bay, near a conical peak which has often served me as a landmark on my sledge-journeys, a great walrus lives in the hills, and crawls out, when there is no moon, to the edge of a ravine, where he bellows with a voice far more powerful than his fellows out to sea. Ootuniah had often heard this walrus, and once, when I was crossing Bedevilled Reach, he stopped me to listen to his dismal tones. I certainly heard them, and Ootuniah said that a good hunt would come of it. I tried to talk to him about echoes; but, as neither of us could understand the other, I listened quietly at last to the Big Walrus, and went my way.

G. White | Engraved at J.M. Butler's establishment 84 Chestnut St | J.C. McRae

WALRUS HUNT OFF PIKANTLIK.

CHAPTER XXII.

THE BAKERY—THE GUITAR GHOST—THE BOAT CAMP—NESSARK'S WIFE — OUT IN A GALE — CAPE MISERY — THE BURROW — THE RETREAT.

THE sledge-party under Mr. Brooks had advanced to within three miles of the hut when I reached them on my return. They had found the ice more practicable, and their health was improving. But their desire for food had increased proportionably; and, as it was a well-understood rule of our commissariat not to touch the reserved provision of the boats, it became necessary to draw additional supplies from the brig. The seven hundred pounds of bread-dust, our entire stock, could not be reduced with safety.

But the dogs were wanted to advance the contents of our Anoatok storehouse to the stations farther south, and I resolved to take Tom Hickey with me and walk back for another baking exploit. It was more of an effort than I counted on: we were sixteen hours on the ice, and we had forgotten our gutta-percha eyautick, or slit goggles. The glare of the sun as we entered the curve of our ice-cumbered harbor almost blinded us.

Tom had been a baker at home; but he assures me, with all the authority of an ancient member of the guild, that our achievement the day we came on board might be worthy of praise in the "old country:" Tom knows no praise more expanded. We kneaded the dough in a large pickled-cabbage cask, fired sundry volumes of the Penny Cyclopedia of Useful Knowledge, and converted, between duff and loaf, almost a whole barrel of flour into a strong likeness to the staff of life. It was the last of our stock; and "all the better too," said my improvident comrade, who retained some of the genius of blundering as well as the gallantry of his countrymen, "all the better, sir, since we'll have no more bread to bake."

Godfrey came on with the dogs three days after, to carry back the fruits of our labor; but an abrupt change of the weather gave us a howling gale outside, and we were all of us storm-stayed. It was Sunday, and probably the last time that two or three would be gathered together in our dreary cabin. So I took a Bible from one of the bunks, and we went through the old-times service. It was my closing act of official duty among my shipmates on board the poor little craft. I visited her afterward, but none of them were with me.

Tom and myself set out soon after, though the wind drove heavily from the south, leaving our companion to recover from his fatigue. We brought on our sledge-load safely, and had forgotten our baking achievement, with things of minor note, in that dreamless sleep which rewards physical exhaustion, when Godfrey came in upon us. He had had a hard chase behind the sledge, and was unwilling to confess at first what had brought him after us so soon. He had tried to forget himself among the debris of a mattress on the cabin floor, when he heard a sound from Mr. Wilson's guitar, sad and flowing in all its unearthly harmonies. He was sure he was awake, for he ran for it on the instant, and the proof was, he had left his coat behind him. The harp of Æolus had not been dreamed of in Bill's philosophy.

I was glad, when I reached the sick-station, to find things so much better. Everybody was stronger, and, as a consequence, more cheerful. They had learned housekeeping, with its courtesies as well as comforts. Their kotluk would have done credit to Aningnah herself: they had a dish of tea for us, and a lump of walrus; and they bestirred themselves real housewife-fashion, to give us the warm place and make us comfortable. I was right sorry to leave them, for the snow outside was drifting with the gale; but after a little while the dogs struck the track of the sledges, and, following it with unerring instinct, did not slacken their

KOTLUK.

pace till they had brought us to our companions on the floe.

They had wisely halted on account of the storm; and, with their three little boats drawn up side by side for mutual protection, had been lying to for the past

BOAT'S CAMP IN A STORM.

two days, tightly housed, and moored fast by whale-lines to the ice. But the drifts had almost buried the "Hope," which was the windward boat; and when I saw the burly form of Brooks emerging from the snow-covered roof, I could have fancied it a walrus rising through the ice.

They had found it hard travel, but were doing well. Brooks's provision-report was the old story,—out of meat and nearly out of bread:—no pleasant news for a tired-out man, who saw in this the necessity of another trip to Etah. I was only too glad, however, to see that their appetites held, for with the animal man, as with all others, while he feeds he lives. Short allowance for working-men on bread diet was of course out of the question. For the past week, each man had eaten three pounds of duff a day, and I did not dare to check them, although we had no more flour in reserve to draw upon. But the question how long matters could go on at this rate admitted of a simple arithmetical solution.

Six Esquimaux, three of them women,—that ugly beauty, Nessark's wife, at the head of them,—had come off to the boats for shelter from the gale. They seemed so entirely deferential, and to recognise with such simple trust our mutual relations of alliance, that I resolved to drive down to Etah with Petersen as interpreter, and formally claim assistance, according to their own laws, on the ground of our established brotherhood. I had thought of this before; but both Marsumah and Metek had been so engrossed with their bird-catching that I was loath to take them from their families.

Our dogs moved slowly, and the discolored ice admonished me to make long circuits. As we neared Littleton Island, the wind blew so freshly from the southwest, that I determined to take the in-shore channel and attempt to make the settlements over land. But I was hardly under the lee of the island, when there broke upon us one of the most fearful gales I have ever experienced. It had the character and the

"ANAK," WIFE OF NESSARK.

force of a cyclome. The dogs were literally blown from their harness, and it was only by throwing ourselves on our faces that we saved ourselves from being swept away: it seemed as if the ice must give way. We availed ourselves of a momentary lull to shoulder the sledge, and, calling the affrighted dogs around us, made for the rocks of Eider Island, and, after the most exhausting exertions, succeeded in gaining terra firma.

We were now safe from the danger that had seemed most imminent; but our condition was not improved. We were out on a blank cliff, the wind eddying round us so furiously that we could not keep our feet, and the air so darkened with the snow-wreaths that, although we were in the full daytime of the Arctic summer, we could neither see each other nor our dogs.

CAPE MISERY.

There was not a cleft or a projecting knob that could give us refuge. I saw that we must move or die. It was impossible that the ice should continue to resist such a hurricane, and a bold channel separated us from the shore. Petersen indeed protested that the channel was already broken up and driving with the storm. We made the effort, and crossed.

We struck a headland on the main shore, where a dark hornblende rock, perhaps thirty feet high, had formed a barricade, behind which the drifts piled themselves; and into this mound of snow we had just strength enough left to dig a burrow. We knew it soon after as Cape Misery.

The dogs and sledge were dragged in, and Petersen and myself, reclining "spoon-fashion," cowered among them. The snow piled over us all, and we were very soon so roofed in and quilted round that the storm seemed to rage far outside of us. We could only hear the wind droning like a great fly-wheel, except when a surge of greater malignity would sweep up over our burial-place and sift the snow upon the surface like hail. Our greatest enemy here was warmth. Our fur jumpers had been literally torn off our backs by the wind; but the united respiration of dogs and men melted the snow around us, and we were soon wet to the skin. It was a noisome vapor-bath, and we experienced its effects in an alarming tendency to syncope and loss of power.

Is it possible to imagine a juncture of more comic annoyance than that which now introduced itself among the terrors of our position? Toodla, our master-dog, was seized with a violent fit; and, as their custom is, his companions indulged in a family conflict upon the occasion, which was only mediated, after much effort, at the sacrifice of all that remained of Petersen's pantaloons and drawers.

We had all the longing for repose that accompanies extreme prostration, and had been fearing every moment that the combatants would bring the snow down upon us. At last down came our whole canopy, and we were exposed in an instant to the fury of the elements. I do not think, often as I have gone up on deck from a close cabin in a gale at sea, that I was ever more struck with the extreme noise and tumult of a storm.

Once more snowed up,—for the drift built its crystal palace rapidly about us,—we remained cramped and seething till our appetites reminded us of the neces-

ICE-BELT BROKEN BY FALLING ROCK.

sities of the inner man. To breast the gale was simply impossible; the alternative was to drive before it to the north and east. Forty miles of floundering travel brought us in twenty hours to the party on the floes.

They too had felt the force of the storm, and had drawn up the boats with their prows to the wind, all hands housed, and wondering as much as we did that the ice still held.

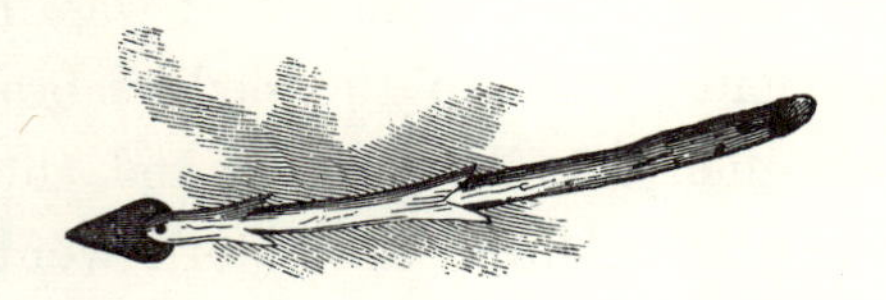

CHAPTER XXIII.

FRESH DOGS—THE SLIDES—ROCKING-STONES—OHLSEN'S ACCIDENT —ICE-SAILING—MOUNTING THE BELT—THE ICE-MARSHES—PEKIUTLIK—HANS THE BENEDICK.

PETERSEN and myself gave up the sledge to Morton, who, with Marsumah and Nessark, set out at once to negotiate at Etah, while I took my place with the sledge-parties.

The ice, though not broken up by the storm, had been so much affected by it, as well as by the advancing season, that I felt we could not spare ourselves an hour's rest. The snow-fields before us to the south were already saturated with wet. Around the bergs the black water came directly to the surface, and the whole area was spotted with pools. We summoned all our energies on the 5th for this dangerous traverse; but, although the boats were unladen and every thing transported by sledge, it was impossible to prevent accidents. One of the sledges broke through, carrying six men into the water, and the Hope narrowly escaped being lost. Her stern went down, and she was extricated with great difficulty.

The 6th saw the same disheartening work. The ice was almost impassable. Both sick and well worked at the drag-ropes alike, and hardly a man but was constantly wet to the skin. Fearing for the invalids at the sick-station in case we should be cut off from them, I sent for Mr. Goodfellow at once, and gave orders for the rest to be in readiness for removal at a moment's notice.

The next day Morton returned from Etah. The natives had responded to the brotherly appeal of the nalegak; and they came down from the settlement, bringing a full supply of meat and blubber, and every sound dog that belonged to them. I had now once more a serviceable team. The comfort and security of such a possession to men in our critical position can hardly be realized. It was more than an addition of ten strong men to our party. I set off at once with Metek to glean from the brig her last remnant of slush, (tallow,) and to bring down the sick men from Anoatok.

As we travelled with our empty sledges along a sort of beaten track or road which led close under the cliffs, I realized very forcibly the influence of the coming summer upon the rocks above us. They were just released from the frost which had bound them so long and closely, and were rolling down the slopes of the debris with the din of a battle-field, and absolutely clogging the ice-belt at the foot. Here and there, too, a large sheet of rocks and earth would leave its bed at once, and, gathering mass as it travelled, move downward like a cataract of ruins. The dogs were terrified by the clamor, and could hardly be driven on till it intermitted.

Just beyond Six-mile Ravine my sledge barely es-

THE SLIDE.

caped destruction from one of these land-slides. Happily Metek was behind, and warned me of the danger just in time to cut loose the traces and drag away the sledge.

But it is not in the season of thaws only that these

wonderful geological changes take place. Large rocks are projected in the fall by the water freezing in the crevices, like the Mons Meg cannon-balls. Our old boat, the "Forlorn Hope," the veteran of my Beechy Island attempt, was stove in by one of these while drawn up under the cliffs of "Ten-mile Gorge."

LIMESTONE ON MICA SLATE.

GREENSTONE ON GNEISS.

The rocks which fell in this manner upon the ice-belt were rapidly imbedded by the action of the sun's heat; and it happened frequently, of course, that one more recently disengaged would overlie another that had already sunk below the surface. This, as the ice-belt subsided in the gradual thaw, had given many examples of the rocking-stone. I have placed in the margin

LIMESTONE ON GREENSTONE.

GNEISS ON GREENSTONE.

SYENITES AND LIMESTONES.

some drawings of these geological puzzles. They were of all sizes, from tons to pounds, often strangely dissimilar in material, though grouped within a narrow area, their diversity depending on the varying strata from which they came. There were some strange illustrations among them of the transporting forces of the ice-raft, which I should like to dwell on, if the character of my book and the haste with which it is approaching its close did not forbid me.

Our visit to the brig was soon over: we had very few stores to remove. I trod her solitary deck for the last time, and returned with Metek to his sledge.

I had left the party on the floes with many apprehensions for their safety, and the result proved they were not without cause. While crossing a "tide-hole," one of the runners of the Hope's sledge broke through, and, but for the strength and presence of mind of Ohlsen, the boat would have gone under. He saw the ice give way, and, by a violent exercise of strength, passed a capstan-bar under the sledge, and thus bore the load till it was hauled on to safer ice. He was a very powerful man, and might have done this without injuring himself; but it would seem his footing gave way under him, forcing him to make a still more desperate effort to extricate himself. It cost him his life: he died three days afterwards.

PORTRAIT OF CHRISTIAN OHLSEN.

I was bringing down George Stephenson from the sick-station, and, my sledge being heavily laden, I had just crossed, with some anxiety, near the spot at which the accident occurred. A little way beyond we met Mr. Ohlsen, seated upon a lump of ice, and very pale. He pointed to the camp about three miles farther on, and told us, in a faint voice, that he had not detained the party: he "had a little cramp in the small of the back," but would soon be better.

I put him at once in Stephenson's place, and drove him on to the "Faith." Here he was placed in the stern-sheets of the boat, and well muffled up in our best buffalo-robes. During all that night he was assiduously attended by Dr. Hayes; but he sank rapidly. His symptoms had from the first a certain obscure but fatal resemblance to our winter's tetanus, which filled us with forebodings.

On Saturday, June 6, after stowing away our disabled comrade in the "Faith," we again set all hands at the drag-ropes. The ice ahead of us bore the same character as the day before,—no better: we were all perceptibly weaker, and much disheartened.

We had been tugging in harness about two hours, when a breeze set in from the northward, the first that we had felt since crossing Bedevilled Reach. We got out our long steering-oar as a boom, and made sail upon the boats. The wind freshened almost to a gale; and, heading toward the depôt on Littleton Island, we ran gallantly before it.

It was a new sensation to our foot-sore men, this sailing over solid ice. Levels which, under the slow labor of the drag-ropes, would have delayed us for hours, were glided over without a halt. We thought it dangerous work at first, but the speed of the sledges made rotten ice nearly as available as sound. The men could see plainly that they were approaching new landmarks and leaving old ones behind. Their spirits rose; the sick mounted the thwarts; the well clung to the gunwale: and, for the first time for nearly a year, broke out the sailor's chorus, "Storm along, my hearty boys!"

We must have made a greater distance in this single day than in the five that preceded it. We encamped at 5 P.M. near a small berg, which gave us plenty of fresh water, after a progress of at least eight miles.

As we were halting, I saw two Esquimaux on the ice toward Life-boat Cove; and the well-known "Huk! huuk!" a sort of Masonic signal among them, soon brought them to us. They turned out to be Sip-su and old Nessark. They were the bearers of good news: my dogs were refreshed and nearly able to travel again; and, as they volunteered to do me service, I harnessed up our united teams, and despatched Nessark to the hut to bring down Mr. Wilson and George Whipple.

We expected now to have our whole party together again; and the day would have been an active cheering one throughout, but for the condition of poor Ohlsen, who was growing rapidly worse.

From this time we went on for some days aided by our sails, meeting with accidents occasionally,—the giving way of a spar or the falling of some of the party through the spongy ice,—and occasionally, when the floe was altogether too infirm, laboring our way with great difficulty upon the ice-belt. To mount this solid highway, or to descend from it, the axes were always in requisition. An inclined plane was to be cut, ten, fifteen, or even thirty feet long, and along this the sledges were to be pushed and guided by bars and levers with painful labor. These are light things, as I refer to them here; but in our circumstances, at the time I write of, when the breaking of a stick of timber was an irreparable harm, and the delay of a day involved the peril of life, they were grave enough. Even on the floes the axe was often indispensable to carve our path through the hummocks; and many a weary and anxious hour have I looked on and toiled

ICE-MARSHES.

while the sledges were waiting for the way to open. Sometimes too, both on the land-ice and on the belt, we encountered heavy snow-drifts, which were to be shovelled away before we could get along; and within an hour afterward, or perhaps even at the bottom of the drift, one of the sledge-runners would cut through to the water.

It was saddening to our poor fellows, when we were forced to leave the ice-belt and push out into the open field, to look ahead at the salt ice-marshes, as they called them, studded with black pools, with only a white lump rising here and there through the lead-colored surface, like tussocks of grass or rushes struggling through a swamp. The labor would have been too much for us, weary and broken as we were, but for the occasional assistance we derived from the Esquimaux. I remember once a sledge went so far under, carrying with it several of the party, that the boat floated loose. Just then seven of the natives came up to us, —five sturdy men, and two almost as sturdy women,— and, without waiting to be called on, worked with us most efficiently for more than half a day, asking no reward.

Still passing slowly on day after day,—I am reluctant to borrow from my journal the details of anxiety and embarrassment with which it abounds throughout this period,—we came at last to the unmistakable neighborhood of the open water. We were off Pekiutlik, the largest of the Littleton Island group, opposite "Kosoak," the Great River. Here Mr. Wilson and George Whipple rejoined us, under the faithful charge of old Nessark. They had broken through twice on the road, but without any serious inconvenience in consequence. It was with truly thankful hearts we united in our prayers that evening.

One only was absent of all the party that remained on our rolls. Hans, the kind son and ardent young lover of Fiskernaes, my well-trusted friend, had been missing for nearly two months. I am loath to tell the story as I believe it, for it may not be the true one after all, and I would not intimate an unwarranted doubt of the constancy of boyish love. But I must explain, as far as I can at least, why he was not with us when we first looked at the open water. Just before my departure for my April hunt, Hans came to me with a long face, asking permission to visit Peteravik: "he had no boots, and wanted to lay in a stock of walrus-hide for soles: he did not need the dogs; he would rather walk." It was a long march, but he was well practised in it, and I consented of course. Both Petersen and myself gave him commissions to execute, and he left us, intending to stop by the way at Etah.

In our labors of the next month we missed Hans much. He had not yet returned, and the stories of him that came to us from Etah were the theme of much conversation and surmise among us. He had certainly called there as he promised, and given to Nessark's wife an order for a pair of boots, and he had then wended his way across the big headland to Peteravik, where Shang-hu and his pretty daughter had their home. This intimation was given with many an explanatory grin; for Hans was a favorite with all, the fair especially, and, as a *match*, one of the greatest men in the country. It required all my recollections of his "old love" to make me suspend my judgment; for the boots came, as if to confirm the scandal. I never failed in my efforts afterward to find his whereabouts, and went out of our way to interrogate this and that settlement; for, independent of every thing like duty, I was very fond of him. But the story was everywhere the same. Hans the faithful—yet, I fear, the faithless—was last seen upon a native sledge, driving south from Peteravik, with a maiden at his side, and professedly bound to a new principality at Uwarrow Suk-suk, high up Murchison's Sound. Alas for Hans, the married man!

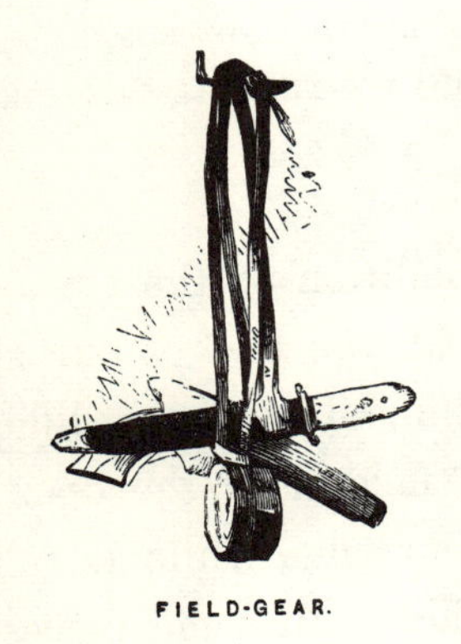

FIELD-GEAR.

CHAPTER XXIV.

THE RED BOAT SINKING — THE LIFE-BOAT CACHE — THE OPEN WATER—OHLSEN'S DEATH—HIS FUNERAL—BARENTZ, OUR PRECURSOR — ACCOMODAH — THE PRESCRIPTION — CAPE WELCOME — THE RESOLVE.

THOUGH the condition of the ice assured us that we were drawing near the end of our sledge-journeys, it by no means diminished their difficulty or hazards. The part of the field near the open water is always abraded by the currents, while it remains apparently firm on the surface. In some places it was so transparent that we could even see the gurgling eddies below it; while in others it was worn into open holes that were already the resort of wild fowl. But in general it looked hard and plausible, though not more than a foot or even six inches in thickness.

This continued to be its character as long as we pursued the Littleton Island channel, and we were compelled, the whole way through, to sound ahead with the boat-hook or narwhal-horn. We learned this

C. Schuessele & J. Hamilton.

Engraved at J.M.Butler's establishment 84 Chestnut St

J.C. Mc Rae

THE BROKEN FLOES

NEARING PIKANTLIK.

(From a sketch by Dr. Kane.)

precaution from the Esquimaux, who always move in advance of their sledges when the ice is treacherous, and test its strength before bringing on their teams. Our first warning impressed us with the policy of observing it. We were making wide circuits with the whaleboats to avoid the tide-holes, when signals of distress from men scrambling on the ice announced to us that the Red Eric had disappeared. This unfortunate little craft contained all the dearly-earned documents of the expedition. There was not a man who did not feel that the reputation of the party rested in a great degree upon their preservation. It had cost us many a pang to give up our collections of natural history, to which every one had contributed his quota of labor and interest; but the destruction of the vouchers of the cruise—the log-books, the meteorological registers, the surveys, and the journals—seemed to strike them all as an irreparable disaster.

When I reached the boat every thing was in confusion. Blake, with a line passed round his waist, was standing up to his knees in sludge, groping for the document-box, and Mr. Bonsall, dripping wet, was endeavoring to haul the provision-bags to a place of safety. Happily the boat was our lightest one, and every thing was saved. She was gradually lightened until she could bear a man, and her cargo was then passed out by a line and hauled upon the ice. In spite of the wet and the cold and our thoughts of poor Ohlsen, we greeted its safety with three cheers.

It was by great good fortune that no lives were lost.

Stephenson was caught as he sank by one of the sledge-runners, and Morton, while in the very act of drifting under the ice, was seized by the hair of the head by Mr. Bonsall and saved.

We were now close upon Life-boat Cove, where nearly two years before we had made provision for just such a contingency as that which was now before us. Buried under the frozen soil, our stores had escaped even the keen scrutiny of our savage allies, and we now turned to them as essential to our relief. Mr. McGary was sent to the cache, with orders to bring every thing except the salt beef. This had been so long a poison to us, that, tainted as we were by scurvy, I was afraid to bring it among those who might be tempted to indulge in it.

On the 12th the boats and sledges came to a halt in the narrow passage between the islands opposite Cape Misery, the scene of our late snow-storm. All our cargo had been gathered together at this spot, and the rocks were covered with our stores. Out of the fourteen hundred pounds not an ounce had been sacrificed. Every thing was cased in its water-proof covering, and as dry and perfect as when it had left the brig.

The Littleton Island of Captain Inglefield is one of a group of four *skiers* which flank the northeast headland of Hartstene Bay. They are of the bottom-series, coarse gneisses and mica schists. When here before, at this time of the year, they were surrounded by water, and the eider-ducks were breeding on their slopes. Now, as if to illustrate the difference of the seasons here, as well as the influence which they exert upon the habits of the migratory wild-fowl, they were thoroughly cased in ice, and not a nest was to be seen.

I ascended some eight hundred feet to the summit of Pekiutlik, and, looking out, beheld the open water, so long the goal of our struggles, spread out before me. It extended seemingly to Cape Alexander, and was nearer to the westward than the south of my position by some five or six miles. But the ice in the latter direction led into the curve of the bay, and was thus

PEKIUTLIK, (THE BOBBING SEAL.)

protected from the wind and swell. My jaded comrades pleaded anxiously in favor of the direct line to the water; but I knew that this ice would give us both safer and better travel. I determined to adopt the inshore route. Our position at Pekiutlik, as we determined carefully by the mean of several observations, is in latitude 78° 22′ 1″ and longitude 74° 10′. We connected it with Cape Alexander and other determined stations to the north and west.

The channel between the islands was much choked with upreared ice; but our dogs had now come back to us so much refreshed that I was able to call their services again into requisition. We carried one entire load to the main which forms the northeast headland of Hartstene Bay, and, the Esquimaux assisting us, deposited it safely on the inner side.

I was with the advance boat, trying to force a way through the channel, when the report came to me from Dr. Hayes that Ohlsen was no more. He had shown, a short half-hour before, some signs of revival, and Petersen had gone out to kill a few birds, in the hope of possibly sustaining him by a concentrated soup. But it was in vain: the poor fellow flushed up only to die a few minutes after.

We had no time to mourn the loss of our comrade, a tried and courageous man, who met his death in the gallant discharge of duty. It cast a gloom over the whole party; but the exigencies of the moment were upon us, and we knew not whose turn would come next, or how soon we might all of us follow him together.

I had carefully concealed Mr. Ohlsen's sickness from the Esquimaux, with every thing else that could intimate our weakness; for, without reflecting at all upon their fidelity, I felt that with them, as with the rest of the world, pity was a less active provocative to good deeds than the deference which is exacted by power. I had therefore represented our abandonment of the brig as merely the absence of a general hunting-party to the Far South, and I was willing now to keep up the impression. I leave to moralists the discussion of the question how far I erred; but I now sent them to their village under pretext of obtaining birds, and lent them our dogs to insure their departure.

The body of Mr. Ohlsen was sewed up, while they were gone, in his own blankets, and carried in procession to the head of a little gorge on the east face of Pekiutlik, where by hard labor we consigned his remains to a sort of trench, and covered them with rocks to protect them from the fox and bear. Without the knowledge of my comrades, I encroached on our little store of sheet-lead, which we were husbanding to mend our leaky boats with, and, cutting on a small tablet his name and age,—

CHRISTIAN OHLSEN,

AGED 36 YEARS,

laid it on his manly breast. The cape that looks down on him bears his name.

As we walked back to our camp upon the ice, the death of Ohlsen brought to my mind the strange parallel of our story with that of old William Barentz, —a parallel which might verify that sad truth of history that human adventure repeats itself.

Two hundred and fifty-nine years ago, William Barentz, Chief Pilot of the States-General of Holland,—the United States of that day,—had wintered on the coast of Novaia Zemlia, exploring the northernmost region of the Old Continent, as we had that of the New. His men, seventeen in number, broke down during the trials of the winter, and three died, just as of our eighteen three had gone. He abandoned his vessel as we had abandoned ours, took to his boats, and escaped along the Lapland coast to lands of Norwegian civilization. We had embarked with sledge and boat to attempt the same thing. We had the longer journey and the more difficult before us. He lost, as we had done, a cherished comrade by the wayside; and, as I thought of this closing resemblance in our fortunes also, my mind left but one part of the parallel incomplete,—*Barentz himself perished.*

CARRYING THE SICK.

We gave two quiet hours to the memory of our dead brother, and then resumed our toilsome march. We kept up nearly the same routine as before; but, as we neared the settlements, the Esquimaux came in flocks to our assistance. They volunteered to aid us at the drag-ropes. They carried our sick upon hand-sledges. They relieved us of all care for our supplies of daily food. The quantity of little auks that they brought us was enormous. They fed us and our dogs at the rate of eight thousand birds a week, all of them caught in their little hand-nets. All anxiety left us for the time. The men broke out in their old forecastle-songs; the sledges began to move merrily ahead, and laugh and jest drove out the old moody silence.

During one of our evening halts, when the congregation of natives had scattered away to their camp-fires, Metek and Nualik his wife came to me privately on a matter of grave consultation. They brought with them a fat, curious-looking boy. "Accomodah," said they, "is our youngest son. His sleep at night is bad, and his *nangah*"—pointing to that protuberance which is supposed to represent aldermanic dignity—"is always round and hard. He eats ossuk (blubber) and no meat, and bleeds at the nose. Besides, he does not grow." They wanted me, in my capacity of angekok-soak, to charm or cure him.

I told them, with all the freedom from mystery that distinguishes the regulated practitioner from the empiric, what must be my mode of treatment: that I must dip my hand into the salt water where the ice cut against the sea, and lay it on the offending nangah; and that if they would bring to me their rotund little companion within three days, at that broad and deep Bethesda, I would signalize my consideration of the kindness of the tribe by a trial of my powers.

They went away very thankful, taking a preliminary

prescription of a lump of brown soap, a silk shirt, and a *taboo* of all further eating of ossuk; and I had no doubt that their anxiety to have the boy duly powwowed, would urge forward our sledges and bring us early to the healing waters. We longed for them

ACCOMODAH.

at least as much as Metek, and needed them more than Accomodah.

My little note-book closes for the week with this gratefully-expanded record:—

"June 16, Saturday.—Our boats are at the open

water. We see its deep indigo horizon, and hear its roar against the icy beach. Its scent is in our nostrils and our hearts.

"Our camp is but three-quarters of a mile from the sea: it is at the northern curve of the North Baffin

CAPE WELCOME.

polynia. We must reach it at the southern sweep of Etah Bay, about three miles from Cape Alexander. A dark headland defines the spot. It is more marked than the southern entrance of Smith's Straits. How magnificently the surf beats against its sides! There are ridges of squeezed ice between us and it, and a broad zone of floating sludge is swelling and rolling sluggishly along its margin:—formidable barriers to boats and sledges. But we have mastered worse obstacles, and by God's help we will master these."

ANOTHER MODE OF CARRYING THE SICK.

CHAPTER XXV.

THE FAREWELL—ATTEMPT TO EMBARK.

We had our boats to prepare now for a long and adventurous navigation. They were so small and heavily laden as hardly to justify much confidence in their buoyancy; but, besides this, they were split with frost and warped by sunshine, and fairly open at the seams. They were to be calked and swelled and launched and stowed, before we could venture to embark in them. A rainy southwester too, which had met us on our arrival, was now spreading with its black nimbus over the bay, and it looked as if we were to be storm-stayed on the precarious ice-beach. It was a time of anxiety, but to me personally of comparative rest. I resumed my journal:—

"July 18, Monday.—The Esquimaux are camped by our side,—the whole settlement of Etah congregated around the 'big caldron' of Cape Alexander, to bid us good-bye. There are Metek, and Nualik his wife, our old acquaintance Mrs. Eider-duck, and their five children, commencing with Myouk, my body-guard, and ending with the ventricose little Accomodah. There is Nessark and Anak his wife; and Tellerk the 'Right Arm,' and Amaunalik his wife; and Sip-su, and Marsumah and Aningnah—and who not? I can name them every one, and they know us as well. We have found brothers in a strange land.

"Each one has a knife, or a file, or a saw, or some such treasured keepsake; and the children have a lump of soap the greatest of all great medicines. The

BABY SLEDGES.

merry little urchins break in upon me even now as I am writing:—'Kuyanake, kuyanake, Nalegak-soak!' 'Thank you, thank you, big chief!' while Myouk is crowding fresh presents of raw birds on me as if I could eat forever, and poor Aningnah is crying beside the tent-curtain, wiping her eyes on a bird-skin!

"My heart warms to these poor, dirty, miserable, yet happy beings, so long our neighbors, and of late so stanchly our friends. Theirs is no affectation of regret. There are twenty-two of them around me, all busy in good offices to the Docto Kayens; and there are only two women and the old blind patriarch Kresuk, 'Drift-wood,' left behind at the settlement.

"But see! more of them are coming up,—boys ten years old pushing forward babies on their sledges. The whole nation is gypsying with us upon the icy meadows.

"We cook for them in our big camp-kettle; they sleep in the Red Eric; a berg close at hand supplies them with water: and thus, rich in all that they value, —sleep and food and drink and companionship,—with their treasured short-lived summer sun above them, the *beau ideal* and sum of Esquimaux blessings, they seem supremely happy.

"Poor creatures! It is only six months ago that starvation was among them: many of the faces around me have not yet lost the lines of wasting suspense. The walrus-season is again of doubtful productiveness, and they are cut off from their brethren to the south, at Netelik and Appah, until winter rebuilds the avenue of ice. With all this, no thoughts of the future cross them. Babies squall, and women chatter, and the men weave their long yarns with peals of rattling hearty laughter between.

"Ever since we reached Pekiutlik, these friends of ours have considered us their guests. They have given us hand-sledges for our baggage, and taken turn about in watches to carry us and it to the water's edge. But for them our dreary journey would have been prolonged at least a fortnight, and we are so late even now that hours may measure our lives. Metek, Myouk,

Nessark, Marsumah, Erkee, and the half-grown boys, have been our chief laborers; but women, children, and dogs are all bearing their part.

"Whatever may have been the faults of these Esquimaux heretofore, stealing was the only grave one. Treachery they may have conceived; and I have reason to believe that, under superstitious fears of an evil influence from our presence, they would at one time have been glad to destroy us. But the day of all this has passed away. When trouble came to us and to them, and we bent ourselves to their habits,—when we looked to them to procure us fresh meat, and they found at our poor Oomiak-soak shelter and protection during their wild bear-hunts,—then we were so blended in our interests as well as modes of life that every trace of enmity wore away. God knows that since they professed friendship, albeit the imaginary powers of the angekok-soak and the marvellous six-shooter which attested them may have had their influence, never have friends been more true. Although, since Ohlsen's death, numberless articles of inestimable value to them have been scattered upon the ice unwatched, they have not stolen a nail. It was only yesterday that Metek, upon my alluding to the manner in which property of all sorts was exposed without pilfering, explained through Petersen, in these two short sentences, the argument of their morality:—

"'You have done us good. We are not hungry; we will not take, (steal.)——You have done us good; we want to help you: we are friends.'"

I made my last visit to Etah while we were waiting the issue of the storm. I saw old Kresuk (Drift-wood) the blind man, and listened to his long good-bye talk. I had passed with the Esquimaux as an angekok, in virtue of some simple exploits of natural magic; and it was one of the regular old-times entertainments of our visitors at the brig, to see my hand terrible with blazing ether, while it lifted nails with a magnet. I tried now to communicate a portion of my wonder-working talent. I made a lens of ice before them, and "drew down the sun," so as to light the moss under their kolupsut. I did not quite understand old Kresuk, and I was not quite sure he understood himself. But I trusted to the others to explain to him what I had done, and burned the back of his hand for a testimony in the most friendly manner. After all which, with a reputation for wisdom which I dare say will live in their short annals, I wended my way to the brig again.

We renewed our queries about Hans, but could get no further news of him. The last story is, that the poor boy and his better half were seen leaving Peter-avik, "the halting-place," in company with Shang-hu and one of his big sons. Lover as he was, and nalegak by the all-hail hereafter, joy go with him, for he was a right good fellow.

We had quite a scene, distributing our last presents. My amputating-knives, the great gift of all, went to Metek and Nessark; but every one had something as his special prize. Our dogs went to the community at large, as tenants in common, except Toodla-mik and

Whitey, our representative dogs through very many trials. I could not part with them, the leaders of my team; I have them still.

But Nualik, the poor mother, had something still to remind me of. She had accompanied us throughout the transit of Etah Bay, with her boy Accomodah, waiting anxiously for the moment when the first salt water would enable me to fulfil my promised exorcisation of the demon in his stomach. There was no alternative now but to fulfil the pledge with faithful ceremony. The boy was taken to the water's edge, and his exorbitant little nangah faithfully embrocated in the presence of both his parents. I could not speak my thanks in their language, but I contributed my scanty stock of silk shirts to the poor little sufferer,—for such he was,—and I blessed them for their humanity to us with a fervor of heart which from a better man might peradventure have carried a blessing along with it.

And now it only remained for us to make our farewell to these desolate and confiding people. I gathered them round me on the ice-beach, and talked to them as brothers for whose kindness I had still a return to make. I told them what I knew of the tribes from which they were separated by the glacier and the sea, of the resources that abounded in those less ungenial regions not very far off to the south, the greater duration of daylight, the less intensity of the cold, the facilities of the hunt, the frequent drift-wood, the kayak, and the fishing-net. I tried to explain to them how, under bold and cautious guidance, they might reach there in a few seasons of patient march. I gave them drawings of the coast, with its headlands and hunting-grounds, as far as Cape Shackleton, and its best camping-stations from Red Head to the Danish settlements.

They listened with breathless interest, closing their circle round me; and, as Petersen described the big ussuk, the white whale, the bear, and the long open-water hunts with the kayak and the rifle, they looked at each other with a significance not to be misunderstood. They would anxiously have had me promise that I would some day return and carry a load of them down to the settlements; and I shall not wonder if—guided perhaps by Hans—they hereafter attempt the journey without other aid.

This was our parting. A letter which I addressed, at the moment of reaching the settlements, to the Lutheran Missions, the tutelar society of the Esquimaux of Greenland, will attest the sincerity of my professions and my willingness to assist in giving them effect. It will be found in the Appendix.

It was in the soft subdued light of a Sunday evening, June 17, that, after hauling our boats with much hard labor through the hummocks, we stood beside the open sea-way. Before midnight we had launched the Red Eric, and given three cheers for Henry Grinnell and "homeward bound," unfurling all our flags.

But we were not yet to embark; for the gale which

had been long brooding now began to dash a heavy *wind-lipper* against the floe, and obliged us to retreat before it, hauling our boats back with each fresh breakage of the ice. It rose more fiercely, and we were obliged to give way before it still more. Our

BIDDING GOOD-BYE.

goods, which had been stacked upon the ice, had to be carried farther inward. We worked our way back thus, step by step, before the breaking ice, for about two hundred yards. At last it became apparent that the men must sleep and rest, or sink; and, giving up for the present all thoughts of embarking, I hauled the boats at once nearly a mile from the water's edge, where a large iceberg was frozen tight in the floes.

But here we were still pursued. All the next night it blew fearfully, and at last our berg crashed away through the broken ice, and our asylum was destroyed. Again we fell to hauling back the boats; until, fearing that the continuance of the gale might induce a ground-swell, which would have been fatal to us, I came to a halt near the slope of a low iceberg, on which I felt confident that we could haul up in case of the entire disruption of the floes. The entire area was already intersected with long cracks, and the surface began to show a perceptible undulation beneath our feet.

It was well for us I had not gratified the men by taking the outside track: we should certainly have been rafted off into the storm, and without an apparent possibility of escape.

I climbed to the summit of the berg; but it was impossible to penetrate the obscurity of mist and spray and cloud farther than a thousand yards. The sea tore the ice up almost to the very base of the berg, and all around it looked like one vast tumultuous caldron, the ice-tables crashing together in every possible position with deafening clamor.

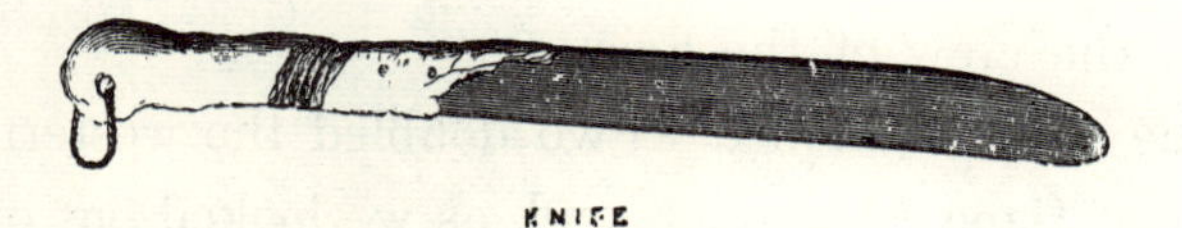

KNIFE

CHAPTER XXVI.

SUTHERLAND ISLAND — HAKLUYT ISLAND — NORTHUMBERLAND ISLAND—FITZ-CLARENCE ROCK—DALRYMPLE ROCK—GIVING OUT — BREAK-UP OF THE FLOE — BROKEN DOWN — WEARY MAN'S REST — THE FOURTH — SHORT COMMONS.

THE gale died away to a calm, and the water became as tranquil as if the gale had never been. All hands were called to prepare for embarking. The boats were stowed, and the cargo divided between them equally; the sledges unlashed and slung outside the gunwales; and on Tuesday the 19th, at 4 P.M., with the bay as smooth as a garden-lake, I put off in the Faith. She was followed by the Red Eric on our quarter, and the Hope astern. In the Faith I had with me Mr. McGary, and Petersen, Hickey, Stephenson, and Whipple. Mr. Brooks was in the Hope, with Hayes, Sontag, Morton, Goodfellow, and Blake. Bonsall, Riley, and Godfrey made the crew of the Eric.

The wind freshened as we doubled the westernmost point of Cape Alexander, and, as we looked out on the expanse of the sound, we saw the kittiwakes and the ivory-gulls and jagers dipping their wings in the curling waves. They seemed the very same birds we had left two years before screaming and catching fish in the beautiful water. We tried to make our first rest at Sutherland Island; but we found it so barricaded by the precipitous ice-belt that it was impossible to land. I clambered myself from the boat's mast upon the platform and filled our kettles with snow, and then, after cooking our supper in the boats, we stood away for Hakluyt. It was an ugly crossing: we had a short chopping sea from the southeast; and, after a while, the Red Boat swamped. Riley and Godfrey managed to struggle to the Faith, and Bonsall to the Hope; but it was impossible to remove the cargo of our little comrade: it was as much as we could do to keep her afloat and let her tow behind us. Just at this time, too, the Hope made a signal of distress; and Brooks hailed us to say that she was making water faster than he could free her.

The wind was hauling round to the westward, and we could not take the sea abeam. But, as I made a rapid survey of the area round me, studded already with floating shreds of floe-ice, I saw ahead the low gray blink of the pack. I remembered well the experience of our Beechy Island trip, and knew that the margin of these large fields is almost always broken by inlets of open water, which give much the same sort of protection as the creeks and rivers of an adverse coast. We were fortunate in finding one of these and fastening ourselves to an old floe, alongside of which our weary men turned in to sleep without hauling up the boats.

When Petersen and myself returned from an unsuccessful hunt upon the ice, we found them still asleep, in spite of a cold and drizzling rain that might have stimulated wakefulness. I did not disturb them till eight o'clock. We then retreated from our breakwater of refuge, generally pulling along by the boat-hooks, but sometimes dragging our boats over the ice; and at last, bending to our oars as the water opened, reached the shore of Hakluyt Island.

It was hardly less repulsive than the ice-cliffs of the day before; but a spit to the southward gave us the opportunity of hauling up as the tide rose, and we finally succeeded in transferring ourselves and all our fortunes to the land-ice, and thence to the rocks beyond. It snowed hard in the night, and the work of calking went on badly, though we expended on it a prodigal share of our remaining white-lead. We rigged up, however, a tent for the sick, and reinforced our bread-dust and tallow supper by a few birds. We had shot a seal in the course of the day, but we lost him by his sinking.

In the morning of the 22d we pushed forward through the snow-storm for Northumberland Island, and succeeded in reaching it a little to the eastward of my former landing-place. Myriads of auks greeted us, and we returned their greeting by the appropriate invitation to our table. A fox also saluted us with an admirable imitation of the "Huk-huk-huk," which among the Esquimaux is the never-unheeded call of distress; but the rascal, after seducing us a mile and a half out of our way, escaped our guns.

Our boats entered a little patch of open water that conducted us to the beach, directly below one of the

MY BROTHER JOHN'S GLACIER.

hanging glaciers. The interest with which these impressed me when I was turning back from my Beechy Island effort was justified very fully by what I saw of them now. It seemed as if a caldron of ice inside the coast-ridge was boiling over, and throwing its crust in huge fragments from the overhanging lip into the sea below. The glacier must have been eleven hundred feet high; but even at its summit we could see the lines of viscous movement which I have endeavored to transfer to my sketch.

We crossed Murchison Channel on the 23d, and encamped for the night on the land-floe at the base of Cape Parry; a hard day's travel, partly by tracking over ice, partly through tortuous and zigzag leads. The next day brought us to the neighborhood of Fitz-Clarence Rock, one of the most interesting monuments that rear themselves along this dreary coast: in a region more familiar to men, it would be a landmark to the navigator. It rises from a field of ice like an Egyptian pyramid surmounted by an obelisk.

I had been anxious to communicate with the Esquimaux of Netelik, in the hope of gaining some further intelligence of Hans. Our friends of Etah had given me, in their own style, a complete itinerary of this region, and we had no difficulty in instructing Godfrey how to trace his way across the neck of land which stood between us and the settlement. He made the attempt, but found the snow-drift impassable; and Petersen, whom I sent on the same errand to Tessiusak, returned equally unsuccessful.

The next day gave us admirable progress. The ice opened in leads before us, somewhat tortuous, but, on the whole, favoring, and for sixteen hours I never left the helm. We were all of us exhausted when the day's work came to a close. Our allowance had been small from the first; but the delays we seemed fated to encounter had made me reduce them to what I then thought the minimum quantity, six ounces of bread-dust and a lump of tallow the size of a walnut: a paste or broth, made of these before setting out in the morning and distributed occasionally through the day in scanty rations, was our only fare. We were all of us glad when, running the boats under the lee of a berg, we were able to fill our kettles with snow and boil up for our great restorative tea. I may remark that, under the circumstances of most privation, I found no comforter so welcome to the party as this. We drank immoderately of it, and always with advantage.

While the men slept after their weary labor, McGary and myself climbed the berg for a view ahead. It was a saddening one. We had lost sight of Cary Island; but shoreward, up Wostenholme Channel, the ice seemed as if it had not yet begun to yield to the influences of summer. Every thing showed how intense the last winter had been. We were close upon the 1st of July, and had a right to look for the North Water of the whalers where we now had solid ice or close pack, both of them almost equally unfavorable to our progress. Far off in the distance—how far I could not measure—rose the Dalrymple Rock, projecting from the lofty precipice of the island ahead; but between us and it the land-ice spread itself from the base of Saunders's Island unbroken to the Far South.

The next day's progress was of course slow and wearisome, pushing through alternate ice and water for the land-belt. We fastened at last to the great floe near the shore, making our harbor in a crack which opened with the changes of tide.

The imperfect diet of the party was showing itself more and more in the decline of their muscular power. They seemed scarcely aware of it themselves, and referred the difficulty they found in dragging and pushing to something uncommon about the ice or sludge rather than to their own weakness. But, as we endeavored to renew our labors through the morning fog, belted in on all sides by ice-fields so distorted and rugged as to defy our efforts to cross them, the truth seemed to burst upon every one. We had lost the feeling of hunger, and were almost satisfied with our pasty broth and the large draughts of tea which accompanied it. I was anxious to send our small boat, the Eric, across to the lumme-hill of Appah, where I knew from the Esquimaux we should find plenty of birds; but the strength of the party was insufficient to drag her.

We were sorely disheartened, and could only wait for the fog to rise, in the hope of some smoother platform than that which was about us, or some lead that might save us the painful labor of tracking. I had climbed the iceberg; and there was nothing in view except Dalrymple Rock, with its red brassy face towering in the unknown distance. But I hardly got back to my boat, before a gale struck us from the northwest, and a floe, taking upon a tongue of ice about a mile to the north of us, began to swing upon it like a pivot and close slowly in upon our narrow resting-place.

J. Hamilton. Engraved at J. M. Butler's establishment 84 Chestnut St: G. Ulman.

"THE ESCAPE OFF WEARY MEN'S REST."

BELT ICE.

(From a sketch by Dr. Kane)

At first our own floe also was driven before the wind; but in a little while it encountered the stationary ice at the foot of the very rock itself. On the instant the wildest imaginable ruin rose around us. The men sprang mechanically each one to his station, bearing back the boats and stores; but I gave up for the moment all hope of our escape. It was not a nip, such as is familiar to Arctic navigators; but the whole platform, where we stood and for hundreds of yards on every side of us, crumbled and crushed and piled and tossed itself madly under the pressure. I do not believe that of our little body of men, all of them disciplined in trials, able to measure danger while combating it,—I do not believe there is one who this day can explain how or why—hardly when, in fact—we found ourselves afloat. We only know that in the midst of a clamor utterly indescribable, through which the braying of a thousand trumpets could no more have been heard than the voice of a man, we were shaken and raised and whirled and let down again in a swelling waste of broken hummocks, and, as the men grasped their boat-hooks in the stillness that followed, the boats eddied away in a tumultuous skreed of ice and snow and water.

We were borne along in this manner as long as the unbroken remnant of the in-shore floe continued revolving,—utterly powerless, and catching a glimpse every now and then of the brazen headland that looked down on us through the snowy sky. At last the floe brought up against the rocks, the looser fragments that hung round it began to separate, and we were able by oars and boat-hooks to force our battered little flotilla clear of them. To our joyful surprise, we soon found ourselves in a stretch of the land-water wide enough to give us rowing-room, and with the assured promise of land close ahead.

As we neared it, we saw the same forbidding wall of belt-ice as at Sutherland and Hakluyt. We pulled along its margin, seeking in vain either an opening of access or a nook of shelter. The gale rose, and the ice began to drive again; but there was nothing to be done but get a grapnel out to the belt and hold on for the rising tide. The Hope stove her bottom and lost part of her weather-boarding, and all the boats were badly chafed. It was an awful storm; and it was not without constant exertion that we kept afloat, baling out the scud that broke over us, and warding off the ice with boat-hooks.

At three o'clock the tide was high enough for us to scale the ice-cliff. One by one we pulled up the boats upon a narrow shelf, the whole sixteen of us uniting at each pull. We were too much worn down to unload; but a deep and narrow gorge opened in the cliffs almost at the spot where we clambered up; and, as we pushed the boats into it on an even keel, the rocks seemed to close above our heads, until an abrupt turn in the course of the ravine placed a protecting cliff between us and the gale. We were completely encaved.

Just as we had brought in the last boat, the Red Eric, and were shoring her up with blocks of ice, a long-unused but familiar and unmistakable sound startled and gladdened every ear, and a flock of eiders flecking the sky for a moment passed swiftly in front of us. We knew that we must be at their breeding-grounds; and, as we turned in wet and hungry to our

WEARY MAN'S REST.

long-coveted sleep, it was only to dream of eggs and abundance.

We remained almost three days in our crystal retreat, gathering eggs at the rate of twelve hundred a day. Outside, the storm raged without intermission, and our egg-hunters found it difficult to keep their feet; but a merrier set of gourmands than were gathered within never surfeited in genial diet.

On the 3d of July the wind began to moderate, though the snow still fell heavily; and the next morning, after a patriotic egg-nog, the liquor borrowed grudgingly from our alcohol-flask, and diluted till it was worthy of temperance praise,—we lowered our boats, and bade a grateful farewell to "Weary Man's Rest." We rowed to the southeast end of Wostenholme Island; but the tide left us there, and we moved to the ice-foot.

For some days after this we kept moving slowly to the south, along the lanes that opened between the belt-ice and the floe. The weather continued dull and unfavorable for observations of any sort, and we were off a large glacier before we were aware that further progress near the shore was impracticable. Great chains of bergs presented themselves as barriers in our way, the spaces between choked by barricades of hummocks. It was hopeless to bore. We tried for sixteen hours together without finding a possibility of egress. The whole sea was rugged and broken in the extreme.

I climbed one of the bergs to the height of about two hundred feet, and, looking well to the west, was satisfied that a lead which I saw there could be followed in the direction of Conical Rocks, and beyond toward Cape Dudley Digges. But, on conferring with Brooks and McGary, I was startled to find how much the boats had suffered in the rude encounters of the last few days. The "Hope" was in fact altogether unseaworthy: the ice had strained her bottom-timbers, and it required nearly all our wood to repair her; bit by bit we had already cut up and burned the runners and cross-bars of two sledges; the third we had to reserve as essential to our ice-crossings.

In the mean time, the birds, which had been so abundant when we left Dalrymple's Island, and which we had counted on for a continuous store, seemed to have been driven off by the storm. We were again reduced to short daily rations of bread-dust, and I was aware that the change of diet could not fail to tell upon the strength and energies of the party. I determined to keep in-shore, in spite of the barricades of ice, in the hope of renewing, to some extent at least, our supplies of game. We were fifty-two hours in forcing this rugged passage: a most painful labor, which but for the disciplined endurance of the men might well have been deemed impracticable.

SEAL-HOLE.

CHAPTER XXVII.

A LOOK-OUT — PROVIDENCE HALT — THE GLACIER — PROVIDENCE DIET.

ONCE through the barrier, the leads began to open again, and on the 11th we found ourselves approaching Cape Dudley Digges, with a light breeze from the north-west. It looked for some hours as if our troubles were over, when a glacier came in sight not laid down on the charts, whose tongue of floe extended still farther out to sea than the one we had just passed with so much labor. Our first resolve was to double it at all hazards, for our crews were too much weakened to justify another tracking through the hummocks, and the soft snow which covered the land-floes was an obstacle quite insuperable. Nevertheless, we forced our way into a lead of sludge, mingled with the comminuted ice of the glacier; but the only result was a lesson of gratitude for our escape from it. Our frail and weather-worn boats were quite unequal to the duty.

I again climbed the nearest berg,—for these ice-mountains were to us like the look-out hills of men at home, —and surveyed the ice to the south far on toward Cape York. My eyes never looked on a spectacle more painful. We were in advance of the season: the floes had not broken up. There was no "western water." Here, in a *cul-de-sac*, between two barriers, both impassable to men in our condition, with stores miserably inadequate and strength broken down, we were to wait till the tardy summer should open to us a way.

I headed for the cliffs. Desolate and frowning as they were, it was better to reach them and halt upon the inhospitable shore than await the fruitless ventures of the sea. A narrow lead, a mere fissure at the edge of the land-ice, ended opposite a low platform: we had traced its whole extent, and it landed us close under the shadow of the precipitous shore.

My sketch intended to represent this wild locality, like that of the "Weary Man's Rest," gives a very imperfect idea of the scene.

Where the cape lies directly open to the swell of the northwest winds, at the base of a lofty precipice there was left still clinging to the rock a fragment of the winter ice-belt not more than five feet wide. The tides rose over it and the waves washed against it continually, but it gave a perfectly safe perch to our little boats. Above, cliff seemed to pile over cliff, until in the high distance the rocks looked like the overlapping scales of ancient armor. They were at least eleven hundred feet high, their summits generally lost in fog and mist; and all the way up we seemed to see the birds whose home is among their clefts. The nests were thickest on the shelves some fifty yards above the water; but both lumme and tridactyl gulls filled the entire air with glimmering specks, cawing and screeching with an incessant clamor.

PROVIDENCE HALT.

To soften the scene, a natural bridge opened on our right hand into a little valley cove, green with mosses, and beyond and above it, cold and white, the glacier.

This glacier was about seven miles across at its

"debouche;" it sloped gradually upward for some five miles back, and then, following the irregularities of its rocky sub-structure, suddenly became a steep crevassed hill, ascending in abrupt terraces. Then came two intervals of less rugged ice, from which the glacier passed into the great *mer de glace.*

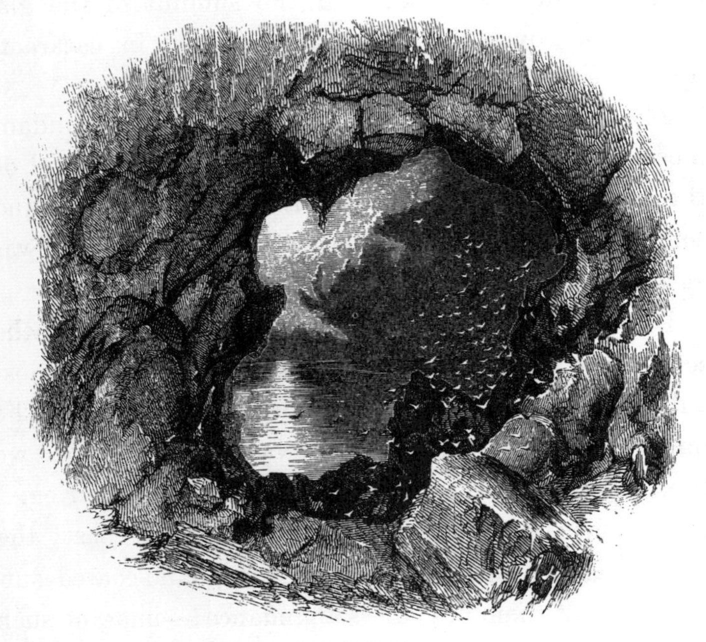

THE BRIDGE.

On ascending a high craggy hill to the northward, I had a sublime prospect of this great frozen ocean, which seems to form the continental axis of Greenland,—a vast undulating plain of purple-tinted ice, studded with islands, and absolutely gemming the horizon with the varied glitter of sun-tipped crystal.

The discharge of water from the lower surface of the glacier exceeded that of any of the northern glaciers except that of Humboldt and the one near Etah. One torrent on the side nearest me overran the ice-foot from two to five feet in depth, and spread itself upon the floes for several hundred yards; and another, finding its outlet near the summit of the glacier, broke over the rocks, and poured in cataracts upon the beach below.

The ranunculus, saxifrages, chickweeds, abundant mosses, and Arctic grasses, flourished near the level of the first talus of the glacier: the stone crops I found some two hundred feet higher. The thermometer was at 90° in the sun; in the shade at 38°.

I have tried to describe the natural features of the scene, but I have omitted that which was its most valued characteristic. It abounded in life. The lumme, nearly as large as canvas-backs, and, as we thought, altogether sweeter and more juicy; their eggs, well known as delicacies on the Labrador coast; the cochlearia, growing superbly on the guano-coated surface;—all of them in endless abundance:—imagine such a combination of charms for scurvy-broken, hunger-stricken men.

I could not allow the fuel for a fire; our slush and tallow was reduced to very little more than a hundred pounds. The more curious in that art which has dignified the memory of Lucullus, and may do as much for Soyer, made experiments upon the organic matters within their reach,—the dried nests of the kittiwake, the sods of poa, the heavy mosses, and the fatty skins of the birds around us. But they would none of them burn; and the most fastidious consoled himself at last with the doubt whether heat, though concentrating flavor, might not impair some other excellence. We

PROVIDENCE CLIFFS.

limited ourselves to an average of a bird a-piece per meal,—of choice, not of necessity,—and renewed the zest of the table with the best salad in the world,—raw eggs and cochlearia.

It was one glorious holiday, our week at Providence

Halt, so full of refreshment and all-happy thoughts, that I never allowed myself to detract from it by acknowledging that it was other than premeditated. There were only two of the party who had looked out with me on the bleak ice-field ahead, and them I had pledged to silence.

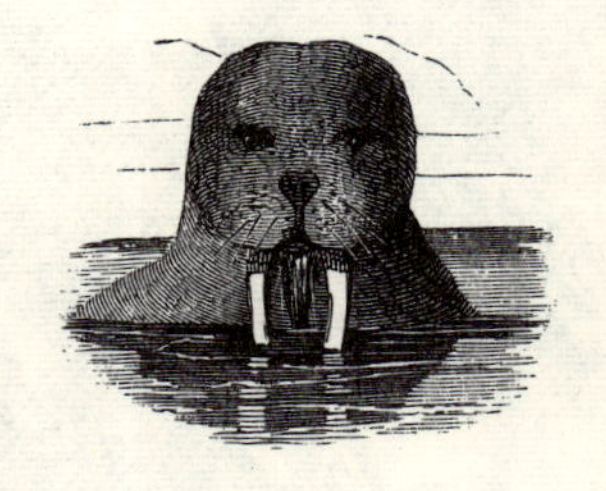

CHAPTER XXVIII.

THE CRIMSON CLIFFS — THE ESQUIMAUX EDEN — DEPRESSION OF THE COAST—INVENTORY—IMALIK—LOSING OUR WAY—AT THE RUE-RADDIES — THE OPEN SEA — EFFECTS OF HUNGER — RESCUE OF THE FAITH.

It was the 18th of July before the aspects of the ice about us gave me the hope of progress. We had prepared ourselves for the new encounter with the sea and its trials by laying in a store of lumme; two hundred and fifty of which had been duly skinned, spread open, and dried on the rocks, as the *entremets* of our bread-dust and tallow.

My journal tells of disaster in its record of our setting out. In launching the Hope from the frail and perishing ice-wharf on which we found our first refuge from the gale, she was precipitated into the sludge below, carrying away rail and bulwark, losing overboard our best shot-gun, Bonsall's favorite, and, worst of all, that universal favorite, our kettle,—soup-kettle, paste-kettle, tea-kettle, water-kettle, in one. I may mention before I pass, that the kettle found its substitute and successor in the remains of a tin can which a good aunt of mine had filled with ginger-nuts two years before, and which had long survived the condiments that once gave it dignity. "Such are the uses of adversity."

PASSING THE CRIMSON CLIFFS.

Our descent to the coast followed the margin of the fast ice. After passing the Crimson Cliffs of Sir John Ross, it wore almost the dress of a holiday excursion,—a rude one perhaps, yet truly one in feeling. Our course, except where a protruding glacier interfered with it, was nearly parallel to the shore. The birds along it were rejoicing in the young summer, and when we halted it was upon some green-clothed cape near a stream of water from the ice-fields above. Our sportsmen would clamber up the cliffs and come back laden with little auks; great generous fires of turf, that cost nothing but the toil of gathering, blazed merrily; and our happy oarsmen, after a long day's work, made easy by the promise ahead, would stretch themselves in the sunshine and dream happily away till called to the morning wash and prayers. We enjoyed it the more, for we all of us knew that it could not last.

This coast must have been a favorite region at one time with the natives,—a sort of Esquimaux Eden. We seldom encamped without finding the ruins of their habitations, for the most part overgrown with lichens, and exhibiting every mark of antiquity. One of these, in latitude 76° 20′, was once, no doubt, an extensive village. Cairns for the safe deposit of meat stood in long lines, six or eight in a group; and the huts, built of large rocks, faced each other, as if disposed on a street or avenue.

The same reasoning which deduces the subsidence of the coast from the actual base of the Temple of Serapis, proves that the depression of the Greenland coast, which I had detected as far north as Upernavik, is also going on up here. Some of these huts were washed by the sea or torn away by the ice that had descended with the tides. The turf, too, a representative of very ancient growth, was cut off even with the water's edge, giving sections two feet thick. I had not noticed before such unmistakable evidence of the depression of this coast: its converse elevation I had observed to the north of Wostenholme Sound. The axis of oscillation must be somewhere in the neighborhood of latitude 77°.

We reached Cape York on the 21st, after a tortuous but romantic travel through a misty atmosphere. Here the land-leads ceased, with the exception of some small and scarcely-practicable openings near the shore, which were evidently owing to the wind that prevailed for the time. Every thing bore proof of the late development of the season. The red snow was a fortnight behind its time. A fast floe extended with numerous tongues far out to the south and east. The only question was between a new rest, for the shore-ices to open, or a desertion of the coast and a trial of the open water to the west.

We sent off a detachment to see whether the Esquimaux might not be passing the summer at Episok, behind the glacier of Cape Imalik, and began an inventory of our stock on hand. I give the result:—

Dried lumme	195	birds.
Pork-slush	112	pounds.
Flour	50	"
Indian meal	50	"
Meat-biscuit	80	"
Bread	348	"

Six hundred and forty pounds of provision, all told, exclusive of our dried birds, or some thirty-six pounds a man. Tom Hickey found a turf, something like his native peat, which we thought might help to boil our kettle; and with the aid of this our fuel-account stood thus:—

Turf, for two boilings a day	7 days.
Two sledge-runners	6 "
Spare oars, sledges, and an empty cask	4 "

Seventeen days in all; not counting, however, the Red Boat, which would add something, and our emptied provision-bags, which might carry on the estimate to about three weeks.

The return of the party from Imalik gave us no reason to hesitate. The Esquimaux had not been there for several years. There were no birds in the neighborhood.

I climbed the rocks a second time with Mr. McGary, and took a careful survey of the ice with my glass. The "fast," as the whalers call the immovable shore-ice, could be seen in a nearly unbroken sweep, passing by Bushnell's Island, and joining the coast not far from where I stood. The outside floes were large, and had evidently been not long broken; but it cheered my heart to see that there was one well-defined lead which followed the main floe until it lost itself to seaward.

I called my officers together, explained to them the motives which governed me, and prepared to re-embark. The boats were hauled up, examined carefully, and, as far as our means permitted, repaired. The Red Eric was stripped of her outfit and cargo, to be broken up for fuel when the occasion should come. A large beacon-cairn was built on an eminence, open to view from the south and west; and a red flannel shirt, spared with some reluctance, was hoisted as a pennant to draw attention to the spot. Here I deposited a

IMALIK.

succinct record of our condition and purposes, and then directed our course south by west into the ice-fields.

By degrees the ice through which we were moving became more and more impacted; and it sometimes required all our ice-knowledge to determine whether a particular lead was practicable or not. The irregularities of the surface, broken by hummocks, and occasionally by larger masses, made it difficult to see far ahead; besides which, we were often embarrassed by the fogs. I was awakened one evening from a weary sleep in my fox-skins, to discover that we had fairly lost our way. The officer at the helm of the leading boat, misled by the irregular shape of a large iceberg that crossed his track, had lost the main lead some time before, and was steering shoreward far out of the true course. The little canal in which he had locked us was hardly two boats'-lengths across, and lost itself not far off in a feeble zigzag both behind and before us: it was evidently closing, and we could not retreat.

Without apprising the men of our misadventure, I ordered the boats hauled up, and, under pretence of drying the clothing and stores, made a camp on the ice. A few hours after, the weather cleared enough for the first time to allow a view of the distance, and McGary and myself climbed a berg some three hundred feet high for the purpose. It was truly fearful: we were deep in the recesses of the bay, surrounded on all sides by stupendous icebergs and tangled floe-pieces. My sturdy second officer, not naturally impressible, and long accustomed to the vicissitudes of whaling life, shed tears at the prospect.

There was but one thing to be done: cost what it might, we must harness our sledges again and retrace our way to the westward. One sledge had been already used for firewood; the Red Eric, to which it had belonged, was now cut up, and her light cedar planking laid upon the floor of the other boats; and we went to work with the rue-raddies as in the olden time. It was not till the third toilsome day was well spent that we reached the berg which had bewildered our helmsman. We hauled over its tongue, and joyously embarked again upon a free lead, with a fine breeze from the north.

Our little squadron was now reduced to two boats. The land to the northward was no longer visible; and whenever I left the margin of the fast to avoid its deep sinuosities, I was obliged to trust entirely to the compass. We had at least eight days' allowance of fuel on board; but our provisions were running very low, and we met few birds, and failed to secure any larger game. We saw several large seals upon the ice, but they were too watchful for us; and on two occasions we came upon the walrus sleeping,—once within actual lance-thrust; but the animal charged in the teeth of his assailant and made good his retreat.

On the 28th I instituted a quiet review of the state of things before us. Our draft on the stores we had laid in at Providence Halt had been limited for some days to three raw eggs and two breasts of birds a day; but we had a small ration of bread-dust besides; and when we halted, as we did regularly for meals, our fuel allowed us to indulge lavishly in the great panacea of Arctic travel, tea. The men's strength was waning under this restricted diet; but a careful reckoning up of our remaining supplies proved to me now that even this was more than we could afford ourselves without an undue reliance on the fortunes of the hunt. Our next land was to be Cape Shackleton, one of the most prolific bird-colonies of the coast, which we were all looking to, much as sailors nearing home in their boats after disaster and short allowance at sea. But, meting out our stores through the number of days that must elapse before we could expect to share its hospitable welcome, I found that five ounces of bread-dust, four of tallow, and three of bird-meat, must from this time form our daily ration.

So far we had generally coasted the fast ice: it had given us an occasional resting-place and refuge, and we were able sometimes to reinforce our stores of provisions by our guns. But it made our progress tediously slow, and our stock of small-shot was so nearly exhausted that I was convinced our safety depended on an increase of speed. I determined to try the more open sea.

For the first two days the experiment was a failure. We were surrounded by heavy fogs; a southwest wind brought the outside pack upon us and obliged us to haul up on the drifting ice. We were thus carried to the northward, and lost about twenty miles. My party, much overworked, felt despondingly the want of the protection of the land-floes.

Nevertheless, I held to my purpose, steering S.S.W. as nearly as the leads would admit, and looking constantly for the thinning out of the pack that hangs around the western water.

Although the low diet and exposure to wet had

again reduced our party, there was no apparent relaxation of energy; and it was not until some days later that I found their strength seriously giving way.

It is a little curious that the effect of a short allowance of food does not show itself in hunger. The first symptom is a loss of power, often so imperceptibly brought on that it becomes evident only by an accident. I well remember our look of blank amazement as, one day, the order being given to haul the "Hope" over a tongue of ice, we found that she would not budge. At first I thought it was owing to the wetness of the snow-covered surface in which her runners were; but, as there was a heavy gale blowing outside, and I was extremely anxious to get her on to a larger floe to prevent being drifted off, I lightened her cargo and set both crews upon her. In the land of promise, off Crimson Cliffs, such a force would have trundled her like a wheelbarrow: we could almost have borne her upon our backs. Now, with incessant labor and standing-hauls, she moved at a snail's pace.

The "Faith" was left behind, and barely escaped destruction. The outside pressure cleft the floe asunder, and we saw our best boat, with all our stores, drifting rapidly away from us. The sight produced an almost hysterical impression upon our party. Two days of want of bread, I am sure, would have destroyed us; and we had now left us but eight pounds of shot in all. To launch the Hope again, and rescue her comrade or share her fortunes, would have been the instinct of other circumstances; but it was out of the question now. Happily, before we had time to ponder our loss, a flat cake of ice eddied round near the floe we were upon; McGary and myself sprang to it at the moment, and succeeded in floating it across the chasm in time to secure her. The rest of the crew rejoined her by only scrambling over the crushed ice as we brought her in at the hummock-lines.

KINGSTON HUTS.

CHAPTER XXIX.

THE SEAL! THE SEAL! — THE FESTIVAL — TERRA FIRMA — PAUL ZACHARIAS — THE FRAULEIN FLAISCHER — THE NEWS — AT THE SETTLEMENTS — THE WELCOME.

THINGS grew worse and worse with us: the old difficulty of breathing came back again, and our feet swelled to such an extent that we were obliged to cut open our canvas boots. But the symptom which gave me most uneasiness was our inability to sleep. A form of low fever which hung by us when at work had been kept down by the thoroughness of our daily rest: all my hopes of escape were in the refreshing influences of the halt.

It must be remembered that we were now in the open bay, in the full line of the great ice-drift to the Atlantic, and in boats so frail and unseaworthy as to require constant baling to keep them afloat.

It was at this crisis of our fortunes that we saw a large seal floating—as is the custom of these animals—on a small patch of ice, and seemingly asleep. It was an ussuk, and so large that I at first mistook it for a walrus. Signal was made for the Hope to follow astern, and, trembling with anxiety, we prepared to crawl down upon him.

Petersen, with the large English rifle, was stationed in the bow, and stockings were drawn over the oars as mufflers. As we neared the animal, our excitement became so intense that the men could hardly keep stroke. I had a set of signals for such occasions, which spared us the noise of the voice; and when about three hundred yards off, the oars were taken in, and we moved on in deep silence with a single scull astern.

He was not asleep, for he reared his head when we were almost within rifle-shot; and to this day I can remember the hard, careworn, almost despairing expression of the men's thin faces as they saw him move: their lives depended on his capture.

I depressed my hand nervously, as a signal for Petersen to fire. McGary hung upon his oar, and the boat, slowly but noiselessly sagging ahead, seemed to me within certain range. Looking at Petersen, I saw that the poor fellow was paralyzed by his anxiety, trying vainly to obtain a rest for his gun against the cutwater of the boat. The seal rose on his fore-flippers, gazed at us for a moment with frightened curiosity, and coiled himself for a plunge. At that instant, simultaneously with the crack of our rifle, he relaxed his long length on the ice, and, at the very brink of the water, his head fell helpless to one side.

I would have ordered another shot, but no discipline could have controlled the men. With a wild yell, each vociferating according to his own impulse, they urged both boats upon the floes. A crowd of hands seized the seal and bore him up to safer ice. The men seemed half crazy: I had not realized how much we were reduced by absolute famine. They ran over the floe, crying and laughing and brandishing their knives. It was not five minutes before every man was sucking his bloody fingers or mouthing long strips of raw blubber.

Not an ounce of this seal was lost. The intestines found their way into the soup-kettles without any observance of the preliminary home-processes. The cartilaginous parts of the fore-flippers were cut off in the *mêlée*, and passed round to be chewed upon; and even the liver, warm and raw as it was, bade fair to be eaten before it had seen the pot. That night, on the large halting-floe, to which, in contempt of the dangers of drifting, we happy men had hauled our boats, two entire planks of the Red Eric were devoted to a grand cooking-fire, and we enjoyed a rare and savage feast.

This was our last experience of the disagreeable effects of hunger. In the words of George Stephenson, "The charm was broken, and the dogs were safe." The dogs I have said little about, for none of us liked to think of them. The poor creatures Toodla and Whitey had been taken with us as last resources against starvation. They were, as McGary worded it, "meat on the hoof," and "able to carry their own fat over the floes." Once, near Weary Man's Rest, I had been on the point of killing them; but they had been the leaders of our winter's team, and we could not bear the sacrifice.

I need not detail our journey any farther. Within a day or two we shot another seal, and from that time forward had a full supply of food.

On the 1st of August we sighted the Devil's Thumb, and were again among the familiar localities of the whalers' battling-ground. The bay was quite open, and we had been making easting for two days before. We were soon among the Duck Islands, and, passing to the south of Cape Shackleton, prepared to land.

"Terra firma! Terra firma!" How very pleasant it was to look upon, and with what a tingle of excited thankfulness we drew near it! A little time to seek a cove among the wrinkled hills, a little time to exchange congratulations, and then our battered boats were hauled high and dry upon the rocks, and our party, with hearts full of our deliverance, lay down to rest.

And now, with the apparent certainty of reaching our homes, came that nervous apprehension which follows upon hope long deferred. I could not trust myself to take the outside passage, but timidly sought the quiet-water channels running deep into the archipelago which forms a sort of labyrinth along the coast.

Thus it was that at one of our sleeping-halts upon the rocks—for we still adhered to the old routine—Petersen awoke me with a story. He had just seen and recognised a native, who, in his frail kayak, was evidently seeking eider-down among the islands. The man had once been an inmate of his family. "Paul Zacharias, don't you know me? I'm Carl Petersen!" "No," said the man; "his wife says he's dead;" and, with a stolid expression of wonder, he stared for a

THE FIRST KAYAK.

moment at the long beard that loomed at him through the fog, and paddled away with all the energy of fright.

Two days after this, a mist had settled down upon the islands which embayed us, and when it lifted we found ourselves rowing, in lazy time, under the shadow of Karkamoot. Just then a familiar sound came to us over the water. We had often listened to the screeching of the gulls or the bark of the fox, and mistaken it for the "Huk" of the Esquimaux; but this had about it an inflection not to be mistaken, for it died away in the familiar cadence of a "halloo."

"Listen, Petersen! oars, men!" "What is it?"—and he listened quietly at first, and then, trembling, said, in a half whisper, "Dannemarkers!"

I remember this, the first tone of Christian voice which had greeted our return to the world. How we all stood up and peered into the distant nooks; and how the cry came to us again, just as, having seen nothing, we were doubting whether the whole was not a dream; and then how, with long sweeps, the white ash cracking under the spring of the rowers, we stood for the cape that the sound proceeded from, and how nervously we scanned the green spots which our experience, grown now into instinct, told us would be the likely camping-ground of wayfarers.

By-and-by—for we must have been pulling a good half hour—the single mast of a small shallop showed itself; and Petersen, who had been very quiet and grave, burst out into an incoherent fit of crying, only relieved by broken exclamations of mingled Danish and English. "'Tis the Upernavik oil-boat! The Fraulein Flaischer! Carlie Mossyn, the assistant cooper, must be on his road to Kingatok for blubber. The Mariane (the one annual ship) has come, and Carlie

Mossyn——" and here he did it all over again, gulping down his words and wringing his hands.

It was Carlie Mossyn, sure enough. The quiet routine of a Danish settlement is the same year after year, and Petersen had hit upon the exact state of things. The Mariane was at Proven, and Carlie Mossyn had come up in the Fraulein Flaischer to get the year's supply of blubber from Kingatok.

Here we first got our cloudy vague idea of what had passed in the big world during our absence. The friction of its fierce rotation had not much disturbed this little outpost of civilization, and we thought it a sort of blunder as he told us that France and England were leagued with the Mussulman against the Greek Church. He was a good Lutheran, this assistant cooper, and all news with him had a theological complexion.

"What of America? eh, Petersen?"—and we all looked, waiting for him to interpret the answer.

"America?" said Carlie; "we don't know much of that country here, for they have no whalers on the coast; but a steamer and a barque passed up a fortnight ago, and have gone out into the ice to seek your party."

How gently all the lore of this man oozed out of him! he seemed an oracle, as, with hot-tingling fingers pressed against the gunwale of the boat, we listened to his words. "Sebastopol ain't taken." Where and what was Sebastopol?

But "Sir John Franklin?" There we were at home

again,—our own delusive little speciality rose uppermost. Franklin's party, or traces of the dead which represented it, had been found nearly a thousand miles to the south of where we had been searching for them. He knew it; for the priest (Pastor Kraag) had a Ger-

ENTERING THE DANISH SETTLEMENT.

man newspaper which told all about it. And so we "out oars" again, and rowed into the fogs.

Another sleeping-halt has passed, and we have all washed clean at the fresh-water basins and furbished up our ragged furs and woollens. Kasarsoak, the snow top of Sanderson's Hope, shows itself above the mists, and we hear the yelling of the dogs. Petersen had been foreman of the settlement, and he calls my attention, with a sort of pride, to the tolling of the workmen's bell. It is six o'clock. We are nearing the end of our trials. Can it be a dream?——

We hugged the land by the big harbor, turned the corner by the old brew-house, and, in the midst of a crowd of children, hauled our boats for the last time upon the rocks.

For eighty-four days we had lived in the open air. Our habits were hard and weather-worn. We could not remain within the four walls of a house without a distressing sense of suffocation. But we drank coffee that night before many a hospitable threshold, and listened again and again to the hymn of welcome, which, sung by many voices, greeted our deliverance.

OOMIAK.

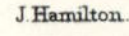

J. Hamilton. Engraved at J. M. Butler's establishment 84 Chestnut St. A. W. Graham.

KASARSOAK. SANDERSON'S HOPE.

UPERNAVIK.

(From a sketch by Dr. Kane.)

CONCLUSION.

We received all manner of kindness from the Danes of Upernavik. The residents of this distant settlement are dependent for their supplies on the annual trading-ship of the colonies, and they of course could not minister to our many necessities without much personal inconvenience. But they fitted up a loft for our reception, and shared their stores with us in liberal Christian charity.

They gave us many details of the expeditions in search of Sir John Franklin, and added the painful news that my gallant friend and comrade, Bellot, had perished in a second crusade to save him. We knew each other by many common sympathies: I had divided with him the hazards of mutual rescue among the ice-fields; and his last letter to me, just before I left New York, promised me the hope that we were to meet again in Baffin's Bay, and that he would unite himself with our party as a volunteer. The French service never lost a more chivalrous spirit.

The Danish vessel was not ready for her homeward journey till the 4th of September; but the interval was well spent in regaining health and gradually accustoming ourselves to in-door life and habits. It is a fact, which the physiologist will not find it difficult to reconcile with established theories, that we were all more prostrated by the repose and comfort of our new condition than we had been by nearly three months of constant exposure and effort.

On the 6th I left Upernavik, with all our party, in the Mariane, a stanch but antiquated little barque, under the command of Captain Ammondson, a fine representative of the true-hearted and skilful seamen of his nation, who promised to drop us at the Shetland Islands. Our little boat, the Faith, which was regarded by all of us as a precious relic, took passage along with us. Except the furs on our backs, and the documents that recorded our labors and our trials, it was all we brought back of the Advance and her fortunes.

On the 11th we arrived at Godhavn, the inspectorate of North Greenland, and had a characteristic welcome from my excellent friend, Mr. Olrik. The Mariane had stopped only to discharge a few stores and receive her papers of clearance; but her departure was held back to the latest moment, in hopes of receiving news of Captain Hartstene's squadron, which had not been heard of since the 21st of July.

We were upon the eve of setting out, however, when the look-out man at the hill-top announced a steamer in the distance. It drew near, with a barque in tow, and we soon recognised the stars and stripes of our own country. The Faith was lowered for the last time into the water, and the little flag which had floated so near the poles of both hemispheres opened once more to the breeze. With Brooks at the tiller and Mr. Olrik at my side, followed by all the boats of the settlement, we went out to meet them.

Not even after the death of the usuk did our men lay to their oars more heartily. We neared the squadron and the gallant men that had come out to seek us; we could see the scars which their own ice-battles had impressed on the vessels; we knew the gold lace of the officers' cap-bands, and discerned the groups who, glass in hand, were evidently regarding us.

Presently we were alongside. An officer, whom I shall ever remember as a cherished friend, Captain Hartstene, hailed a little man in a ragged flannel shirt, "Is that Dr. Kane?" and with the "Yes!" that followed, the rigging was manned by our countrymen, and cheers welcomed us back to the social world of love which they represented.

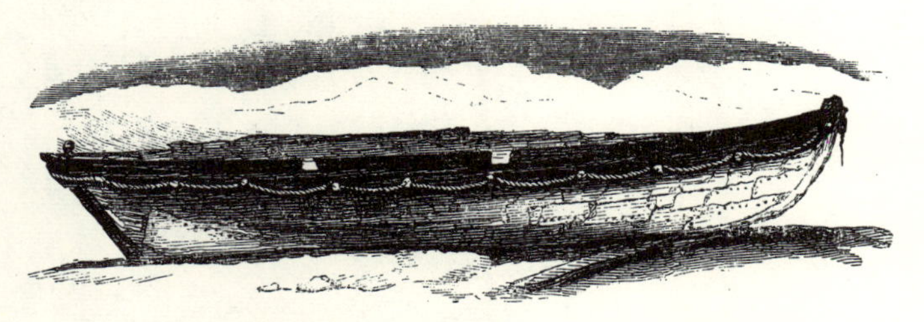

THE FAITH, NOW AT THE BROOKLYN NAVY-YARD.

APPENDIX.

No. I.

Instructions of the Secretary of the Navy to Passed Assistant Surgeon Kane.

NAVY DEPARTMENT, November 27, 1852.

SIR :—Lady Franklin having urged you to undertake a search for her husband, Sir John Franklin, and his companions, and a vessel, the Advance, having been placed at your disposition by Mr. Grinnell, you are hereby assigned to special duty for the purpose of conducting an overland journey from the upper waters of Baffin's Bay to the shores of the Polar seas

Relying upon your zeal and discretion, the Department sends you forth upon an undertaking which will be attended with great peril and exposure. Trusting that you will be sustained by the laudable object in view, and wishing you success and a safe return to your friends, I am, respectfully, your obedient servant,

JOHN P. KENNEDY.

Passed Assistant Surgeon E. K. Kane,
United States Navy, Philadelphia.

NAVY DEPARTMENT, February 9, 1853.

SIR :—In connection with the special duty assigned to you by the order of this Department bearing date November 27, 1852, your attention is invited to objects of scientific inquiry; particularly to such as relate to the existence of an open Polar sea, terrestrial magnetism, general meteorology, and subjects of importance in connection with natural history.

You will transmit to the Department, when opportunities offer, reports of your progress and the results of your search, and, on your return to the United States, a full and detailed narrative of the incidents and discoveries of your exploration by land and sea, as matters of the scientific observations herein referred to.

Repeating my best wishes for your success, I am, very respectfully, &c.

JOHN P. KENNEDY.

Passed Assistant Surgeon E. K. Kane,
United States Navy, New York.

No. II.

Preliminary Report of Passed Assistant Surgeon Kane to the Secretary of the Navy

HON. JAMES C. DOBBIN, *Secretary of the Navy:*

SIR:—The expedition to which I was assigned by orders from the Department, under date the 27th of November, 1852, left New York in the brig Advance, one hundred and twenty tons burden, on the 30th of May following. Our company consisted of eighteen persons in all; of whom ten were regularly attached to the naval service, the others being engaged by private liberality.

Our destination was to the highest penetrable point of Baffin's Bay, from which, according to instructions from the Department, we were to attempt a search for the missing vessels of Sir John Franklin. This region was then entirely unexplored, and it was selected on that account.

The copies which I annex of my letters heretofore addressed to the Department indicate my course up to the time of leaving Upernavik, in latitude 72° 47′ N. It will be seen from them that I engaged at that point an Esquimaux hunter and an interpreter, deeming their aid essential to the success of our expedition. I had also purchased supplies of fresh meat and fish, which were carefully dried and set aside to meet emergencies.

On reaching Melville Bay I found the shore-ices so decayed that I did not deem it advisable to attempt the usual passage along the fast floes of the land, but stood directly to the northward and westward, as indicated by my log, until I met the Middle Pack. Here we headed nearly direct for Cape York, and succeeded in crossing the bay without injury in ten days after first encountering the ice. On the 7th of August we reached the headland of Sir Thomas Smith's Sound, and passed the highest point attained by our predecessor, Captain Inglefield, R. N.

So far our observations accorded completely with the experience of this gallant officer in the summer of 1852. A fresh breeze, with a swell setting in from the southward and westward; marks upon the rocks indicating regular tides; no ice visible from aloft, and all the signs of continuous open water.

As we advanced, however, a belt of heavy stream-ice was seen,—an evident precursor of drift; and a little afterward it became evident that the channel to the northward was obstructed by a drifting pack.

We were still too far to the south to carry out the views I had formed of our purposed search, and it became my duty, therefore, to attempt the penetration of this ice. Before doing this, I selected an appropriate inlet for a provision-depôt, and buried there a supply of beef, pork, and bread; at the same place we deposited our Francis's life-boat, covering it carefully with wet sand, and overlaying the frozen mass with stones and moss. We afterward found that the Esquimaux had hunted around this inlet; but the *cache*, which we had thus secured as our own resort in case of emergency, escaped detection.

No one having yet visited this coast, I landed on the most prominent western headland of a group of small islands,—the Littleton Islands of Inglefield,—and erected there a flagstaff and beacon; near this beacon, according to preconcerted arrangement, we deposited official despatches and our private letters of farewell.

My first design in entering the pack was to force a passage to the north; but, after reaching latitude 78° 45′ N., we found the ice hugging the American shore, and extending in a drifting mass completely across the channel. This ice gradually bore down upon us, and we were forced to seek the comparatively open spaces of the Greenland coast. Still, we should have inevitably been beset and swept to the south, but for a small landlocked bay under whose cliffs we found a temporary asylum. We named it Refuge Inlet: it carries fifty fathoms of water within a biscuit-toss of its northern headland, and, but for a glacier which occupies its inner curve, would prove an eligible winter harbor.

We were detained in this helpless situation three valuable days, the pack outside hardly admitting the passage of a boat. But, on the 13th, fearing lest the rapidly-advancing cold might prevent our penetrating farther, we warped out into the drift, and fastened to a grounded berg.

That the Department may correctly apprehend our subsequent movements, it is necessary to describe some features peculiar to our position. The coast trended to the N.N.E. It was metamorphic in structure, rising in abrupt precipitous cliffs of basaltic greenstone from eight hundred to twelve hundred feet in perpendicular height. The shore at the base of this wall was invested by a permanent belt of ice, measuring from three to forty yards in width, with a mean summer thickness of eighteen feet. The ice clung to the rocks with extreme tenacity; and, unlike similar formations to the south, it had resisted the thawing influences of summer. The tidal currents had worn its seaward face into a gnarled mural escarpment, against which the floes broke with splendid displays of force; but it still preserved an upper surface comparatively level, and adapted as a sort of highway for further travel. The drifting ice or pack outside of it was utterly impenetrable; many bergs recently discharged were driving backward and forward with the tides; and thus, pressing upon the ice of the floes, had raised up hills from sixty to seventy feet high. The mean rise and fall of the tide was twelve feet, and its rate of motion two and a half knots an hour.

In this state of things, having no alternative but either to advance or to discontinue the search, I determined to take advantage of a small interspace which occurred at certain stages of the tide between the main pack and the coast, and, if possible, press through it. I was confirmed in this purpose by my knowledge of the extreme strength of the Advance, and my confidence in the spirit and fidelity of my comrades. The effort occupied us until the 1st of September. It was attended by the usual dangers of ice-penetration. We were on our beam-ends whenever the receding tides left us in deficient soundings; and on two of such occasions it was impossible to secure our stoves so as to prevent the brig from taking fire. We reached latitude 78° 43′ N. on the 29th of August, having lost a part of our starboard bulwarks, a quarter-boat, our jib-boom, our best bower-anchor, and about six hundred fathoms of hawser; but with our brig in all essentials uninjured.

We were now retarded by the rapid advance of winter: the young ice was forming with such rapidity that it became evident that we must soon be frozen in. At this juncture my officers addressed to me written opinions in favor of a return to a more southern harbor; but, as such a step would have cost us our dearly-purchased progress and removed us from the field of our intended observations, I could not accede to their views. I determined, therefore, to start on foot with a party of observation, to seek a spot which might be eligible as a starting-point for our future travel, and, if such a one were found, to enter at once upon the fall duties of search.

This step determined on, the command of the brig was committed to Mr. Ohlsen, and I started on the 29th of August with a detachment, carrying a whale-boat and sledge. The ice soon checked the passage of our boat; but I left her, and proceeded with a small sledge along the ledge of ice which, under the name of "ice-foot," I have before described as clinging to the shore.

We were obliged, of course, to follow all the indentations of the coast, and our way was often completely obstructed by the discharge of rocks from the adjacent cliffs. In crossing a glacier we came near losing our party, and were finally compelled to abandon the sledge and continue our journey on foot. We succeeded, however, in completing our work, and reached a projecting cape, from which, at an elevation of eleven hundred feet, I commanded a prospect of the ice to the north and west as high as latitude 80° N. A black ridge running nearly due north, which we found afterward to be a glacier, terminated our view along the Greenland coast to the eastward. Numerous icebergs were crowded in masses throughout the axis of the channel; and, as far as our vision extended, the entire surface was a frozen sea. The island named Louis Napoleon on the charts of Captain Inglefield does not exist. The resemblance of ice to land will readily explain the misapprehension.

The result of this journey, although not cheering, confirmed me in my intention of wintering in the actual position of the brig; and I proceeded, immediately on our return, to organize parties for the fall, with a view to the establishment of provision-depôts to facilitate the further researches of the spring. In selecting sites for these and the attendant travel, our parties passed over more than eight hundred miles. The coast of Greenland was traced one hundred and twenty-five miles to the north and east, and three caches were established at favorable points. The largest of these (No. III. of chart) contained eight hundred pounds of pemmican; it was located upon an island in latitude 79° 12′ 6″ N., longitude 65° 25′ W., by Messrs. McGary and Bonsall.

These operations were continued until the 20th of November, when the darkness arrested them.

Our brig had been frozen in since the 10th of September. We had selected a harbor near a group of rocky islets in the southeastern curve of the bay, where we could establish our observatory, and had facilities for procuring water and for daily exercise. We were secure, too, against probable disturbance during the winter, and were sufficiently within the tidal influences to give us a hope of liberation in the spring.

As we were about to winter higher north than any previous expedition, and, besides a probable excess of cold, were about to experience a longer deprivation of solar light, the arrangements for the interior were studied carefully.

The deck was housed in with boards and calked with oakum. A system of warmth and ventilation was established: our permanent lamps were cased with chimneys, to prevent the accumulation of smoke; cooking, ice-melting, and washing arrangements were minutely cared for; the dogs were kennelled in squads, and they were allowed the alternate use of snow-houses and of the brig, as their condition might require. Our domestic system was organized with the most exact attention to cleanliness, exercise, recreation, and withal to fixed routine.

During the winter which followed, the sun was one hundred and twenty days below the horizon; and, owing to a range of hills toward our southern meridian, the maximum darkness was not relieved by apparent twilight even at noonday.

The atmospheric temperatures were lower than any that had been recorded by others before us. We had adopted every precaution to secure accuracy in these observations, and the indications of our numerous thermometers—alcoholic, ethereal, and mercurial—were registered hourly.

From them it appears that the mean annual temperature of Rensselaer Harbor, as we named our winter home, is lower than that of Melville Island, as recorded by Parry, by two degrees. In certain sheltered positions, the process of freezing was unintermitted for any consecutive twenty-four hours throughout the year.

The lowest temperature was observed in February, when the mean of eight instruments indicated minus 70° Fahrenheit. Chloroform froze; the essential oils of sassafras, juniper, cubebs, and winter-green, were resolved into mixed solid and liquid; and on the morning of February 24 we witnessed chloric ether congealed for the first time by a natural temperature.

In the early part of this winter I erected an astronomical observatory, and mounted our "transit" and theodolite upon pedestals of stone cemented by ice. Great care was taken by Mr. Sontag, the astronomer to the expedition, in determining our geographical position. The results for the determination of longitude, as based upon moon culminations, are in every respect satisfactory; they are corroborated by occultations of planets and the late solar eclipse of May, 1855. An occultation of Saturn simultaneously observed by Mr. Sontag and myself, at temperatures of minus 60° and 53°, differed but two seconds. This is the lowest temperature at which such an observation has ever been taken.

The position of our observatory may be stated as in latitude 78° 37′ N., longitude 70° 40′ 6″ W.

A room artificially heated was attached to the observatory as a magnetic station. The observations were both absolute and relative, and were sustained by a corps of volunteers among the officers.

A strong tendency to tonic spasm, probably induced by the lengthened cold and darkness, was the chief trial of our party. General disease was readily controlled by a careful hygiene; and the unremitting and intelligent exertions of Dr. I. I. Hayes, the surgeon of the expedition, kept the scurvy in complete subjugation.

But this anomalous form of spasmodic disease was encountered with difficulty. It extended to our dogs, assuming the aspect of tetanus: in spite of every effort, no less than fifty-seven perished, many of them with symptoms not unlike those of hydrophobia.

The loss of these animals interfered seriously with my original scheme of search. They had been collected at various points of the coast of Greenland, and had been trained for their office with extreme care and labor. I had contemplated employing them in following the coast, and with this view had devoted the labors of the fall to the organization of a chain of depôts. Now, however, a new system of operations was to be established, with different appliances. New sledges were to be built, and cooking-utensils and field-equipments provided, suited to larger parties and of more portable character. The latter period of darkness was entirely occupied with these new preparations.

Our party was unhappily too small for an extended system of field-operations by unassisted human labor; and the only remaining hope of continuing the search was to be found in a passage through or over the great ice-fields to the north,—an effort the success of which was rendered very doubtful by the crowded bergs and distorted ice of this frozen area. With this object I organized a party of our strongest men (all volunteers) under my personal charge, and sent an advanced corps under Mr. Brooks, the energetic first officer of the expedition, to place a relief-cargo of provisions at ten days' journey from the brig.

On the 27th of March, the ninth day of their absence, a heavy gale from the north-northeast broke upon this party. The thermometer fell to 57° below zero; and the ice-ridges (hummock-lines) were so obstructed by snow-drift that they could not deposit their stores beyond fifty miles from the brig. Four of the most valuable members of the party, Messrs. Brooks and Wilson, Jefferson Baker, and Peter Schubert, were frozen at the extremities; and, a single man being left to attend them, the others returned to the brig in a state of extreme exhaustion. The name of the brave fellow who remained with his comrades was Thomas Hickey, an Irishman.

The main company under my own command started at once for the floes, with but little hope of rescuing our comrades; Mr. Ohlsen, one of the returned party, volunteering to guide us. He was sewed up in furs, and strapped upon a small sledge, which we dragged after us; but symptoms of mental disturbance rendered his heroism unavailing, and, but for striking the trail of the party, we must all of us have perished.

On this occasion I was deeply touched by the confidence of the disabled men in the certainty of their relief. Although they were nearly concealed by snow-drift, and dependent for warmth upon their sleeping-bags, they had patiently and hopefully awaited our arrival. The discovery of a small canvas tent in the midst of these immense plains of ice I must remember as providential.

I mention gratefully the endurance and self-denial of my comrades upon this fearful march. They had been eighty-one out of eighty-four hours without sleep, and had halted for the purpose of melting ice for drink. The tendency to sleep could only be overcome by mechanical violence; and when at last we got back to the brig, still dragging the wounded men instinctively behind us, there was not one whose mind was found to be unimpaired.

This disastrous effort cost us two valuable lives, Jefferson Baker and Peter Schubert. The first of these was a native of Delaware county, Pennsylvania, a trustworthy and faithful follower; he died of locked-jaw, thirty-six hours after his return to the brig. The other was cook to the expedition, and a volunteer upon the duty which caused his death. Our little party had throughout, from the nature of the service, been in close relations with one another, and these men are remembered by us all with sympathy and respect.

As soon after this as the health of our company could justify, I set out with my original party to renew the attempt from a higher point on the Greenland coast, carrying with me an India-rubber boat. This journey was undertaken in the latter part of April, and continued into May. It was followed by others, which extended the search, almost without intermission, until the 10th of July. These journeys may be thus summed up:—

March....................Mr. Brooks and Dr. Kane.
April, May.............Dr. Kane, Messrs. McGary and Bonsall.
June.......................Dr. Hayes and William Godfrey.
June, July.............William Morton, and Hans Heindrick, our native hunter.

The arrival of the Esquimaux in April enabled us to add four dogs to the three that remained of our original stock, and thus to equip a slender team. The value of these animals for Arctic ice-travel can hardly be overestimated. The earlier journeys of March, April, and May, proved incomparably more arduous and exposing than those performed with dogs, while their results were entirely disproportionate to the labor they cost us. It was invariably the case that the entire party, on its return from the field, passed at once upon the sick-list.

Out of nearly three thousand miles of travel, no less than eleven hundred were made by the dog-sledge; and during the fall, winter, and spring of the ensuing year (1854–55) I made, in person, no less than fourteen hundred miles with a single team.

Setting out from our winter quarters, three expeditions effected the passage of the bay:—1. To the north, with Messrs. McGary and Bonsall, along the base of a great glacier which issued from the coast of Greenland in latitude 79° 12′. A copy of this glacier, as surveyed by me in 1855, accompanies this report. 2. To the southwest, by Dr. Hayes and William Godfrey. 3. To the northwest, and along the shores of a new channel, by W. Morton and our Esquimaux hunter, Hans. The original reports of these journeys, with my own observations, are now under seal and subject to the orders of the Department. I give only a summary of results, referring for particulars to the track chart projected on the spot from the original field-notes, which I have the honor to transmit with this report.

Greenland reaches its farthest western point at Cape Alexander, in the neighborhood of latitude 78° 10′ N., and, after passing longitude

70° W. of Greenwich, trends nearly due east and west, (E. 20° N.) This northern face of Greenland is broken by two large bays, at the base of which are numerous granitoid islands, which, as you approach longitude 65° W., assume the form of an archipelago. Fifteen islands were surveyed and located here. The aspect of the coast is imposing, abutting upon the water-line in headlands from eight hundred to fourteen hundred feet high, and one range of precipice presenting an unbroken wall of forty-five miles in length. Its geological structure is of the older red sandstones and silurian limestones, overlying a primary basis of massive syenites. The sandstones to the south of 78° seem to form the floor of the bay. They are in series, with intercalated greenstones and other ejected plutonic rocks, and form the chief girders of the coast. Upon this and collateral subjects I shall, with your permission, address a special report to the Department.

The further progress of our parties toward the Atlantic was arrested by a great glacier, which issued in latitude 79° 12′ N., longitude 64° 20′ W., and ran directly north. This forms an insuperable barrier to exploration in this direction: it is continuous with the *mer de glace* of interior Greenland, and is the largest true glacier known to exist. Its great mass adapts itself to the configuration of the basis-country which it overlies. Its escarpment abutting upon the water presents a perpendicular face varying from three to five hundred feet in height.

The lines of crevasse and fracture are on an unexampled scale of interest. The bergs, which are ejected in lines, arrange themselves in a sort of escalade, which confers a character of great sublimity upon the landscape.

It was followed along its base, and traced into a new and northern land, trending far to the west. This land I have named *Washington.* The large bay which separates it from the coast of Greenland and the glacier I have described bears on my chart the name of our liberal countryman, Mr. Peabody.

The coasts of this new territory, adjoining Peabody Bay, have been accurately delineated by two parties, whose results correspond. Its southwestern cape is in latitude 80° 20′ N., by observation with artificial horizon; its longitude, by chronometer and bearings, 66° 42′ W. of Greenwich. The cape was doubled by William Morton and our Esquimaux, with a team of dogs, and the land to the north traced until they reached the large indentation named Constitution Bay. The whole of this line was washed by open water, extending in an iceless channel to the opposite shores on the west. This western land I have inscribed with the name of Henry Grinnell.

The course of this channel at its southern opening was traced, by actual survey, in a long horseshoe curve, sharply defined against the solid ice of Smith's Sound, and terminating at its extremes against two noble headlands about forty miles apart. The western coast was followed, in subsequent explorations, to a mural face of nine hundred feet elevation, preserving throughout its iceless character. Here a heavy surf, beating directly against the rocks, checked our future progress.

This precipitous headland, the farthest point attained by the party, was named Cape Independence. It is in latitude 81° 22′ N. and longitude 65° 35′ W. It was only touched by William Morton, who left the dogs and made his way to it along the coast. From it the western coast was seen stretching far toward the north, with an iceless horizon, and a heavy swell rolling in with white caps. At a height of about five hundred feet above the sea this great expanse still presented all the appearance of an open and iceless sea. In claiming for it this character I have reference only to the facts actually observed, without seeking confirmation or support from any deduction of theory. Among such facts are the following:—

1. It was approached by a channel entirely free from ice, having a length of fifty-two and a mean width of thirty-six geographical miles.

2. The coast-ice along the water-line of this channel had been completely destroyed by thaw and water-action; while an unbroken belt of solid ice, one hundred and twenty-five miles in diameter, extended to the south.

3. A gale from the northeast, of fifty-four hours' duration, brought a heavy sea from that quarter, without disclosing any drift or other ice.

4. Dark *nimbus* clouds and water-sky invested the northeastern horizon.

5. Crowds of migratory birds were observed thronging its waters.

Two islands on the threshold of this sea, the most northern islands known, bear the names of Sir John Franklin and his associate, Captain Crozier, the leaders of the gallant party for which we had been in search.

To the northwest the coasts became mountainous, rising in truncated cones, like the Magdalena Cliffs of Spitzbergen. The farthest distinctly-sighted point was a lofty mountain, bearing N. 5° E., (solar;) its latitude, by estimate and intersection, was E. 2° 30′. Its longitude, as thus determined, would give 66° W., (approximative.)

I would suggest for it the name of the late Sir Edward Parry, who, as he has carried his name to the most northern latitude yet reached, should have in this, the highest known northern land, a recognition of his pre-eminent position among Arctic explorers.

The extension of the American coast to the southwest, as it appears upon the chart, was the work of Dr. Hayes and William Godfrey, renewed and confirmed by myself in April of the present year. It completes the survey of the coast as far as the Cape Sabine of Captain Inglefield. The land is very lofty, sometimes rising at its culminating peaks to the height of two thousand five hundred feet. The travel along the western and northwestern coast was made for the most part upon the ice-foot. One large bay, in latitude 79° 40′ N., longitude 73° W., by estimate, extended forty miles into the interior, and was terminated by a glacier. A large island occupies the southwestern curve of that bay.

A summary of the operations of the expedition will therefore comprehend—

1. The survey and delineation of the north coast of Greenland to its termination by a great glacier.

2. The survey of this glacial mass and its extension northward into the new land named Washington.

3. The discovery of a large channel to the northwest, free from ice, and leading into an open and expanding area equally free. The whole embraces an iceless area of four thousand two hundred miles.

4. The discovery and delineation of a large tract of land forming the extension northward of the American continent.

5. The completed survey of the American coast to the south and west as far as Cape Sabine, thus connecting our survey with the last-determined position of Captain Inglefield, and completing the circuit of the straits and bay heretofore known at their southernmost opening as Smith's Sound.

The summer of 1854 had brought with it few changes bearing toward the liberation of our brig. The melted snows did not run in the water-channels until the 30th of June, and our limited flora showed a tardy and inauspicious season.

On the 12th of July, the ice being still unbroken as far as Anoatok, I set out in a whaleboat with five volunteers, to communicate, if possible, with our English brethren whom we supposed to be at Beechy Island. The declining state of our resources suggested this attempt, although it promised many difficulties.

It occupied us until the 6th of August. We found a solid pack extending from Jones's to Murchison Sounds, between Clarence Head and Northumberland Island. To the west the ice still invested the American shore, extending some twenty miles from Cape Isabella. Between this and Mitie Island was a solid surface, the curved shoreline occupied by an extended glacier.

After endeavoring several times to bore, we were forced to make Hakluyt Island, on the Greenland side, and landed there to rest and renew our stock of provisions. The pack still filled the channel between that island and Cape Parry; and it was only with extreme effort that we were able to carry our boat over the ice. We had approached in this manner within ten miles of the latter point, when, seeing no chance of success, the winter rapidly advancing upon us, I reluctantly gave orders for our return to the brig. During this journey, which was full of exciting contingencies, we passed over the track of Bylot and Baffin, the explorers of 1616.

Our preparations for the second winter were modified largely by controlling circumstances. The physical energies of the party had sensibly declined. Our resources were diminished. We had but fifty gallons of oil saved from our summer's seal-hunt. We were scant of fuel; and our food, which now consisted only of the ordinary marine stores, was by no means suited to repel scurvy. Our molasses was reduced to forty gallons, and our dried fruits seemed to have lost their efficiency.

A single apartment was bulkheaded off amidships as a dormitory and abiding-room for our entire party, and a moss envelope, cut with difficulty from the frozen cliffs, made to enclose it like a wall. A similar casing was placed over our deck, and a small tunnelled entry—the *tossut* of the Esquimaux—contrived to enter from below. We adopted as nearly as we could the habits of the natives, burning lamps for heat, dressing in fox-skin clothing, and relying for our daily supplies on the success of organized hunting-parties.

The upper tribes of these Esquimaux had their nearest winter settlement at a spot distant, by dog-journey, about seventy-five miles. We entered into regular communication with this rude and simple-minded people, combining our efforts with theirs for mutual support, and interchanging numerous friendly offices. Bear-meat, seal, walrus, fox, and ptarmigan, were our supplies. They were eaten raw, with a rigorous attention to their impartial distribution.

With the dark months, however, these supplies became very scanty. The exertions of our best hunters were unavailing, and my personal attempts to reach the Esquimaux failed less on account of the cold (minus 52°) than the ruggedness of the ice, the extreme darkness, and the renewal of tetanic diseases among our dogs. Our poor neighbors, however, fared worse than ourselves: famine, attended by frightful forms of disease, reduced them to the lowest stages of misery and emaciation.

Our own party was gradually disabled. Mr. Brooks and Mr. Wilson, both of whom had lost toes by amputation, manifested symptoms of a grave character. William Morton was severely frozen; and we were deprived of the valuable services of the surgeon by the effects of frost-bite, which rendered it necessary for him to submit to amputation.

Scurvy with varying phases gradually pervaded our company, until Mr. Bonsall and myself only remained able to attend upon the sick and carry on the daily work of the ship, if that name could still appropriately designate the burrow which we inhabited. Even after this state of things had begun to improve, the demoralizing effects of continued debility and seemingly hopeless privation were unfavorably apparent among some of the party. I pass from this topic with the single remark that our ultimate escape would have been hazarded, but for the often painfully-enforced routine which the more experienced among us felt the necessity of adhering to rigorously under all circumstances.

In the latter part of March the walrus again made their appearance among the broken ice to the south, and we shared with the Esquimaux the proceeds of the hunt. The hemorrhages which had much depressed our party subsided, and we began slowly to recover our strength. The sun came back to us on the 21st of February; and by the 18th of April the carpenter and several others were able to resume their duties.

In view of the contingencies which I had long apprehended, I found it necessary to abandon the brig. We had already consumed for firewood her upper spars, bulwarks, deck-sheathing, stanchions, bulkheads, hatches, extra strengthening-timbers—in fact, every thing that could be taken without destroying her sea-worthiness. The papers which I append show the results of the several surveys made at this time by my orders. It will be seen from them that we had but a few weeks' supply left of food or fuel; that the path of our intended retreat was a solid plain of ice, and that to delay a third winter, while it could in no wise promote the search after Sir John Franklin, would prove fatal to many of our party.

Our organization for the escape was matured with the greatest care.

Three boats—two of them whaleboats twenty-four feet in length, and the third a light cedar dingy of thirteen feet—were mounted upon runners cut from the cross-beams of the vessel and bolted, to prevent the disaster of breakage. These runners were eighteen feet in length, and shod with hoop-iron. No nails were used in their construction; they were lashed together so as to form a pliable sledge, and upon it the boats were cradled so as to be removable at pleasure.

A fourth sledge, with a team of dogs, was reserved for the transport of our sick, four of whom were still unable to move, and for carrying on our stock of provisions. An abandoned Esquimaux hut, about thirty-five miles from the brig, was fitted up as well as our means permitted, to serve as an *entrepôt* of stores and a wayside shelter for those of the party who were already broken down, or who might yield to the first trials of the journey.

The cooking-utensils were made from our old stove-pipe. They consisted of simple soup-boilers, enclosed by a cylinder to protect them from the wind. A metal trough to receive fat, with the aid of moss and cotton canvas, enabled us to keep up an active fire. My provisions were packed in water-proof bags, adapted in shape to the sheer of the boats, and in no case rising above the thwarts. They consisted, with the exception of tea, coffee, and small stores for the sick, exclusively of melted fat and powdered biscuit.

The clothing was limited to a fixed allowance. Moccasins for the feet were made of our woollen carpeting, which had been saved for the purpose, and numerous changes of dry blanket-socks were kept for general use. For bedding, our buffalo-robes were aided by eider-down quilted into coverlets: the experience of former travel having assured us that, next to diet and periodical rest, good bedding and comfortable foot-gear were the most important things to be considered.

I took upon myself the office of transporting the sick and our reserve of provisions, employing for this purpose a dog-sledge and our single team of dogs. I carried down my first load of stores in April, and on the 15th of May began the removal of the sick. By the middle of June, all our disabled men and some twelve hundred pounds of stores had in this manner been transferred by a series of journeyings equal in the aggregate to eleven hundred miles.

On the 17th of May, having authenticated by appropriate surveys the necessities of our condition and made all our preparations for the journey, the sledge-boats left the vessel, dragged by the officers and men, under the immediate charge of Mr. Henry Brooks; a duty which he fulfilled with unswerving fidelity and energy.

My collections of natural history were also carried as far as the sick-station at Anoatok; but, under a reluctant conviction that a further effort to preserve them would risk the safety of the party, they were finally abandoned. It is grateful to me to recollect the devotion of my comrades, who volunteered to sacrifice shares of both food and clothing to secure these records of our labors.

We were able, not without difficulty, to carry our chronometers and the various instruments, magnetic and others, which might allow me still to make and verify our accustomed observations. We left behind the theodolite of the United States Coast Survey and the valuable self-registering barometric apparatus furnished by the American Philosophical Society. Our library, as well those portions which had been furnished by the government and by Mr. Grinnell as my own, were necessarily sacrificed. We preserved only the documents of the Expedition.

The first portions of our journey filled me with misgivings, as the weakness of the party showed itself in dropsical swellings and excessive difficulty of respiration. In spite of a careful system of training, the first exposure to temperatures ranging about zero and below it were to an invalid party extremely trying; and for the first eight days the entire distance accomplished from the ship did not exceed fifteen miles. Although the mean rate of transportation was afterward increased, it never exceeded three and a half miles a day over ice. Some idea may be formed by the Department of the nature of this journey from the fact that every three and a half miles thus attained cost us from twelve to fifteen miles of actual travel.

To sustain the party by the aid of fresh food required dog-journeys to the south settlements of the Esquimaux, distant from us about seventy-five miles. I found it necessary, also, to return from time to time to the brig, with the view of augmenting our supplies. My last visit to her was on the 8th of June, for the purpose of procuring some pork to serve for fuel. She was then precisely as when we left her on the 17th of May, immovably frozen in, with nine feet of solid ice under her bows. We availed ourselves of the occasional facilities which these visits allowed us to increase our stock of bread, of which we succeeded in baking four hundred and eighty pounds.

Continuing our southward progress, we neared Littleton Island. Our sick, first left at Anoatok, were gradually brought down to the boats as some of them gained strength enough to aid in the labor of dragging. The condition of the ice as it became thinner and decaying made this labor more difficult; and, in the course of our many breaks through, several of the party narrowly escaped being carried under by the tides. In the effort to liberate our sledges from the broken ice after one of these accidents, Acting Carpenter Ohlsen received an internal injury. Paralysis of the bladder was rapidly followed by tetanic symptoms, and he died on the 12th of June, three days after his attack. He has left behind him a young wife, who depended entirely upon him for support. He was buried upon Littleton Island, opposite a cape which bears his name.

From this stage of our journey up to the time of reaching the first open water, which was near Cape Alexander, we were comforted by the friendly assistance of the Esquimaux of Etah. These people faithfully adhered to the alliance which we had established during the winter. They brought us daily supplies of birds, helped us to carry our provisions and stores, and in their daily intercourse with us exhibited the kindest feeling and most rigid honesty. When we remembered that they had been so assuming and aggressive upon our first arrival that I was forced to seize their wives as hostages for the protection of our property, their present demeanor was not without its lesson. Once convinced of our superiority of power, and assured of our disposition to unite our resources with theirs for mutual protection and support, they had relied upon us implicitly, and strove now to requite their obligations toward us by ministering to our wants.

We left them on the 18th of June, at the margin of the floe. In thirty-one days we had walked three hundred and sixteen miles, and had transported our boats over eighty-one miles of unbroken ice. The men, women, and children of the little settlement had also travelled over the ice to bid us good-bye, and we did not part from them without emotion.

The passage between this point and one ten miles northwest of Hakluyt Island was in open water. It was the only open water seen north of Cape York, in latitude 75° 59′ N. We ran this under sail in a single day, hauling upon the ice to sleep. This ice was a closed pack, hanging around the north and south channels of Murchison Sound, and seemingly continued to the westward. The land-ices were still unbroken, and we were obliged to continue our journey by alternate movements over ice and water. So protracted and arduous were these, that between the 20th of June and the 6th of July we had advanced but one hundred miles.

Our average progress was about eight miles a day, stopping for our hunting-parties and for sleep. Great care was taken not to infringe upon the daily routine. We had perpetual daylight; but it was my rule, rarely broken even by extreme necessity, not to enter upon the labors of a day until we were fully refreshed from those of the day before. We halted regularly at bedtime and for meals. The boats, if afloat, were drawn up, the oars always disposed on the ice as a platform for the stores; our buffalo-skins were spread, each man placed himself with his pack according to his number, the cook for the day made his fire, and the ration, however scanty, was formally measured out. Prayers were never intermitted. I believe firmly that to these well-sustained observances we are largely indebted for our final escape.

As we moved onward, we were forced to rely principally on our guns for a supply of food. We suffered, when off the coast immediately north of Wostenholme Sound, from a scarcity of game, and were subjected to serious sickness in consequence. But at Dalrymple Island, a little farther south, we recruited rapidly on eggs of the eider-duck; and from this point to Conical Rock we found birds in abundance. Again, at the most uncertain period of our passage, when our stock of provisions was nearly exhausted, we were suddenly arrested in our course by high and rugged land-ice, which hugged a glacier near Cape Dudley Digges. We were too weak to drag our boats over this barrier, and were driven in consequence to land under the cliffs. To our joyful surprise, we found them teeming with animal life. This transition from enfeebling want to the plenty which restored our strength, we attributed to the direct interposition of Providence. The *lumme* (Uriæ, Brunichii, and Troile) was the fowl which we here found in greatest numbers. We dried upon the rocks about two hundred pounds of its meat, which we carefully saved for the transit of Melville Bay.

The rest of the coast, except under the glaciers, was followed with less difficulty. We found peat of good quality, and plenty of food. Our daily allowance of birds was twelve to a man. They were boiled into a rich soup, to which we added a carefully-measured allowance of six ounces of bread.

On the 21st we reached Cape York, and, finding no natives, made immediate preparations for crossing Melville Bay. An extended view showed the land-ice nearly unbroken, and a large drift of pack to the southward and westward. A beacon-cairn was built, and strips of red flannel fastened to a flagstaff so placed as to attract the attention of whalers or searching-parties. I deposited here a notice of our future intentions, a list of our provisions on hand, and a short summary of the discoveries of the cruise.

Up to the 26th of July our traverse of Melville Bay was along the margin of the land-ice, with only twice a resort to portage. We came then upon comparatively open drift extending to the southward and westward, which, after mature consideration, I determined to follow. There were arguments in favor of a different course, perhaps for the time less hazardous; but the state of health among my comrades admonished me that it was best to encounter the risks that were to expedite our release. The reduced bulk of our stores enabled us now to consolidate the party into two boats, breaking up the remaining one for fuel, of which we were in need. Our lengthened practice of alternating boat and sledge-management had given us something of assurance in this mode of travel, and we were, besides, familiarized with privation. It was a time of renewed suffering; but, in the result, we reached the north coast of Greenland, near Horse's Head, on the 3d of August, and, following thence the inside passage, arrived on the 6th at Upernavik, eighty-three days after leaving the Advance. We did not intermit our observations by sextant and artificial horizon as we came down the bay, and succeeded in adding to our meteorological and magnetic registers. These, including a re-survey of the coast as laid down in the Admiralty charts, will be included in a special report to the Department.

We were welcomed at the Danish settlements with characteristic hospitality. The chief trader, Knud Gelmeyden Fleischer, advanced to us from the stores of the Royal Greenland Trading Company at Upernavik whatever our necessities required; and when we afterward reached Godhavn, the seat of the royal inspectorate, Mr. Olrik, the inspector, lavished the kindest attentions upon our party.

We had taken passage at Upernavik in the Danish brig Marianne, then upon her annual visit to the Greenland colonies, Captain Amandsen, her very courteous and liberal commander, having engaged to land us at the Shetland Isles on his return route to Copenhagen. But, touching for a few days at Disco, we were met by the vessels which had been sent after us, under the command of Lieutenant Hartstene. I have no words to express the gratitude of all our party toward that noble-spirited officer and his associates, and toward our countrymen at home who had devised and given effect to the expedition for our rescue.

I have the honor to be, very respectfully, sir, your most obedient servant,

E. K. Kane.

FISKERNAES, SOUTH GREENLAND, July 6, 1853.

SIR:—We reached this place on the 5th instant, after a run of twelve days from St. John's, Newfoundland.

By means of special facilities extended to our expedition by the Danish government, we have been able to obtain from the Royal Greenland Company supplies of fresh dried codfish, as also a native Esquimaux as hunter. This boy will take with him his kayak, and is expected to prove of essential service.

We have as yet encountered no ice. It is my intention to stop at Sukkertoppen to purchase reindeer-skins.

I am, sir, very respectfully, your obedient servant,

E. K. KANE.

HON. SECRETARY OF THE NAVY, *Washington.*

UPERNAVIK, NORTH GREENLAND, July 24, 1853.

SIR:—I have the honor to report the safe arrival of myself and party at Upernavik.

Being much delayed by calms, I deemed it unadvisable to stop at Godhavn, but have lost no time in proceeding north. Our full complement of dogs is now on board, and we leave in a few hours for Melville Bay.

I have engaged the valuable services of Mr. Carl Johan Petersen, late interpreter to Captain Penny's expedition of search. If we should meet the Esquimaux north of Cape Alexander, he will be essential to our party.

The officers and men are in excellent health and spirits.

I am, sir, very respectfully, your obedient servant,

E. K. KANE.

HON. SECRETARY OF THE NAVY, *Washington.*

[Deposited in Cairn—lat. 78° 24′ N.—August 7, 1853.]

ADVANCE, August 7, 1853.

SIR:—I have the honor to report our successful transit of Melville Bay, and safe arrival within the waters of Sir Thomas Smith's Sound.

This letter will be deposited in a cairn on Littleton Island, in latitude 78° 24′ N. The prospects of a farther progress have led me to leave near this spot a metallic life-boat, with a supply of stores, as a means of retreat should our vessel be imprisoned in the ice.

The course of our party will be from this date along the coast of Greenland, trending to the north and east. If a possible chance presents itself of forcing the brig into a northern sea, I will endeavor, before availing myself of such a chance, to leave another cairn, announcing my point of departure.

Our officers and men are in excellent health and spirits, and no cases have yet occurred of scurvy or other serious disease.

After the brig is obliged to go into winter quarters, I intend to start with a carefully-equipped party to establish a depôt for the final labors of next season. Our dogs are in admirable condition, and well broken to harness.

I am, sir, very respectfully, your obedient servant,

E. K. KANE.

HON. SECRETARY OF THE NAVY, *Washington.*

No. III.

SURVEYS BEFORE ABANDONING THE BRIG.

Orders to Mr. McGary to examine the State of the Ice.

TO SECOND OFFICER, JAMES MCGARY.

SIR:—William Godfrey and the sledge will be placed at your disposition. After sleeping at Anoatok, proceed on the next day to Cape Hatherton and Flagstaff Point, returning to the brig on Monday, 14th of May.

The object of this journey is that you may compare the ice of this season with that seen in your last year's inspection. You are requested to note accurately the condition and advance of the open water, and report in writing your opinion as to the possibility of its reaching our brig in time to escape during the coming year.

Respectfully yours,

E. K. KANE, *Commanding Expedition.*

BRIG ADVANCE, April 12, 1855.

Second Officer McGary's Report.

BRIG ADVANCE, May 15, 1855.

To E. K. KANE, Esq., *Commanding Grinnell Expedition.*

SIR:—By your orders I examined the ice at this time last year from the point at which I now renew my inspection.

Last year the open water was about a mile south of Fog Inlet, and the ice broken into floes or drift for about two miles farther: the water along the ice-foot reached to Esquimaux Point. The surface-ice of the channel was thin and wet, and broken into small pools. Water was seen in the offing as far as the eye could reach with your telescope, (a 20-diam. Fraunhöfer.)

At the present date from the same stations no water can be seen, but heavy, rank ice, very hummocky to westward, and covered with snow-drifts. By going to Littleton Island, (Flagstaff Point,) about fifteen miles farther down the channel, I found the water between six and eight miles off; beyond it the sky was dark and every thing clear and open. To the westward the water met the ice about ten miles distant.

My opinion is that there is no possible chance of the water coming within twenty miles of the brig. The floe is old and heavy, and it breaks slowly. It is now more than twice as far from the brig as it was at this time last year. It will have to break up faster than ever I saw ice break to reach us this season. I regard it therefore as impossible for the vessel to be liberated with the coming year.

Yours respectfully,

JAMES MCGARY, *Second Officer.*

Orders for a full Inspection of the remaining Stock of Provisions.

TO MESSRS. BROOKS, RILEY, MORTON.

GENTLEMEN:—You will hold a survey upon the beef, pork, flour, and bread, remaining in the stores of the expedition, and report in writing upon their condition and the quantity on hand fit for use.

Very respectfully, your obedient servant,

E. K. KANE, *Commanding Expedition.*

BRIG ADVANCE. May 16, 1855.

Report of Inspection.

BRIG ADVANCE, May 16, 17.

TO E. K. KANE, Esq., *Commander Grinnell Expedition.*

SIR:—In accordance with your order of the 16th inst., we have carefully examined the condition and quantity of the provisions remaining on board, viz.: beef, pork, flour, and bread, and report the following:—

Seven barrels beef unfit for use;
Six barrels pork entirely unfit for eating;

and since June, 1854, with the nicest selection, we got but sixty pounds eatable pork.

Four barrels flour in good condition;
Bread there is none left;

and in our opinion thirty-six days provisions is the most there is.

Very respectfully, your obedient servants,

HENRY BROOKS,
GEORGE RILEY,
WILLIAM MORTON.

Orders to Carpenter, Second Officer, and Mr. Bonsall, to examine and report on the condition of the Brig.

MESSRS. OHLSEN, MCGARY, BONSALL.

GENTLEMEN:—You will do me the favor to hold a careful survey upon the brig, and give me your opinion in writing whether it be possible to cut from her more firewood without rendering her unseaworthy.

Have we one month's firewood on board or in the ship?

Respectfully, your obedient servant,

E. K. KANE, *Commanding Expedition.*

BRIG ADVANCE, May 16, 1855.

Report on Condition of the Brig.

BRIG ADVANCE, May 17, 1855.

SIR:—In accordance with your orders, we have held a careful survey upon the brig, and give it as our decided opinion that we cannot cut from her more firewood without rendering her unseaworthy.

We have computed the present amount of firewood on board, including the trebling, to be equal to fourteen days' consumption.

We are, respectfully, your obedient servants,

CHRISTIAN OHLSEN, *Carpenter.*
J. McGARY, *Second Officer.*
AMOS BONSALL.

To E. K. KANE, Esq., *Commanding Expedition.*

No. IV.

Letter from the Hon. Secretary of the Navy to Lieut. Hartstene.

NAVY DEPARTMENT, May 25, 1855.

SIR:—A resolution of Congress, approved February 3, 1855, authorizes the Secretary of the Navy "to provide and despatch a suitable naval or other steamer, and, if necessary, a tender, to the Arctic seas, for the purpose of rescuing or affording relief to Passed Assistant Surgeon E. K. Kane, of the United States Navy, and the officers and men under his command."

The barque Release and steamer Arctic having been procured and especially fitted and equipped for this service under your supervision and inspection, with full rations and extra provisions for two years, and clothing peculiarly adapted for the climate of the Arctic regions, and such officers and men detailed as the Department, as well as yourself, considered necessary and sufficient, and the command of the expedition having been already assigned to you, you will, so soon as the above-named vessels are in all respects ready for sea, proceed with them, by all means as early as the first of June, in the prosecution of the object of the resolution of Congress, economizing as much as possible in the use of coal.

It is understood from reliable sources that you can renew your supply of coal at Waigat Island, at which point it would seem to be advisable that you should touch, unless unforeseen circumstances admonish you to do otherwise, or some more practicable point should be ascertained by you. I will endeavor to procure and forward to you letters of introduction from the representative of Denmark to the governor of the Danish settlements, at which it may be useful and prudent that you should touch, for the purpose of making inquiry and procuring information.

Dr. Kane sailed from New York in the Advance early in June, 1853, since which time the Department has received no information from him. It is believed, however, that intelligence was received of him at Upernavik in July, 1853, by his father, Judge Kane, of Philadelphia. The expedition was then going north; and this is the last that has been heard from it. The Department, however, learns, and deems it proper to put you in possession of the information, that it was the intention of Dr. Kane, after leaving Upernavik, on his way up to make a depot of provisions and erect a beacon, &c. at Cape Alexander, the east cape of Smith's Sound, or at Cape Isabella,—most probably the former. The department further learns that it was then the intention of Dr. Kane to pass up Smith's Sound and proceed west; and in case it was necessary for him to abandon his vessel he would make for Beechy Island.

Should you fall in with any of Franklin's party, your own humane feelings will suggest the propriety of extending to them all the relief in your power.

Before sailing, you will acquaint Lieutenant C. C. Simms, who has been ordered to command the Arctic, and whom of course you will consider as your second in command, fully with all your plans and intentions, and appoint places of rendezvous, so that, in case the two vessels of the expedition may at any time become separated, each may know where to look for the other.

You will seize any opportunity that may offer of communicating with the Department, informing it of your progress and your future movements; and you will also take particular care to avail yourself of every occasion for leaving, as you proceed, records and signs to tell of your condition and intentions. For this purpose you will erect flagstaffs, make piles of stones, or other marks, in conspicuous places, burying a bottle at the base containing your letters. Should the two vessels be separated, you will direct Lieutenant Simms to do likewise.

The Department has every confidence in your judgment, and relies implicitly upon your sound discretion. You are aware of the generous considerations which prompted Congress to authorize this mission of humanity. I have determined to trust you with its execution, *untrammelled by stringent directions, which might embarrass you and conflict with the suggestions of circumstances and developments of the future.* Judge Kane, the father of the doctor, is in possession of much important information left by his son, to be used in the event of a search for him. This will aid you much. I would suggest, however, that you should, unless constrained by strong hopes of future success, avoid passing a winter in the Arctic regions, and on no account uselessly hazard the safety of the vessels under your command, or, what is of more importance, unnecessarily expose to danger the officers and men committed to your charge. Your attention is also especially directed to the care and preservation of their health, for which hygienics have been abundantly furnished.

I transmit herewith, for your information and guidance, a copy of the instructions to Dr. Kane, dated November 27, 1852, as also copies of a series of letters from Sir Edward Parry, Sir Francis Beaufort, and other Arctic authorities, written by command of the British Admiralty, and kindly furnished to Dr. Kane, with the object of advancing the interests of the expedition to which he had been assigned by the Department.

Sincerely trusting that you may be enabled to carry out successfully the objects of the expedition under your command, and that a divine Providence will protect you in the hazardous enterprise for which you and your companions have so nobly volunteered,

I am, respectfully, your obedient servant,

J. C. DOBBIN.

Lieut. HENRY J. HARTSTENE,
U. S. Navy, Commanding Expedition for Relief of Dr. Kane and Companions, New York.

Report of Lieut. Hartstene to the Hon. Secretary of the Navy.

UNITED STATES BARQUE RELEASE,
LIEVELY, ISLE OF DISCO, GREENLAND, July 9, 1855.

SIR:—I have the honor to inform you of the arrival of the Arctic expedition here on the 5th instant, after a most boisterous passage, during most of which we were enveloped in dense fogs, and were much retarded by towing the Arctic nearly to the southern point of Greenland, where it was deemed advisable to separate, that this vessel might hasten on to make some necessary arrangements; but, much to my agreeable surprise, by good management and favorable winds, our consort came in a few hours after us, having used steam but for a short time.

The first iceberg was seen in latitude 51° 30′ N., longitude 51° 40′ W.; and about sixty miles farther north we found thick extreme ridges of "sailing ice," so heavy as to make it necessary to avoid them, which we successfully managed during daylight; but, after dark, while going under all sail six knots, we ran suddenly into one of them, bringing us up all standing, and caused our consort, towing astern, to foul us, without, however, doing any material damage. Pressing on, we bored through, and had but fairly relieved ourselves, when we encountered a heavy blow, with much sea and ice in all directions, requiring incessant care and manœuvring to prevent being thrown against, to the inevitable destruction of the vessels. Since then, we have had bergs daily in sight. The numbers increased as we advanced north to this place, off where there are now several hundred, stalking quietly and majestically.

The accounts of the extreme severity of the present winter have induced me to remain here a few days to have a quantity of fur clothing prepared, to enable us to winter, as we shall probably be compelled to do, with more safety in the Arctic ice. Through the many facilities offered, and the obliging kindness of Mr. Olrik, the government agent, we have succeeded in effecting all, and are now ready and will leave this day for the Waigat Strait, to take as much coal as possible, and proceed north to Cape Alexander, touching off Upernavik for information.

Our records and communications, at the different points touched at after entering the ice-barrier, will be deposited in bottles buried within twelve feet north by compass of cairns erected on the most conspicuous and accessible points.

To avoid further risk of human life in a search so extremely hazardous, I would suggest the impropriety of making any efforts to relieve us if we should not return, feeling confident that we shall be able tc accomplish all necessary for our own release under the most extraordinary circumstances.

In conclusion, it affords me much pleasure to state that we are all well and in full spirits.

Very respectfully, &c., your obedient servant,

H. J. Hartstene,

Lieutenant commanding Arctic Expedition.

Hon. J. C. Dobbin,

Secretary of the Navy, Washington, D. C.

Report of Lieut. Hartstene to the Hon. Secretary of the Navy.

UNITED STATES BARQUE RELEASE, OFF UPERNAVIK, July 16, 1855.

SIR:—Herewith enclosed is a duplicate of my last communication, left at Lievely, to be sent to its destination by the first opportunity.

On the 10th, in company with the Arctic, we started from the latter place for the coal-district in Waigat Strait; but, on arriving off the supposed position of it, the weather became so boisterous and thick that, after several times narrowly escaping running on shore by shaving the coast too close, I reluctantly abandoned the idea of losing time here on an uncertainty, and made immediately for this port, where we have just arrived. While becalmed off Hare Isle, at the northwest entrance of the Waigat Strait, I succeeded in obtaining there about nine tons of inferior coal, which, however, will answer very well for cooking-purposes.

On our passage up we fell in with two English whalers who had been up as far as Horsehead Isle, and, after ineffectual efforts to enter Melville Bay, had given it up, and were on their way to try the western coast. They represented the last winter as having been very severe and the ice now unusually close, and think we shall not be able to enter for several weeks.

I shall remain here but a few hours, to obtain some furs, and by to-morrow morning will be at the ice-barrier, as we have a strong favorable wind.

There is no news of the missing party. We are all well.

Very respectfully, your obedient servant,

H. J. HARTSTENE,

Lieutenant commanding Arctic Expedition.

Hon. J. C. DOBBIN,

Secretary of the Navy, Washington, D. C.

Report of Lieut. Hartstene to the Hon. Secretary of the Navy.

UNITED STATES BARQUE RELEASE, BAFFIN'S BAY,
Lat. 69° 39′ N., lon. 63° 30′ W., September 8, 1855.

SIR:—We have suddenly and unexpectedly fallen in with an English whaler, which necessitates me to draw up, rather hastily, an account of our efforts since my last communication of the 16th of July, from Upernavik, on the afternoon of which date both vessels stood to the northward, and in a few hours met the ice drifting down in an extended floe, but so loose as to permit of our working along under sail some forty miles to Wedge Island, where its compactness obliged us to moor to bergs and await several days, when suddenly, and without any apparent cause but the remarkably mysterious currents, it disappeared and left us open water, through which we steamed uninterruptedly to Sugar-Loaf Island, and entered the closely-packed floe of Melville Bay, through which, by strenuous and untiring efforts, and being so fortunate as never to have entered a false lead or to have lost any by drifts, we forced a passage into the North Water on the morning of the 13th August, twenty-eight days after our entrance of the barrier. With our invaluable little "Arctic" ahead, we passed within good view of the coast from Cape York to Wostenholme Island, when I deemed it advisable and hastened on in the steamer (leaving this vessel in charge of Lieutenant Simms, to follow with all despatch) to Cape Alexander, which, with Sutherland Island near to, both most conspicuous points, beyond the reach of Esquimaux, were thoroughly examined; but not the slightest evidence was found to indicate that they had ever before been trodden by civilized men. Much chagrined and disappointed, I deposited a record of our visit, and further instructions for the "Release;" then rounded the cape with a strong head-wind, and ice extending in a compact mass to the western shore and as far north as could be seen, leaving, however, a narrow lead so near the land as to allow us to discern the smallest objects. We passed on; but naught was seen until we reached the most northwestern point in sight, which we supposed to be Cape Hatherton, but was afterward proved to be Pelham Point, where a few stones were observed together. A party, with Acting Master Lovell and Dr. Kane, of the steamer, landed immediately, and found beneath this carelessly-erected mark a small vial with the letter K cut in the cork, containing a large mosquito, with a small piece of cartridge-paper for one of Sharpe's rifles, prepared in Philadelphia, the ball of which was lying by it: on this was written, apparently with the point of the ball, "Dr. Kane, 1853." This was extremely perplexing, but assured us of his having been there, and I determined to push on as far north as possible. But, on rounding this point, which was found to be in latitude 78° 32′ N.,—farther, it is believed, than any one before had ever reached on this side,—we were opposed by a solid, hummocky field of very heavy ice, to which no limit was visible, interspersed with many bergs, all drifting to the southward. Under sail, we dropped with it, anxiously watching for an opening, examining Cape Hatherton and Littleton Island in our retrograde, without any success, though Dr. Kane, in his last letter to his brother, which I have adopted as my guide, emphatically says, "On Cape Alexander or Cape Hatherton I will deposit my boat and erect a 'cairn.'" We finally took refuge under a projecting point, some fifteen miles northwest of Cape Alexander, when we were startled by the hail of human voices. A party, including myself and the surgeon of the "Arctic," brother of Dr. Kane, started off forthwith, exultingly, with light hearts, confident that they were of the missing party; but, after a long and anxious pull, we were met by two Esquimaux, who appeared very anxious to go off to the brig; but, on being refused, they significantly pointed up a deep, most beautiful, and finely-sheltered bay, inducing us to think that there was there a settlement; and, as we should lose no time, I assented. And well were we compensated for our trouble; for, after reaching the bottom of it, some three miles distant, we landed, and soon reached a settlement of some thirty of them, in seven tents, all covered with canvas. We now discovered many other articles, such as tin pans and pots, canvas, and iron spikes, preserved-meat cans, a knife and fork, bake-pan for a vessel's galley, various spools of thread, several Guernsey frocks, and a cotton shirt, with the initials "H. B." marked with red thread, which was supposed to have been undoubtedly the property of the boatswain of the "Advance," whose wife was a Mahonese, and the marking was evidently her handiwork. There were also broken oars and pieces of slats; and, finally, we found the tube of a telescope, which was recognised as having belonged to Dr. Kane. A close examination of the most intelligent of them, at three separate periods, by myself, Mr. Lovell, and Dr. Kane's brother, aided by an Esquimaux vocabulary and representations in drawing of vessels, persons, and boats, put us in possession of what I believe to be the fact,—viz.: that Dr. Kane, (whose name the natives pronounced very distinctly, and described most unmistakingly his appearance,) having lost his vessel in the ice somewhere to the north of this, had been here, with Carl Petersen (his interpreter) and seventeen others, in two boats and a sled, and, after remaining ten days, they went south, to Upernavik. With all these evidences, I deemed it my duty to return south, touching again at Cape Alexander and Sutherland Islands; and, joining the barque, towed her to Hakluyt Island to water ship and examine for relics. In the mean time the south side of Northumberland Island was passed and repassed by the "Arctic," she returning; and with the barque we stood over to the entrance of Lancaster Sound, and, thinking possibly he may have gone to Beechy Island, I left the barque, to examine the coast between Capes Horsburg and Warrander, and, in the "Arctic," attempted to reach the island; but, after passing Cape Bullin, found the field-ice firmly packed, which we coursed from shore to shore, without any opening to induce a further attempt. In the mean time we became firmly beset; and the weather, becoming thick with snow, led me to suppose for a time that we were in our winter quarters; but, by dint of steam and a powerful bow, we succeeded, after twenty-four hours' heavy battering, in relieving ourselves. Returning off the cruising-ground of our consort, and not seeing her, I ran north as far as Cape Combermere, where we were again opposed by a solid barrier of the firmest ice; thus having made nearly the whole circuit of the northern part of Baffin's Bay, with the exception of a deep indentation between Capes Combermere and Isabella, which, from its ice-bound and cheerless appearance, forbade the idea of any one having attempted to land on its shores. We then returned, and, in company, visited and examined Possession and Pond's Bays, firing guns, burning blue-lights, and throwing up rockets; but here again we were disappointed, and I unhesitatingly deemed it my duty to proceed forthwith to Upernavik, feeling confident that the party had gone there through Melville Bay,—no uncommon undertaking, as the crews of many whalers lost in the ice had done so before. Therefore, on the morning of the 31st of August we again pushed on for the ice-barrier, which we passed, after many difficulties and narrow escapes, in one of which the vessel was, in a snow-storm, brought in collision with an iceberg, against whose sides she was thrown most ruthlessly for several hours, to our apparent inevitable destruction, but from which she was finally released, with slight damages to her starboard upper works.

In conclusion, I would add, we are all well; and, should we not meet with the missing party at Upernavik, shall ágain proceed north and winter in the ice.

Very respectfully, your obedient servant,

H. J. Hartstene,
Lieutenant commanding Arctic Expedition.

Hon. J. C. Dobbin,
Secretary of the Navy, Washington, D. C.

Report of Lieut. Hartstene to the Hon. Secretary of the Navy.

United States Barque Release, New York, October 11, 1855.

Sir:—I have the honor to report the arrival here, this day, of the Arctic expedition, with Dr. Kane and his associates, who were received on board at Lievely, where they had arrived several days previous, having deserted their brig in Smith's Sound, about thirty miles to the northward and eastward of the farthest point reached by us, and, by unprecedented energy and determination, made their way down in boats and sledges.

In five days after my last communication to the Department (a copy of which, as well as of all others since leaving, are herewith enclosed) we succeeded in "boring" a passage through the middle "pack" of Baffin's Bay, and in reaching Lievely, where we were detained until the 18th ultimo, coaling, watering, and preparing to receive our increased numbers. Sailing on that day in company with the "Arctic," we have, without any incident worthy of note, returned all in health.

No traces whatever of Sir John Franklin or his party were discovered.

Our vessels have both proved themselves all that could have been desired, particularly the "Arctic," she having, in addition to her steam-motive power, the qualities of a good, weatherly, moderate-sailing vessel. They have been pretty severely nipped and chafed by the ice, but are generally in good condition.

I enclose a list of the officers, men, and crews of the "Release" and "Arctic," as well as of Dr. Kane's party.

As the crews of both vessels were shipped with the understanding that they were to be discharged on the return of the expedition to the United States, I respectfully request authority from the Department to pay them off.

I am, very respectfully, your obedient servant,

H. J. HARTSTENE,

Lieutenant commanding Arctic Expedition.

Hon. J. C. DOBBIN,

Secretary of the Navy, Washington, D. C.

List of the Officers and Crew of the United States barque Release.

H. J. Hartstene, lieutenant commanding.
James Laws, acting assistant surgeon.
Wm. S. Lovell, acting master.
Jos. P. Fyffe, passed midshipman.
Van R. Hall, boatswain.
Charles Sever, captain's clerk.

Thomas Franklyn, purser's steward.
Richard M. Clarke, surgeon's steward.
Robert Bruce, boatswain's mate.
William Smith do.
David Batey, captain of foretop.
Charles Johnson, captain of maintop.
George Devys, gunner's mate.
Thomas Ford, do.
William Phinney, quartermaster.
Joseph Morris, do.
Benjamin Moore, sailmaker's mate.
Charles Williams, carpenter's mate.
Francis Taylor, captain of hold.
William Henry, ship's cook.
Louis Lawrence, seaman.
Andrew Lawson, do.
Byron Potter, do.
John Haley, do.
John Smith, do.
George Bidwold, do.

PASSENGERS.

Passed Assistant Surgeon E. K. Kane, United States Navy.

John W. Wilson,
Amos Bonsall,
I. I. Hayes,
August Sontag,
Henry Goodfellow,
William Morton,
Geo. Stephenson,
Thomas Hickey,
} Belonging to Dr. Kane's party.

List of the officers and crew of the United States steam-brig Arctic.

Charles C. Simms, lieutenant commanding.
John K. Kane, acting assistant surgeon.
Watson Smith, acting master.
Harman Newell, 1st assistant engineer.

William Johnston, acting 3d assistant engineer.
John Van Dyke, purser's steward.
Abraham W. Kendell, surgeon's steward.
Samuel Whiting, acting boatswain.
William Richardson, acting carpenter.
William Carey, boatswain's mate.
John Blinn, do.
William Grover, quartermaster.
Walter Wilkinson, do.
Richard Hartley, captain of hold.
Joseph Brown, ship's cook.
John Fox, 2d class fireman.
John Gilbert, do.
George Tyler, do.
John Thompson, seaman.
John Brown. do.
George Price, do.
James Botsford, do.

PASSENGERS BELONGING TO DR. KANE'S PARTY.

Boatswain Henry Brooks, U. S. Navy.
James McGary.
George Riley.
William Godfrey.
Charles Blake.
George Whipple.

No. V.

Report of a Journey by Messrs. Bonsall and McGary to establish Provision-Depôts along the Greenland Coast.

SIR:—We have the honor to submit the following report, taken from the journal and field-notes of our party.

September 20, Tuesday.—We left the ship about one o'clock with the "Sledge Faith" and seven men, and arrived at Coffee Gorge at eight o'clock. As it was low-water, we were unable to gain the land-ice, and encamped on the floe. You accompanied us for the first stage of our journey with the dogs.

September 21, Wednesday.—Started this morning about eight o'clock and travelled until noon, when, as we were about to halt for dinner, we came upon weak ice, which gave way. The after-part of the sledge went down, but the floats prevented it from sinking. In order to draw it out without breaking the ice, we unlashed and took off part of the load. Our thermometer was broken, and some few of the articles were wet; every thing else was uninjured. At 2 P.M. we concluded to pitch our tent, as we could not get on the land-ice until high-water; besides, Mr. McGary and two of the men were very wet. By 4 P.M. we succeeded in drawing up the sledge, and reloaded for an early start the next morning.

September 22, Thursday.—At 8 A.M. we set off on the land-ice, and at the expiration of two hours found we had travelled only two miles. We then spent two hours in lowering down the sledge and cargo upon the bay-ice, which we found perfectly strong. But by this time the ice had set off from the shore, and four of us were forced to walk about a mile up the land-ice before we found a suitable place of descent. We then travelled about five miles on the floe, when we were stopped by an open crack. We attempted to get on the land-ice again, but, finding that impossible, we started out into the bay, hoping to cross it on the old floe; but this we failed to do, as the crack ran through it to an indefinite extent. We therefore determined to return to the point we had left and await the flood-tide, which would close the crack. We encamped near the land-ice, with a strong wind blowing from the S.E. accompanied by snow.

September 23, Friday.—This morning Mr. McGary started off shore to search for a crossing-place, the ice being not yet closed. He returned at 7 A.M. and reported that the lead was closing, and in half an hour crossed it in perfect safety. We travelled quite rapidly over the smooth ice for two miles, when we came to more thin ice, but by careful search and trial found a place sufficiently strong to bear us. At this point we found an open crack running off shore, and were forced to unship the cargo from the sledge and get it upon the land-ice, on which we progressed with difficulty about a mile, when we found it necessary to divide our load and transport half of it at a time. In this manner we travelled until 6 P.M., when we encamped on the land-ice, and Mr. McGary and one of the men returned about four miles to procure water.

September 24, Saturday.—Started at 7.30 A.M., and found, after walking a few hundred paces, that we should be able to regain the floe-ice. This occupied us about an hour and a half. The ice was from twelve to sixteen inches thick. Encamped at 5 P.M. about ten miles from Chimney Rock.

September 25, Sunday.—We did not start till 9 A.M., as it was Sunday. We then pushed forward toward Cape Russell over old floe-ice well covered with snow and quite smooth. About 2 P.M. we made the cairn, and proceeded to cache the pemmican, (bag No. 5, weight 105 lbs.,) also one-half of our meal and half a bag of bread, at the base of the rock on which the cairn is built, being about one thousand paces from a prominent cape, and the same distance from the cape west of it. Encamped near the cliffs at 4 P.M., having travelled about fourteen miles. We took no observations, the weather being cloudy.

September 26, Monday.—We started at 7.30 A.M., and, having smooth ice, made about two and a half miles per hour. The coast has nearly the same trend as that of yesterday, (E.S.E.) About 11 A.M. we discovered a deep gorge running into the land, and stopped there a short time to find water, but without success. We named this spot "Sunny Gorge;" as its course was S.E. and N.W., the sun shone directly upon it, while at the same time we were in the shadow of the cliffs. We discovered the remains of five Esquimaux huts, which, though very old and in ruins, appeared to be larger and better constructed than any we had seen before. We also met with our first bear tracks to-day; but they were apparently a week old. This morning our cook shot a silver-gray fox near our tent. During the night the wind blew quite strong from the E., and this morning changed to N.E. with a light breeze; but I took compass-bearings and approximate distances of the most prominent objects along the line of coast. At noon when we halted for dinner we were forced to melt ice to drink, as we were very thirsty. At 4 P.M. we came to some running water in a gorge, the first we had seen since we left Glacier Bay. From this point we discovered an island or point, apparently about six miles in length, running out from the cliffs, and partly forming the coast of a bay. After making preparations for repelling the bears in case they should discover our pemmican, we turned in, having travelled from sixteen to eighteen miles.

September 27, Tuesday.—Set off at 8 A.M., and walked about twenty miles over the bay toward yesterday's station, where we arrived about 3 P.M. From this point the land changes, from the high cliffs of limestone and greenstone, to rolling hills of red granite, which trend a little to the S. of E., and are intersected by small bays and islands. We have been looking out, but without success, for the dark mass seen by you from Cape George Russell when on the first travelling party. Encamped about 4 P.M., having made about fifteen miles.

September 28, Wednesday.—Left our encampment about 8 A.M., and pushed on in the face of an easterly snow-storm, which fell so thick that we could not see the coast-line more than a few yards ahead; but, having taken bearings on the preceding day, we were not at a loss. Last night, owing to the thawing of the ice, our buffalo-skin became very wet, which rendered us extremely cold and uncomfortable. In the afternoon we arrived at a suitable point for making the second cache, and deposited the pemmican bag No. 3, weighing 110 lbs., and half a bag of bread. We built a cairn upon the rock above the cache, to mark the spot, which bears from the centre of the cairn E. by N.¼N. distant ten paces. It being late, we pitched our tent, having travelled this day about fourteen miles. By placing some loose articles under the buffalo, we were much more comfortable than on the preceding night. The temperature was so much lower than we had yet experienced, that our stockings froze to the soles of our boots; yet none of us were frost-bitten.

September 29, Thursday.—We could not set out till 8 A.M., owing to the sickness of two of our men, who got better, however, after travelling an hour or two. About twenty miles above our encampment the glacier comes down to the shores of the sound, covering the land completely, and extending as far as the eye can reach toward the N. by E. The weather was extremely cold. We made about twelve miles to-day.

September 30, Friday.—It was clear and very cold all the day. Mr. McGary, myself, and two of the men, were slightly frost-bitten. We passed almost parallel with the glacier, (about N. by E.;) but, as the refraction was very great, we were not a little confused as to our coast-line, though we thought we saw dark land to the northward. At

4.30 P.M. we halted and pitched our tent, having travelled eleven or twelve miles. As the sun went down the cold increased, so that it was nearly morning by the time we felt comfortable.

October 1, Saturday.—We started at 8.15 A.M., and travelled N. by E. over very heavy floe. The snow, which had been gradually deepening, was about six or seven inches in depth, and very cold to our feet, although none of us were frost-bitten to-day. The cold, being so intense, induced us to halt earlier than usual, having travelled only about ten miles. We have had but little encouragement to-day, as we can see nothing but glacier as far as the eye can reach. The men complain of cold at night, and we get but little sleep. Owing to the severe cold, I found it impossible to write my log: I wrote it this morning in the sunshine. To-day we burned the last of our alcohol, though we used it with the greatest economy. We attempted to burn rum, but found it was not sufficiently strong. We then had recourse to the staves of the cask and other small pieces of wood, together with a few pounds of lard. We progressed about ten or twelve miles to-day, having struck a lead of smooth ice which ran in our course.

October 2, Sunday.—We found the travelling much better than yesterday, as we followed the lead of last evening. We are still looking out for land to the northward, none being in sight even from the highest bergs. The nights become sensibly colder as we advance, and lately some of us have suffered considerably from cramp in the limbs, though no serious cases have occurred. Mr. McGary, who has not slept for several nights, is now quite unwell. We made to-day about twelve miles, having had comparatively good travelling, although the snow is deep.

October 3, Monday.—Last night we slept more comfortably than we had done for some time. This morning an easterly gale sprung up directly off the glacier, which blew the snow so much as to make the travelling impracticable; and, my frozen feet rendering me quite lame, we resolved to remain in our tent. Mr. McGary and two men walked to a berg about two miles distant, and in two hours returned with the news that they saw land at a long distance to the north of us.

October 4, Tuesday.—This morning, the gale having subsided, we prepared for an early start. We dug our sledge out of the drift and made for the land sighted yesterday. The wind, having packed the snow, made it more firm, and rendering the travelling easier. About 3 P.M. we halted to melt snow for drink, but the high wind made it difficult to keep the fire burning. While some of the party were cooking supper, others climbed a high berg, and on their return reported better ice than we have had for some time; also, from present appearances, a fair prospect of making land in two days more. We have advanced about ten or twelve miles. The wind is east, and weather cloudy. All our fuel is expended.

October 5, Wednesday.—Started about 7 A.M.; but, as I lost my watch-key, we could only guess the time by the sun. About 11 A.M. we came to an almost impenetrable mass of bergs, and were soon stopped by an open crack running nearly E. and W. for several miles in each direction from our position. It was about thirty fathoms wide. We sent parties out to seek a crossing; but, finding it was a tide-crack extending probably many miles, we concluded to await the turn of the tide, which would close it. On the opposite side we could discern nothing but high icebergs with narrow passages between them choked up by hummocks and squeezed ice. Finding it impossible to make land to the eastward, we attempted to cross to the westward; but, seeing no change in the appearance of the ice, we pitched our tent and turned in, as it was near sunset. We begin to fear we shall be obliged to return to the other side of the glacier, owing to the bad appearance of the ice; besides, as the men are growing weaker, and are still affected with cramp, they are less able to draw the sledge over the increasing difficulties of the way. With all our toil, we made this day but eight miles in a straight line.

October 6, Thursday.—The crack closed last night. To-day we rose early, crossed it about 6 A.M., and commenced forcing our way among hummocks and squeezed ice. After twisting about among the bergs for two or three hours and advancing only about a mile, we came to a full stop; and, as we found it impossible to proceed, we left the sledge. Five of the party started on foot through the ravines between the bergs, crossed three more cracks, but found great difficulty in walking, on account of the broken character of the ice. After travelling about two miles through the gorges we ascended to the top of an iceberg, whence a desolate scene burst upon our view. Before us, at the distance of twenty-five or thirty miles, the land, which runs about W.N.W. and E S.E., assumed the character of the coast near Cape Frederick VII.;* but between us and the land was a solid mass of bergs having narrow passages between them similar to those we had just passed through. In taking the bearings of the most prominent points with the sextant, I froze my fingers severely. Finding it impossible to progress farther in our course toward the land, we turned

* This name was applied by my predecessor to a supposed cape. We retained the name during our early parties for a large headland in lat. 78° 55·8′, long. 68° 50′.—E. K. K.

back very reluctantly, as our near approach to it had raised our hopes. In the mean time Mr. McGary had been in another direction, but returned equally unsuccessful. We therefore concluded to make for the first land on the S. side of the glacier and deposit the pemmican. After hard labor we regained the crack we had crossed this morning, but, finding it open, we were forced to wait till it closed. This morning our cook wounded a fox, which gave two of the men a long chase before they secured it. Baker is quite unwell to-day.

October 7, Friday.—Last night the crack closed, but we feared to cross it in the dark. This morning we rose about five o'clock, but were obliged to wait till eight, as the crack was not sufficiently close to admit of our crossing. We had just passed over it when it began to open, and before we had finished lashing our sledge it had opened several feet. About 9 A. M. we pursued our way outside of the bergs on the S. side of the crack, and found the ice much better for travelling. We headed directly for the point on the S. side of the sound. Encamped about 4 P.M., the weather excessively cold. Some of the men complain of frozen feet. Baker is much better.

October 8, Saturday.—Started this morning at sunrise and travelled fast over the floe, which was comparatively smooth. It was so cold that we could not stop to rest, and for the same reason took a very short time for dinner. Yesterday we took more of the alcohol for cache, as the gallon we first took had been consumed. I think we lost both rum and alcohol by evaporation. This evening I opened the thermometers which were sent for deposit at the cache, and found, much to my regret and disappointment, that they were both broken, although they were packed securely. I had my nose and two of my fingers frozen to-day. I was not aware of my nose being frozen until I was informed of it, when I had it rubbed with snow, which seemed to make it worse. Mr. McGary's feet were frozen again to-day. A strong breeze sprung up from the E. about 7 P.M. We made about fifteen miles.

October 9, Sunday.—The wind ceased during the night, and this morning we started at sunrise. We had smooth ice, and made good speed. About 10 A.M. a white fox came in view. I shot him without injuring the skin. We had hoped to make the cache-point this evening, but at sunset we were still several miles from it; and, as it became very cold, we concluded to encamp. We travelled about seventeen miles to-day.

October 10, Monday.—We started at 7 A.M.; and, as the sun had not yet risen, the cold was so severe that we could scarcely prevent our faces from being frozen. About 9 A.M. we made the point of the island, to which we carried our bags of pemmican and our heaviest stores, which we covered with the largest stones we could find, to prevent the animals from attacking our meat. This was laborious work, as the stones had to be carried some distance up the hill. After stopping up every crevice a fox could work through, we covered it with loose stones and moss. While we were employed in building the cache, Mr. McGary was engaged in making a stew of one of the foxes we had shot, in which operation he froze his finger severely. We built the cairn on a point of rock thirty paces E.½S. from the cache, and at the same distance from the point of a remarkable rock on the highest part of the island, bearing S. by W.½W. There were two small islands about two thousand paces from the cache, the larger bearing E. by N.½N., and the smaller E.N.E. Owing to the severity of the cold, I was unable to take sextant-bearings of these points; but, from the situation of the island and positions of the cache and cairn, as well as the fixed points, it could readily be found. As it was nearly night by the time we had finished our cache, we concluded to encamp on the island. This was the coldest day we had yet experienced.

October 11, Tuesday.—After a cold and sleepless night, we set out very early, and travelled fast, in order to reach the cache where we had left half a bag of bread. We arrived there after a hard day's travel of about twenty-five miles.

October 12, Wednesday.—Started very early this morning, and travelled fast, stopping at noon only, to melt snow, as we were all very thirsty. Made about fifteen miles this day.

October 13, Thursday.—Set out early, and walked fast, in order to gain a stream of water we had passed on our outward journey. We reached it about 10 A.M., but found it frozen solid. We then took some moss, and melted enough for a drink. We hurried on, hoping to meet Cape Frederick before nightfall; but in about an hour we came to an open crack, which checked our progress for the time, as we tried in vain to get on the land-ice. We waited until after dark; but, as the crack did not close, we pitched our tent. Just then a white fox came in sight, which was soon shot, making the fifth since leaving the vessel. The day closed with a high wind and a snow-storm. We made about twelve miles.

October 14, Friday.—Rose this morning at peep of day, crossed the crack, which was now closed, and pushed on for Cape Frederick. We were arrested by cracks and bay-ice every half mile; and, as this was all solid floe when we passed it in going out, there must have been a strong gale here since then. Opposite Sunny Gorge we came to an open crack, which delayed us about half an hour; but, finding a loose piece of ice sufficiently large to bear us and our sledge, we ferried ourselves over without difficulty. About camping-time we arrived opposite to our first cache, but were unable to get upon the land-ice, owing to the low tide. In passing the place where we cached the fox on our outward journey, we found foxes and ravens had eaten the carcass, leaving scarcely a vestige of it. We made to-day about fifteen miles.

October 15, Saturday.—Early this morning, the tide having risen, we endeavored to secure some bread from the cache. This we accomplished by one man standing upon the shoulders of another. We immediately set off, but were soon stopped by a crack, which we crossed about a mile farther up. We then came to the bay, and, steering direct for the opposite cape, would have crossed without difficulty; but, as we neared the cape, the ice was broken up, and about sunset we came to a crack about one hundred fathoms wide, which it seemed impossible to cross; but in about half an hour we succeeded in detaching a large piece of ice, on which we ferried ourselves over as before. We travelled on over the smooth ice till near dark, when we came to another crack, which we did not attempt to cross, but pitched our tent and turned in. On the return of flood-tide the cracks closed, and, by sending a man ahead to try the strength of the ice, we succeeded in crossing fifteen cracks in the space of four or five miles. We encamped for the night, having travelled about twenty-five miles.

October 16, Sunday.—We set off at daylight, determined, if possible, to reach the vessel to-day. We headed directly for the cape of the bay in which our vessel was lying. About two hours after starting, we discovered an object nearly three miles from us in-shore, which on a nearer approach proved to be a tent. Before reaching it, we discovered it to belong to our commander, who, with one of the men and the Newfoundland dogs and sledge, were coming to meet us; and we were very glad to see them after our long absence. We soon had a warm drink,—a luxury we had not tasted for a week. The party then took upon our sledge the tent and baggage of the dog-sledge; and, leaving the man with them, I returned to the vessel with you, after having fallen into the water,—no very pleasant affair with the thermometer below zero. We arrived at the vessel at half-past twelve o'clock, and Mr. McGary and party joined us about half-past three.

We remain your obedient servants,

James McGary,
Amos Bonsall.*

To Dr. E. K. Kane, *Commanding Arctic Expedition.*
Brig Advance, Smith's Sound, October 30, 1853.

* Compiled by me from the original field-notes.—A. Bonsall.

Field-Notes to the Journey of Messrs. McGary and Bonsall, September and October, 1853.

Date.		Time of starting.	Time of halt.	Course, (true.)	Distance. Stat. Miles.	REMARKS.
		h. m.	h. m.			
Sept.	20	1 0 P.M.	8 0 P.M.	N.N.E.	9	Halted at Coffee Gorge.
"	21	7 45 A.M.	12 0 M.	N.E.½E.	6	
"	22	8 0 A.M.	......	N.E.	7	
"	23	8 40 A.M.	6 0 P.M.	N.E. by E.	7	Crossed Bancroft Bay.
"	24	9 30 A.M.	5 30 P.M.	N.E. by E.	7	
"	25	9 0 A.M.	2 30 P.M.	N.E. by E.	9	Halted at cape.
"	25	4 30 P.M.	6 0 P.M.	E.N.E.	3	
"	26	7 30 A.M.	4 30 P.M.	E.N.E.	16	Passed Sunny Gorge at 11 A.M.
"	27	7 0 A.M.	3 0 P.M.	E.N.E.	15	Camped opposite bay.
"	28	8 0 A.M.	......	E.N.E.	14	Made Cache No. 2 at N.E. point of bay.
"	29	8 0 A.M.	......	N.E. by E.	12	Reached the large glacier.
"	30	......	......	N. by E.	11	Parallel with the glacier.
Oct.	1	8 15 A.M.	......	N. by E.	10	" " "
"	2	......	......	N. by E.	12	" " "
"	3	......	......	......	...	Gale from the E. laying up.
"	4	......	3 0 P.M.	N. by E.	10	Strong east wind.
"	5	7 0 A.M.	......	N. by E.	8	Parallel with the glacier.
"	6	......	......	N. by E.	1	Stopped by icebergs.
"	7	8 0 A.M.	4 0 P.M.	S. by W.	10	" "
"	8	8 30 A.M.	......	S. by W.	15	Parallel with glacier. Strong east wind.
"	9	8 30 A.M.	......	S. by W.	7	
"	10	7 0 A.M.	9 0 A.M.	S.	4	Reached Cache Island at 9 A.M.
"	11	......	......	S.S.W.	25	Reached Cache No. 2.
"	12	......	......	W.S.W.	15	Crossed opposite to cape of bay.
"	13	6 30 A.M.	......	W.S.W.	12	Snow and strong wind.
"	14	......	......	W.S.W.	25	Camped near cape.
"	15	......	......	S.W.byW.	25	Crossed bay.
"	16	......	3 30 P.M.	S.S.W.	...	Reached the brig.

Oct.	6	Angle between last Cape I. to the N.W. and the next cape to the right II.	18° 30′
		Angle between Cape II. and the next cape to the right III., Cape III. bearing true N. from place of observation	24° 30′
		Angle between Cape III. and bottom of bay to the right IV....	15° 18′
		" " IV and cape to the right of bay....................	15° 30′
"	10	POSITION.—Cache Island. Large island bearing E. by N.½N., (true.) Distance, 2000 yards. Small island bearing E.N.E., (true.)	

Journal of a Travelling Party into the Interior eastward from Rensselaer Harbor.

Party consisting of Mr. Wilson, Dr. Hayes, and Hans, the Esquimaux.

BRIG ADVANCE, March 29, 1854.

To DR. E. K. KANE, *Commanding American Arctic Expedition.*

The subjoined journal is a copy from a rough note-book kept daily, and the accompanying chart is projected from the field-notes.

Respectfully submitted, your obedient servant,

I. I. HAYES, *Surgeon to Expedition.*

September 8, Thursday.—Left the brig at 7 P.M., equipped by order as follows:—two buffalo-robes sewed together and covered with India-rubber cloth, to serve as a tent; thirty pounds of pemmican, two of bread, one of meat-biscuit, one of chocolate, and one of coffee, constituted our stock of provisions. Each man carried a tin-cup strapped to his waist, an extra pair of boots, (Esquimaux,) a Lady Franklin gun, and a Danish rifle. The tent weighed twenty-six pounds.

Our course lay due east, but from this we were obliged to deviate on meeting the inlet at the termination of the bay. We followed the course of a ravine, which afforded us a more level track, and encamped about eight miles from the brig, beside a small stream, which opened into a plain half a mile long by about a hundred yards broad, and covered with rich grass. One hare was seen during our march, and I observed a few single specimens of a saxifrage still in full bloom. A heath—Andromeda tetragona—which grew luxuriantly about the rocks and protected places afforded us a plentiful supply of fuel; and, had it not been completely saturated with snow, would have made us an admirable fire. At 11 P.M. our thermometer showed +17°.4 Fahrenheit.

September 9, Friday.—Set out at eleven o'clock, having first ascended the highest bluff within reach, from which I could sight the headlands of the bay, for the purpose of connecting our route with them and with the plateau beyond. We therefore travelled as nearly due east as the winding path among the rough syenitic bluffs would allow. We reached the base of the greenstone debris, and ascended it, at an angle of from 25° to 30°, to an elevation nearly equal to that of the headland before mentioned. A half mile brought us to the termination of a talus, which seemed to be succeeded by another beyond, and above a partially broken-down escarpment. We encamped in a gorge at 8.30 P.M., having travelled by rude estimate fifteen miles. A hare shot by

Mr. Wilson afforded us a good supper, cooked Esquimaux-fashion by Hans, on a flat stone, with the burning rags from around our pemmican. Thermometer at 3 P.M., +23°, at 11 A.M., +16°.2.

September 10, Saturday.—Ready and on our march at 10.30 A.M. A heavy fog which hung over the bay obscured the headlands, and prevented our connecting our position with that of any known point. We were, I supposed, at least two points to the south of east from the vessel. We ascended to the highest point of the plateau by a succession of steps, three in number, which brought us to an elevation one-third higher than the terminating headland. From this point we could see the syenites we had just left again cropping out much less bluffy, and terminating the table-land to the eastward by a continuous line, trending generally northwest and southeast. The opposite shore of the sound could be distinguished by high conical peaks; and a headland of the eastern shore was distinctly visible, with its table-land, which ran back until it was lost in the syenitic outcropping, which terminated the eastern view by a range of long bluffs, trending apparently north and south. To the southeast and south was visible a long continuous mist-bank, reaching 4° or 5° of altitude, and terminating below in vertical lines, alternately light and dark. This I supposed to be a great internal glacier, from fifty to sixty miles distant. Its upper line or surface was lost in the mist, and could in no place be determined. We reached the ridge to the eastward at 9 P.M., and encamped. As neither water nor fuel could be found, we were obliged to content ourselves with raw pemmican and a little brandy,—a meal by no means unpalatable after a hard journey of at least twenty miles.

September 11, Sunday.—Our route lay due east over a gently undulating country. Nearly every two miles we found a lake or pool, from which we procured water by breaking ice six or eight inches thick. The travelling was more tedious than over the unbroken plain of yesterday, as we had often to jump from rock to rock. But a single high bluff was seen. It was hemispherical, and from one hundred to one hundred and fifty feet high. Having made about eight miles, we encamped at 8 P.M. Thermometer at midnight, +9°.5. I found it impossible to lay down our track by a series of triangulations, as at the distance of a mile one point could not be distinguished from another. Many reindeer and fox-tracks were seen during the day, but no living thing passed within view.

September 12, Monday.—Set out at 10.30 A.M. Our route growing more interrupted by fissures and gorges, added to the difficulties of travel. On one occasion I tumbled headforemost down some rocks;

but happily the tent which I was carrying saved me from injury. The stock of my gun and my pocket-thermometer were broken. Hans expressed a determination to proceed no farther in our present course. He pointed east, exclaiming, "No good;" "Esquimaux none;" and, looking west, he said "Sloopkie," and started in the latter direction. On ascending the highest point in our vicinity, we discovered a river about three miles distant, running nearly northwest. This we showed our Esquimaux friend, whereupon he set off immediately and reached its banks at 8 P.M.—half an hour before we arrived. We travelled about ten miles to-day, and during our journey found the most luxuriant growth of andromeda which we have met with in North Greenland. Besides serving for fuel, a quantity of it spread under our tent made a much softer bed than the stones.

September 13, Tuesday.—Hans having expressed his unwillingness to go any farther, we thought it best to leave him in charge of the tent, &c., and, without the encumbrance of baggage, to proceed up the river. in order to find its source, which I hoped to do in one day's travel. I felt certain that the glacier we had sighted on the 10th could not be very distant. I supposed the river to be a continuation of that crossed by Dr. Kane with his first full party. About a mile from the tent we came to a fork in the river, one branch of which ran northwest, the other west. We followed the latter, and after ten miles' travel we came to a succession of terraced plains, occasionally appearing on either side of the stream, generally covered with rich grass, and marked in every direction by reindeer-tracks. We saw five of these animals feeding along the borders of the stream. These meadow-lands (for such they really seemed) indicated by their vegetable life a temperature much warmer than that along the coast, and in their apparent richness contrasted strangely with the desolate scenery around. This plain was at least two miles in diameter and about five in length. From this point we obtained the first sight of the glacier, which is about fifteen miles distant. We could see its upper surface in one continuous and unbroken line, through an arc of more than 90°. When within about half a mile of the glacier, a beautiful meteor fell directly before us, revealing in the dim twilight the real character of the huge mirror beneath us. From the glacier rose loud reports like distant thunder. It was nearly midnight when we reached its base, and we immediately undertook its ascent. Along the base, to the height of fifty or sixty feet, was a bank of snow continuous with the face of the glacier, and rising at an angle of 30°. This we ascended without difficulty; but the smooth surface of the ice baffled us in our attempts to scale it. I now wished for our tent, that we might rest here the following day and make further attempts to reach the summit of the glacier. We were already tired and cold.

September 14, Wednesday.—As constant exercise is necessary in order to keep warm, we set out on our return, and reached our encampment about noon, after a walk of twenty miles. The trend of this glacier is north-northeast, its altitude above the general level of the country from three hundred to four hundred feet, and the distance between its crevasses from twenty to forty feet. These crevasses are generally small, being from one to three feet wide, and about the same in depth, and partially filled with snow. The face of the glacier rose, at an angle of about 35°, to an elevation of one hundred and sixty feet, when it rounded off as it gradually approached the *mer de glace* above.

September 15, Thursday.—Having accomplished the object of our journey, we determined upon returning to the vessel, although we had been absent less than half the allotted time. We kept our old track until we reached the camping-ground of the fourth night out, when we struck off to the north of east. We saw three deer; but, with all the dexterity of an experienced hunter, Hans failed to approach them near enough for a shot. An old and weather-worn skull of a musk-ox was found during the day's march.

September 16, Friday.—We reached the brig at 3 A.M., after a continuous walk of nineteen hours, during which time we halted but for one meal.

Respectfully submitted,

I. I. HAYES, M.D., *Surgeon to the Expedition.*

Journal of a Party sent out to deposit a Self-Registering Thermometer at some available point to the northward of Marshall Bay, under charge of Dr. I. I. Hayes.

October 21, Friday.—Left the brig at a quarter-past eleven, the party consisting, besides myself, of Mr. Morton, steward, and John Blake, seaman. A sledge drawn by four Newfoundland dogs carried our tent, buffalo-robes, sleeping-bags, provisions,—in short, every thing practicable and necessary for comfort and convenience in Arctic travelling. Our only extra weight was a keg of alcohol, to be deposited in cache. I carried a pocket-sextant and portable compass strapped to my waist. For the first two miles we found the travelling excellent, over newly-formed ice intermingled with heavy pieces and hummocks. Our load being light, the dogs drew the sledge in a half-trot, causing us to keep up a brisk walk. On meeting with rough hummocky ice, we unharnessed the dogs and drew the sledge ourselves for the next two or three miles, passing Coffee Gorge and camping for the night about five miles beyond. It was the work of half an hour to pitch our tent, unharness our dogs, collect snow for water, and carefully stow our dogs in one side of our tent and ourselves in the other. On opening our provision-bag we were not a little mortified to find our fresh beef and pemmican had been forgotten, and were forced to make out with a much less palatable dish than our commander had kindly intended,—a stew of pork and bread.

October 22, Saturday.—Roused Morton and John at six, it being not yet quite light. A pot of coffee and pork-stew constituted our breakfast. By half-past eight we were on our march, and at twelve we halted to melt snow for the dogs opposite to the point to the eastward of Marshall Bay. I took sextant-altitudes of the cliffs, called by Commander Kane Tennyson Monument, stepping a base-line of two hundred yards. The results are:—height of cliffs to top of debris, seven hundred and twelve feet; height of debris, three hundred and fifty feet. Upon a rude estimate, the debris runs out at an angle of forty degrees. At half-past twelve we were off again on a "dog-trot," keeping a straight course for the outermost point of a large cape, hoping to reach it by noon of the following day. About three o'clock we pitched our tent in the centre of a large old floe, about ten miles from the nearest point of the opposite shore. We were here in full view of the bay, in the centre of which rose the rugged faces of the syenites,—the same range crossed in my inland journey in September. Chimney Rock was recognised as the same headland sighted from the plateau in that journey, bearing N. 50° E. By half-past five we were ready to turn in. On unwrapping the thermometer, to my great mortification and astonishment, I found it broken,—an accident which must have occurred in the lashing of the sledge. It was, however, most carefully wrapped in woollen, and placed in the centre of the sleeping-bags and buffalo-robes, so that I thought there could be no danger of accident. As I was much interested in the results to be obtained, the defeat was no small disappointment, and the idea of turning back, which appeared the only alternative, no less unpleasant. As endeavoring to obtain sights of the opposite coast-line and make a survey of this was secondary to the other object, I thought that, in the uncertainty of having clear weather, and the great probability that another effort would be made by Dr. Kane to obtain a result so desirable, it would be useless to proceed farther at present, except to deposit the keg of alcohol at the first cache made by Messrs. McGary and Bonsall near Chimney Rock. This I determined to do the next day. By immersing the broken thermometer in melting snow to ascertain rudely its correction, I found the temperature of the air to be —21° 5′, the wind, which had been blowing stiffly from the eastward, having nearly subsided. Morton and I had our hands severely frost-bitten during the day,—he in melting snow, and I in carelessly exposing my hands in manipulating with the sextant at Tennyson Monument. Alternate pounding and rubbing brought us off with each a single blister.

October 23, Sunday.—Were ready to start by 8.10 A.M. Morton and I occupied the place of the dogs in drawing the sledge, leaving John in charge of the dogs, tent, &c. We reached the cache at half-past twelve, a distance of fifteen miles. The cache remained undisturbed; but the numerous tracks around, and the efforts made to undermine the pile of stones, showed the necessity of great precaution in depositing provisions. The keg of alcohol was placed at one end of the bag of pemmican, and the cache additionally strengthened. The debris was mostly of limestone, and not extending so high as is common in those already passed. I was very anxious to fulfil the desire of Dr. Kane to obtain a suite of specimens of the cliffs and debris; but the cliffs were difficult to ascend, and, by the time I had reached half-way, I found it would be impossible to gain the top without first descending. Specimens of the rock, as far as I ascended, were carefully wrapped in paper and marked in series. A stiff breeze was blowing around the point, and, by the time I reached the bottom, I was so chilled that I felt little like making another effort; besides, I had already gone up by a gorge to take a look, without doing any good, and it was growing late. Sextant-altitudes were taken of the top of the greenstone and the debris, with a stepped base of two hundred paces, which gave severally six hundred and three hundred feet. Started back at three o'clock, a light snow falling. Reached the tent about 7 P.M.

October 24, Monday.—Commenced my journey at 10 A.M., passing over nearly the same track as on the 22d. We made the land-ice, to avail ourselves of the lee of the cliffs against the strong wind, and pitched our tent at a quarter-past three. We found, on unpacking the sledge, that a stanchion and top-bar had been broken. One of the dogs having made his exit at one corner of the tent two nights previously, John soon had us safely fastened in. We ate our stew, drank our coffee, and I smoked my last cigar; after which we pulled into our blanket-bags.

October 25, Tuesday.—Were ready and on our way to the brig by 9.45 A.M., keeping along the land-floe to Coffee Gorge. Dr. Kane had previously called my attention to a set of rocking-stones, the phenomena of which he explained satisfactorily. As soon as we sighted the vessel, the dogs kept us on a half-run until half-past one, at which time we reached it.

Very respectfully,

I. I. HAYES, *Surgeon to Expedition.*

To DR. E. K. KANE, *Commanding Arctic Expedition.*

Report of the Advance Party, and attempt to reach the Northern Shore, in charge of Henry Brooks.

RENSSELAER HARBOR, April 4, 1854.

SIR:—I have the honor to submit the subjoined abstract from our field-notes:—

March 19.—This day we left the brig at 1 P.M., and travelled in a northerly direction three miles, over very good new floes nearly parallel with the northeastern shore of Rensselaer Bay, and about two miles distant from it. The sledge dragged so heavily that at times it became immovable except by a standing pull. This was probably the effect of the intense cold, which causes the runners to adhere to the snow. Mr. Brooks desired me to return to the brig and inform you of our slow progress. At half past one o'clock you arrived with five men from our camp, bringing the big sledge as a substitute for the Esquimaux sledge, and the large India-rubber boat with two canisters of pemmican, which added greatly to our load.

March 20.—We started at 10 A.M., travelling over good ice; but the sledge dragged so heavily that Mr. Brooks first ordered the boat, and afterward the two canisters of pemmican, to be taken off. The latter were deposited on the south side of a hummock, on the top of which was placed a small red flag. I took the bearings of the neighboring icebergs and headlands, to aid in finding this spot again. To-day I noted two large icebergs which I saw last summer to the south of their present position. About the middle of August one was situated near Refuge Inlet, the other near Bedevilled Reach, (Force Bay,) and about four miles from shore. Mr. McGary and I ascended the latter in company with you. It is now situated about four miles from Coffee Gorge, and two miles from shore.

This afternoon we encountered the chain of icebergs which extends without interruption from the north point of Bedevilled Reach to first cape beyond Chimney Rock, or perhaps even farther north. These icebergs, which are very numerous, are generally long and flat, and situated close together. We crossed this chain from S.S.E. to N.N.W., and north from the north headland of Rensselaer Bay, its mean breadth being about three miles. These icebergs run parallel to the land except where bays are formed, in which case they stretch directly across from one headland to the other. Single icebergs are scattered on both sides of the chain to the distance of six miles.

To-day we travelled due north only two miles and a half; but following, as we did, a very tortuous road between hummocks and icebergs, our walk was increased to more than five miles. The latitude of our camp this night was 78° 44′; and the magnetic variation to-day was 111° S.W.

March 21.—A thick fog this morning made it impracticable to start before 10.30 A. M. We continued our course due north, winding round icebergs and hummocks. At noon I ascended an iceberg about eighty feet in height: the horizon was still obscured by fog, but as far as the eye could reach I could discover no level floes. The icebergs, moved by wind or tide, are driven against the floes and break them; which appears to be the cause of the formation of hummocks. The snow being in many places above our knees rendered the walking very fatiguing. In the afternoon we found the hummocks so high that we were forced to divide our load and draw only half of it over them at a time. By this arrangement we progressed but one mile and a half, although we walked more than four times that distance. At 6 P.M. the fog partially disappeared, when Mr. Petersen and I climbed to the summits of some icebergs, from whence we could see nothing but hummocks in every direction, though to the N.N.E. they seemed rather lower, and occasionally interrupted by small level floe-pieces.

March 22.—On setting out to-day we altered our course from due N. to N.N.E., crossing heavy hummocks during the first two hours. At 11 A.M., the hummocks becoming less, we again changed our course to due N., dragging our sledge over the deep snow which had accumulated in the ravines. In the afternoon we travelled over good new floes interspersed with hummocks, at one of which we found a seal-hole covered with thin ice. About 4 P.M. the fog became so thick as to conceal the land. We travelled by compass until 7 P.M., when we encamped in lat. 78° 49′ 5″, being four miles due north from our last station.

March 23.—This morning, seeing nothing but hummocks in our course, we took a N.W. direction over a very old floe, which made the sledging exceedingly heavy. At noon, after crossing some high hummocks, we came to another old floe, the extent of which could not be discerned on account of the fog. Here the sledge was so obstructed by snow that at times it could only be moved by a standing pull. By 4 P.M. we had crossed this floe, the diameter of which is about two miles. On its northern side it had come in contact with a new floe having tables seven feet thick, with sharp edges. The mean level of the old floe was about six feet higher than that of the new one. The remainder of the day we had a good road on new floes, but, having seen no land since morning, we were forced to pursue our course by compass. In the afternoon a fine breeze sprung up from the N.E., accompanied by light snow. We encamped at 7 P.M.

March 24.—Baker was too sick to walk, and as it still blew a strong breeze from the N.E., we resolved to lay to. No land visible.

March 25.—We set out this morning at 9.20 A.M., and, after crossing some hummocks, travelled to the northward on good floes. I found our latitude at noon, by the artificial horizon, to be 78° 56′ 8″; the dead reckoning for the same hour being 78° 56′ 0″. The north headland of Rensselaer Bay bore exactly south about fifteen miles distant. At 1 P.M. we reached a ridge of hummocks, one of which Mr. Brooks, Mr. Petersen, and I ascended, and found they extended round the horizon from S.S.W. through N. to N.N.E. The western shore could be traced to a point bearing north from us, where it disappeared, leaving an open space of about 50° on the horizon, at which point the lowlands on the eastern side of the bay commenced. The west land appeared very high to the W. by S. and W. from us, but a fog near shore disclosed only the tops of the mountains. A little to the N. of W. it becomes low, and apparently more distant; to the W. by N. it appears dark, and therefore must be in shadow at 1 P.M., which makes the trend of the coast there W. of N. and E. of S.; but it is possible that it is only the mountain-wall forming the western boundary of a glacier, which seems here to descend into the sound. From W.N.W. toward N.W. the land increases in height, and appears to be much traversed by ravines and valleys, judging from the black lines of shadow which interrupt the coast-line in many places, but which was greatly distorted by refraction. On the E. side, at the point where the Esquimaux hut is situated, the land could be distinctly seen south of Force Bay, an indentation of which forms a large bay. Rensselaer Bay bears a little W. from S., and the mountains which lie between it and Glacier Bay (which bears S.E.) appear dark and lofty. The middle of Marshall Bay bears a little S. from E. From this point toward the N.E. the land becomes gradually lower till it disappears in E.N.E. This portion of the eastern shore was not sufficiently distinct to take exact bearings.

In the afternoon we crossed with difficulty some old floes and hummocks. At 3 P.M. we found good new floes leading us toward the N.N.E. along the line of hummocks. We encamped at 7 P.M., having travelled seven miles in a northerly direction.

March 26.—We continued our journey N.N.E. along the hummocks, which run without interruption nearly in a straight line extending N. and W. to the boundary of the horizon. It blew a strong breeze from the N., which in the afternoon increased to a light gale and compelled us to lay to, at 2.30 P.M., having advanced on our journey two and a half miles.

March 27.—This morning we started at 11.30 A.M., against a moderate N. wind, which had blown very strong during the night. As the thick weather did not permit us to see more than a mile ahead, we continued to follow the edge of the ridge of hummocks. These hummocks consist of pieces of ice from one to two feet thick, having sharp edges, and piled up from ten to fifteen feet high. Single piles sometimes exceed thirty feet in height, and when seen at a distance have the appearance of icebergs. Occasionally higher ridges are seen running nearly parallel to each other and at right angles to the outer edge of the hummocks. They seem to have been formed by the meeting of floes which have been drifted N.N.E. and S.S.W. This would indicate that two currents met here coming from opposite directions. Near the middle the sound seems to be entirely free from icebergs; we passed not a single one since the 23d of March, and toward the W. and N. there were none in sight.

We could see no land to-day: the fog increased so much that we were obliged to halt at 3 P.M. in lat. 79° 4′, only one mile and a half to the N.N.E. from our last camp.

March 28.—We were forced to lay to during the entire day, owing to thick weather, and a strong breeze from N. by E. which blew in squalls.

March 29.—This morning was clear and very cold, with a light breeze from the N.

On ascending some of the highest hummocks, Mr. Petersen and I failed to perceive a single opening in their chain, which still extended to the N.N.E. Nearly in the same direction a faint white line could be discerned near the horizon, which was probably the Great Glacier, elevated by refraction.

We were at this time about thirty miles from the opposite (west) shore; and, as the limit of our outward journey was the second of April, it was obvious we could not reach it; for we had now only four days left, and very little can be accomplished in that time among these hummocks. Mr. Brooks, therefore, gave orders to return to the brig; we started at 11.30 A.M., and, after crossing some hummocks, travelled S.S.E. on a good new floe five miles in diameter. This course was chosen with the intention of crossing the chain of icebergs and hummocks which runs parallel to the land farther north, and then to take the smooth land-ice (ice-foot) for the rest of our journey; but at 4 P.M. we were stopped by a very old floe, the surface of which appeared to be covered with old rounded hummocks about ten feet high. The spaces between them being partially filled with deep loose snow rendered the travelling very difficult; but we soon reached new floe, which afforded a good road. We halted at 8 P.M. between hummocks at the S. end of the floe, having travelled nearly S.S.E. about seven miles.

March 30.—This morning Mr. Brooks, Mr. Wilson, Baker, and Peter were unable to walk, on account of frost-bites. Mr. Brooks sent me to the brig, accompanied by Ohlsen and Petersen, to inform you of the condition of the party. We started at 10.20 A.M., and arrived on board at 11 P.M., having walked nearly S. about thirty miles.

This report, and the accompanying table of observed temperatures, are abstracts from field-notes taken on the journey. They also contain some material for the projection of the shores of this sound.

Respectfully submitted, your obedient servant,

A. SONTAG, *Astronomer to the Expedition.*

Temperatures observed on the Sledge-Journey during the month of March, 1854.

Date.	Time of Day.	Observed Temp.	Temp. of Winter Quarters.	Diff.	Lat. at Noon.	REMARKS.
20	10 A.M.	—43·4°	—40·6°	— 2·8°	78° 43′	Calm and clear during the day.
"	12 M.	—37·2	—33·8	— 3·4		
"	2 P.M.	—35·0	—35·6	+ 0·6		
"	6 "	—41·0	—30·1	—10·9		
21	7 A.M.	—16·8	—20·0	+ 3·2	78° 45′	Heavy fog. Calm.
"	10 "	—20·8	—20·8	0·0		Fog clearing away. Calm.
"	1 P.M.	—13·4	—16·4	+ 3·0		Fog increasing. Calm.
"	5 "	—13·4	—15·4	+ 2·0		Calm.
22	6 A.M.	—23·8	—18·5	— 5·3	78° 47·5′	Sky covered, and foggy around horizon. Calm.
"	9 "	—15·5	— 3·8	—11·7		
"	1 P.M.	+ 1·4	+ 2·3	— 0·9		Fine breeze (3) from S.W.
"	2 "	+ 0·2	+ 0·9	— 0·7		Heavy fog. No land visible during the afternoon.
"	7 "	— 1·8	— 5·3	+ 3·5		
23	5 A.M.	—11·4	— 7·1	— 4·3	78° 51·5′	Fog. Land in S.W. dimly seen.
"	9 "	— 5·0	— 9·9	+ 4·9		Light snow. Calm.
"	2 P.M.	— 7·4	— 8·4	+ 1·0		Heavy fog. Snow. Fine breeze (3) from N. by E. during afternoon.
"	7 "	—13·4	— 8·7	— 4·7		
24	9 A.M.	—14·5	—14·4	— 0·1	78° 53·5′	Sky covered. No land visible. Foggy. Strong breeze (6) from N. by E. during the day.
"	12 M.	—17·5	—14·9	— 2·6		
"	4 P.M.	—18·6	—17·8	— 0·8		
"	7 "	—22·9	—21·6	— 1·3		
"	9 "	—25·7	—23·2	— 2·5		
25	6 A.M.	—43·4	—34·5	— 8·9	78° 56·8′	Clear and calm.
"	9 "	—26·7 S.	—23·7	— 3·0		
"	12 M.	—13·4 S.	—19·8	+ 6·4		
"	2 P.M.	—15·5 S.	—16·4	+ 0·9		
26	6 A.M.	—51·5	—47·2	— 4·3	79° 0·0′	Clear sky. Strong breeze from N., which, in the afternoon, increased to a light gale.
"	9 "	—25·7 S.	—34·5	+ 8·8		
"	12 M.	—23·8 S.	—26·4	+ 2·6		
"	6 P.M.	—30·1	—43·4	+ 7·3		
"	8 "	—38·5	—45·7	+ 7·2		
27	5 A.M.	—43·4	—39·8	— 3·6	79° 3·0′	Light mist. Parhelion faintly visible. Light breeze (3) from N.
"	8 "	—29·6	—35·6	+ 6·0		
"	12 M.	—25·7	—30·1	+ 4·4		Thick weather. Strong breeze (6).
"	4 P.M.	—27·7	—28·3	+ 0·6		Gale (8) from N. after 8 P.M.
28	6 A.M.	—31·6	—35·2	+ 3·6	79° 4·0′	Calm at 6 A.M., after which a strong breeze from N. (6) at noon. High gale (7) continued till 8 P.M. Misty.
"	10 "	—27·7	—32·2	+ 4·5		
"	12 M.	—26·7	—32·2	+ 5·5		
"	4 P.M.	—29·6	—31·7	+ 2·1		
29	6 A.M.	—57·5	—45·1	—12·4	79° 0·0′	
"	7 "	—43·4 S.	—38·6	— 4.8		Fresh breeze (5) from N. by E.
"	8 "	—30·6 S.	—36·4	+ 5·8		Clear sky.
"	9 "	—43·4	—44·0	+ 0·6		At noon a light mist, which increased till at 4 P.M. it entirely obscured the sun.
"	12 M.	—43·4	—36·5	— 8·9		
"	7 P.M.	—41·0	—35·6	— 5·4		
"	9 "	—46·6	—43·2	— 3·4		

NOTE.—The observed temperatures are corrected for the errors of the thermometer. The temperatures at winter quarters are the correct readings of the spirit-standard at the same time. The mean difference between the outside temperatures and those of the winter quarters is —1·14°. Outside colder.

Report of Surgeon upon Condition of Rescue-Party, March, 1854.

To E. K. Kane, U.S.N., *Commanding Second American Arctic Expedition.*

Sir:—I have the honor respectfully to submit the following report of the state of health on board the Brig Advance, agreeably to your order:—

Of the six men left on board at the time of your departure five were invalids. Messrs. J. Carl Petersen and Augustus Sontag had, in addition to the fatigue of their long journey, premonitory symptoms of scurvy. Mr. Goodfellow, G. Stephenson, and G. Whipple, had all suffered more or less from scorbutic attacks during the winter, and from which they had not yet recovered. The two latter were, however, able, and did render efficient service to the sick after your return, —Stephenson as nurse, and Whipple as cook.

Mr. Bonsall was the first to arrive at the vessel. He came about two hours in advance of the remainder of your party. From him I learned you were advancing, and that he was sent forward by your orders to give directions for the reception of the sick.

The necessary preparations being completed, I went out on the floe to meet you. Messrs. Brooks and Wilson, J. T. Baker, and Pierre Schubert, lay on the sledge sewed up in buffalo-robes and other furs. The remainder of the party were drawing the sledge. As they passed me, I was startled by their ghastly appearance. They gave me not even a glance of recognition, and when I hailed them they met me only with a vacant, wild stare. Their persons were covered over with frost; from their beards were suspended large lumps of ice; their tread was slow and feeble; and it was a sad sight to see what had three days previous been a party of strong and vigorous men now all bent down as with the weight of years.

For sixty-six hours they had been constantly on foot and exposed in the low temperatures of from 35° to 50° below zero. They had had no rest since leaving the vessel. The loss of sleep, the constant exposure, the depressing effects of the extreme cold, and the great fatigue consequent upon their long journey, had produced alarming prostration. They were almost to a man delirious. Keeping the direction of the vessel as if by instinct, they knew of nothing that transpired. When they arrived at the ship, and when you gave the order to halt, they all dropped the lines and made for the ship's side, the same instinct directing them to their beds.

There was therefore some difficulty in getting force enough to attend to the sick, and it was with a little delay that they were carried to the upper deck, where they were properly allowed to remain some time before taking them into the warm air of the cabin.

Having placed them in their bunks, that had previously been fitted up with as much care as possible, dressed their wounds, and attended to their present wants, my attention was directed to the remainder of the party. I found they had rolled into their bunks "booted and spurred" just as they had come in from the ice, and were all now fast locked in a heavy sleep, from which it seemed impossible to awake them; and, indeed, I made no effort. With them, as with the wounded, what they most needed was rest and quiet.

Reaction soon commenced. What had before assumed only the form of the simplest mental aberration now broke out in raving delirium, and for two days the ship presented all the appearances of a mad-house. Not an individual of the party escaped, although some were much more seriously affected than others. Many of them seemed to think themselves out on the ice perishing with cold, and when they at last awoke most of them had not the least remembrance of what had occurred during the last twenty hours of the journey. Except small doses of morphine, it seemed impolitic to do any thing for them at the first outset of their wild raving. The excessive sleepiness had completely overpowered them, and they would only partially arouse at intervals, and give vent to an imploring cry for aid or an exhortation to hurry on.

At last, after twenty-four hours, they began one by one to awake and ask for food. They were in this state for forty-eight hours; and Mr. Ohlsen, who had been eighty hours constantly exposed, and had travelled not less than one hundred and twenty miles, was unconscious of what was taking place for the greater part of two and a half days. He would ask for food frequently, eat with great voraciousness, and again fall back into a torpid sleep, seeming to recognise while awake nothing but the meal which he was eating. His brain-symptoms were accompanied by strabismus. During his sleep his mind ran continually upon the tent on the ice, and he seemed to think himself pushing forward, guiding the party to it; conscious still, seemingly, of being the only one who knew where *it* was.

You were the last one affected, and among the first to recover. After seeing that the sick were comfortably cared for, you laid down in your cot, and I began to congratulate myself that you had escaped; but after two or three hours I heard you suddenly cry out, "Halloo on deck there!" On going aft to ascertain what was wanted, I received instructions to "call all hands to lay aft and take two reefs in the stove-pipe." As to all hands being now temporarily crazy I had no further doubts; for I would respectfully submit that your mind might perhaps have been at this moment a little wandering.

At this time the frost-bitten patients are all doing well. They have rallied as well as can be expected in the short time after so great prostration. No prognosis of the cases can, however, be ventured upon safely. Pierre will probably lose part of one of his feet. Baker, part of one, or perhaps both. Messrs. Wilson and Brooks are in the same condition, being frozen above the phalangeal joints.

Mr. Ohlsen has a frost-bite on one of his toes, but it will prove only a flesh-wound. Mr. Petersen's symptoms grow more unpleasant. Mr. Sontag has an acute attack of scurvy, with pericarditis. Of the original party of eight, Thomas Hickey alone remains well and sound.

The remainder of the ship's company are all in a very reduced condition. Symptoms of scurvy are visible in every one, and the severe exposure of this trying journey has favored its development. Mr. Bonsall, Mr. Morton, William Godfrey, J. Blake, and Hans Hendrick, are those least affected and most able for duty.

I think, however, that there is every reason to hope for a speedy restoration to perfect health of the major part of the ship's company. Allow me to express a hope also that you may soon be enabled under Providence to again take the field for the further conduct of your explorations.

Respectfully submitted, your obedient servant,

I. I. HAYES, *Surgeon to the Expedition.*

BRIG ADVANCE, RENSSELAER HARBOR, April 5, 1854.*

---

* Jefferson Temple Baker and Peter Schubert, affected as by the above report, died on the 7th of April and 22d of May.

I. I. HAYES.

EASTERN COAST OF SOUND:
Report of Messrs. McGary and Bonsall, June–July, 1854.

BRIG ADVANCE, July 3, 1854.

SIR:—According to your orders, Mr. McGary and I took charge of a party sent out to explore the eastern coast of Smith's Sound and the Great Glacier which terminates it.

June 4.—We left the vessel at 4.30 P.M., and reached the land-ice on the eastern shore of our bay in about two hours. A strong wind set in from the N., and at 8.30 P.M., when about two miles south of Coffee Gorge, we concluded to encamp. The thermometer in the shade stood at 26°.

June 5.—This morning was calm, the thermometer at 25°. After getting breakfast, we started at 7.45 A.M., and travelled up the land-ice about half-way to the terminus of Glacier Bay, where we took the floe, and reached the opposite side at 4.30 P.M., when we encamped. Thermometer, 27°.

June 6.—Started at 7.30 A.M., feeling quite cold, the thermometer being at 15°. We passed up the coast of Marshall Bay as far as the two gorges, when we took the floe and crossed to Chimney Rock, the road being much clearer of hummocks than any before travelled across this bay.

We arrived at 6 P.M., and found the cache at this place had been destroyed by a bear. He had eaten the bread, and with a stroke of his paw had destroyed the can of alcohol. We encamped near the rocks, with a strong northerly breeze accompanied by snow. Thermometer, 23°. Thomas complained very much of his knees, and several bluish spots appeared in the skin, evidently caused by scurvy. Mr. McGary's eye was very painful, though better than during the day.

June 7.—We started at 8 A.M., with a light N. breeze and the thermometer at 24°. Soon after passing Cape Russell, although the sun shone on our backs, the reflection of his rays from the land-ice was very painful to our eyes. Morton and Riley were both snow-blind, and suffered great pain.

We reached the cache about 5 P.M., and found that this one had also been visited by a bear. He had rolled one of the barrels of bread over the ice-foot into the water, had eaten a can of chocolate, some potatoes, &c., and in his search had torn several of the bags. Thermometer this evening, 35°. Made twenty miles to-day.

June 8.—We did not start to-day until 12 M., as we were fatigued from our long march yesterday. We went seven miles up the coast to the ravine near the W. cape of the large bay, at which place we encamped, as I wished to take solar bearings from this position. Before supper, I returned to the cache, a distance of seven miles, in order to procure some articles we had forgotten.

June 9.—This morning the thermometer stood at 30°, with a clouded sky and a cool breeze from the S.W. We left at 7.20 A.M., and, crossing the ice-foot about a mile from our encampment, started across the bay for the low point of land on the opposite side of it. At noon I took solar bearings of the prominent points in the interior of the bay.

After nine hours' travel over hummocks and deep snow, we reached a point of land running out into the bay about a mile and a half. From this point a crack twelve feet wide ran in a northerly direction into the bay. This we crossed on the ice-foot, and encamped on the opposite side. Thomas is better, and Morton and Riley complained less of their eyes. Mr. McGary is no better. I here took an observation for longitude. Thermometer at 34°.

June 10.—Just after midnight, while asleep in our tent, we were suddenly surprised by a visit from a bear. Mr. McGary was awakened by the scratching of the snow near his head. He soon aroused us; but, to our consternation, there was not a gun within reach, they having been carelessly left on the sledge. In the mean time the bear had walked leisurely around the tent, and finally thrust his head inside, when we assailed him with burning matches and paper without effect. Thomas, with more presence of mind than any of us, proposed to cut a hole in the back part of the tent and get the boat-hook. The bear was at this time eating the remainder of our seal, which we had buried in the snow in front of our tent-door. Thomas rushed out and struck him on the nose with the boat-hook, which forced him to recede to the other side of the sledge. He then seized the rifle and handed it to me. The bear had gone about twenty-five yards from us when I fired and sent the ball through his lungs. He ran about a hundred yards and fell dead. We then skinned him, and at the expiration of two hours were ready to turn in again.

We rested longer than usual, and, after breakfast, cut up the bear, took part of the hind-quarters, and left the remainder for the dogs when they should arrive.

We travelled over very deep snow, and, after crossing two cracks, encamped at 3 P.M. Mr. McGary's eyes are so much worse as to render him entirely blind. He also suffers from pain in his legs. Riley's eyes are quite well to-day, Morton's much better, and Thomas's rather worse.

We saw several burgomaster-gulls, as well as other varieties, around the cracks we crossed. The ice in one of these cracks was only three feet thick. Thermometer, 36°.

June 11.—The weather this morning was quite warm, the thermometer being at 43°. Last evening we cooked a large quantity of bear-liver, and ate heartily of it, after which we turned in as well as usual. This morning we all suffered severe pains in our bones, and headache, but did not know whether to attribute it to having eaten the bear's liver or to the hot sun of yesterday. We were not able to proceed until 3 P.M., when, feeling rather better, we set off, and made ten miles over very deep snow.

At 10 P.M. we encamped near an iceberg about two miles from Cache No. 2. A dense fog now set in from the N., and obscured all objects at more than a few yards' distance. We are all better this evening, except Mr. McGary and Morton. Thermometer, 45°.

June 12.—We started to-day at noon, having waited for the sun to go round so far as not to shine in our faces. At about 1.30 P.M. we reached our cache, which we found safe. We took all the provisions on our sledge, for fear our northern cache should have been destroyed. We found the water in many places several inches deep under the snow, which caused us to sink through it at every step, making the travelling very difficult. We keep regular watch since our adventure with the bear. Thomas was not so well this evening. Thermometer, 34°.

June 13.—The thermometer stood at 40° at 10 A.M., at which time we started. We found the snow deeper and the travelling more difficult than yesterday. We worked hard to reach the islands, and, after crossing several cracks in their vicinity, arrived at the foot of the land-ice at 6 P.M. We found this ice broken up and very difficult to cross. We pitched our tent on it, and went to examine the cache, which we discovered had been destroyed by the bears, the tin canister only left untouched.

As the bear-tracks were numerous and recent, I was led to suppose it had not been long since the cache was destroyed. The flagstaff was torn down and dragged some distance, but the cairn remained almost entire. We ate a supper of bear-steaks, not satisfied to pronounce the meat unfit for food without giving it a further trial. Thermometer, 40°.

June 14.—This morning is quite warm, the thermometer standing at 46°. I took a meridian-altitude, and devoted the day to washing, as there were numerous pools of water on the rocks. This evening I took an observation for longitude, and hope to get a corresponding one to-morrow morning.

The sun has been very severe upon us on our journey, every one being more or less blistered. Morton lost all the skin of his face; Riley and Mr. McGary complain of their eyes. Thermometer, 37°.

June 15.—This morning we rose early and prepared for a start; but, as the wind blew heavy from the S.E., and Mr. McGary being yet quite sick, we deferred it until to-morrow. I took bearings by compass of all the prominent points visible from the island. The weather continues very fine. Thermometer, 42°.

June 16.—As the fog was so thick this morning as to prevent us from seeing more than a few yards ahead of us, we concluded to wait until it should clear away. We did not get off until 11.30 A.M., having first taken a meridian-altitude. Mr. McGary and I set off for the glacier, and reached an island within two hundred yards of the perpendicular face, a nearer approach being prevented by the accumulation of bergs, berg-ice, and precipitous hummocks, interspersed with holes of water. This island was about the same height of the perpendicular face at this point, (two hundred and fifty feet;) and I think I had a better opportunity for observation than upon the glacier itself. From this point the glacier appears to have gradually covered the land with a sheet of ice twenty or thirty feet thick, in a succession of ridges and knolls, until it reaches the shore, where, still pushing outward, large flakes are precipitated to the foot, and others, sliding over them, descend into the water and remain stationary, until in their turn they are forced by other discharges into a depth sufficient to float them, and are then carried away by currents into the sea. Their manner of breakage appears to be into long flakes, which are forced over the descent until, their overhanging weight overcoming the tenacity of the ice, the piece becomes detached. Above the perpendicular face it is split into a succession of parallel cracks and corresponding indentations, forming a series of steps, sometimes horizontal, but more frequently following the inclinations of the ground under them and extending back to where the glacier becomes almost level. Beyond this are seen numerous fissures, where the ice has cracked upon taking a new angle of descent and been forced onward to the final launch.

We were fortunate in reaching this point, as an approach at any other would have been impossible, owing to the discharge of bergs and hummocks, which appeared to extend out into the sound for several miles in all directions from our position.

The glacier above its face has a gradual ascent of a few feet to the mile, until in the interior it reaches an apparent altitude of six or seven hundred feet; but the quantity of snow and deep chasms upon its surface prevent travelling upon it.

As an indication of the motion of the ice, deep muttered sounds and crashes are heard at intervals, resembling sharp thunder and distant cannon. At some points masses of small blocks and round pieces are seen, as though crushed by the weight of the mass above. The surface appears to take the formation of the land under it, as it is broken into valleys and indentations, carrying the surface-water off in streams in the same manner as land-drainage. The heads of the valleys and the dividing ridge were not distinctly visible. I here made a sketch of the opposite face, showing the character of the discharge of bergs; and I also took compass-bearings of the islands and glacier.

On arriving at our encampment, we found that Hans had reached it at one o'clock, after two days' travel from the vessel. As the dogs were tired, Mr. McGary concluded to let them rest over to-morrow, although we should then have started on our return if the sledge had not arrived. Thermometer, 49°.

June 17.—This morning it was thick weather, and snowed quite fast during the greater part of the day. We remained in camp until 10 P.M., when we commenced packing our sledges and preparing for a start. We were ready by midnight, and, after getting on the floe, both sledges started together at 12.30 A.M.

June 18.—Morton and Hans followed our old tracks until clear of the cracks near the islands, and then turned toward the N., at about double our speed. They both walked, as the snow was too soft and deep for them to ride, their load being heavy. We travelled until 7.30 A.M., when we encamped, having made about twelve miles. Mr. McGary's eye was very painful this morning. We started again in the evening and walked fast, the snow bearing us quite well. We fell into our old tracks a little to the westward of Cache No. 2, and, afterward following them, we encamped at 5.30 in the morning of

June 19,—Having made about thirteen miles. Mr. McGary suffered very much from the pain in his eye this morning. We started at 9 A.M., and the day being warm rendered the snow soft; but the travelling improved as we advanced. We crossed several cracks, in one of which we shot a long-tailed duck. Thomas fell in to-day in attempting to jump across one of these cracks. We passed our old encampment about 2 A.M.; we there filled our water-cans from pools on the ice.

June 20.—At 5 A.M. we arrived at Bear Point, our encampment of the 10th. We found the carcass of the bear had been eaten by the gulls. We encamped within gun-shot, hoping to get some gulls; but they were too shy, and would not alight while we stayed. We found the can of blubber safe, which would afford us fuel sufficient to last till we should reach the vessel. After breakfast we turned in and slept until 6 P.M., and at 9.30 P.M. we started across the bay.

June 21.—We reached the land-ice at 3 A.M., and deposited some pemmican for Morton on his return. We then travelled on six miles farther to Dr. Kane's Cache, where we encamped at 5 A.M., very tired, after a day's travel of twenty miles. We found all safe, and after supper—or more properly breakfast—we turned in, the wind blowing strong from the west, (true.) At 11 P.M. we loaded our sledge and started toward the vessel on the land-ice. Our sledge ran very heavily, owing to a light fall of snow.

June 22.—We travelled on until 6 A.M., when we encamped, having made but ten miles. I here took an altitude of the cliffs. We started again at 9 P.M., a slight snow falling, accompanied by a north wind. This soon increased, and about 11 P.M. we stopped to take an altitude of the cliffs, and found the water running from them and forming pools on the land-ice. This is the first appearance of running water, though yesterday we observed several wet places on the cliffs and small pools on the ice. The ice-foot is much broken, and in some places the pieces are from twenty to thirty feet off shore, leaving quite a canal.

June 23.—We continued on until we reached the cliffs of the bay, at 2 A.M. We were very tired, as we had not halted to rest since nine o'clock last evening. We had difficulty in pitching our tent, owing to the violence of the wind. We turned in and rested until 7 P.M., but could not cross the ice-foot until 10 P.M., as the tide was too low. The snow was very deep, and, as there was a sheet of water between the snow and ice, we sank to our knees at every step. After eight hours of toil we reached the shore.

June 24.—We passed up the ice-foot at 6.30 A.M., and encamped, having travelled about fourteen miles since ten o'clock last evening. We started again about 9 P.M., and travelled down the land-ice.

June 25.—At 12.30 A.M. we reached the headland, and then took the floe crossing Glacier Bay, where we encamped at 4.30 A.M. The floe on the bay was worse travelling than any we have had since leaving the vessel. The snow was so very soft that we sank to our hips in the drifts, which had four or five inches of water under them. This travelling continued for thirty or forty miles at a time, wetting our feet and causing the sledge to sink in to the bottom. The water was standing in pools in all directions, and surrounding every hummock. We made to-day about twelve miles. We started this morning at ten o'clock, and pushed on toward Coffee Gorge, the land-ice being covered with ponds. About three o'clock we passed the gorge, and encamped at the Black Cliff, two miles south of it, at 4 A.M. of June 26. We started this afternoon at three o'clock, and, after sighting the vessel, a thick fog set in, which very materially obscured our vision; but by following our old tracks we crossed the bay and reached the vessel at 7 P.M. Yours, &c., A. BONSALL.

To DR. E. K. KANE, *Commanding Arctic Expedition.*

July 8, 1854.

Abstract of Journal of Messrs. Bonsall and McGary, June, 1854.

Date.		Time of Starting.	Time of Halting.	True Course.	Distance in miles.	Temperature.		REMARKS.
						Morning.	Evening.	
		h. m.	h. m.					
June	4	4 30 P.M.	8 30 P.M.	N.N.E.	7	...	+26°	Strong N. wind.
"	5	7 45 A.M.	4 30 P.M.	N.E.½E.	16	+25°	+27°	Crossed Glacier Bay.
"	6	7 30 A.M.	6 0 P.M.	N.E. by E.	13	+15°	+23°	Crossed bay.
"	7	8 0 A.M.	5 0 P.M.	E.N.E.	20	+24°	+35°	Light N. wind in the morning.
"	8	12 0 M.	......	E.N.E.	7	...	+28°	Camped at W. cape of bay.
"	9	7 0 A.M.	4 0 P.M.	E.N.E.	12	+30°	+36°	Breeze W.—Crossed bay.
"	10	......	3 0 P.M.	E.N.E.	7	...	+36°	" "
"	11	3 0 P.M.	10 0 P.M.	E.N.E.	10	+43°	+43°	" "
"	12	12 0 M.	1 30 P.M.	E.N.E.	2	...	+34°	Reached Cache No. 2.
"	13	10 0 A.M.	6 0 P.M.	E.N.E.	14	+40°	+40°	Reached Cache Island.
"	14	......	......	......	...	+46°	+37°	Remained at Cache Island.
"	15	......	......	......	...	+42°	...	Attempted to ascend glacier.
"	16	......	......	......	...	...	+49°	" "
"	17	......	......	......	...	...	...	" "
"	18	0 30 A.M.	7 30 A.M.	W.S.W.	12	...	...	Started on return.
"	18	9 0 P.M.	5 30 A.M.	W.S.W.	13	...	...	" "
"	19	9 0 P.M.	5 0 A.M.	W.S.W.	12	...	...	Crossed bay.
"	20	9 30 P.M.	5 0 A.M.	W.S.W.	20	...	...	Reached Dr. Kane's Cache.
"	21	11 0 P.M.	6 0 A.M.	W.S.W.	10	...	...	
"	22	9 0 P.M.	2 30 A.M.	W.S.W.	7	...	...	Blowing a gale.
"	23	10 0 P.M.	6 30 A.M.	S.W. by W.	14	...	...	Crossed bay.
"	24	9 0 P.M.	4 30 A.M.	S.W.½W.	13	...	...	Crossed Glacier Bay.
"	25	10 0 P.M.	4 0 A.M.	S.W.	12	...	...	Camped two miles S. Coffee Gorge.
"	26	3 0 P.M.	7 0 P.M.	S.S.W.	6	...	...	Reached the brig.

Extracts selected from Observations of Latitude.

			°	′
June 7,	Double Altitude	$\overline{\odot}$	68	16
		$\underline{\odot}$	67	8
		$\odot$	67	42
	Index Error	—		2·95
			67	39·05
	Altitude	$\odot$	33	49·52
	Refraction	—		1·43
	Parallax	+		0·12
			33	48·21
	Declination		22	46·60
	Latitude		78	58·39

			°	′
June 14,	Double Altitude	$\underline{\odot}$	67	43·5
		$\overline{\odot}$	68	47·5
			68	15·5
	Index Error	—		3·5
			68	12·0
	Altitude ⊙ centre		34	6·0
	Refraction	—		1·42
	Parallax	+		0·12
			34	4·70
	Declination		23	17·07
	Latitude		79	12·37

			°	′
June 16,	Double Altitude	$\underline{\odot}$	67	54·0
		$\overline{\odot}$	68	57·5
			68	25·75
	Index Error	—		3·90
			68	21·85
	Altitude ⊙ centre		34	10·92
	Refraction	—		1·42
	Parallax	+		0·12
			34	9·62
	Declination		23	22·11
	Latitude		79	12·49

Selected Longitudes.

June 9,	Chronometer.	Double Altitude.
	h. m. s.	° ′
	10 39 16	43 18·5 $\underline{\odot}$
	10 44 29	43 54·8 $\overline{\odot}$
		Index Error — 3·0

June 14,	Chronometer.	Double Altitude.
h. m.	h. m. s.	° ′
(7 30 P.M.)	11 54 58	36 43·5 $\underline{\odot}$
	11 57 49	37 31·8 $\overline{\odot}$
		Index Error — 3·5

June 15,	Chronometer.	Double Altitude.
h. m.	h. m. s.	° ′
(7 40 A.M.)	11 59 20	54 42·3 $\underline{\odot}$
	12 5 10	56 16·3 $\overline{\odot}$
		Index Error — 3·9.

Report of a Sledge Journey to the Northwest Coasts of Smith's Strait by Dr. I. I. Hayes and William Godfrey.

To Dr. E. K. Kane, U.S.N.

Sir:—I have the honor respectfully to submit the following report of a journey made by me under your orders for the purpose of determining the northern coasts of Smith's Strait:—

May 20.—I left the vessel at 2.30 P.M., accompanied by William Godfrey, seaman. Our equipment was as follows:—a light sledge and team of seven dogs, 80 lbs. of pemmican, 16 lbs. of bread, 18 lbs. of lard and rope-yarn for fuel; a reindeer-skin sleeping-bag for each, a lamp and pot for cooking, sextant, pocket-compass, telescope, Sharpe's rifle, two extra pairs of stockings and one of boots for each.

For the first ten miles our course lay nearly due N., after which we encountered ridges of hummock running parallel with the axis of the channel, and through which we worked our way by running off a little to the eastward. Halted at 8 P.M., having made about fifteen miles.

May 21.—Started at 6 A.M.; the travelling generally smooth, with occasional ridges of hummocks, generally running in parallel lines. I was obliged frequently to run off to the westward, as no other passage could be seen, and was thus prevented making as much easting as your orders required. A meridian-altitude gave me lat. 79° 8′ 6″. From this point I obtained excellent sights of the S.E. coast of the channel, and took solar bearings of the several capes. During the afternoon our track was more rough and tortuous, sometimes running to the W. and again to the E. of N. By rude estimate we made fifty miles, and at 5.10 P.M. were brought to a halt by a wall of broken ice ranging from five to thirty feet in height above the general level of the floe, and running in a direction N.E. by E. From this point the north headland of Rensselaer Bay bore S. 4° W. (true.)

May 22.—This morning we set out at six o'clock, and on ascending the highest neighboring pinnacle I found this line of hummocks to extend as far as the eye could reach N.E. by E. and S.W. by W., no termination or break appearing in its surface to the N. and W.

This prospect cast a sudden damper on the hope I had yesterday entertained of a speedy passage to the shore. The land was distinctly visible, and appeared not more than twenty or twenty-five miles distant. I supposed the ridge of broken ice to be the same which had baffled Messrs. Bonsall and McGary last fall; and as I did not see that any thing could be gained by pushing along this barricade, which appeared to run parallel with the coast, I determined to enter it at the first break, and reach the land which loomed high through the disappearing fog.

After travelling along the borders of this formidable barrier about three miles, I succeeded in effecting an entrance, and at the end of a day's journey of twenty or twenty-five miles I found, to my disappointment, that instead of encamping, as I had hoped, under the high cliffs of the shore, we were forced to build our snow-house in the midst of this wilderness of broken ice.

Our linear distance from our last encampment was not more than ten miles, as our track was very tortuous; and, moreover, we had not a foot of level travelling. Huge masses of ice from twenty to forty feet in height were heaped together, around which the fierce winds of winter had piled the drifting snow. In crossing these ridges our sledge would frequently capsize, and roll over and over, dogs, cargo, and all, into the drift below. Sometimes the sledge would be half buried in the hard snow into which it had fallen, in which case its liberation would be attended with difficulty.

The dogs were continually breaking their harness or lines, and, owing to the character of the road, this day's travel tired them more than three times that distance over smooth ice. A meridian-altitude gave me lat. 79° 23′ 5″, but this result I obtained with difficulty, and it is scarcely reliable. Future observations made at this point determined the latitude more accurately. The general course I endeavored to pursue was N. 20° W. in the direction of a headland of the coast made on the 27th. But to this it was never possible to adhere for five minutes consecutively. We ran E., W., N., and even S., as we were occasionally forced to retrace our steps in order to penetrate at another point. I had already, so early as yesterday noon, felt the premonitory symptoms of snow-blindness, and to-day my eyes were so weak as to render the use of the sextant painful.

May 23.—This morning I could not see in the least, and as riding on the sledge was not possible, we were obliged to lay to. My eyes improved a little during the day, and at 9.30 P.M. I managed to get one open. We immediately set out again; but an hour's use closed it, and we encamped.

May 24.—Continued in camp during the day. I have never in my life had the misfortune to have crowded into the short space of thirty-six hours so much bodily pain as I suffered from this attack. William fared better. A pair of light-blue glasses had been loaned me by Mr. Petersen, and, thinking William's eyes as driver were of more account than my own, I desired him to wear them. Although I do not think glasses are always of service, yet they are useful when the sun shines brightly, especially on the face; but on a cloudy or misty day they are of no value whatever.

May 25.—Set out at 4 A.M., and during the first two hours made nearly due N.; then, until 11.30 A.M., our course bore N.W. over the same description of road we had yesterday. I then halted to fix our position and lay down the coast-line as it trended to the northward.

The meridian-observation gave me lat. 79° 24′ 4″ with artificial (mercurial) horizon. The most distant visible headland of the coast bore N. 120 E. (magn.) Bluff sighted on the 22d, N. 100 E. (magn.) This has since been our course. Intermediate bluff, N. 110 E. (magn.) The dogs were pretty well rested by 1.30 P.M. and we again got under way, and at 5.30 we halted, having travelled during the day about five miles in a direct line from the bluff, but not less than twenty in our tortuous course.

May 26.—Started at 6 A.M., our course being N. by N.N.E. Made about the same distance as yesterday, and halted at 4 P.M. At the close of this day William was completely exhausted. The dogs were broken down, and almost unable to drag along. Their harness, having been repeatedly broken, would scarcely hold together. Every spare line we had was brought into requisition; and finally we had recourse to strips cut from the waistbands and extremities of the legs of our seal-skin pantaloons. It now became a question with me as to the possibility of reaching the land. Seven days' provisions had already been consumed, and we were fitted out for but ten. The severe nature of our journey precluded any abatement in our daily allowance. The deceptive nature of the country rendered it very uncertain when we could reach the shore, having made no perceptible advance toward it during the three preceding days. I was by no means certain that it would not require as long a time to return to the vessel as we had already been out, in which event our only plan would be to kill one of the dogs for food for the others, as well as for ourselves. Feeling confident, however, that you would rather such a sacrifice should be made than that I should fail to effect a landing on the shore, I determined to push on to-morrow as far as possible.

After having cooked and eaten our simple supper of coffee and pemmican, and attended as well as I could to the necessities of my sick comrade, I left him at the sledge and walked on with the view of exploring the track for our travel to-morrow. For eight miles I found it similar to that which we had encountered for the last five days; but to my great joy I then struck upon the borders of an old floe, which appeared to run in-shore. I travelled on this smooth plain about two miles, and ascended a high hummock, from whence I could see this field locked against the bluffy headland toward which we had been for several days directing our course. On my return to the sledge I selected the best track, carefully walking through every chasm and around every point which I thought passable, leaving conspicuous markings by my foot-tracks. My determination was to push my way forward as far as possible, by drawing William on the sledge in case he should not be able to walk.

May 27.—Reached the sledge at 2 A.M., after a walk since my last night's rest of not less than forty miles, over rough masses of ice and drifts of snow. I then turned into my sleeping-bag. At 7.30 A.M. rose, cooked our breakfast, and started by 9.30 A.M., one hour having been consumed in mending our harness. As the dogs had had no food on the previous evening, two of them had eaten their harness-lines to satisfy their hunger, and a third had consumed all his harness which was within his reach. An extra whip-lash furnished a line; a belt cut into strips, and a slice of William's pantaloons, fitted out the harness.

This morning William was able to travel, his cramps having left him. In three hours and a half we reached the old floe, and in three hours more we made the land, at the bluffy headland toward which we had directed our course since the 22d, and to which bearings were made on the 25th. This point is to the north and east of a little bay which seemed to terminate about ten miles inland. The dogs were tired and worn down, and their harness in a sad condition. It would require several hours to repair our sledge, as one of the runners was broken and nearly all the rivets lost. On examining our provisions, I found we had but about eighteen pounds of pemmican left. Eight days had been spent in making the passage of the channel, and I had no reason to suppose better fortunes would attend us on our return.

As yet we had seen no bear, and since leaving the eastern coast not a single seal. The extreme improbability of taking any of these animals was too great to base upon it any plan of operations. The propriety of sacrificing part of the dogs for the sustenance of the remainder was very doubtful; especially as it was impossible for me to know how far that might interfere with your future plans.

The travelling to the northward was good. The land-ice was broad and smooth, and the floe outside much less hummocky than at a greater distance from the shore. I felt assured that I was at or near the mouth of the channel you had so confidently predicted would be found opening to the northward of the so-called Smith's Sound. Every thing seemed favorable to our progress, except our short allowance of food. Had I possessed the whole world, I would have given it for fifty pounds of pemmican.

There was now no alternative; and, after a halt of sufficient length to fix our position and rest the dogs, I reluctantly put about for the brig. I conjectured that we were at least one hundred and fifty or two hundred miles to the north and east of previous explorations. To make a survey of this new coast could now be my only object.

May 28.—We rose this morning by two o'clock. I left William to repair the harness and mend the sledge, while I ascended a neighboring peak. But, before I could reach a point which would command an extended view, a thick fog set in, and, as it rolled along the sides of the mountain, it completely shut me out from the scene beneath. I had, however, a fine view of the interior. Peak after peak rose above the misty sea, and a great mountain-chain seemed to follow the trend of the coast-line.

Returning in time for the noonday observation, I found our position on the land-ice to be lat. 79° 42′ 9″ N., and lon. 71° 17′ W. The coast-line to the south trended S. 171 W. (magn.,) W. 27 S. (true;) to the north, N. 151 E. (magn.,) W. 43 E. (true.) Got under way at 10 A.M.; travelled along the land-ice, which averaged from fifty to one hundred and fifty feet in width, covered with light snow, which made the travelling pretty good. With both of us on the sledge, the dogs made from five to six miles an hour.

At 5 P.M. we halted at the north cape of a deep bay. The land between these two stations falls 5° more off to the west than the general trend of the coast.

The observation to determine the positions of the different points along this line, as well as the capes, bays, and headlands that follow, you will find in tabular form appended to this report.

May 29.—Started again to cross the bay at 6 A.M. We found the snow two feet deep and wet, making it impossible for the dogs to draw us on the sledge.

The coast between the first and second halting-stations, as far down as Cape Sabine, consists of high cliffs of magnesian limestone. The debris was usually low, rising at an angle of about forty degrees, and the cliffs generally rose smooth and unbroken to a height of not less than one thousand feet, terminating above in gentle slopes which rose into lofty peaks whose sides were mostly covered with snow and ice, while the deep valleys separating them were often filled with glacier.

Below the points marked *x y* on the chart, the cliffs presented a series of escarpments, rising step after step to a height of six hundred feet above a debris of about two hundred. The centre was depressed about fifty feet below either end; and the graceful sweep of outline of this semi-basin, with the beautiful regularity of the steps, gave a symmetrical beauty to the cliffs which those of the southern side of the channel did not possess. I would respectfully suggest them as being well worthy of a name.

(*Sketches enclosed.*)

After observing the meridian-altitude of the sun at noon, we started again. Unlike yesterday, the land-ice was narrow and covered with deep snow. The dogs made but little headway, the travelling being very laborious. William's cramps were increasing; and, with the hope of finding a smoother road, I took the floe, which proved to be little better. The snow was not quite so deep; but, as we had ridges of hummocks to pass, we were both obliged to walk most of the way, and reached the opposite shore after a continuous journey of seven hours.

At 4.30 P.M. we halted to melt snow and refresh ourselves with a cup of coffee, having made about twelve miles' course S. 5 E. We now lay under the cape bounding the deep bay we crossed yesterday. With the exception of Sanderson's Hope, south of Upernavik, this mass of rock is the most majestic I have ever beheld. Its longest face, presenting on Smith's Sound, is at least five miles; and the face presenting N. about three miles without a break. At the point its altitude is fifteen hundred feet, measured by sextant-angles with a base-line stepped upon the floe. The background is much higher. We this day gave our dogs our last scrap of pemmican.

May 30.—We got under way at 6 A.M., having deemed it expedient to lighten our load as much as possible by leaving behind us our sleeping-bags and every article which could at all be dispensed with; among which was a suite of geological specimens which I had taken the trouble to collect from the broken cliffs of the bluff reached on the 27th. I retained a pair of seal-skin boots, which I thought might serve as a breakfast for the dogs, our stockings, the compass, sextant, telescope, rifle, and lamp. All else was thrown off, to the amount of about forty pounds.

My reasons for this sacrifice I have before stated. I knew full well the service the sleeping-bags would be to you during your future journey; but, as William could no longer walk, I found it impossible to drag him and all our cargo on the sledge. In dispensing with those articles so valuable to us, I hoped to facilitate our arrival at the vessel, and thereby avoid the necessity of killing one of our dogs, thus causing a loss which could not be replaced.

Our travelling for the first few miles to-day was very rough; but the farther we receded from the shore we had harder snow and less sludge. We rode alternately until we reached the middle of the channel, when the dogs could drag us both at the rate of five miles an hour.

The general trend of the coast from the cape last described is W. 27° S. At a mile from the shore five headlands were distinctly visible nearly on a line; at five miles farther, another headland appeared; and at ten miles more, another. Our course was S.S.W., (true.) A thick fog soon appeared, and I did not get another sight of the shore until noon, when a meridian-altitude gave me lat. 79° 6′. I obtained good bearings to the cape where I left the land-ice, and the intermediate points between it and Cape Sabine to the south. These, together with observations previously made, enable me to chart the coast-line from Cape Sabine to thirty miles north of the farthest point reached by me. This material, together with the chart projected therefrom, is now in your possession.

(*Track-Chart accompanies.*)

Between the seventh cape mentioned above, and the next point of land to the south, is a bay which I was at first inclined to believe might be a channel opening to the westward; but as the fog cleared away I could distinctly see the land around the greater part of its margin, which convinced me it was only a deep bay having a narrow entrance. I had no means whereby to determine the true bearing of the land from this point, and in projecting the chart could only place it in connection with my last positively-determined position and Cape Sabine, previously the most northern determined point of land. To-day I called into requisition the pair of old Esquimaux boots which I had already anticipated might prove serviceable. By cutting them into strips, and mixing with them a little of the lard we had for our lamp, the hungry animals made quite a hearty meal.

May 31.—Soon after leaving this station we encountered ridges of hummocks which materially interrupted our progress; but they were neither so high nor difficult to pass as those farther up the channel. We had, however, comparatively smooth travelling, the hummocks being about twenty miles from the west shore. This smooth floe seems to be continuous along the shore to the bluff where I effected my first landing, at which place it runs to a point.

Our course across the channel was as near S.E. as the sluggishness of the compass and the motion of the ice would allow. As we were enveloped in a dense fog, the compass was our only guide. At 6 P.M. the land began to loom up through the fog, and I soon determined it to be Esquimaux Point. We then shaped our course more to the northward, and at 10 P.M. made the land-ice on the north side of Bedevilled Reach.

We gave the dogs the shakings of the bread-bag and the scrapings of the lard-cloth, mixed up with scraps of a pair of skin mittens, and some strips cut from the lower extremities of our pantaloons.

June 1.—We continued pushing our way along the shore without halting, and reached the vessel at 1 A.M.

In our journey down the west coast but two icebergs were seen, and none in crossing the channel until we came within eight miles of the east coast. The belt seems to hug the eastern shore and to widen and thicken as you advance up the channel, being eight miles in width at Force Bay.

Very little animal life was seen. We discovered foot-tracks of several bears, but came in contact with none. Foot-marks of fox and ptarmigan were seen at different points along the west coast, and occasionally a seal was observed on the ice; but they were too timid to allow our approach.

It affords me great pleasure to speak well of the services of my companion. He is an excellent driver, and understands well the management of the dogs.

In presenting this report, I beg to express my regret that I have not been able to do so at an earlier date, as well as that the observations for the survey of the newly-discovered coast-line are given so little in detail. But when you are apprised that after my first attack of snow-blindness I had not the proper use of my eyes,—often not being able to see ten fathoms from me, sometimes being totally blind,—you will, I trust, excuse both the delay and the deficiency. The data are, however, sufficient to enable me to fix the positions of the landmarks with reliable accuracy. The new coast-line which I am enabled to add to the chart is about two hundred miles in extent, and in the twelve days' absence, during two of which we were inactive, the dogs travelled not less than four hundred miles. The last day's travel was seventy miles, and after disposing of our sleeping-fixtures our rest was procured by basking in the sun, lying on the snow, or on the sledge, under the lee of a snow-bank.

Respectfully submitted, your obedient servant,

I. I. HAYES.

DR. E. K. KANE, U.S.N., *Commanding Arctic Expedition in search of, &c. &c.*

BRIG ADVANCE, RENSSELAER HARBOR, July 12, 1854.

Mr. Morton's Report of Journey to north and east during the months of June and July, 1854.

SIR:—

June 4.—I left the vessel at 4 P.M. in company with the party of Messrs. McGary and Bonsall, and arrived at Cache Island on the 14th. The details of this journey are fully given in Mr. Bonsall's report.

I remained at this place with Messrs. McGary and Bonsall's party, waiting for Hans, who arrived with the dog-sledge two days later.

June 18.—Allowing twenty-four hours' rest for Hans and the dogs, we set out at 0.30 A.M. in company with the other party, with whom we were forced to travel a mile on their way to the west, in order to avoid some cracks and openings in the ice near the glacier.

After leaving them we pursued a northerly course nearly parallel with the glacier, and from five to seven miles distant from it, according to the condition of the ice.

The snow was deep and free from hummocks; but, as the travelling was very heavy, we averaged only about three and a half miles per hour; which, in a continued journey of seven and a half hours, made our total distance but little more than twenty-six miles.

The appearance of the glacier is accurately described in Mr. Bonsall's report.

When about twelve miles out I took a back-bearing to Cache Island, and found it N. 284° E. magn. (N. 176° E. true.) We encamped at 8 A.M., our course having been N. 103° E. magn. (N. 5° W. true.) A back-bearing from the camp to Cache Island gave N. 285° E. magn. (N. 177° E. true.)

We started again at 9.30 P.M., and halted at midnight in order to take observations.

June 19.—We resumed our journey at 1 A.M. During three successive hours the travelling was very heavy: the sledge would sometimes be buried in the snow, notwithstanding all our exertions to prevent it. Afterward the travelling became better, and we moved off at the rate of four miles per hour until 4.20 A.M., when we were suddenly checked by meeting the barrier of icebergs mentioned by Mr. Bonsall in his journey in September, 1853. The icebergs and hummocks were so close together that we could not see one hundred yards in any direction. We pursued a westerly course about five miles along the edge of the hummocks and icebergs, when we discovered an opening between them, which we entered, and after a short circuitous route struck again on the right course. We halted at 5.45 A.M., and after supper climbed a high iceberg to select our course for the next day. From this point I discovered some rocks projecting from the face of the glacier, and also some hills on its surface. The sun was so much obscured that I could not obtain a solar bearing.

At 10.30 P.M. we resumed our journey, our course being N. 76° E. magn. (N. 32° W. true;) but at the end of three miles our progress was arrested by icebergs, hummocks, and cracks. We therefore were forced to retrace our steps, and at midnight arrived again at our last encampment. We then followed a westerly course, and four miles brought us to a group of icebergs, between which we found great difficulty in making our way, having to ferry ourselves occasionally over the numerous lanes of water, or to make bridges over them from the floe-pieces which were piled up in hummocks on the edges of the cracks.

June 20.—We succeeded in getting through the bergs by 2.30 A.M. Hans shot a dovekie in one of the cracks. At the same time we first sighted the west land with three prominent capes. We soon got on better ice than we had yet passed over, and made good headway to the N. and E. to within twelve miles of the glacier and about forty miles of the west shore.

The level surface of the glacier was interrupted by rocks and land-hills, excepting which, the background was nothing but snow or glacier. The land becomes continuous to the N., and has an appearance similar to the hills west of our winter quarters, only the debris is comparatively not so high.

No seals were seen during the two preceding days, but to-day we saw several, and three dovekies. We encamped at 7.20 A.M., and at 11.20 P.M. started again and stood for a point of land which I supposed to be a cape, as there was a vacancy between it and the west land. The ice was good and free from bergs; only two or three in sight.

The weather became very thick and misty. We suffered from cold, a strong N.E. wind blowing off the glacier at the time. Temp. +20°. The west land which I saw faintly yesterday was soon obscured, and the cape for which I stood vanished from our view; only a small portion of the east shore remaining faintly visible. I steered my course entirely by bearings of the cape which I took yesterday.

June 21.—At 7 A.M. we reached the mouth of a channel having to the northward and westward a fine headland. Here stretching ahead we found open water, and before I was aware of it we had gone some distance on rotten ice, which was so weak that we could not get within a mile and a half of the open water. My first intention was to go up the channel on the ice, but the water prevented it. We retraced our steps carefully, calling the dogs after us, as they were very much frightened. Birds, apparently ducks, were seen in great numbers flying over the open water.

On reaching the safe ice we travelled in an easterly direction, standing for the cape on the east side of the channel, and halted a mile from it at 7.40 A.M.

After supper, or more properly breakfast, I went to the cape, and around it at the distance of four miles from our camp. The temperature of the water was +40°. I found it would be difficult to pass the cape with a sledge, as the ice-foot was scarcely broad enough; but beyond the cape the ice-foot became better, and would apparently afford good travelling. We returned, fed the dogs, and turned in, after taking a meridian-altitude of the sun.

We started at 11.30 P.M. One of us climbed up the ice-belt, while the other handed up the dogs and provisions, making a ladder of the sledge. While here we saw a large flock of geese.

We then prepared for a journey up the channel, by making a cache of half our provisions, which would be enough to take us to the vessel on our return. It was very difficult to get around the cape, as the ice-foot was nearly all worn away, and the cliffs were very steep. This caused me to reflect what could be done in case the narrow ice-foot should be washed away before my return. I observed a ledge on the face of the cliffs about seventy feet above the ice-belt, over which I could escape myself, and leave the dogs and sledge behind.

We put the sledge on one runner, and thus passed around the most narrow part of the ice-foot. The water under us was very deep and transparent. Its temperature was 36° close alongside the ice-foot, but in a rapid tideway. We here lost our thermometer.

June 22.—At 0.30 A.M. we got around the cape and found good travelling; we went freely at the rate of six miles per hour. After passing three or four bluffs with small inlets, we got beyond the cliffs, where a low country opened on us. Here we saw nine seals in a small bay.

The land-ice across this shallow bay or inlet extended in some places two miles from the water's edge, where piles of gravel were formed; so that the sledge was drawn between hummocks of gravel. On account of this broad land-ice, we were enabled, in some places, to make a short cut, instead of following all the indentations of the coast. About two miles in-shore were cliffs which appeared perpendicular, and not unlike the broken walls of houses. About midnight I observed pieces of ice moving up the channel, toward the north, at the rate of four knots per hour; and now when we are encamping they are moving down the channel at the same rate.

The ice here is entirely broken up, and the channel is navigable for vessels of any size. Eider-ducks are so numerous that Hans killed two at one shot. Large flocks of geese are flying in-shore and up the channel, and the rocks are covered with tern, who are now breeding. Dovekies are very numerous, and ivory-gulls and burgomasters have made their appearance.

We have travelled fifty miles to-day, and must be forty-five miles up the channel. It has been very cold, and so cloudy that I have not been able to see the sun since I entered the channel, which runs north (true) and seems to be about thirty-five miles wide. The opposite (western) shore runs apparently in a straight line, and is very high;

the mountains, having a form resembling a sugar-loaf, extend far back in the interior. This coast-line is interrupted by only two bays.

June 23.—In consequence of a gale, we did not start until 0.30 A.M. After travelling about six miles we were arrested by floe-ice in an inlet, which was pressed over the land-ice against the mountains to the height of one hundred feet. Beyond this there was no ice-belt. We secured the dogs and left the sledge, as it would be impossible to transport them over these hummocks, which we succeeded in ourselves crossing with great difficulty. Our object was to ascertain the state of the travelling on the other side. We found it worse, with few landing-places, the cliffs overhanging the water and broken masses of ice. On these we ferried ourselves over to such pieces of ice as were attached to the coast. In this manner we travelled about four miles, and returned, after sighting a high cape on the north side of a bay before us, opposite to which lay an island. On reaching the sledge we made ourselves as comfortable as possible, and resolved to go on to-morrow without it. Here the ducks were less numerous, but gulls were seen in numbers.

June 24.—We started on foot at 3 A.M., taking with us a small stock of provisions. We found great difficulty in crossing some places, where, in the absence of land-ice, we were forced to crawl over the rocks, or get on loose floating pieces of ice and jump from one to another, or else ferry ourselves until we could again reach the land.

When about nine miles on our way to-day, we saw a bear with a young one at a short distance from us. Five of our dogs had followed us, and, seeing the bear, gave chase to it. The bears ran a considerable distance in-shore. The young one, which could not move fast enough, was pushed ahead by the old one, which sometimes turned round and faced the dogs in order to enable the little one to gain ground. Finally she stopped, and, taking the cub between her fore-legs, guarded it, and at the same time kept the dogs at a distance. She would sometimes make a jump at them, but always kept her eye on the little one, and never left it unprotected. She was thus fighting them off when we came up, and Hans shot her dead and then killed the cub. We skinned both of them, and gave the old one to the dogs, but cached the young one, to be eaten on our return. The skins we wished to take with us to the ship. We found at this place the runner of an Esquimaux sledge. Many small pieces of willow, about an inch and a half in diameter, had drifted up the eastern slope of this bay. Much grass was seen, as well as many plants, all of which I have reported to Dr. Kane. We had wood enough, including the sledge-runner, to cook a large part of the bear.

After this delay we started, in the hope of being able to reach the cape to the north of us. At the very lower end of the bay there was still a little old fast ice, over which we went without following the curve of the bay up the fiord, which shortened our distance considerably. Hans became tired, and I sent him more inland, where the travelling was less laborious. As I proceeded toward the cape ahead of me, the water came again close in-shore. I endeavored to reach it, but found this extremely difficult, as there were piles of broken rocks rising on the cliffs, in many places to the height of one hundred feet. The cliffs above these were perpendicular, and nearly two thousand feet high. I climbed over the rubbish; but beyond it the sea was washing the foot of the cliffs, and, as there were no ledges, it was impossible for me to advance another foot. I was much disappointed, because one hour's travel would have brought me round the cape. The knob to which I climbed was over five hundred feet in height, and from it there was not a speck of ice to be seen. As far as I could discern, the sea was open, a swell coming in from the northward and running crosswise, as if with a small eastern set. The wind was due N.,—enough of it to make white caps,—and the surf broke in on the rocks below in regular breakers. The sky to the N.W. was of dark rain-cloud, the first that I had seen since the brig was frozen up. Ivory-gulls were nesting in the rocks above me, and out to sea were mollemoke and silver-backed gulls. The ducks had not been seen N. of the first island of the channel, but petrel and gulls hung about the waves near the coast.

June 25.—As it was impossible to get around the cape, I retraced my steps, and soon came up to Hans, who had remained a short distance behind.

When we returned to the spot where the bears were killed, the dogs had another feed; they had not followed us any farther, but remained near the carcass of the bear. Three of them were lying down, having eaten so much they were unable to run.

After a difficult passage around the southern cape of the bay, we arrived at our camp, where we had left the sledge at 5 P.M., having been absent thirty-six hours, during which time we had travelled twenty miles due north of it.

June 26.—Before starting I took a meridian-altitude of the sun, (this being the highest northern point I obtained it except one, as during the last two days the weather had been cloudy, with a gale blowing from the north,) and then set off at 4 P.M. on our return down the channel to the south.

I cannot imagine what becomes of the ice. A strong current sets it almost constantly to the south; but, from altitudes of more than five hundred feet, I saw only narrow strips of ice, with great spaces of open water, from ten to fifteen miles in breadth, between them. It must therefore either go to an open space in the north, or dissolve. The tides in-shore seemed to make both north and south; but the tide from northward ran seven hours, and there was no slack-water. The wind blew heavily down the channel from the open water, and had been freshening since yesterday nearly to a gale; but it brought no ice with it.

To-day we again reached the entering cape of the channel, and camped at the place where we deposited half of our provisions on our journey to the north. I here found the thermometer which I had lost on the 21st. The water, five feet deep, taken from a rock, gave +40°, the tide setting from northward. The air in the shade was +34°.

June 27.—We started at 2 P.M. and travelled four hours; but the snow was so soft, in consequence of the warm sun, that we made slow progress. We camped at 6 P.M., intending to commence our night-travelling again.

June 28.—We started at 2 A.M., and travelled along the land, in order to discover more accurately where the glacier joins it. About thirty miles from the entrance of the channel it overlaps the land, which here becomes gradually lower. This land is of low round knobs, about eight hundred feet high.

Two large cracks running east and west caused us some delay. We had to go a great distance to the west near one of them, until we found a loose piece in it large enough to ferry ourselves and the sledge over. A great number of seals were around the cracks. We halted at 9.45 A.M., opposite the place where the land and glacier unite.

June 29.—We started at 0.40 A.M., and went to the south between the icebergs. We were detained by two cracks which we met with to-day. We saw the west shore to the south-of-west from us, which, as far as the eye could reach, did not appear to alter its trend.

June 30.—We started at 1.40 A.M., and soon got clear of the icebergs. We found better travelling-ice; but the snow was soft, and melting very fast. In a few days more it will be impossible to travel here.

This morning we sighted Cache Island, and shaped our course for Sunny Gorge. I saw the western shore to-day, and think it was about sixty miles distant.

July 1.—We started at 2.30 A.M. The travelling to-day was very heavy, the snow being so soft that we sometimes sank to our knees in water; yet we got along safely. A great number of seals were on the ice, and the west shore in sight.

July 2.—We started at 0.30 A.M., and travelled fast toward Sunny Gorge. The places between the old hummocks were filled with water. The dogs were sometimes actually swimming, and the sledge floating. At 8 A.M. we halted, being very much exhausted; we gave the dogs half feed. After a short rest we started again at 1 P.M., and reached the belt at 2.30 P.M. This belt-ice was firm and solid, twenty paces wide and eighteen feet thick. We reached Sunny Gorge at 3.40 P.M., where we encamped.

July 3.—We started at 4.40 A.M., and travelled along the land-ice, which, in some places, is completely overflowed by water falling in cascades and torrents from the tops of the cliffs. It has already made trenches for itself in some places by cutting the land-ice completely through down to the gravel.

When we passed Cape George Russell I saw the alcohol-keg sticking out of the land-ice, and tried to get it; but this was impossible. I then made a hole in it and tasted the contents, but found the alcohol much diluted by snow-water. The dogs' feet were considerably cut by the honey-combed ice. We camped near Chimney Rock at 11 A.M.

We started again at 7 P.M. and crossed Marshall Bay, which was covered with water. Minturn River had made for itself a channel more than one hundred yards wide, over which we ferried ourselves, sledge, and dogs, on a large loose piece of ice. To the west of Marshall Bay a torrent of water came down every ravine, which obliged us to go off the ice-foot and on the floe around it.

July 4.—At 7 A.M. we arrived at the brig, after an absence of thirty days.

I am, sir, respectfully, your obedient servant,

WILLIAM MORTON.

ABSTRACT FROM FIELD-BOOK.

Table of Courses and Estimated Distances.

Date.	Time of starting.	Time of halting.	Course, (magnetical.)	Distance Stat. miles.	REMARKS.
	h. m.	h. m.			
June 18	0 30 A.M.	8 0 A.M.	N.	1	
			N. 103° E.	25	
" "	9 30 P.M.	......	N. 85° E.	20	
" 19	......	5 45 A.M.	N. 18° E.	5	
" "	10 30 P.M.	......	N. 76° E.	3	
			N. 256° E.	3	
" 20	......	7 20 A.M.	N. 18° E.	4	
			N. 120° E.	20	
" "	11 20 P.M.	......	N. 65° E.	25	
" 21	......	7 40 A.M.	N. 280° E.	1	Halted at S. cape of channel.
" "	11 30 P.M.	......	N. 94° E.	45	
" 22	......	8 30 A.M.			
" 23	0 30 A.M.	2 30 A.M.	N. 117° E.	6	
" 24	3 0 A.M.	8 50 P.M.	N. 148° E.	20	Reached the northernmost cape.
" 25	Midnight.	5 0 P.M.	N. 330° E.	20	On our return.
" 26	4 0 P.M.	......	N. 274° E.	45	Reached S. cape of channel.
" 27	......	12 20 A.M.			
" "	2 0 P.M.	6 0 P.M.	N. 303° E.	14	
" 28	2 0 A.M.	9 45 A.M.	N. 216° E.	26	
" 29	0 40 A.M.	7 30 A.M.	N. 324° E.	26	
" 30	1 40 A.M.	9 0 A.M.	N. 314° E.	24	
July 1	2 30 A.M.	8 0 A.M.	N. 318° E.	15	
" 2	0 30 A.M.	8 0 A.M.	N. 349° E.	30	Reached the land-ice at 2.30 P.M.
" "	1 0 A.M.	3 40 P.M.	N. 349° E.		
" 3	4 40 A.M.	11 0 A.M.	N. 350° E.	18	Reached Cape George R. Russell.
" "	7 0 P.M.	......	N. 335° E.	40	
" 4	......	7 0 A.M.	......	...	Reached the brig.

II.

SOLAR BEARINGS.

At the entering cape of the channel.

Date	h. m. s.		
June 21	8 12 50 Chron.	Angle from the sun to last visible cape of west shore	31° 0′
	8 14 0 "	Angle from sun to inlet west coast	72° 0′
		Trend of coast to the north of the entering cape, N. 110° E. magn.; N. 2° E. (true.)	
June 24		From point of bay to high cliff	99° 30′
		From same to N. 2	46° 45′
	9 10 45 Chron. A.M.	From N. 2 to ⊙ (sun)	28° 15′
	9 13 8 " "	From sun to N. cape	43° 15′
	9 15 4 " "	From sun to island	46° 0′
June 26		From snow-valley to inlet	36° 45′
	5 35 10 Chron.	From inlet to ⊙	69° 25′
	5 37 55 "	From ⊙ to Gravel Point	32° 45′
	5 42 30 "	From ⊙ to bluff of bay	132° 20′
		From bluff to lower island	33° 40′
		From north cape to upper island	11° 0′
		From north cape to lower island	30° 40′
		The north cape bears from the position N. 143° E. magn.; N. 35° E. (true.)	
		The middle of the bay bears N. 155° E. magn.; N. 47° E. (true.)	
		Last visible point of W. coast to the north N. 128° E. magn.; N. 20° E. (true.)	
		Last visible point of W. coast to the south, N. 335° E. magn.; N. 227° E.= S. 47° W. (true.)	
		Trend of E. coast to the S. of Gravel Point, N. 270° E. magn.; N. 162° E. (true.)	

III.

OBSERVATIONS WITH POCKET-SEXTANT.

Date	Observation		°	′	Result
June 21	Latitude at noon by dead reckoning one mile from the entering cape of the channel				80° 33.7′
	The observation gives—				
	Double Altitude	$\underline{\odot}$	66	21·5	
		$\overline{\odot}$	67	27·5	
			66	54·5	
	Altitude $\odot$ centre		33	27·25	
	Refraction—Parallax			1·25	
	Correct Altitude	$\odot$	33	26·0	
	Declination		23	27·5	
	Latitude		80	1·5	80° 1·5′
June 24	The latitude by dead reckoning is				81° 24·8′
	The observation gives—				
	Double Altitude	$\underline{\odot}$	64	59·5	
		$\overline{\odot}$	66	04·0	
			65	31·75	
	Altitude $\odot$ centre		32	45·09	
	Refraction—Parallax			1·03	
	Correct Altitude	$\odot$	32	44·06	
	Declination		23	25·08	
	Latitude		80	41·02	80° 41·02′

The observations for Longitude are—

Chronometer. h. m. s.	Double Altitude. ° ′
7 11 12	60 18 $\underline{\odot}$
7 37 35	59 35 $\overline{\odot}$

Date	Observation		°	′	Result
June 26	The latitude by dead reckoning is				80° 55·6′
	The observation gives—				
	Double Altitude	$\underline{\odot}$	65	35·0	
		$\overline{\odot}$	66	40·0	
			66	07·5	
	Altitude $\odot$ centre.		33	03·7	
	Refraction—Parallax			1·3	
	Correct Altitude	$\odot$	33	02·4	
	Declination		23	22·6	
	Latitude		80	20·2	80° 20·2′

The observations for Longitude are—

Chronometer. h. m. s.	Double Altitude. ° ′
12 30 5	55 40·7 $\underline{\odot}$
12 39 32	67 26·8 $\overline{\odot}$

The index error is applied in all the preceding observations.

No. VI.

Table of Geographical Positions determined by the Expedition.

The following signs are used :—

> For theodolite stations for primary triangulation.

S. For positive observations by double altitude and artificial horizon.

△ For positions determined by triangulation or intersecting bearings.

R. For positions determined by dead reckoning, corrected, where possible, by triangulation.

The bearings are always solar, and the positions are arranged nearly according to latitude, commencing with the northernmost.

The Roman numerals refer to the positions as indicated upon the official chart presented to the Navy Department.—E. K. K.

No.	Designation.	Latitude.	Longitude.	Method.
		° ′	°	
XLIV. *a.*	Mount Edward Parry...........................	82 30, ap.	66, ap.	R.
XLIII.	Mount Francis Beaufort.......................	82 27	67 2′	
XLII.	Cape Beechy			
XLI.	Cape Roderick Murchison.....................			
XL.	Cape Bellot...	82 1·9	68 10	△
XXXIX.	Lady Franklin Bay			
XXXVIII.	Cape Sophia Cracroft.........................	81 51·8	68 26	△
XXXVII.	Cape Romain-Desfossés.......................	81 39·0	69 33	△
XXXVI.	Mount James C. Ross			
XXXV.	Cape George Back	81 18·9	70 30	△
XLIV. *b.*	Cape Constitution	81 22 0	... ...	R.
XLV.	Sir John Franklin Island Bay..............	81 17·1	66 12	△
XLVI.	Cape Independence			
XLVII.	Crozier Island			
XLIX.	Lafayette Bay....................................			
XXXIV.	Bay of Carl Ritter..............................	81 12·1	71 10	△
XXXIII.	Cape Von Buch	81 5·4	70 57	△
LI.	Cape Jefferson....................................	81 00	67 40	△ S.
XXXII.	Sir John Richardson Bay.....................	80 58·1	71 10	△
LII.	Cape Hamilton....................................	80 56·3	67 42	△ R.
	Kennedy Channel.			
XXXI.	McClure Bay......................................	80 52·1	70 53	△
XXX.	Cape Collinson..................	80 50·0	70 46	△
LIII.	Mount John Adams			
LIV.	Cape Madison	80 00	66 40	S. R.
XXIX.	Cape McClintock................................	80 00	70 41	△
XXVIII.	Scoresby Bay.....................................			
XXVII.	Cape Norton Shaw..............................	80 00	70 36	△
LV.	Robert Morris Bay			
LVI.	Cape John C. Calhoun.........................	80 00	66 38	△ R.
LIX.	Bay of Silas Wright............................			
LVII.	Cape Andrew Jackson..........................	80 17·6	66 40	R. S.

Table of Geographical Positions—Concluded.

No.	Designation.	Latitude.	Longitude.	Method.
		° ′	° ′	
XXVI.	Cape John Barrow	80 17·3	69 58	Δ
LXI.	Bay of Lewis Cass			
LX.	Cape Daniel Webster	80 15·2	65 52	Δ
LXII.	Cape Henry Clay	80 12·8	65 26	Δ
LXIII.	Bay of Thomas H. Benton			
LXV.	Cape Forbes	80 7·0	64 57	Δ R.
XXV.	Maury Bay			
XXIV.	Cape de la Roquette.	79 55·0	70 57	Δ
XXIII.	Cape John F. Frazer	79 42·9	71 17	S.
XXII.	Cape Joseph Leidy	79 40·0	71 59	R.
XXI.	Cape Hayes	79 38·8	72 00	R.
XIX.	Bay of James C. Dobbin			
XX.	Cape Prescott	79 35·2	72 44	Δ S.
XVII.	Cape Schott	79 34·8	73 42	Δ
XVI.	Washington Irving Island	79 28·6	73 18	R.
XV.	Cape Francis L. Hawks	79 00	73 41	Δ S.
XIV.	Cape Dumont D'Urville	79 00	74 8	R.
XI.	Bay of Franklin Pierce	79 25·3	75 5	Δ
XIII.	Louis Napoleon Promontory of Inglefield	79 16·0	74 36	Δ
LXVI. *a.*	Cape Agassiz	79 14·5	65 14	Δ
LXVI. *b.*	McGary Island			
LXVII. *b.*	Advance Bay	79 12·6	65 23	S.
X.	Cape R. M. T. Hunter	79 11·2	75 54	Δ
LXVII. *a.*	Brooks Island	79 8·5	66 10	Δ R.
LXVIII.	Cape Winfield Scott	79 6·8	66 49	Δ R.
IX.	Cape Alexander Dallas Bache	79 5·0	76 14	Δ
VIII.	Buchanan Bay			
LXX.	Cape James Kent	79 0.5	67 38	Δ R.
LXXI.	Cape William Wood	78 59·4	68 7	Δ S.
LXIX.	George M. Dallas Bay	78 58·8	67 0	Δ
VII.	Cape Joseph Henry	78 57·5	76 25	Δ
LXXII.	Cape George R. Russell	78 56·8	68 50	
LXIII.	John Marshall Bay			
VI.	Cape Sabine	78 50·8	76 15	Δ
LXXIV.	Cape Roger B. Taney	78 50·3	69 35	Δ R.
LXXV.	Bancroft Bay	78 48·0	69 22	Δ R.
V.	Cape Faraday			
IV.	Rosse Bay	78 45·8	76 58	Δ
LXXVI.	Cape De Haven	78 45·3	69 00	Δ R.
LXXVII.	Cape John W. Francis			
III.	Cape Dunglison			
LXXVIII.	Cape Thomas Leiper			
LXXXIX.	Rensselaer Bay	78 38·0	71 14	Δ R
⚓	Winter Quarters of Advance, 1853–54–55	78 37·0	70 40	S. >
II.	Herschell Bay	78 36·0	77 23	Δ
LXXIX.	Force Bay			
LXXX.	Cape Inglefield	78 34·5	72 51	>
I.	Cape Robert M. Patterson			
LXXXI.	Anoatok			
LXXXII.	Refuge Harbor			
LXXXIII.	Cape Hatherton	78 26·4	74 0	Δ R.
LXXXIV.	Life-boat Cove			
LXXXVI.	Hartstene Bay	78 20·0	73 43	Δ
LXXXV.	Cape Ohlsen	78 17·0	74 5	Δ S.
LXXXVII.	Cape Francis Patrick Kenrick	78 13·9	74 0	Δ

Notes to the preceding Geographical Positions.

1.

LXVII. Cache Island.

Position determined by Mr. Bonsall, from two sets of observations for latitude and two for longitude. The observations for latitude are:

	°	′	
1854, June 14	67	43·5	Double Altitude.
	68	47·5	
Mean	68	15·5	
Index Error —		3·5	
	68	12·0	
Altitude ⊙ centre	34	6·0	
Refraction —		1·42	
Parallax +		0·12	
Correct Altitude	34	4·70	
Declination	23	17·07	
	10	47·63	Lat. 79° 12·37′.

	°	′	
June 16 ⊙̲	67	54·0	
⊙̄	68	57·5	
	68	25·75	
Index Error —		3·90	
	68	21·85	
Altitude ⊙ centre	34	10·92	
Refraction —		1·42	
Parallax +		0·12	
Correct Altitude	34	9·62	
Declination	23	22·11	
	10	47·51	Lat. 79° 12·49′.

2.

LXXI. Cape William Wood.

Position determined by Mr. Bonsall. The observations for latitude are:

	°	′	
1854, June 7 ⊙̄	68	16	Double Altitude.
⊙̲	67	8	
	67	42	
Index Error —		2·95	
	67	39·05	
Altitude ⊙ centre	33	49·52	
Refraction —		1·43	
Parallax +		0·12	
Correct Altitude	33	48·21	
Declination	22	46·60	
	11	1·61	Lat. 78° 58·39′.

3.

THE POSITION OF THE WINTER QUARTERS.

The latitude depends on seven sets of circum-meridian-altitudes, taken in September, 1853, and May, 1854, each set consisting of eight to twelve single observations; the first set with theodolite, the rest with sextant and artificial horizon.

	°	′	″		
Latitude of winter quarters..........	78	37	6·0	Difference	—5·9
		37	7·0		—6·9
		37	3·0		—2·9
		36	53·0		+7·1
		37	0·7		—0·6
		36	59·0		+1·1
		36	52·0		+8·1
Mean..........................	78°	37′	00·1″		
Probable uncertainty			+4		

The longitude is derived principally from moon-culminations and moon-culminating stars, by three occultations of Saturn, December 13, 1853, January 8 and February 5, 1854, and an occultation of Mars, February 13, 1854, and a solar eclipse, May 15, 1855.

4.

The latitude of Littleton Island is determined by a set of circum-meridian-altitudes of the sun, made on the east end of the island; the single observations give, (corrected for refraction,)

		°	′	″	
1855, June 12,	Altitude ⊙ centre.................	34	47	27	
				32	
				25	
				22	
				38	
				26	
				26	
				35	
	Mean.............................	34	47	29	
	Parallax.........................+			7	
	Correct Altitude ⊙ centre...	34	47	36	
	Declination	23	9	37	
		11	37	59	Lat. 78° 22′ 1″.

5.

Position LI.

The latitude is the mean of the uncorrected dead reckoning and observation with pocket-sextant and artificial horizon. The dead reckoning gives latitude 81° 24·8′.

The observation is—

		°	′
1854, June 24	$\underline{\odot}$	64	59·5
	$\overline{\odot}$	66	4·0
		65	31·8
Altitude ⊙ centre		32	45·9
Refraction—Parallax	—		1·3
Correct Altitude		32	44·6
Declination		23	25·8
		9	18·8
Latitude		80°	41·2′ by observation.

6.

Position LIV.

The latitude is determined in the same way as the preceding; the dead reckoning gives latitude 80° 55·6′.

The observation is—

		°	′
1854, June 26	$\underline{\odot}$	65	35·0
	$\overline{\odot}$	66	40·0
		66	7·5
Altitude ⊙ centre		33	3·7
Refraction—Parallax	—		1·3
Correct Altitude ⊙		33	2·4
Declination		23	22·6
Latitude		80°	20·2′ by observation.

7.

Position LVII.

The position is determined in the same way as the preceding. The dead reckoning gives latitude 80° 33·7′.

The observation is—

		°	′
June 21	$\underline{\odot}$	66	21·5
	$\overline{\odot}$	67	27·5
		66	54·5
Altitude ⊙ centre		33	27·3
Refraction—Parallax	—		1·3
Correct Altitude ⊙		33	26·0
Declination		23	27·5
		9	58·5
Latitude		80°	1·5′ by observation.

8.

Position XXIII.

This position is determined by an observation with sextant and ice-horizon.
The dead reckoning makes it 4′ more to the north.
The observation is—

			°	′
1854, May 28,	Altitude	$\underline{\odot}$	31	33·5
		$\overline{\odot}$	32	5·5
	Altitude ⊙ centre......................		31	49·5
	Dip + Refraction—Parallax ....—			3·0
	Correct Altitude ⊙.....................		31	46·5
	Declination..............................		21	29·4
	Latitude		78°	42·9′

9.

Position XX.

The latitude is obtained by an observation with sextant and artificial horizon.

			°	′
1854, May 29, noon.	Double Altitude	$\overline{\odot}$	64	42·0
		$\underline{\odot}$	63	38·0
	Mean		64	10·0
	Altitude ⊙ centre...................		32	5·0
	Refraction—Parallax.............—			1·4
	Correct Altitude ⊙................		32	3·6
	Declination		21	38·8
	Latitude..............................		79°	35·2′

10.

Position XV.

This position is determined by bearings from Position XX. and a place on the floe, of which the latitude was obtained from the following observation with sextant and artificial horizon.

			°	′
1854, May 30, noon.	Double Altitude.....................	$\overline{\odot}$	65	58
		$\underline{\odot}$	64	55
	Mean		65	26·5
	Altitude ⊙ centre...................		32	43·2
	Refraction—Parallax.............—			1·4
	Correct Altitude ⊙................		32	41·8
	Declination..........................		21	47·9
	Latitude..............................		79°	6·1′

11.

Position LXIII.

This position is obtained by an observation with theodolite and a solar bearing. The sun was during the observation constantly so obscured by clouds that no sun-glass could be used.

The observations are—

1853, September 3. Circle		Chronometer. h.	m.	s.	Level.	Reading. °	′	″
E.	$\underline{\odot}$	4	13	27	7·0	199	7	10
					15·0		6	45
							6	45
							7	5
E.	$\underline{\odot}$	4	20	25	11·18	199	7	20
					11· 7		6	50
							6	40
							6	55
W.	$\overline{\odot}$	4	27	22	12·0	71	52	5
					11·3		51	55
							51	50
							52	10
W.	$\overline{\odot}$	4	43	0	10·0	71	52	15
					13·0		52	10
							51	50
							52	25
E.	$\overline{\odot}$	4	59	50	10·8	199	35	50
					12·3			30
								35
								50
W.	$\underline{\odot}$	5	8	9	10·0	72	31	30
					13·0			30
								35
								40

Temperature of air, + 27·5°.

Barometer, (Aneroid,) 29·98.

The north end of the level always read first.

The latitude follows, from these observations, 78° 52′ 0″.

The bearing gives the longitude 1° 59′ east from the winter quarters.

12.

Position LXXX.

The position is obtained by observations for latitude and longitude with theodolite. The observations for latitude are—

1853, August 12. Circle	Chronometer. h.	m.	s.	Level.	Reading. °	′	″
W. $\underline{\odot}$	4	53	32	10·0	206	45	50
				11·5			25
							30
							45
W. $\overline{\odot}$	4	57	32	12·2	207	17	55
				9·2			45
							36
							50
E. $\overline{\odot}$	5	2	2	6·2	64	5	10
				14·8			30
							30
							25
E. $\underline{\odot}$	5	5	24	15·3	64	37	0
				5·0			5
							10
							10
W. $\underline{\odot}$	5	10	52	10·0	206	42	25
				11·0		41	50
						42	0
						42	10
W. $\overline{\odot}$	5	14	37	10·3	207	13	5
				10·3		12	50
						12	30
						13	0
E. $\overline{\odot}$	5	19	36	15·8	64	10	10
				4·2			30
							20
							25
E. $\underline{\odot}$	5	23	7	8·0	64	44	5
				12·4			20
							20
							20

Temperature of air, 33·1°.
Aneroid Barometer, 29·79.
Latitude 78° 34′ 5″.

13.

Position of the West Cape of Fog Inlet.

This position is obtained by two sets of sextant observations and artificial horizon, and a set of theodolite observations for latitude. These are—

1853, August 11.

Circle	Chronometer. h.	m.	s.	Level.	Reading. °	′	″
W. $\overline{\odot}$	4	18	17	12·2	207	6	10
				11·0		5	55
						5	55
						6	15
W. $\overline{\odot}$	4	21	17	12·0	207	8	0
				11·3		7	40
						7	50
						7	55
W. $\underline{\odot}$	4	27	6	10·8	206	38	15
				12·9		37	55
						37	55
						38	10
E. $\underline{\odot}$	4	35	8	11·2	63	54	0
				11·8			5
							10
							5
E. $\underline{\odot}$	4	38	16	9·5	63	53	35
				13·2			40
							45
							50

Circle	Chronometer. h.	m.	s.	Level.	Reading. °	′	″
E. $\overline{\odot}$	4	44	2	13·19	63	20	50
				8·2		20	55
						21	10
						21	5
E. $\overline{\odot}$	4	47	47	9·2	63	20	35
				13·4			55
							50
							50
W. $\overline{\odot}$	4	58	41	12·0	207	14	30
				11·0			5
							5
							16
W. $\underline{\odot}$	5	1	52	11·8	206	42	25
				12·0		41	55
						42	0
						42	10
E. $\underline{\odot}$	5	7	6	11·8	63	54	20
				11·0			30
							35
							35

Temperature of air, 35·6°.

Aneroid Barometer, 29·85.

Latitude, 78° 31′ 0″.

The north end of the level is by these and the preceding observations always read first. The instrument was carefully protected from the rays of the sun by a paper screen fitting around the object-glass of the telescope.

14.

Position of Cape Alexander.

This position is obtained by an observation at a point on the ice 5′ distant and N. 7° 26′ E. from the cape.

		°	′
1855, June 17	$\overline{\odot}$	70	45
	$\underline{\odot}$	69	41
		70	13
Index	+		8·7
		70	21·7
Altitude ⊙ centre		35	10·8
Refraction—Parallax	—		1·4
Correct Altitude ⊙		35	9·4
Declination		23	23·7
Latitude		78°	14·3′

No. VII.

Abstract of the Log-Book.

This abstract contains the position of the ship at noon each day as found by dead reckoning and by astronomical determinations, and the true direction of the surface-current, with the corresponding velocity in miles per hour.

1853.	Lat. D. R.	Long. D. R.	Lat. Obs.	Long. Obs.	Wind.			Atmosphere.	Current.	
					4h.	12h.	20h.		True Direction.	Velocity.
	° ′	° ′							°	′
June 1	39 47	73 33	......	......	E.	E.	E.N.E.	f.	......	......
2	39 29	72 58	......	......	S.E.	S.E.	S.	f.	......	......
3	40 1	71 42	39 28	72 7	S.W.	S.W.	W.	b.	S. 30 W.	0·58
4	40 16	69 42	......	......	N.	N.E.	N.E.	c. f.	......	......
5	40 14	67 58	40 3	67 3	N.E.	N.E.	E.	b.	S. 75 E.	0·91
6	40 2	66 31	40 3	66 30	S.	S.	S.	b.	N. 39 E.	0·05
7	40 49	65 11	41 8	65 8	S.	S.	S.	b. v.	N. 7 E.	0·80
8	42 9	63 18	42 15	63 2	S.	S.	S.	b. f.	N. 63 E.	0·56
9	43 3	61 21	......	......	Variable.	Calm.	Variable.	f.	......	......
10	43 8	60 56	43 18	60 19	Calm.	Calm.	Calm.	b. f.	N. 70 E.	0·60
11	43 19	60 14	......	......	Calm.	N.E.	N.E.	v. f.	......	......
12	43 13	58 34	43 9	58 12	N.N.E.	N.N.E.	N.N.E.	b.	S. 76 E.	0·34
13	43 13	56 23	43 17	55 59	Calm.	S.W.	S.W.	b.	N. 77 E.	0·75
14	44 38	54 44	44 44	54 30	Variable.	W.	W.	b. c.	N. 59 E.	0·49
15	45 38	53 38	45 44	53 30	W.	W.	......	b. c.	N. 43 E.	0·34
16	Harbor of St. John's, Newfoundland.				......	......	......	...	......	......
17					......	W.2	S.W.2	b.	......	......
18	48 17	52 16	48 26	52 8	S.W.5	S.W.5	W.S.W.5	b.	N. 31 E.	0·88
19	51 12	52 8	......	......	Calm.	S.E.5	S.E.2	o.	......	......
20	52 20	52 12	......	......	Calm.	Calm.	W.S.W.1	o.	......	......
21	52 50	52 12	52 57	......	W.S.W.3	W.N.W.5	W.4	b. o.	......	......
22	55 16	52 12	......	......	W.3	W.1	W.2	o.	......	......
23	56 7	52 12	56 28	50 31	Calm.	E.6	E.7	b. c.	N. 69 E.	0·49
24	57 11	51 58	57 20	......	E.5	Calm.	N.5	b. c.	......	......
25	58 37	51 35	58 25	51 21	N.4	N.4	N.2	b. m.	S. 32 E.	0·29
26	59 48	50 3	59 35	49 27	S.W.3	S.3	S.2	b.	S. 55 E.	0·94
27	61 0	49 33	61 12	49 44	S.2	N.1	E.1	b. m.	N. 24 W.	0·55
28	61 55	50 27	62 14	50 6	N.3	S.E.1	S.E.2	b. f.	N. 44 W.	1·10
29	......	......	Harbor of Fiskernaes.		......	......	......	b.	......	......
30	......	......			......	......	......	b.	......	......
July 1	......	......			......	N.E.5	N.N.E.5	b.	......	......
2	......	......	62 46	52 24	N.4	N.4	N.3	o.	......	......
3	63 26	53 14	63 24	52 8	N.2	N.2	N.E.1	o. f.	S. 86 E.	1·25
4	63 48	52 14	63 47	......	N.2	N.N.E.2	N.N.E.2	o. f.	......	......
5	64 5	52 59	63 49	52 25	N.2	N.E.1	N.E.1	o.	S. 43 E.	0·50
6	64 6	52 43	......	......	Calm.	N.E.3	N.N.E.3	o. f.	......	......
7	64 39	53 29	64 8	53 30	N.N.E.2	N.1	S.1	b.	S. 1 E.	0·65
8	64 35	53 16	......	......	N.2	S.1	S.1	b. f.	......	......
9	65 7	53 40	Near Sukkertoppen		N.W.4	N.N.E.2	N.E.6	b. c.	......	......
10	......	......			N.E.5	N.E.5	N.N.E.3	o. f.	......	......
11	......	......	65 37	53 16	N.3	N.N.E.5	N.2	b.	......	......
12	65 56	54 23	65 51	53 30	Variable.	S.W.3	S.4	b. c.	S. 77 E.	0·94
13	67 47	55 19	67 46	......	S.W.5	S.W.5	S.W.4	o.	......	......
14	69 53	57 6	70 0	......	S.W.1	Calm.	N.E.3	o.	......	......
15	70 36	57 48	70 33	56 41	N.E.1	W.3	E.N.E.4	o. f.	S. 83 E.	0·35
16	71 25	56 55	......	......	Variable.	Calm.	E.1	b. c.	......	......
17	72 8	57 21	......	......	Calm.	Variable.	Calm.	b. c.	......	......
18	......	......	......	......	E.4	......	......	b. c.	......	......

Abstract of Log-Book—Concluded.

1853.	Lat. D. R.	Long. D. R.	Lat. Obs.	Long. Obs.	Wind. 4h.	Wind. 12h.	Wind. 20h.	Atmosphere.	Current. True Direction.	Current. Velocity.
	° ′	° ′	° ′	° ′					°	′
July 19	Harbor of Proven.				......	......	......	b. f.	......	......
20	Among small islands from Proven to Upernavik.				N.E.1	Variable.	Calm.	b. f.	......	......
21					N.N.W.1	Calm.	E.N.E.2	c. f.	......	......
22					Calm.	Variable.	Calm.	b. m.	......	......
23					W.4	S.W.2	N.N.E.2	b. c.	......	......
24	73 47	57 27	......	......	N.E.1	E.2	N.E.1	b. c.	......	......
25	73 59	57 16	......	......	Calm.	N.1	Calm.	b. c.	......	......
26	74 20	57 31	74 14	......	Calm.	N.W.2	Calm.	o. f.	......	......
27	74 23	57 57	......	......	N.E.2	N.E.3	N.4	o. f.	......	......
28	74 38	61 26	......	......	N.W.1	Calm.	S.W.3	o. f.	......	......
29	75 18	62 47	......	......	S.W.4	S.6	S.W.3	o. f.	......	......
30	75 34	63 5	......	......	S.3	S.3	S.3	b. m.	......	......
31	75 34	63 5	......	......	E.N.E.2	N.E.2	E.1	b. m.	......	......
Aug. 1	75 34	63 5	75 40	62 12	N.E.2	Calm.	S.3	b.	......	......
2	75 40	62 12	75 44	62 20	N.3	Calm.	Variable.	b. f.	N. 27 W.	0·19
3	75 44	62 20	75 48	62 33	N.N.E.4	N.3	Variable.	b. f.	N. 39 W.	0·21
4	75 48	62 33	......	......	S.5	S.S.W.5	S.S.W.4	o. f.	......	......
5	76 59	71 44	......	......	S.E.3	Calm.	Calm.	o. f.	......	.....
6	77 23	72 56	......	......	E.3	S.E.1	S.W.3	o. f.	......	......
7	77 53	72 52	78 22	......	S.E.2	S.E.2	S.E.4	o. f.	N.	1·20
8	Refuge Inlet.		......	......	N.	N.	N.N.W.	o.	......	......
9			......	......	S.W.2	S.W.2	S.W.	b_2m_p	......	......
10			78 31·1	73 47	N.6	E.4	E.2	b. f.	......	......
11			......	......	W.5	W.1	Calm.	b.	......	......
12	......	......	78 34·6	72 51	Calm.	Calm.	Calm.	b.	......	......
13	......	......	78 34·6	72 51	Calm.	Calm.	Calm.	b. f.	......	......
14	Godsend Island.				Calm.	N.W.6	N.W.3	b. c.	......	......
15					N.W.4	Calm.	Calm.	b. c.	......	......
16					Calm.	S.W.1	Calm.	o.	......	......
17					N.3	N.W.7	N.E.6	b. c.	......	......
18					Calm.	Calm.	Calm.	o.	......	......
19					Calm.	S.E.5	S.S.E.	o.	......	......
20	Working along the coast.				S.S.E.8	Calm.	Calm.	b. c.	......	......
21	78 40	72 0	......	......	Calm.	Calm.	Calm.	f.	......	......
22	78 41	71 40	......	......	Calm.	Calm.	Calm.	b. f.	......	......
23	78 38	71 0	......	......	Calm.	Calm.	Calm.	o. f.	......	......
24	78 37	70 40	......	......	Calm.	Calm.	Calm.	o. f.	......	......
25	78 40	70 40	......	......	Calm.	Calm.	S.4	b. c.	......	......
26	78 41	70 35	......	......	N.3	Calm.	Calm.	b. c.	......	......
27	78 42	70 35	......	......	Calm.	Calm.	S.1	o.	......	......
28	78 43	70 35	......	......	N.2	Calm.	Calm.	b. c.	......	......
29	78 43	70 35	......	......	Calm.	Calm.	Calm.	c.	......	......
30	78 40	70 40	......	......	Calm.	Calm.	Calm.	o.	......	......
31	78 37	70 40	......	......	Calm.	Calm.	N.W.3	o. f.	......	......
Sept. 1	......	......	......	......	W.4	N.W.4	N.N.W 2	o. f.	......	......
2	......	......	......	......	N.W.5	N.W.3	Calm.	o.	......	......
3	......	......	......	......	Calm.	Calm.	Calm.	o.	......	......
4	......	......	......	......	Calm.	Calm.	Calm.	o.	......	......
5	......	......	......	......	S.W.1	Calm.	S.W.1	o.	......	......
6	......	......	......	......	S.W.5	S.W.7	S.W.3	o.	......	......
7	......	......	......	......	......	......	......	......	......	......
8	Entered winter quarters, Rensselaer Bay.					......	......	......	......	......

No. VIII.

Observations for Longitude of Rensselaer Harbor.

RECORD OF OBSERVATIONS OF MOON-CULMINATIONS AND MOON-CULMINATING STARS.

TRANSIT-INSTRUMENT. OBSERVATORY, FERN ROCK.—A. SONTAG, *Observer.*

November 28, 1853. *Circle West. Pocket-Chronometer.*

Object Observed.	Wire I.	II.	III.	IV.	V.	Mean.
	h. m. s.	m. s.	m. s.	m. s.	h. m. s.	h. m. s.
☾ II. S. P.	6 49 16·0	49 37·0	50 1·5	50 24·0	50 45·5	6 50 1·00
μ Geminorum, S. P.	7 5 39·5	6 1·5	6 23·0	6 44·5	7 6·5	7 6 23·00
ε " S. P.	26 24·0	26 45·5	27 7·0	27 29·5	27 51·5	27 7·50
After these observations changes azimuth and inclination.						
Polaris, R.	14 16 44·0	2 39·0	49 21·0	36 50·0	13 22 55·0	13 49 29·80
η Ursæ Major, S. P.	32 12·0	32 41·5	......	33 42·5	34 15·0	14 33 12·70
α Arietis	50 26·5	50 5·0	49 44·0	49 23·0	......	49 44·00
α Boötis, S. P.	59 19·0	59 39·0	0 0·5	0 21·0	0 42·5	15 0 0·40
γ Ceti	15 27 14·0	26 54·0	26 34·5	26 14·5	25 54·0	26 34·20
Circle East.						
β Ursæ Min. S. P. refl.	45 17·0	44 1·5	42 47·0	41 31·5	40 14·0	42 46·00
Approximate azimuth, —92s.; inclination, + 5.6s. c = 0.						
November 21. *Circle East.*						
	h. m. s.	m. s.	m. s.	m. s.	m. s.	h. m. s.
51 Cephis, S. P. R.	7 0 0·0	16 42·5	9 18·5	2 45·0	......	7 9 35·33
β Lyræ	23 3·0	23 29·0	23 53·5	24 14·5	24 37·5	23 51·50
ζ Aquilæ	37 14·5	37 34·5	37 54·0	38 16·0	38 37·0	37 55·20
δ Geminorum, S. P.	51 32·5	51 12·0	50 50·0	50 29·5	50 7·0	50 50·20
δ Aquilæ	56 41·5	57 2·0	57 19·5	57 43·0	58 2·5	57 21·70
γ Cancris, ☾ * S. P.	9 14 44·0	14 24·0	14 2·5	13 42·5	......	9 14 3·00
☾ II. S. P.	20 1·0	......	19 15·0	18 52·5	18 28·5	19 14·83
ι Ursæ Major, S. P.	29 35·0	29 6·5	28 37·0	28 7·5	27 35·0	28 36·20
ζ Cygni	44 46·5	45 9·0	45 30·5	45 53·5	46 17·0	45 31·30
α Cephis, R.	52 49·0	53 30·0	54 13·5	54 55·0	55 38·5	54 13·20
λ Leonis, S. P.	10 3 11·0	2 50·5	2 28·5	2 7·0	1 44·0	10 2 28·20
November 23. *Circle East.*						
η Draconis, R.	4 53 44·0	54 27·0	55 6·5	55 50·0	56 32·5	4 55 8·00
α Tauri, S. P.	5 1 11·0	0 51·0	0 29·5	0 9·0	59 47·0	5 0 29·50
α Aurigæ, S. P.	40 1·0	39 33·0	39 4·5	38 35·0	38 6·5	39 4·40
γ Draconis, R.	6 24 56·5	25 31·0	26 2·0	26 33·0	27 7·0	6 26 1·90
α Lyræ	7 3 12·5	3 39·0	4 4·0	4 30·0	4 56·0	7 4 4·30
β "	15 2·0	15 25·0	15 47·0	16 12·0	16 35·0	15 48·20 + 1 m.
ζ Aquilæ	30 16·5	30 36·5	30 57·0	31 17·0	31 37·5	30 56·90
δ Geminorum, S. P.	44 40·0	44 21·0	43 59·0	43 36·0	43 14·5	43 58·10
α Leonis, ☾ *	22 29 44·5	30 4·0	30 25·5	30 45·0	31 5·5	22 30 24·90
γ Leonis, ☾ *	40 56·0	41 16·0	41 37·0	41 59·0	42 23·0	41 38·20
☾ II.	23 18 25·0	18 45·0	19 7·0	19 29·0	19 49·5	23 19 7·10

Observations of Moon-Culminations, &c.—Continued.

Object Observed.	Wire I.	II.	III.	IV.	V.	Mean.
	December 8. Circle East.					
	h. m. s.	m. s.	m. s.	m. s.	m. s.	h. m. s.
ε Piscium	11 3 55·0	4 15·0	4 35·0	4 54·0	5 15·0	11 4 34·80
α Andromedæ	31 46·0	32 8·0	32 31·0	32 54·0	33 16·5	32 31·10
γ Pegasi	36 57·0	37 17·0	37 37·0	37 57·5	38 19·0	37 37·50
☾ I.	54 49·0	55 11·0	55 31·0	55 53·5	56 13·0	55 31·60
Piscium, ☾✱	12 12 23·0	12 41·0	13 3·5	13 22·0	13 42·5	12 13 2·40
	December 9. Circle East.					
α Andromedæ	11 27 52·0	28 15·0	28 36·0	29 0·0	29 21·5	11 28 36·90
γ Pegasi.	33 2·0	33 22·5	33 42·0	34 3·5	34 24·0	33 42·80
☾ I.	36 57·5	37 17·0	37 38·0	37 58·5	38 20·0	37 38·20
	December 12. Circle East.					
δ Arietis, ☾✱	2 0 0·0	18 41·0	19 3·5	19 25·0	19 44·0	2 19 3·20
☾ I.	44 30·0	44 53·5	45 15·0	45 36·5	45 58·0	45 14·60
η Tauri, ☾✱	53 38·5	54 0·0	54 23·5	54 44·5	55 7·0	54 22·70
Plegadæ?	55 20·0	55 41·0	56 4·0	56 25·5	56 48·0	56 3·70
α^1 Tauri	3 10 55·5	11 17·0	11 38·5	12 0·0	12 22·0	3 11 38·60
	December 13. Circle East.					
Polaris, R.	11 51 56·0	4 10·0	17 39·5	......	......	......
	Circle West.					
Polaris, R.	12 41 37·0	28 36·5	......	......	......	11 17 39·00
α Arietis, R.	1 11 27·0	11 6·0	10 44·5	10 23·5	10 4·0	1 10 45·00
α Boötis, S. P.	20 4·5	20 26·0	20 46·5	21 8·0	21 29·5	20 46·90
γ Ceti	48 10·0	47 51·0	47 30·0	47 11·0	46 49·5	47 30·30
β Ursæ Min. S. P. R.	2 0 0·0	1 38·0	2 56·5	4 13·0	5 28·0	2 2 55·80
α Coronæ, S. P.	39 20·0	39 42·0	40 3·5	40 25·0	40 48·0	40 3·70
η Tauri	51 5·5	50 43·5	50 22·5	50 2·0	49 38·0	50 22·30
Plegadæ?	52 45·0	52 25·0	52 3·0	51 39·0	51 20·0	52 2·40
α^1 Tauri	3 8 18·5	7 57·0	7 30·5	7 12·0	6 50·5	3 7 34·70
☾ I.	31 20·5	30 59·5	30 38·0	30 17·0	29 52·5	30 37·50
	December 14. Circle West.					
ζ Ursæ Min. S. P. R.	4 3 52·5	6 27·0	9 21·5	......	......	4 9 21·00
☾ I.	19 1·0	18 41·5	18 16·5	17 56·0	17 35·5	18 16·70
☾ II.	21 15·0	20 52·5	20 31·0	20 7·5	19 44·5	20 30·10
						moon nearly full.
δ Tauri, ☾✱	26 56·0	26 34·5	26 13·0	25 50·5	25 30·0	26 12·80
δ Orionis	32 36·5	32 16·5	31 57·0	31 36·5	31 16·5	31 56·60
ζ Tauri, ☾✱	36 58·0	36 35·5	36 15·5	35 53·5	35 31·5	36 14·80
α Orionis	55 15·5	54 54·0	54 35·0	54 14·0	53 53·5	54 34·40
μ Geminorum	5 22 5·5	21 43·5	21 23·0	21 1·0	20 29·5	5 21 22·50

Observations of Moon-Culminations, &c.—Concluded.

Object Observed.	Wire I.	II.	III.	IV.	V.	Mean.
December 15. *Circle West.*						
	h. m. s.	m. s.	m. s.	m. s.	m. s.	h. m. s.
Polaris, R.	12 33 22·0	20 13·5	7 32·5	54 18·5	41 27·0	12 7 22·70
η Ursæ Major, S. P.	44 55·5	45 27·5	45 57·0	46 29·0	46 58·5	45 57·50
η Boötis, S. P.	51 5·5	51 26·5	51 47·5	52 9·0	52 31·0	51 47·90
α Arietis, R.	1 3 40·0	3 18·5	2 58·0	2 35·5	2 13·0	1 2 57·00
α Boötis, S. P.	12 19·5	12 40·5	13 1·0	13 23·0	13 43·0	13 1·40
γ Ceti	40 18·5	39 59·0	39 39·0	39 19·0	38 59·5	39 39·00
β Ursæ Min. S. P. R.	52 49·0	54 6·0	55 20·0	56 35·0	57 52·5	55 20·50
ο Tauri, ☾✱	4 23 2·0	22 39·0	22 19·5	21 57·5	21 35·5	4 22 18·70
ζ Tauri, ☾✱	33 2·5	32 41·5	32 20·0	31 58·5	31 37·0	32 20·00
α Orionis	51 17·0	50 57·5	50 37·0	50 17·5	49 58·0	50 37·40
γ Draconis, S. P.	55 38·0	56 10·5	56 42·5	57 15·0	57 47·5	56 42·70
☾ II.	5 10 42·0	10 19·0	9 56·5	9 34·0	9 11·0	5 9 56·50
Gemini, ☾✱	18 7·5	17 46·5	17 25·5	17 3·5	16 41·0	17 24·80
January 8, 1854. *Circle West.*						
α Boötis, S. P.	......	37 34·0	37 55·0	38 16·5	38 37·5	11 37 55·17
B. A. C. 485, ☾✱	12 6 34·5	6 14·0	5 54·5	5 33·5	5 12·5	12 5 53·80
π Arietis, ☾✱	10 39·5	10 18·5	9 58·5	9 38·0	9 15·5	9 58·00
α Ceti	24 6·5	23 45·5	23 27·0	23 6·5	22 45·5	23 26·20
☾ I.	42 42·5	42 20·5	41 57·0	41 37·5	41 15·0	41 58·50
Saturn, centre	1 2 41·5	2 20·5	1 59·0	1 39·5	1 18·0	1 1 59·10
17 Tauri, ☾✱	5 36·5	5 15·0	4 53·0	4 31·0	4 8·5	4 52·80
Taurus ? (parallel of 17 T.)	8 12·5	7 50·5	7 29·0	7 7·5	6 45·0	7 28·90
27 Tauri, ☾✱	9 53·5	9 31·5	9 9·5	8 47·5	8 26·0	9 9·40
January 9. *Circle West.*						
γ Pegasi	9 31 42·5	31 23·0	31 2·5	30 40·0	30 19·0	9 31 2·40
α Cassiopeia, R.	59 8·5	58 34·0	57 58·5	57 23·0	56 46·5	57 58·10
Polaris, R.	9 0·0	56 12·0	43 10·0	30 9·5	17 54·5	10 43 17·20
η Ursæ Major, S. P.	5 45·0	6 17·5	6 46·0	7 18·0	7 49·5	11 6 47·20
α Arietis	24 39·5	24 18·5	23 58·0	23 36·5	23 13·0	23 57·10
January 10. *Circle West.*						
γ Pegasi	9 27 48·5	27 28·0	27 7·0	26 47·5	26 27·0	9 27 7.60
α Cassiopeia, R.	55 15·0	54 41·5	54 5·5	53 30·0	52 52·5	54 4·90
Polaris, R.	11 6 9·5	53 6·0	39 30·0	26 11·0	13 22·0	10 39 39·70
α Boötis, S. P.	29 20·5	29 42·0	30 2·5	30 24·0	30 46·0	30 3.20

Notes to the preceding Observations with the Transit-Instrument.

The time was noted by pocket-chronometer, showing nearly mean time, and within a few minutes of Greenwich time.

There are five wires in the telescope, which are numbered I., II., III., IV., V. in the order as a star passes them in the upper culmination when the circle is on the east side of the telescope. The mean of broken transits refers to the middle wire, and not the mean wire.

The sign R. after the name of the observed object denotes that its transit was observed by means of a mercurial horizon. This was necessary for the determination of the inclination of the axis, on account of the bubble in the level becoming too long in consequence of the intense cold. At temperatures lower than —40° no use could be made of the instrument.

An approximate computation of the transit-observation gave for the longitude 4h. 42m. 40s. W. of Greenwich. The latitude was found to be 78° 37′. The observations from which this position is derived will be found in the table of geographical positions.

A. S.

No. IX.

Observations for Longitude of Rensselaer Harbor—Continued.

OCCULTATIONS.

Observations of Occultations of Planets and of an Eclipse of the Sun at Rensselaer Harbor, in latitude 78° 37′ *and approximate longitude* 70° 40′ *W. of Greenwich.*

The time is mean Rensselaer Harbor time, already corrected for error and rate; the observers, Dr. Kane and A. Sontag: initials are inserted.

1. *Occultation of Saturn, December* 12, 1853.

Total immersion	14h.	21m.	25·8s.	—A. S.
" "			22·5	—Dr. Hayes.
" emersion	14	54	54·2	—A. S.

At immersion the time was noted when the last point of Saturn's ring disappeared behind the moon's limb; at the emersion the time is given when the last point of the ring parted from the moon's limb.

2. *Occultation of Saturn, January* 7–8, 1854.

Total immersion	17h.	27m.	55·0s.	—A. S.
" emersion	18	24	31·5	—A. S.

The immersion is doubtful, Saturn perhaps obscured by a cloud. For the points of contact, see note above.

3. *Occultation of Saturn, February* 4–5, 1854.

Immersion: moment of total disappearance	23h.	42m.	14·6s.	—A. S.
			16·3	—E. K. K.
Emersion, (February 5:) Saturn's centre	0	40	13·1	—A. S.
Last contact of ring		40	34·3	—E. K. K.

The moon's limb was much undulating. The temperature at immersion was —56°, and at emersion —55°.

4. *Occultation of Mars, February* 13, 1854.

Immersion: first contact	20h.	21m.	48·4s.	—A. S.
" total disappearance		22	50·9	—A. S.
" " "		22	37·5	—E. K. K.
Emersion: total reappearance	20	52	54·9	—A. S.

The emersion is uncertain.

5. *Eclipse of the Sun, May* 15, 1855.

Time of beginning	9h.	13m.	38s.	—A. S.
			41	—E. K. K.
" ending	10	55	44	—E. K. K.
			52	—A. S.
Altitude of sun at beginning	10° 17′			
" " end	8			

The time was obtained by means of corresponding altitudes of the sun; while for the occultations the chronometer's error and rate was determined by means of an eighteen-inch transit-instrument mounted in a small observatory built of ice. The phenomena were observed by means of two thirty-inch telescopes.

AUGUST SONTAG.

No. X.

Methods of Survey.

It is proposed in the following sketch to give a general account of the methods used in surveying the coasts of Smith's Straits, and of Greenland, as far south as Melville Bay. For a large portion of this labor I am indebted to my assistant, Mr. Sontag.

It will be seen that the survey conducted by the returning expedition has more claims to accuracy than is attainable by a mere running or flying survey, although the operations were limited by the peculiar condition of the party.

The means employed were, of course, not new; yet a short and precise account of the methods used to secure as perfect a delineation of the shore-line as circumstances would permit may be properly given, with a view to a comparison of results with other surveys of the same region.

It may be remarked at the outset that the geographical results of the expedition depend altogether for their longitude on the meridian of Rensselaer Harbor. The establishment of this prime meridian was therefore an object of great attention.

As a general rule, the geographical positions were determined on shore whenever practicable; on some occasions on large floes, which afforded a firm basis for the artificial horizon. On several occasions, in Smith's Straits, observations for latitude and longitude were made by means of a theodolite. This instrument was provided with a vertical circle of ten inches diameter, and its limb was divided to four seconds; attached to it was a very sensitive level, the value of a scale-division of which had been determined at Washington, and was found to equal 1·13″.

For latitude, a number of measurements of the altitude of the sun's upper and lower limb were taken, commencing about twenty minutes before and ending twenty minutes after the culminations. An equal number of readings of both limbs were taken with the instrument in the direct and reversed position. A screen of pasteboard protected the instrument from the direct action of the sun's rays.

Observations for time (and longitude) were taken about 9 o'clock A.M. or 3 o'clock P.M.

The apparent path of the sun in these high latitudes is but slightly inclined to the horizon; and the azimuth of any object was determined from the transit of the sun's first and second limb over the vertical wires of the instrument. The time being known, the azimuth of the zero of the limb is easily calculated, and nothing remained but to measure the horizontal angle between that direction and any object the astronomical bearing of which was desired. The azimuth is reckoned from north by east round to 360°. As objects for azimuthal determination, well-defined glaciers, bluffs, islands, prominent capes, and the most distant headlands, were selected; and, in order to make sure of the stability of the instrument during the period of observation, a second set of observations of the sun for azimuth of zero of limb was obtained.

By means of two positions thus determined, a number of objects were located by the intersections of the bearings of the known points, and whenever practicable a third or check azimuth was obtained; in this latter case any discrepancy was properly taken into account according to known principles.

In observing with the sextant for altitude of the sun, the usual precautions were taken, and in particular the parallelism of the upper and lower surfaces of the covering-glass of the artificial mercurial horizon was tested. An error of ten seconds, it is thought, cannot exist on this account, although another roof gave results differing as much as fifteen minutes in the direct and reversed position, and consequently had to be rejected.

The sextants used were made by Gambey, and divided to ten seconds. They were provided with an astronomical telescope, which has invariably been made use of in connection with the artificial horizon. When observing for latitude, multiplied observations were generally taken: first, three of the sun's upper limb; next, three of the lower; and, finally, again three of the upper limb. These observations were commenced about eight or ten minutes before noon. The corresponding index error was always determined.

Observations for longitude were never made nearer than three hours from noon; and, whenever weather and time permitted, corresponding observations in the forenoon and afternoon were secured. On these occasions twelve observations, divided into four groups, and an equal number for the upper and lower limb, were taken.

In observing corresponding altitudes, the index was set to an even five or ten minutes, and the time noted when the contact was perfect. The successive changes of the index were regulated according to the sun's relative changes in altitude.

To illustrate the above by an example, the following is subjoined:—

Approximate latitude. A.M. Time by pocket-chronometer.	78° 37′ Double altitude of sun.	May 16, 1854. P.M. Time by pocket-chronometer.
h. m. s.	° ′	h. m. s.
0 46 18	$\underline{\odot}$ 49 30	8 25 21·5
47 24	35	24 21
48 17·5	40	23 29
0 49 33	$\overline{\odot}$ 50 50	8 22 0·5
50 35·5	55	21 11
51 31	51 00	20 10·5
0 53 16·5	$\underline{\odot}$ 50 5	8 18 31·5
54 15	10	17 36
55 16·5	15	16 33·5
0 56 22·5	$\overline{\odot}$ 51 25	8 15 20·5
57 33·5	30	14 19·5
58 32·5	35	13 8·5

Index error on arc +0′ 24″. Same, P.M., +0′ 20″.

Barometer, 30·04 inches; attached thermometer, +49°; temperature of air, +7° 5′ in the morning, and 30·02 inches; 50° 5′ and +13°; the same respectively in the afternoon.

In working up the observations, index error, refraction, and change of the sun's declination, during the interval, were properly taken into account.

In a few instances, when the weather or other causes prevented an observation for latitude at noon, two sets of observations were taken, as far distant from one another as practicable, and latitude and longitude deduced accordingly. Such was the case at Fiskernaes and Refuge Inlet. This method proved very accurate, provided one set was not more than two hours from noon, and the other at least two hours distant from the first.

Time was noted by a pocket-chronometer, which was compared before and after each set of observations with four box-chronometers, the rates of which had been determined at New York before leaving port. At St. John's, Newfoundland, and at different times in our winter quarters, the box-chronometers were rated by Mr. Sontag by means of a transit-instrument. The mean rate of the pocket-chronometer as found by comparison with each box-chronometer was adopted. As an approximate longitude of the prime meridian of Rensselaer Harbor, 70° 40′ W. of Greenwich has at present been adopted. A slight change is anticipated from some observed occultations of planets by the moon and a solar eclipse: these observations have not yet been worked up. Any change made hereafter in this longitude will, as has already been remarked, equally affect all the other longitudes.

For the determination of azimuths by means of a sextant, the angle between the sun's centre and the object was measured, and the corresponding time noted. For this purpose the smaller telescope was used, and sometimes a pocket-sextant. Whenever the object, the azimuth of which was to be found, was farther removed than 120° from the sun, the angular distance of an intermediate object, about 90° from the sun, was introduced. At the same time the altitude of the sun was observed, to allow for the reduction of the arc of the horizon: this reduction was always small, since the sun was seldom higher than 30°, and in no case higher than 36°.

When the azimuth of an object was thus determined, a number of other conspicuous objects were connected with it by horizontal angles. Two determinations of the azimuth of an object, obtained from two astronomically-determined points, seldom differed more than seven minutes.

The principal points of the coast have thus become known, either by direct observations of latitude and longitude, by latitude and a solar bearing, or by the intersection of two azimuths, according to methods explained above.

The filling in of the minor or secondary points remains yet to be explained. Their position was generally obtained by solar or compass bearings and estimated distances. In regard to the solar bearings, it may be remarked that their frequent application rendered the construction of a table of double entry for every degree of altitude of the sun from 5° to 36°, and for every degree of angular distance from 10° to 125°, quite an acceptable improvement in facilitating the reduction. In regard to magnetic bearings, it is to be remarked that they were taken with a pocket-compass, the face of which, divided into degrees, was fastened to the bottom of the box to allow the needle free play. The magnetic declination (variation of compass) observed with this instrument at different times at the same place seldom differed more than three degrees, while, on the contrary, other compasses, with the card fastened to the needle, would remain stationary in any position in which they were placed, in consequence of the small horizontal force in the region traversed. Care was taken to keep the compass perfectly level, and in sighting, the eye was kept directly over the north end of the needle.

The estimation of distances of intermediate points was the only thing loosely obtained; but it must be remembered, however, that these distances were always checked by means of astronomically-determined positions, and hence no error of this kind, although they were of frequent occurrence, could be propagated. Distances estimated at the same time have in some instances received a proportionate correction, obtained from the check of any single line directly from comparison with astronomical data. At other times, distances paced were found to agree remarkably well with their distance astronomically determined. In this way a journey undertaken in March, 1854, was found correct to within one-thirtieth of the whole distance travelled over in six days.

The survey of bays and harbors was conducted in the ordinary way by means of a base-line, measured either with a cord properly stretched or by pacing. Angles were then measured at each extremity, and occasionally another point was determined trigonometrically. The headlands, prominent bluffs, and islands for these maps generally were determined astronomically.

The above exposition refers to a complete horizontal survey; but the measurement of prominent elevations was not neglected. This was done by means of a base-line parallel with the foot of the cliff, and the measurement of the necessary angles. Some barometric altitudes were obtained with an aneroid,—an instrument peculiarly fitted for such measurements, and which was compared with a mercurial barometer before leaving and immediately after returning to the brig. In one instance, in March, 1854, the aneroid for a short time after returning on board pointed to the same mark which it had indicated while on the top of the cliff. It had there been exposed to a temperature of 50° below zero; and, after the instrument had attained its former higher temperature, the index returned to its proper place within one-hundredth of an inch.

The whole survey, made as explained above, embraces that portion of the coast north of Capes Alexander and Sabine. That portion of it included between Cape Alexander and Upernavik, which was in revision of the work of our English predecessors, as laid down in the Admiralty charts, was made during the escape of the party in boats. For the greater portion of this labor I am indebted to Mr. Sontag.

E. K. K.

No. XI.

Determination of Temperatures.

Our expedition was without any special organization for purposes of scientific inquiry; and the constant call upon the services of its members which the exigencies of our situation made necessary threw the duties of observation upon a few of the more intelligent. I could not have been justified in imposing such a task on them; but they volunteered to perform it, and did so most faithfully.

Our meteorological observatory was erected on the ice-floe, one hundred and fifty yards from the brig. It was enclosed by a system of wooden screens, so arranged that the seats of suspension of the several thermometers should be affected by external changes alike, and errors dependent on wind, sun, and local radiation, guarded against as far as possible. Such errors as were unavoidable at a single station were still further eliminated by corrective observations on the islands and elsewhere.

These precautions were very necessary. Sir Edward Parry, and more recent Arctic voyagers, have shown that there is a difference amounting sometimes to two degrees between the temperatures adjacent to, and at a distance from the vessel. This was abundantly confirmed by our experience. During the intense cold of our winters, the instruments became very impressible to artificial elevation of temperature. The approach of the observer, the use of the lantern, the neighborhood of articles taken from a heated apartment, &c. &c. were at once perceptible in our records.

Except in naval expeditions, Arctic temperatures, whether Asiatic or American, have been recorded with a limited number of instruments. The results of these must be received with extreme caution; for the differences which alcoholic thermometers exhibit at temperatures below the freezing-point of mercury are so varying as to require a large number of comparisons, and upon many instruments, to determine their proper correction. It was not uncommon for thermometers which had given us correct and agreeing temperatures as low as —40° to show at —60° differences of from fifteen to twenty degrees. Such too was the case with the well-constructed instruments of Sir James Ross at Leopold Harbor.

To give an example of this, I may refer to the record of six thermometers, suspended near each other as above described, and observed for purposes of comparison at noon, February 5, 1854.

—71°, —63°, —54°, —53°, —50° and —50°.

All of these at temperatures above —40° agreed within 1·8°, and were selected as the most consistent of nearly thirty spirit thermometers.

At 9 A.M. of the same day eleven similar thermometers gave under like circumstances a mean of 68°, the extreme readings being —56·4° and —80°. For the purpose of obtaining the most probable temperature from these conflicting records, my first impulse was to reject the lowest (coldest) extremes, and take the mean of those which accorded best; but upon advising with our astronomer, Mr. Sontag, I determined to take the mean of all, without rejecting any,—the view which he took being simply that those instruments which indicated the extremes in the low scale had never in temperatures above —40° shown any anomaly which deprived them of an equal claim to confidence with the rest, and that there was no reason *a priori* to consider the results which they gave as less probable than those shown by the others.

In a word, I adopted the views of Professor Airy, as published in the 95th number of the American Astronomical Journal. The causes which had produced the errors were mostly unknown, and the quantity to which these errors might amount was entirely so.

Our thermometers were made with great care by Taliabue, of New York. But, independently of other mechanical sources of error, I am obliged to say that I do not regard the contraction of colored alcohol at very low temperatures as sufficiently investigated to enable us to arrive at the causes or the quantity of error. In most of the spirit thermometers the uniform thickness of the tube was tested before leaving New York; and the freezing of carefully-distilled mercury which I had taken with me for the purpose, gave excellent determinations of absolute temperature.

But it may not be uninteresting to state that the freezing-point of this metal varied between —38·5° and —41·5°, and that its rate of contraction as a solid was so uniform, that in our long and excellent 36-inch standards it descended after freezing as low as —44°. This result is in accordance with that obtained by Sir Edward Belcher, whose experiments go even further than my own,—the mercury having been observed by him to descend as low as 46° below zero.

I may mention the fact as in some degree confirming the propriety of not excluding an eccentric result from the computation of means, that two or more instruments may agree well together and still differ considerably from the most probable temperatures. This was the case with two long spirit thermometers, which never, even at the lowest temperatures, showed differences amounting to one degree, but which at 68° varied 7·7° from the mean of eleven others. The cause was in this instance easily explained. The two instruments were fac-similes of each other; any errors of division of the scale or from the unequal contraction of the fluid, which was the same in both and the same in quantity, and probably taken from the same preparation of spirits, were of course common to both. The error induced by the coloring matter of the fluid adhering in small particles to the sides of the tube became very marked at low temperatures.

Our routine of daily observation was as follows:—Two 36-inch register spirit thermometers were noted hourly, as well as a varying number of instruments of smaller size. For purposes of comparison, the long spirit thermometers, and from five to twelve of the others in selected groups were generally read at the same time. The difference between the mean of these observations and the reading of any one instrument gave the correction which was applied to that instrument, in order to get the true or most probable temperature.

I add here a table, containing the comparisons from which the corrections of the spirit thermometers actually in use between the temperatures of —68° and —20° are derived. The comparisons for temperatures between —20° and +36° are not given in the table, as they are very numerous; and the corrections of all our thermometers ran so regularly within these limits that their details would have little interest.

In the following table S denotes the long 36-inch spirit thermometers, M the mercurial of the same construction. All the rest are alcoholic thermometers of from twelve to eighteen inches in length of scale.

The appended table was compiled by Mr. Sontag directly from the original register. It is arranged according to the temperatures, commencing with the lowest.

Table of Comparisons of Spirit Thermometers.

1854. February 5.			February 5.			February 4.		
Therm.	Read.	Corr.	Therm.	Read.	Corr.	Therm.	Read.	Corr.
No. 12	—80·0°	+12·0°	No. 12	—77·9°	+13·0°	No. 12	—78·2°	+14·0°
1	—75·5	+ 7·5	4	—72·7	+ 7·8	4	—74·0	+ 9·8
4	—75·0	+ 7·0	2	—69·0	+ 4·1	C	—63·0	— 1·2
2	—72·0	+ 4·0	8	—67·5	+ 2·6	SS	—57·8	— 6·4
8	—70·5	+ 2·5	C	—62·5	— 2·4	A	—56·2	— 8·0
9	—69·8	+ 1·8	S	—58·3	— 6·6	B	—56·0	— 8·2
9	—67·0	— 1·0	A	—56·0	— 8·9	Mean	—64·2	
C	—64·6	— 3·4	B	—55·5	— 9·4			
S	—60·3	— 7·7	Mean	—64·9				
A	—57·0	—11·0						
B	—56·4	—11·6						
Mean	—68·0							

Table of Comparisons of Spirit Thermometers—Continued.

January 20.

Therm.	Read.	Corr.
No. 12	—73·0°	+13·5°
4	—66·5	+ 7·0
C	—57·0	— 2·5
S	—54·8	— 4·7
A	—53·0	— 6·5
B	—52·5	— 7·0
Mean	—59·5	

February 5.

Therm.	Read.	Corr.
No. 12	—71·0°	+14·2°
4	—63·0	+ 6·2
C	—54·0	— 2·8
S	—53·0	— 3·8
A	—50·0	— 6·8
B	—50·0	— 6·8
Mean	—56·8	

March 14.

Therm.	Read.	Corr.
No. 12	—64·4°	+11·0°
4	—58·7	+ 5·3
S	—50·2	— 3·2
A	—47·2	— 6·2
B	—46·7	— 6·7
Mean	—53·4	

February 6.

Therm.	Read.	Corr.
No. 12	—57·8°	+ 9·0°
4	—55·5	+ 6·7
S	—46·6	— 2·2
C	—45·0	— 3·8
A	—44·5	— 4·3
B	—43·6	— 5·2
Mean	—48·8	

February 6.

Therm.	Read.	Corr.
	—57·3°	+ 9·0°
	—55·0	+ 6·7
	—46·3	— 2·0
	—44·0	— 4·3
	—44·0	— 4·3
	—43·0	— 5·3
Mean	—48·3	

March 3.

Therm.	Read.	Corr.
	—54·5°	+ 7·7°
	—53·5	+ 6·7
	—45·0	— 1·8
	—43·0	— 3·8
	—42·9	— 3·9
	—42·0	— 4·8
Mean	—46·8	

February 9.

Therm.	Read.	Corr.
No. 12	—54·0°	+ 7·4
4	—53·5	+ 6·9
S	—44·8	— 1·8
C	—43·0	— 3·6
A	—42·5	— 4·1
B	—42·0	— 4·6
Mean	—46·6	

March 3.

Therm.	Read.	Corr.
	—47·5°	+ 5·0°
	—46·1	+ 3·6
	—41·2	— 1·3
	—40·5	— 2·0
	—40·0	— 2·5
	—39·9	— 2·6
Mean	—42·5	

March 3.

Therm.	Read.	Corr.
	—46·7°	+ 4·7°
	—45·5	+ 3·5
	—40·8	— 1·2
	—40·2	— 1·8
	—39·7	— 2·3
	—39·0	— 3·0
Mean	—42·0	

March 16.

Therm.	Read.	Corr.
No. 12	—44·1°	+ 3·9°
4	—43·2	+ 3·0
9	—41·4	+ 1·2
SS	—39·1	— 1·1
C	—38·8	— 1·4
A	—37·6	— 2·6
B	—37·2	— 3·0
Mean	—40·2	

March 16.

Therm.	Read.	Corr.
No. 12	—43·7°	+ 4·0°
4	—42·9	+ 3·2
9	—41·0	+ 1·3
S	—38·7	— 1·0
M	—38·4	— 1·3
C	—38·2	— 1·5
A	—37·7	— 2·0
B	—37·2	— 2·5
Mean	—39·7	

February 25.

Therm.	Read.	Corr.
	—41·0	+ 3·6°
	—40·6	+ 3·0
	—38·9	+ 1·5
	—36·6	— 0·8
	—36·3	— 1·1
	—35·6	— 1·8
	—35·2	— 2·2
	—34·8	— 2·6
Mean	—37·4	

February 26.

Therm.	Read.	Corr.
No. 12	—37·7°	+ 3·2°
4	—37·0	+ 2·5
9	—35·7	+ 1·2
S	—34·0	— 0·5
M	—33·8	— 0·7
C	—32·8	— 1·7
A	—32·9	— 1·6
B	—32·2	— 2·3
Mean	—34·5	

February 7.

Therm.	Read.	Corr.
No. 12	—35·0°	+ 3·0°
4	—34·2	+ 2·3
9	—33·0	+ 1·0
8	—32·9	+ 0·9
2	—32·4	+ 0·4
S	—31·8	— 0·2
M	—31·3	— 0·7
C	—29·5	— 2·5
A	—30·2	— 1·8
B	—29.8	— 2·2
Mean	—32·0	

February 24.

Therm.	Read.	Corr.
No. 12	—33·8°	+ 2·8°
4	—33·3	+ 2·3
9	—32·0	+ 1·0
S	—31·0	0·0
M	—30·4	— 0·6
C	—29·0	— 2·0
A	—29·5	— 1·5
B	—29·0	— 2·0
Mean	—31·0	

Table of Comparisons of Spirit Thermometers—Concluded.

February 18.		
Therm.	Read.	Corr.
No. 12	—33·2°	+2·9°
4	—32·6	+2·3
S	—30·2	—0·1
M	—29·6	—0·7
C	—28·8	—1·5
A	—29·0	—1·3
B	—28·5	—1·8
Mean	—30·3	

February 23.		
Therm.	Read.	Corr.
No. 12	—31·7	+2·5
4	—31·2	+2·0
9	—30·2	+1·0
S	—29·0	—0.2
M	—28·6	—0·6
C	—27·3	—1·9
A	—28·0	—1·2
B	—27·5	—1·7
Mean	—29·2	

February 20.		
Therm.	Read.	Corr.
	—27·9°	+2·2
	—27·5	+1·8
	—26·9	+1·2
	—25·2	—0·5
	—24·7	—1·0
	—24·4	—1·3
	—24·7	—1·0
	—24·3	—1·4
Mean	—25·7	

February 19.		
Therm.	Read.	Corr.
No. 12	—27·0°	+2·0°
4	—27·0	+2·0
9	—26·0	+1·0
S	—24·5	—0·5
M	—23·9	—1·1
C	—23·6	—1·4
A	—24·2	—0·8
B	—23·5	—1·5
Mean	—25·0	

February 15.		
Therm.	Read.	Corr.
	—25·0°	+2·2°
	—24·3	+1·5
	—24·0	+1·2
	—22·1	—0·7
	—21·5	—1·3
	—22·0	—0·8
	—21·6	—1·2
	—22·0	—0·8
Mean	—22·8	

February 19.		
Therm.	Read.	Corr.
	—23·8°	+1·8°
	—23·5	+1·5
	—23·3	+1·3
	—21·2	—0·8
	—20·8	—1·2
	—21·0	—1·0
	—20·8	—1·2
	—21·3	—0·7
Mean	—22·0	

February 18.		
Therm.	Read.	Corr.
No. 12	—22·7°	+2·0°
4	—21·9	+1·2
9	—21·2	+0·5
S	—20·0	—0·7
M	—19·5	—1·2
C	—20·0	—0·7
A	—19·7	—1·0
B	—20·2	—0·5
Mean	—20·7	

February 17.		
Therm.	Read.	Corr.
	—21·7°	+1·5°
	—21·7	+1·5
	—21·0	+0·8
	—19·4	—0·8
	—19·1	—1·1
	—19·6	—0·6
	—19·3	—0·9
	—19·6	—0·6
Mean	—20·2	

From these comparisons the corrections of each thermometer for the different temperatures between —68° and —20°, at which they were observed, was extracted and put together, and generally two or three of these corrections which correspond to nearly the same temperatures were united to a mean. Between those means the correction for every degree of the scale was interpolated and all brought into a continuous series. In this way the following table of corrections was obtained:—

Table of Corrections for the Thermometers in actual use for every degree lower than —20°.

12.

Scale.	Corr.	Scale.	Corr.	Scale.	Corr.	Scale.	Corr.	Scale.	Corr.
—78°	+13·5°	—66°	+11·8°	—54°	+7·5°	—42°	+3·7°	—30°	+2·4°
—77	+13·5	—65	+11·4	—53	+7·1	—41	+3·6	—29	+2·3
—76	+13·6	—64	+11·0	—52	+6·7	—40	+3·5	—28	+2·2
—75	+13·6	—63	+10·6	—51	+6·3	—39	+3·4	—27	+2·1
—74	+13·7	—62	+10·3	—50	+5·9	—38	+3·3	—26	+2·0
—73	+13·7	—61	+10·0	—49	+5·5	—37	+3·2	—25	+1·9
—72	+13·8	—60	+ 9·7	—48	+5·1	—36	+3·1	—24	+1·9
—71	+13·8	—59	+ 9·4	—47	+4·8	—35	+2·9	—23	+1·8
—70	+13·6	—58	+ 9·2	—46	+4·5	—34	+2·8	—22	+1·8
—69	+13·2	—57	+ 9·0	—45	+4·2	—33	+2·7	—21	+1·7
—68	+12·7	—56	+ 8·5	—44	+4·0	—32	+2·6	—20	+1·7
—67	+12·2	—55	+ 8·0	—43	+3·8	—31	+2·5		

4.

—74°	+8·2°	—63°	+6·3°	—52°	+6·5°	—41°	+3·0°	—30°	+2·1°
—73	+8·0	—62	+6·0	—51	+6·1	—40	+2·9	—29	+2·0
—72	+7·9	—61	+5·7	—50	+5·6	—39	+2·8	—28	+1·9
—71	+7·8	—60	+5·4	—49	+5·2	—38	+2·7	—27	+1·9
—70	+7·7	—59	+5·3	—48	+4·8	—37	+2·6	—26	+1·8
—69	+7·5	—58	+5·6	—47	+4·4	—36	+2·5	—25	+1·6
—68	+7·4	—57	+6·0	—46	+3·6	—35	+2·4	—24	+1·5
—67	+7·3	—56	+6·4	—45	+3·4	—34	+2·4	—23	+1·4
—66	+7·1	—55	+6·7	—44	+3·2	—33	+2·3	—22	+1·3
—65	+6·9	—54	+6·8	—43	+3·1	—32	+2·2	—21	+1·2
—64	+6·6	—53	+6·8	—42	+3·0	—31	+2·1	—20	+1·2

9.

—67°	—1·0°	—37°	+1·3°	—32°	+1·0°	—27°	+1·1°	—22°	+1·0°
—41	+1·3	—36	+1·2	—31	+1·0	—26	+1·2	—21	+0·8
—40	+1·4	—35	+1·2	—30	+1·0	—25	+1·2	—20	+0·6
—39	+1·5	—34	+1·1	—29	+1·0	—24	+1·2		
—38	+1·4	—33	+1·1	—28	+1·0	—23	+1·2		

C.

—63°	—2·3°	—54°	—2·8°	—45°	—3·8°	—36°	—1·6°	—27°	—1·9°
—62	—2·4	—53	—2·9	—44	—3·9	—35	—1·6	—26	—1·7
—61	—2·4	—52	—3·0	—43	—3·6	—34	—1·7	—25	—1·5
—60	—2·5	—51	—3·1	—42	—3·0	—33	—1·7	—24	—1·3
—59	—2·5	—50	—3·2	—41	—2·4	—32	—1·8	—23	—1·1
—58	—2·5	—49	—3·3	—40	—1·9	—31	—1·8	—22	—0·9
—57	—2·6	—48	—3·4	—39	—1·7	—30	—1·9	—21	—0·8
—56	—2·6	—47	—3·5	—38	—1·5	—29	—2·0	—20	—0·7
—55	—2·7	—46	—3·7	—37	—1·5	—28	—2·0		

Table of Corrections—Concluded.

S.

Scale.	Corr.	Scale.	Corr.	Scale.	Corr.	Scale.	Corr.	Scale.	Corr.
—60°	—7·5°	—51°	—3·3°	—42°	—1·4°	—33°	—0·3°	—24°	—0·6°
—59	—7·0	—50	—3·1	—41	—1·3	—32	—0·2	—23	—0·7
—58	—6·4	—49	—2·8	—40	—1·2	—31	—0·0	—22	—0·8
—57	—5·9	—48	—2·5	—39	—1·1	—30	—0·1	—21	—0·8
—56	—5·4	—47	—2·3	—38	—1·0	—29	—0·2	—20	—0·8
—55	—4·9	—46	—2·0	—37	—0·8	—28	—0·3		
—54	—4·3	—45	—1·8	—36	—0·7	—27	—0·4		
—53	—3·8	—44	—1·7	—35	—0·6	—26	—0·4		
—52	—3·6	—43	—1·6	—34	—0·5	—25	—0·5		

M.

Scale.	Corr.	Scale.	Corr.	Scale.	Corr.	Scale.	Corr.	Scale.	Corr.
—37°	—1·2°	—33°	—0·7°	—29°	—0·6°	—25°	—1·0°	—21°	—1·2°
—36	—1·0	—32	—0·7	—28	—0·6	—24	—1·1	—20	—1·2
—35	—0·8	—31	—0·7	—27	—0·7	—23	—1·1	—19	—1·1
—34	—0·7	—30	—0·7	—26	—0·9	—22	—1·2		

A.

Scale.	Corr.	Scale.	Corr.	Scale.	Corr.	Scale.	Corr.	Scale.	Corr.
—57°	—9·8°	—49°	—6·3°	—41°	—2·8°	—33°	—1·9°	—25°	—1·0°
—56	—9·4	—48	—6·2	—40	—2·4	—32	—1·8	—24	—0·9
—55	—9·0	—47	—6·2	—39	—2·3	—31	—1·6	—23	—0·9
—54	—8·5	—46	—5·7	—38	—2·3	—30	—1·5	—22	—1·0
—53	—8·0	—45	—5·0	—37	—2·3	—29	—1·4	—21	—1·1
—52	—7·5	—44	—4·2	—36	—2·2	—28	—1·3	—20	—1·1
—51	—7·0	—43	—3·6	—35	—2·1	—27	—1·2	—19	—1·2
—50	—6·5	—42	—3·2	—34	—2·0	—26	—1·1		

B.

Scale.	Corr.	Scale.	Corr.	Scale.	Corr.	Scale.	Corr.	Scale.	Corr.
—56°	—9·7°	—48°	—6·7°	—40°	—3·5°	—32°	—2·3°	—24°	—1·3°
—55	—9·2	—47	—6·7	—39	—3·1	—31	—2·2	—23	—1·2
—54	—8·7	—46	—6·3	—38	—2·8	—30	—2·1	—22	—1·0
—53	—8·0	—45	—5·8	—37	—2·7	—29	—1·9	—21	—0·8
—52	—7·4	—44	—5·4	—36	—2·6	—28	—1·8	—20	—0·6
—51	—6·9	—43	—5·0	—35	—2·6	—27	—1·6	—19	—0·5
—50	—6·8	—42	—4·5	—34	—2·5	—26	—1·5		
—49	—6·8	—41	—4·0	—33	—2·4	—25	—1·4		

Similar tables were, as I before remarked, constructed for the corrections of thermometer-readings at temperatures between —20° and +36° from 5° to 5°.

The corrections of the small mercurial thermometers were obtained at +32° by Mr. Taliabue and Mr. Sontag in New York. These thermometers were generally only used at temperatures near the freezing-point and for observing the temperatures of the sea. Their corrections at lower temperatures were therefore of less importance.

E. K. KANE.

No. XII.

Meteorological Abstracts.

The temperatures in the second column are means of the hourly readings corrected for errors of thermometers, and are expressed in degrees of Fahrenheit's scale. The sign — is prefixed to temperatures below zero.

In the fifth column the mean temperature of the surface-water has been noted; and after October 1, 1853, this column contains the mean reading of the barometer at temperatures recorded in the following column.

The next columns contain the state of the weather, recorded three times a day:—at the hours 4, 12, and 20. The force of the wind is indicated by figures from 1 to 10,—the former expressing light airs, the latter a hurricane; the letter *c* stands for calm. The direction of the wind is given uncorrected for variation of compass. From June 1, 1853, to September 11, 1853, the state of the weather is to be found in the abstract of the log-book.

To indicate the condition of the atmosphere the following abbreviations were used:—*b* for clear sky; *o* for sky entirely covered with clouds; *f* for fog, *r* for rain, and *s* for snow; *bm*1 for sky covered one-third with mist or clouds, and *bm*2 for the same covered two-thirds with mist or clouds.—E. K. K.

Date. June, 1853.	Mean Temp. of Air.	Maximum.	Minimum.	Mean Temp. of Water.	Mean Height of Barometer.	Attached Thermometer.	Remarks. Position of Ship at Noon. Latitude.	Longitude.
	°	°	°	°	inch.	°		
1	....	......	......	....	....	......	39° 47′	73° 33′
2	....	......	......	....	....	......	39 29	72 58
3	....	......	......	....	....	......	39 28	72 7
4	....	......	......	....	....	......	40 16	69 42
5	+67·08	......	......	+69·05	....	......	40 3	67 3
6	67·35	......	......	64·25	....	......	40 3	66 30
7	64·87	......	......	61·05	....	......	41 8	65 8
8	59·52	+65·0	+55·0	53·58	30·394	+65·8	42 15	63 2
9	53·72	57·0	50·5	50·72	30·166	57·8	43 3	61 21
10	53·63	61·0	49·0	50·72	30·153	58·0	43 18	60 19
11	55·00	62·0	50·0	53·30	30·075	58·9	43 19	60 14
12	51·58	55·0	50·0	53·96	30·177	55·2	43 9	58 12
13	54·14	59·0	51·0	53·98	30·119	58·2	43 17	55 59
14	49·11	54·0	45·0	49·72	30·143	56·6	44 44	54 30
15	52·88	70·0	44·0	43·71	30·016	55·9	45 44	53 30
16	....	......	......	....	....	......	Harbor of St. John's,	
17	48·85	56·0	47·5	43·42	29·942	54·2	Newfoundland.	
18	46·27	51·0	43·0	40·04	29·800	50·1	48 26	52 8
19	43·68	48·0	38·0	39·02	29·750	46·2	51 12	52 8
20	39·90	42·0	39·0	37·44	29·625	42·6	52 20	52 12
21	39·00	40·0	37·5	38·31	29·282	42·0	52 57	52 12
22	39·28	40·0	38·5	42·08	29·183	42·0	55 16	52 12
23	43·57	46·0	42·0	42·20	29·425	46·4	56 28	50 31
24	41·65	48·0	41·5	41·28	29·757	67·3	57 20	51 58
25	43·14	45·0	42·0	41·69	29·701	73·0	58 25	51 21
26	43·23	46·0	42·0	42·23	29·568	71·0	59 35	49 27
27	42·60	48·0	38·0	39·13	29·944	72·7	61 12	49 44
28	37·67	42·0	36·0	38·35	30·087	72·7	62 14	50 6
29	38·95	44·0	35·0	42·02	30·139	......	Harbor of Fiskernaes.	
30	39·16	45·0	35·0	41·55	30·128	......	" " "	
	+48·63	+70·0	+35·0	+46·91	29·890	+55·73		

Date. July, 1853.	Mean Temp. of Air.	Maximum.	Minimum.	Mean Temp. of Water.	Mean Height of Barometer.	Attached Thermometer.	Remarks. Position of Ship at Noon. Latitude.	Longitude.
	°	°	°	°	inch.	°		
1	....	......	......	....	....	......	Harbor of Fiskernaes.	
2	+36·78	+41·0	+32·0	+37·50	29·982	......	62° 46′	52° 24′
3	37·88	44·0	34·0	37·85	29·910	+68·2	63 24	52 8
4	37·80	39·0	37·0	37·83	29·930	68·4	63 47	52 14
5	37·05	40·0	36·0	37·73	29·989	70·6	63 49	52 25
6	37·37	41·0	36·0	38·08	29·947	70·0	64 6	52 43
7	39·55	44·0	37·0	39·10	29·736	67·1	64 8	53 30
8	38·42	40·0	37·0	40·67	29·863	69·3	64 35	53 16
9	42·42	51·0	36·0	45·85	29·884	70·9	65 7	53 40
10	41·12	49·0	33·0	38·09	29·907	70·8	Near Sukkertoppen.	
11	36·85	40·0	33·0	39·54	29·839	64·7	65 37	53 16
12	40·50	44·0	37·0	40·62	29·830	70·5	65 51	53 30
13	41·96	46·0	40·0	39·79	29·812	67·1	67 46	55 19
14	39·21	42·0	35·0	39·25	29·925	69·6	70 0	57 6
15	36·88	41·0	33·0	37·87	29·783	66·1	70 33	56 41
16	37·42	40·0	35·0	35·33	29·779	68·8	71 25	56 55
17	39·17	44·0	32·0	36·62	29·807	65·5	72 8	57 21
18	40·08	46·0	33·0	38·75	29·630	72·0	Near Proven.	
19	40·19	44·0	36·0	39·91	29·547	67·8	Harbor of Proven.	
20	37·08	42·0	34·0	38·02	29·521	73·8		
21	33·98	44·0	30·0	37·83	29·366	71·2	From Proven to	
22	40·04	43·0	33·0	37·33	29·521	70·8	Upernavik.	
23	38·67	42·0	37·0	34·50	29·546	69·4		
24	35·83	44·0	33·0	36·42	29·615	67·2	73 47	57 27
25	39·17	41·0	37·0	38·42	29·642	69·7	73 59	57 16
26	39·75	45·0	37·0	40·00	29·261	71·4	74 14	57 30
27	37·37	40·0	34·0	39·40	29·679	71·0	74 23	57 57
28	32·98	35·0	31·5	34·51	29·443	65·6	74 38	61 26
29	32·52	35·0	30·0	32·11	29·692	68·2	75 18	62 47
30	33·46	37·0	31·0	31·74	29·730	69·7	75 34	63 5
31	33·40	35·5	31·0	30·35	29·683	69·4	75 34	63 5
	+37·83	+51·0	+30·0	+37·70	29·727	+68·83		

Date. Aug. 1853.	Mean Temp. of Air.	Maximum.	Minimum.	Mean Temp. of Water.	Mean Height of Barometer.	Attached Thermometer.	Remarks. Position of Ship at Noon. Latitude.	Longitude.
	°	°	°	°	inch.	°		
1	+35·00	+39·5	+31·0	+31·05	29·411	+68·9	75° 40′	62° 12′
2	31·58	34·0	27·0	31·06	29·526	68·6	75 44	62 20
3	33·44	35·0	32·0	33·25	29·501	68·5	75 48	62 33
4	33·62	35·7	31·0	32·12	29·498	71·1	75 48	62 33
5	35·40	37·5	34·0	36·67	29·437	73·5	76 59	71 44
6	35·96	38·5	34·0	36·81	29·481	71·3	77 23	72 56
7	31·98	34·5	29·0	33·48	29·500	71·4	78 22	72 52
8	31·58	33·5	30·0	31·30	29·445	67·2	Refuge Inlet.	
9	32·56	34·5	31·0	30·57	29·470	66·3		
10	32·08	33·5	30·0	30·27	29·722	67·0		
11	34·96	38·5	31·0	31·40	29·642	65·3	78 31	73 47
12	30·27	40·0	25·0	31·25	29·748	69·2	78 35	73 13
13	29·60	31·5	28·0	31·08	29·790	68·8	78 35	73 13
14	32·54	36·0	30·0	31·53	29·755	71·8	Force Bay.	
15	34·26	40·0	30·5	31·80	29·822	70·5		
16	30·10	32·5	28·0	30·67	29·920	74·2		
17	38·52	46·0	30·0	32·42	29·742	70·4		
18	33·45	38·0	29·5	31·58	29·798	68·5		
19	37·95	40·5	34·0	32·26	29·600	69·7		
20	37·08	41·5	34·0	30·92	29·681	67·0	78 41	71 40
21	32·46	39·0	28·0	30·79	29·783	67·9	78 41	71 40
22	27·98	31·5	25·5	29·80	29·783	68·1	78 37	70 50
23	30·55	32·0	30·0	30·53	29·742	68·1	78 44	70 40
24	31·21	32·2	30·0	30·67	29·681	66·9		
25	37·26	42·0	30·2	31·37	29·723	70·5		
26	39·09	44·0	34·5	31·12	29·790	66·1		
27	35·10	37·0	32·5	31·57	29·680	68·5		
28	35·87	43·0	32·5	31·78	29·736	69·0		
29	30·73	33·0	28·5	31·35	29·711	68·6		
30	31·90	33·5	29·0	31·23	29·655	66·5		
31	31·60	34·0	28·5	31·31	29·725	67·2		
	+33·41	+46·0	+25·0	+31·71	29·661	+68·92		

Date. Sept. 1853.	Mean Temp. of Air.	Maximum.	Minimum.	Mean Temp. of Water.	Mean Height of Barometer.	Attached Thermometer.	Wind: Direction and Force.			Weather.		
	°	°	°	°	inch.	°						
1	+29·96	+31·0	+28·7	+30·69	29·412	+68·0						
2	28·89	31·0	28·0	30·15	29·573	66·9						
3	28·71	30·0	28·0	30·46	29·648	68·4						
4	28·67	29·5	28·0	30·40	29·732	67·6						
5	28·29	30·0	27·5	30·02	29·735	65·4						
6	30·71	32·0	28·0	30·05	29·696	66·0						
7	22·09	30·7	18·5	29·95	29·241	68·6						
8	20·54	22·5	19·5	29·50	29·200	66·2						
9	18·58	22·0	14·5	29·50	29·323	63·1						
10	16·82	19·0	15·0	29·50	29·402	64·8						
11	16·78	19·8	14·2	29·50	29·428	65·1	c.	c.	c.	b.m.1	b.m.2	o.
12	17·83	21·0	12·5	29·50	29·567	64·7	S.E.2	c.	W.4	b.	o.	b.m.1
13	15·83	24·0	12·5	29·50	29·480	64·0	c.	c.	c.	b.	o.	b.
14	14·02	15·5	11·5	28·96	29·487	48·7	S.E.1	c.	N.E.1	o. s.	o. s.	b. f.
15	13·76	17·7	10·8	28·67	29·587	21·7	E.2	E.1	c.	o.	o.	b.m.1
16	13·90	20·0	8·5	28·69	29·720	20·7	N.E.1	c.	c.	o.	o.	o.
17	12·13	16·0	9·0	28·81	29·860	24·4	W.1	c.	c.	b.m.1	b.m.1	b.m.1
18	11·10	19·0	5·5	28·68	29·930	21·6	c.	c.	c.	b.	b.	b. f.
19	8·40	12·2	4·5	28·71	29·836	46·5	N.E.2	c.	c.	b.	o.	b.
20	9·37	15·2	3·7	28·75	29·828	55·4	c.	c.	N.W.2	b.	b.	o.
21	9·34	15·0	3·7	....	29·802	57·6	S.1	c.	S.W.3	b.	b.	b.
22	14·54	20·0	4·0	....	29·882	53·0	S.1	S.1	S.3	b.	o.	o. s.
23	20·83	24·2	18·0	....	29·898	52·7	S.W.2	S.W.1	S.1	o. s.	o. s.	o. s.
24	17·37	20·2	11·0	....	29·242	59·4	S.1	S.W.1	c.	o.	b.m.1	b.m.1
25	20·79	24·0	16·5	....	30·006	59·3	S.1	S.1	S.W.1	o. s.	o. s.	b.m.2
26	12·52	20·0	8·7	....	30·011	58·0	c.	c.	S.E.2	b.m.1	b.m.1	b.m.1
27	10·45	13·5	6·2	....	29·937	57·7	E.2	N.E.1	c.	o. s.	o.	o.
28	8·54	10·7	7·7	....	29·934	60·2	N.W.1	N.3	S.1	o. s.	o. s.	o. s.
29	9·04	10·2	6·2	....	29·920	63·7	W.2	c.	c.	b.m.1	b.m.1	b.m.1
30	4·87	11·0	—2·2	....	30·009	56·9	c.	E.1	c.	b.m.2	o.	o.
	+17·16	+32·0	—2·2	+29·50	29·678	+55·86						

Date. Oct. 1853.	Mean Temp. of Air.	Maximum.	Minimum.	Mean Height of Barometer	Attached Ther mometer.	Wind: Direction and Force.			Weather.		
	°	°	°	inch.	°						
1	+ 0·73	+ 5·4	— 3·0	29·951	+63·0	c.	c.	S.E.2	b.m.1	o.	b.m.1
2	+ 0·66	+ 4·3	— 2·8	29·674	65·8	S.E.3	N.1	E.1	b.m.1	b.m.2	b.
3	+ 6·32	+13·7	— 1·5	29·263	66·0	S.1	E.1	S.4	b.m.2	b.m.1	b.m.1
4	+14·82	+17·8	+12·3	29·368	65·5	S.5	S.E.2	S.4	b.m.2	b.m.1	b.m.1
5	+13·32	+16·8	+11·0	29·462	66·1	S.3	S.2	S.3	b.m.1	b.m.1	b.m.1
6	+13·69	+15·1	+12·1	29·495	68·7	S.3	S.E.2	S.E.1	o.	b.m.2	o.
7	+ 9·60	+13·3	+ 6·4	29·731	71·9	S.E.2	S.3	c.	b.	b.m.1	o.
8	+ 8·28	+11·5	+ 4·0	29·802	67·5	N.W.5	c.	S.W.6	o.	o.	b.m.1
9	+ 4·42	+ 9·7	+ 0·5	30·164	70·1	S.E.1	S.E.1	c.	b.m.1	o.	o.
10	— 2·97	+ 4·3	— 7·4	30·181	71·7	S.2	S.E.2	S.E.1	o.	o.	b.
11	— 5·24	— 1·9	— 8·7	30·361	67·2	S.E.1	S.E.1	c.	b.	o.	o.
12	+11·00	+13·1	+ 4·4	30·178	68·3	S.W.1	S.W.1	c.	b.m.2	o.	o.
13	+11·35	+13·4	+ 8·7	29·900	67·7	S.1	S.1	S.E.2	o. f.	o.	b.m.2
14	+13·34	+14·1	+11·5	29·709	70·9	S.E.1	c.	S.1	o.	o. s.	o.
15	+11·36	+13·8	+ 8·4	29·652	71·3	c.	c.	c.	b.m.2	b.m.1	b.m.2
16	+ 1·56	+ 5·4	— 0·8	29·860	69·6	S.2	c.	c.	b.	b.m.1	b.m.1
17	+ 0·44	+ 5·0	— 3·8	29·878	65·4	c.	S.1	c.	b.m.2	b.m.2	b.m.1
18	+ 5·32	+12·6	— 3·7	29·821	69·0	c.	S.E.1	c.	b.	o. f.	o. s.
19	+12·35	+16·8	— 1·3	29·765	70·6	S.W.1	S.W.1	S.W.1	o.	o.	o.
20	— 5·02	— 1·8	— 9·3	29·742	71·0	S.2	S.1	c.	b.	b.m.2	b.m.1
21	—10·46	— 6·0	—14·8	29·823	70·4	S.1	S.1	S.E.1	b.	b.	b.
22	—19·85	—16·2	—22·5	30·015	71·7	S.E.1	S.E.2	S.E.1	b.	b.m.1	o. s.
23	—12·60	— 1·8	—23·7	29·913	66·9	S.E 1	S.W.5	c.	o. s.	o.	o. s.
24	+ 3·97	+ 8·7	— 2·8	29·733	74·9	S.E.2	S.E.2	c.	o.	b.	b.m.2
25	+ 7·23	+10·4	+ 3·3	29·787	74·7	S.1	c.	S.E.1	b.	b.	b.
26	+ 0·48	+ 7·4	— 8·5	30·031	72·2	c.	S.E.1	c.	o.	b.	b.
27	—11·40	— 0·8	—18·0	29·865	73·8	c.	c.	c.	b.m.1	b.	b.
28	—16·05	—10·9	—18·2	29·761	72·7	c.	S.1	c.	b.	b.	b.
29	—19·04	—16·8	—20·1	29·735	71·2	c.	c.	c.	b.	b.	b.
30	—15·46	—11·9	—18·8	29·566	73·7	c.	c.	c.	b.	o.	b.m.2
31	—15·17	—10·9	—17·3	29·654	73·0	c.	S.E.1	c.	b.m.1	o.	b.
	+0·55	+17·8	—23·7	29·801	+69·76						

Date. Nov. 1853.	Mean Temp. of Air.	Maximum.	Minimum.	Mean Height of Barometer.	Attached Ther- mometer.	Wind: Direction and Force.			Weather.		
	°	°	°	inch.	°						
1	—14·40	—10·1	—21·3	29·791	+30·2	c.	c.	c.	b.	b.	b.
2	21·60	—20·0	23·5	29·849	31·9	c.	c.	c.	b.	b.	b.
3	20·88	—18·5	23·2	29·746	30·7	c.	c.	c.	b.	b.	b.
4	17·40	—13·1	19·6	29·741	33·8	c.	c.	c.	b.	b.	b.
5	13·96	—10·9	22·0	29·670	36·9	c.	c.	c.	b.	b.m.1	b.
6	18·02	—15·5	25·1	29·647	35·6	W.1	W.1	c.	f.	o.	o.
7	16·03	—10·9	23·7	29·789	37·7	c.	c.	c.	o.	o.	b.m.1
8	17·60	—11·5	25·1	29·986	37·5	c.	c.	N.2	b.m.1	o.	o.
9	25·99	—23·5	29·4	29·719	35·2	c.	c.	c.	o.	b.m.1	b.m.1
10	19·50	— 7·9	30·6	29·375	34·5	c.	S.1	c.	b.	b.	b.
11	15·30	— 8·5	24·4	29·281	34·6	c.	E.1	S.E.2	b.	b.	b.
12	11·80	— 3·2	17·8	29·628	35·8	c.	c.	N.3	b.	b.	b.m.1
13	20·20	—16·8	24.4	30·155	35·2	S.S.W.4	S.S.W.4	N.2	o.	o.	b.
14	25·35	—22·1	27·9	30·211	35·5	c.	S.S.W.4	c.	b.	b.	b.
15	27·20	—25·5	28·5	30·101	29·5	c.	c.	c.	b.	b.	b.
16	27·66	—25·9	29·6	29·863	30·7	c.	c.	c.	b.	b.	b.m.1
17	27·80	—26·3	29·9	29·849	30·4	c.	c.	S.1	b.	b.m.1	b.
18	28·80	—24·6	33·5	29·766	31·6	c.	S.1	S.4	b.	b.m.1	b.m.1
19	33·20	—31·5	34·5	29·736	35·0	S.2	S.E.1	c.	b.	b.m.1	b.
20	32·42	—27·4	35·6	29·672	34·6	c.	c.	c.	b.	b.	b.
21	32·14	—27·4	36·7	29·733	32·0	c.	c.	S.E.2	b.	b.	b.
22	35·82	—31·0	38·4	29·809	29·4	c.	c.	c.	b.	h.	h.
23	38·00	—35·6	41·2	29·922	33·3	c.	c.	c.	b.	b.	b.
24	39·92	—36·9	43·2	29·971	32·8	c.	S.1	c.	b.	b.	b.
25	29·61	—20·9	39·1	29·681	34·6	c.	N.E.2	N.E.1	b.	b.	b.
26	26·55	—17·6	29·6	29·569	35·8	c.	S.E.1	S.E.2	m.	b.m.2	b.m.2
27	23·46	—20·6	28·7	29·272	36·3	c.	S.1	S.W.1	b.	b.	b.m.1
28	13·57	— 2·8	21·6	29·178	39·7	c.	c.	S.E.1	b.	b.m.2	b.m.2
29	9·06	+ 0·2	24·6	29·412	40·2	S.1	c.	c.	b.m.1	b.m.2	o.
30	7·00	— 4·3	11·9	29·661	39·5	N.W.2	c.	c.	o. s.	b.m.2	b.m.2
						c.	N.W.1	N.W.1	o.	o. s.	b. h.
	—23·01	+ 0·2	—43·2	29·726	+34·35						

Date. Dec. 1853.	Mean Temp. of Air.	Maximum.	Minimum.	Mean Height of Barometer.	Attached Thermometer.	Wind: Direction and Force.			Weather.		
	°	°	°	inch.	°						
1	—25·69	—17·3	—33·3	29·655	+37·8	S.1	S.E.1	c.	o.	b.m.1	b.
2	—27·88	—21·8	—35·8	29·531	37·9	S.E.2	S.E.2	S.E.1	b.	b.	b.
3	—29·70	—25·1	—34·1	29·648	37·9	c.	c.	c.	o.	b.m.1	b.m.2
4	—19·84	—10·4	—27·7	29·807	37·2	S.S.W.1	S.W.2	S.2	b.	b.	b.m.1
5	—25·34	— 9·4	—33·9	29·636	36·1	S.4	c.	c.	o.	b.m.1	b.
6	—30·16	—24·1	—34·1	29·456	35·4	c.	S.1	c.	b.	b.	b.m.1
7	—29·69	—24·6	—43·4	29·675	32·7	c.	S.1	S.S.E.1	b.	b.	b.
8	—41·72	—35·6	—45·7	29·715	31·3	c.	c.	c.	b.	b.	b.
9	—29·44	—21·3	—35·6	29·705	28·7	o.	S.1	S.E.3	b.	b.	b.m.1
10	—16·86	—10·4	—26·4	29·861	38·0	S.E.2	S.E.6	S.E.5 N.6	o.	o.	o. f.
11	—25·19	—14·4	—31·0	29·863	36·2	S.S.E.2	S.5	S.S.E.1	b.	b.	b.
12	—27·30	—24·5	—30·2	29·978	33·1	S.E.4	E.5	S.S.E.6	b.	b.m.1	b.
13	—35·10	—29·2	—40·6	30·017	34·4	S.E.2	S.E.1	S.1	b.	b.	b.
14	—41·20	—38·3	—44·1	30·014	35·0	S.E.1	S.E.1	S.S.W.1	b.	b.	b.
15	—42·30	—38·4	—45·1	29·906	33·3	c.	S.S.E.1	S.E.1	b.	b.	b.
16	—42·40	—35·0	—44·2	29·821	31·7	E.1	c.	c.	b.	b.	b.
17	—41·61	—38·4	—45·2	29·814	33·3	c.	c.	c.	b.	b.	b.
18	—28·10	—22·4	—40·6	30·017	35·0	c.	c.	c.	o.	o. s.	o.
19	—22·98	—17·3	—35·6	29·886	39·5	N.W.2	N.W.1	c.	o. s.	b.m.2	b.m.1
20	—33·29	—28·0	—41·4	29·537	37·4	c.	c.	E.2	b.	b.	o.
21	—33·75	—28·8	—41·2	29·995	37·4	c.	c.	S.1	h.	b.m.2	b.
22	—35·42	—29·2	—39·0	29·504	38·9	S.E.2	c.	c	b.	b.	b.m.2
23	—16·89	—10·6	—29·0	29·750	40·1	S.E.2	c.	S.E.1	b.m.1	h.	h.
24	—13·06	—11·0	—16·4	30·182	37·9	S.S.W.6	S.S.W.6	S.3	o.	b.m.2	b.m.2
25	—25·10	—18·8	—30·2	30·254	37·5	c.	c.	c.	b.	b.	b.
26	—21·86	—17·3	—27·9	30·147	38·6	S.1	c.	c.	o.	o. s.	o. s.
27	—11·56	— 7·3	—15·4	29·367	42·0	c.	S.1	c.	o.	o.	o.
28	+ 7·04	+15·8	+ 0·3	29·665	37·4	S.W.7	S.5	S.E.6	o.	o.	o.
29	—11·21	+ 0·6	—21·0	30·442	38·9	S.S.E.2	S.E.1	S.E.1	o.	b.m.2	b.
30	—18·14	—11·7	—22·8	30·290	36·6	c.	c.	c.	b.	o. s.	o. s.
31	— 9·30	— 6·4	—12·4	29·962	39·9	N.W.2	N.W.1	c.	o. s.	o.	o. s.
	—25·99	+15·8	—45·7	29·842	+36·36						

Date. Jan. 1854.	Mean Temp. of Air.	Maximum.	Minimum.	Mean Height of Barometer.	Attached Thermometer.	Wind: Direction and Force.			Weather.		
	°	°	°	inch.	°						
1	— 1·63	+ 1·7	— 5·3	29·614	+40·7	S.E.2	S.W.1	c.	o.	o.	o.
2	+ 3·76	+11·0	3·2	29·637	40·6	E.1	S.S.W.4	c.	o.	o.	o. s.
3	+ 1·55	+ 6·4	5·3	29·497	39·6	E.2	E.2	c.	o. s.	o. s.	o. s.
4	—11·92	— 9·9	14·9	29·333	38·0	S.E.2	c.	c.	o.	o.	o.
5	—11·90	— 6·4	16·5	29·472	39·7	c.	c.	c.	o.	b.m.2	b.m.2
6	— 8·70	— 3·0	13·0	29·561	43·7	c.	c.	S.W.4	b.m.2	b.m.2	o.
7	— 8·97	— 5·6	10·7	29·756	41·6	S.4	S.4	S.E.3	b.m.2	f. o.	o. s.
8	—20·80	—13·5	26·9	29·788	42·0	c.	c.	S.3	b.m.1	b.m.1	b.
9	—29·37	—23·7	34·7	29·893	42·0	c.	c.	c.	b.m.1	b.m.2	b.m.2
10	—33·63	—28·3	39·6	29·714	40·8	S.E.1	c.	S.1	b.	b.	b.
11	—36·66	—29·7	39·6	29·555	39·1	c.	c.	c.	b.	b.	b.
12	—30·17	—21·8	37·3	29·543	35·0	c.	c.	c.	b.	b.m.2	o.
13	—25·16	—22·6	29·7	29·659	33·6	N.W.2	c.	c.	h. s.	h.	h.
14	—37·49	—25·5	42·9	29·505	23·7	c.	c.	c.	h.	b.m.2	b.
15	—41·82	—35·0	48·0	29·371	16·2	c.	c.	c.	b.	b.m.2	b.m.2
16	—48·04	—39·3	52·6	29·562	14·0	c.	c.	c.	b.m.2	b.m.1	b.m.1
17	—38·83	—36·7	50·8	29·572	16·3	c.	c.	c.	b.m.2	b.m.2	b.m.1
18	—47·34	—41·2	51·2	29·601	16·4	c.	c.	c.	b.	b.	b.
19	—52·16	—49·5	55·6	29·601	15·6	c.	S.1	c.	b.	b.	b.
20	—50·58	—46·2	59·9	29·620	14·9	c.	c.	c.	b.	b.	b.
21	—43·15	—29·7	45·7	29·287	22·3	c.	c.	S.E.3	b.	b.	b.
22	—34·81	—23·7	46·8	29·265	27·9	N.N.W.2	c.	c.	o.	b.	b.m.1
23	—33·80	—27·2	42·3	28·946	23·9	c.	c.	c.	b.	b.	b.
24	—36·08	—30·1	41·0	28·979	28·0	c.	c.	c.	b.	b.	b.
25	—28·62	—22·8	40·1	28·955	29·1	c.	S.2	c.	b.	b.m.2	o. s.
26	—26·76	—20·3	35·2	29·122	29·9	N.1	W.N.W.1	c.	b.m.2	b.m.2	b.m.2
27	—32·80	—28·8	38·6	29·200	30·5	S.1	S.1	c.	b.m.1	b.m.2	b.
28	—38·89	—27·9	48·7	29·247	23·9	c.	c.	c.	o.	b.	b.m.1
29	—46·39	—43·4	48·7	29·387	23·7	c.	S.E.2	c.	b.m.2	b.	b.
30	—45·58	—37·3	53·1	29·500	21·6	c.	c.	c.	b.	b.	b.m.1
31	—40·57	—29·7	45·9	29·548	25·3	c.	c.	c.	b.m.1	b.m.2	b.
	—30·24	+11·0	—59·9	29·461	+29·66						

Date. Feb. 1854.	Mean Temp. of Air.	Maximum.	Minimum.	Mean Height of Barometer.	Attached Thermometer.	Wind: Direction and Force.			Weather.		
	°	°	°	inch.	°						
1	—40·91	—36·4	—49·3	29·523	+23·2	c.	c.	c.	b.	b.	b.
2	46·77	40·6	56·8	29·674	23·9	S.1	c.	c.	b.	b.	b.
3	48·02	37·8	58·3	29·470	22·4	c.	c.	S.E.1	b.	b.	b.
4	55·74	46·8	64·4	29·642	18·9	c.	c.	c.	b.	b.	b.
5	58·01	50·5	68·0	29·327	14·9	c.	S.1	c.	b.	b.	b.
6	51·50	45·7	60·8	29·521	16·4	c.	S.S.E.3	S.E.3	b.	b.	b.
7	27·65	21·9	56·8	29·913	20·3	S.7	S.8	S.3	b.m.2	b.m.2	b.m.2
8	37·62	28·1	51·4	30·212	19·4	c.	S.E.2	c.	b.	b.	b.
9	45·94	43·2	50·5	29·567	19·0	c.	S.E.1	c.	b.	b.	b.m.1
10	30·10	22·0	49·9	29·742	19·5	S.W.3	S.W.4	S.W.6	o.	o.	h.
11	31·04	29·7	34·5	29·855	22·1	c.	S.4	S.4	h.	h.	b. h.
12	25·60	21·9	35·3	30·208	24·5	S.S.E.2	S.S.W.4	S.W.4	o. f.	f. s.	o.
13	33·51	26·4	36·9	29·970	25·1	S.S.E.2	S.S.E.2	S.1	b.m.2	b.m.2	b.m.1
14	29·61	21·8	35·4	29·812	25·1	E.1	S.W.2	S.S.W.1	b.	o.	o.
15	20·77	11·3	32·2	29·517	27·2	c.	S.5	S.S.W.7	b.m.1	o.	o.
16	14·94	11·4	17·3	29·962	30·9	S.1	S.1	E.2	o.	o.	o.
17	16·36	12·4	21·7	29·855	31·6	c.	c.	c.	o.	o.	b.m.1
18	21·88	17·3	26·6	29·028	32·8	c.	c.	c.	o.	o.	o.
19	20·60	17·5	27·5	28·965	33·6	c.	c.	c.	o.	o.	b.m.1
20	27·48	21·6	31·0	29·229	32·0	c.	c.	c.	o.	o.	b.
21	26·79	22·8	32·5	29·220	30·4	S.E.3	S.E.2	S.S.E.2	b.m.1	b.m.2	o. f.
22	25·15	21·8	28·8	29·469	31·4	c.	c.	c.	o.	o.	b.m.2
23	34·45	28·5	39·3	29·686	27·3	S.E.1	S.E.1	S.1	b.	b.	b.
24	31·80	27·9	34·7	30·051	28·6	S.S.E.2	S.4	S.4	b.	b.	b.
25	32·96	24·2	42·5	29·969	24·0	S.E.1	c.	c.	b.m.1	b.	b.
26	34·68	30·6	31·5	29·412	21·6	c.	c.	c.	o.	b.m.1	b.m.1
27	34·91	31·6	40·0	29·595	23·4	S.1	c.	c.	b.m.1	b.m.1	b.
28	36·08	31·0	39·4	29·592	21·7	S.S.W.1	c.	c.	b.	b.m.1	b.
	—33·60	—11·3	—68·0	29·642	+24·69						

Date. Mar. 1854.	Mean Temp. of Air.	Maximum.	Minimum.	Mean Height of Barometer.	Attached Thermometer.	Wind: Direction and Force.			Weather.		
	°	°	°	inch.	°						
1	—34·77	—31·0	—39·9	29·521	+22·1	c.	c.	c.	b.m.2	b.m.2	b.m.2
2	38·80	—36·4	40·2	29·737	19·9	c.	c.	c.	b.	b.	b.
3	37·80	—33·3	45·4	30·161	14·1	c.	c.	c.	b.	b.	b.
4	45·86	—43·1	48·0	30·400	15·5	c.	c.	c.	b.	b.	b.
5	46·60	—43·4	50·5	30·123	20·0	c.	c.	c.	b.	b.	b.
6	45·71	—42·5	48·0	29·917	13·7	c.	N.1	c.	b.	b.	b.
7	46·84	—41·2	49·9	29·694	16·6	c.	c.	c.	b.	b.	b.
8	45·32	—40·6	49·9	29·660	12·3	c.	c.	N.1	b.m.1	b.	b.m.1
9	39·43	—26·7	49·3	29·779	14·5	c.	c.	c.	b.	b.	b.
10	48·03	—43·4	52·1	29·842	7·0	c.	c.	c.	b.	b.m.1	b.m.1
11	47·50	—45·7	49·9	29·800	10·8	c.	c.	c.	b.	b.	b.
12	48·83	—44·6	51·2	29·661	6·6	c.	c.	c.	b.	b.	b.m.1
13	48·76	—44·0	53·3	29·538	8·4	c.	c.	c.	b.	o.	b.m.1
14	48·85	—40·7	55·6	29·437	12·4	c.	c.	N.1	b.m.1	b.	b.m.1
15	39·48	—29·4	53·1	29·488	14·3	S.E.5	S.S.W.4	S.5	o.	b.m.1	b.m.2
16	32·24	—26·9	45·4	29·825	17·5	S.S.E.5	S.W.2	W.1	b.m.1	b.m.1	b.m.1
17	44·56	—39·6	50·1	30·064	15·0	S.1	S.1	c.	b.m.1	b.m.1	b.
18	42·74	—32·2	49·3	29·822	14·4	c.	c.	c.	b.	b.	b.
19	42·31	—36·7	46·3	29·811	23·8	c.	c.	c.	b.	b.	b.
20	35·40	—22·8	43·7	29·865	17·7	c.	c.	c.	b.m.1	b.m.2	o.
21	19·37	—15·9	23·7	29·610	23·7	c.	c.	c.	o. s.	o.	o.
22	7·47	+ 0·9	18·5	29·682	24·3	S.E.3	S.1	c.	b.m.2	o. s.	o.
23	9·07	— 6·4	14·2	29·789	20·9	S.E.2	c.	W.2	o.	o. s.	o. s.
24	18·32	—13·9	29·6	29·876	15·4	W.2	W.3	N.W.3	o.	o. s.	o. s.
25	34·80	—28·5	43·4	30·033	14·8	c.	c.	c.	b.	b.	b.m.1
26	42·90	—37·8	44·6	30·007	10·5	c.	c.	c.	b.	b.	b.
27	34·38	—28·8	42·5	29·749	5·5	S.E.2	S.E.1	c.	b.	o.	b.m.1
28	35·32	—30·1	45·7	29·380	9·9	S.E.1	c.	c.	b.m.2	o.	o.
29	40·12	—29·7	45·7	29·210	9·4	S.E.1	S.W.1	c.	b.m·2	o.	b.m.2
30	41·29	—32·8	47·6	29·559	9·6	c.	c.	c.	b.m.1	b.	b.
31	38·05	—23·7	44·8	29·515	9·7	c.	c.	S.4	b.	b.	b.m.1
	—38·09	+ 0·9	—55·6	29·760	+14·52						

Date. April 1854.	Mean Temp. of Air.	Maximum.	Minimum.	Mean Height of Barometer.	Attached Thermometer.	Wind: Direction and Force.			Weather.		
	°	°	°	inch.	°						
1	—17·20	—11·9	—21.0	29·795	+ 8·6	S.3	S.1	S.E.2	o.	o.	o.
2	—22·84	—19·6	—26·0	29·783	15·6	S.E.3	S.E.1	S.E.1	o.	b.m.1	b.
3	—34·24	—25·1	—43·0	29·333	24·7	c.	c.	c.	b.	b.	b.
4	—19·51	— 9·9	—41·4	29·355	28·1	S.E.2	S.1	S.E.1	b.m.1	b.	o. s.
5	—12·92	— 9·9	—14·9	29·397	28·1	S.1	S.W.2	S.W.1	o.	o. m.	o.
6	—16·18	—10·5	—28·0	29·905	25·3	S.W.2	S.1	c.	o.	b.	b.
7	—26·12	—22·6	—35·2	30·193	23·5	S.1	S.2	S.1	o.	b.m.1	b.
8	—23·02	—15·7	—35·2	30·113	24·1	c.	S.1	c.	b.	b.	b.m.1
9	—11·16	— 3·3	—21·3	30·078	29·5	c.	c.	c.	b.m.2	o.	o.
10	— 9·99	— 3·8	—16·8	30·239	29·0	c.	S·E.2	S.3	o.	o.	b.m.2
11	—18·88	—12·7	—25·5	30·105	27·8	c.	c.	c.	b.	b.m.1	b.
12	—13·52	— 2·3	—26·2	29·970	29·5	c.	c.	c.	b.	b.m.1	b.
13	— 2·36	+ 4·3	—14·7	29·936	32·4	c.	c.	S.2	b.m.2	o.	o.
14	+ 1·50	+ 3·7	— 6·9	29·894	32·2	S.W.6	S.W.6	S.W.6	o.	o.	o.
15	— 0·91	+ 6·4	— 8·4	30·042	30·4	S.E.3	S.E.2	S.W.8	b.	o.	o. s.
16	+ 4·15	+ 7·9	— 7·9	30·094	34·7	S.1	c.	c.	b.	b.	b.m.1
17	— 7·08	— 1·8	—14·9	30·172	33·6	S.1	c.	c.	b.	b.	b.m.1
18	— 8·82	— 2·8	—15·4	30·240	30·7	c.	c.	c.	b.	b.	b.
19	— 6·99	+ 2·0	—17·8	30·307	29·5	c.	N.1	c.	b.	b.m.1	b.
20	— 6·20	+ 4·3	—17·8	30·311	30·0	c.	c.	c.	b.	b.	b.
21	— 8·32	+ 2·3	—14·4	30·077	31·0	W.1	c.	S.W.3	b.	b.	b.
22	+ 1·04	+14·3	—12·2	29·926	32·4	c.	c.	c.	b.	b.m.1	o.
23	+ 0·93	+ 6·4	— 7·9	29·959	35·0	c.	c.	c.	o.	b.	b.
24	— 3·96	+ 2·7	—11·4	29·926	33·4	c.	c.	N.W.2	b.	b.	b.
25	— 3·64	+ 6·4	—10·1	29·983	33·1	c.	c.	S.E.2	b.	b.	b.
26	+ 3·31	+ 8·4	— 5·0	30·127	33·8	c.	c.	S.1	b.	b.	b.m.1
27	— 0·11	+ 6·4	— 5·9	30·146	36·9	c.	c.	c.	b.m.1	b.	b.
28	— 0·33	+ 4·1	— 8·2	30·130	36·7	c.	c.	S.E.2	b.	b.	b.m.1
29	+ 0·19	+ 5·1	— 4·8	29·901	36·0	c.	c.	S.E.1	b.	b.	b.
30	+ 5·07	+10·5	+ 1·2	29·985	35·8	c.	c.	c.	b.	b.	b.m.1
	— 8·60	+14·3	—43·0	29·981	+29·71						

Date. May, 1854.	Mean Temp. of Air.	Maximum.	Minimum.	Mean Height of Barometer.	Attached Thermometer.	Wind: Direction and Force.			Weather.		
	°	°	°	inch.	°						
1	+11·70	+18·6	+ 1·5	29·982	+39·4	S.1	N.W.1	c.	b.m.1	b.m.1	o.
2	3·90	8·9	— 2·5	29·930	38·5	N.W.1	N.W.2	c.	o. s.	o. s.	b.m.1
3	1·50	6·3	— 7·4	29·749	49·5	N.W.1	N.W.1	c.	o. s.	b.	b.m.1
4	2·32	5·6	— 1·8	29·333	47·1	S.E.1	N.W.2	c.	b.m.1	b.m.1	b.m.1
5	1·70	7·0	— 3·8	29·466	44·5	c.	c.	c.	o. s.	o. s.	o.
6	2·90	4·3	— 0·8	29·730	43·6	c.	c.	c.	b.	b.m.2	o.
7	9·60	13·6	+ 4·8	29·988	55·4	S.E.5	S.6	S.2	b.m.1	o.	b.m.1
8	11·80	16·8	+ 4·3	30·292	54·4	S.4	S.2	S.3	o.	b.m.2	b.
9	7·60	11·0	+ 4·3	30·160	56·6	S.3	c.	S.W.3	b.	b.	b.
10	8·30	13·9	+ 4·8	29·841	57·7	S.W.1	N.2	N.1	o.	o. s.	o. s.
11	7·60	14·1	+ 2·3	29·723	57·1	W.1	N.W.1	N.W.1	o.	b.m.1	b.m.1
12	4·50	9·7	— 0·8	29·995	54·4	N.W.1	c.	c.	b.	b.m.1	o.
13	1·60	6·6	— 8·7	30·001	56·3	N.W.1	N.W.1	N.W.1	b.m.1	b.	b.
14	5·30	10·7	— 0·8	29·874	53·5	c.	c.	c.	b.	b.	b.
15	6·90	13·7	+ 2·3	29·933	46·4	S.W.1	N.W.1	S.1	b.m.1	b.m.1	b.
16	10·00	14·5	+ 3·3	30·055	48·7	E.1	N.W.2	c.	b.	b.	b.
17	9·10	13·6	+ 6·6	29·990	43·5	c.	N.W.2	c.	b.	b.m.1	o.
18	13·50	19·4	+ 3·3	30·023	52·6	c.	N.1	S.W.2	o. s.	o. s.	o. s.
19	12·00	20·3	+ 4·3	30·134	51·2	c.	c.	S.W.2	b.m.2	o.	b.m.2
20	11·90	15·7	+ 5·6	30·265	49·1	S.W.1	c.	S.W.2	b.	b.	b.
21	14·20	18·4	+ 7·7	30·438	49·0	S.W.2	S.W.3	S.W.4	b.m.1	b.m.1	b.
22	11·80	22·4	+ 7·4	30·419	54·4	S.2	N.2	c.	b.	b.	b.
23	14·90	20·1	+12·9	30·168	54·7	c.	N.1	c.	b.	o.	b.m.2
24	17·10	20·1	+12·0	30·108	55·6	c.	c.	c.	b.m.1	b.	o.
25	21·85	25·7	+17·8	29·926	55·6	c.	c.	S.W.1	o. s.	o.	o.
26	28·50	32·2	+22·9	29·982	55·3	c.	N.1	N.W.1	o. s.	o. f.	o. s.
27	32·59	37·9	+27·6	30·042	55·3	c.	c.	c.	o. s. f.	o. s. f.	o. f.
28	32·32	39·4	+26·6	30·090	54·9	c.	c.	c.	o. s.	o. f.	o. f.
29	31·02	38·3	+23·8	30·153	57·5	c.	c.	c.	o. s.	o.	o.
30	28·47	35·3	+20·1	30·215	55·9	c.	N.1	c.	b. f.	b. f.	f.
31	23·06	33·5	+17·2	30·070	52·5	c.	c.	c.	b. f.	b. f.	b. f.
	+12·89	+39·4	— 8·7	29·970	+51·62						

Date. June, 1854.	Mean Temp. of Air.	Maximum.	Minimum.	Mean Height of Barometer.	Attached Thermometer.	Wind: Direction and Force.			Weather.		
	°	°	°	inch.	°						
1	+24·05	+26·6	+19·1	29·896	+51·0	c.	c.	c.	b.	f.	b. f.
2	28·73	32·2	22·1	29·852	54·6	S.W.1	N.W.1	c.	b.	o.	b.
3	27·13	30·0	25·2	29·986	55·4	N.1	N.W.3	N.W.2	b.	b.m.1	o.
4	24·36	25·9	21·0	29·993	61·0	N.4	N.5	c.	b.	b.	b.
5	22·90	26·7	19·1	29·940	49·4	N.W.1	N.W.2	N.W.2	b.m.1	b.m.2	o.
6	23·30	28·6	17·7	29·751	51·1	c.	N.N.W.3	N.W.2	o.	b.m.2	o.
7	24·00	28·6	20·5	29·552	54·3	c.	N.W.3	c.	b.m.1	b.m.1	b.m.1
8	28·10	33·8	20·1	29·793	53·2	c.	c.	N.W.1	b.m.1	b.m.2	b.m.1
9	26·00	31·6	22·9	29·822	54·0	N.W.1	N.W.2	c.	o.	b.m.1	b.m.1
10	25·00	34·8	22·2	29·640	53·5	c.	c.	c.	b.	o.	o.
11	26·10	27·6	24·1	29·686	53·7	N.W.1	N.W.1	c.	o.	b.m.2	b.
12	24·30	27·6	21·5	29·645	54·1	N.W.1	N.W.1	N.W.3	f.	b.	o.
13	25·00	29·4	20·1	29·637	54·6	W.N.W.1	N.W.6	N.W.1	b.m.2	b.m.1	b.
14	27·40	31·7	21·9	29·590	55·1	c.	c.	c.	b.	b.	b.
15	27·20	30·0	21·9	29·681	56·4	c.	c.	c.	b.	b.	b.
16	31·60	33·8	24·3	29·653	56·0	c.	c.	c.	b.m.1	b.m.2	o. s.
17	33·60	34·9	31·1	29·732	55·1	S.W.3	c.	c.	b.	b.	b.
18	32·90	39·4	27·1	29·940	55·0	c.	c.	c.	b.	b.m.1	b.m.1
19	33·60	38·9	29·5	29·987	58·7	c.	c.	c.	o.	b.	b.
20	28·10	30·0	25·4	29·772	57·5	c.	c.	c.	b.	b.	b.
21	32·20	34·9	27·6	29·847	54·2	c.	c.	c.	b.	b.	b.
22	31·37	35·4	28·1	29·849	44·7	c.	c.	N.W.3	o. s.	o.	f.
23	30·50	32·2	27·1	29·766	42·5	N.W.4	N.W.4	W.1	o. s.	b.m.1	b.m.1
24	33·90	38·9	28·3	29·779	55·8	c.	c.	c.	o.	o.	o.
25	33·50	37·4	30·6	29·851	56·8	c.	c.	N.W.1	o.	o.	o.
26	35·10	39·9	32·2	29·713	57·1	c.	c.	c.	b.m.2	o.	o. f.
27	31·70	38·7	26·2	29·744	55·4	c.	c.	c.	b.	b.	f.
28	33·20	38·2	30·9	29·628	55·1	c.	c.	c.	b.	o.	b.m.1
29	36·10	38·4	33·0	29·778	52·1	c.	c.	c.	o.	b.m.1	b.
30	37·10	41·9	34·1	29·891	52·0	c.	c.	N.W.1	b.m.2	b.m.2	b.m.2
	+29·23	+41·9	+17·7	29·780	+53·98						

Date. July, 1854.	Mean Temp. of Air.	Maximum.	Minimum.	Mean Height of Barometer.	Attached Thermometer.	Wind: Direction and Force.			Weather.		
	°	°	°	inch.	°						
1	+38·30	+42·9	+34·3	29·948	+47·2	c.	c.	N.W.1	o.	b.m.2	o.
2	42·70	48·9	36·9	29·911	47·6	S.E.5	S.3	c.	o.	o.	o.
3	39·40	41·9	34·9	29·850	50·4	c.	c.	c.	o.	o.	b.m.2
4	45·60	53·9	36·9	29·899	55·7	N.1	c.	c.	b.m.1	b.m.2	b.m.1
5	40·30	41·9	37·9	29·785	55·1	c.	c.	c.	b.m.1	b.m.1	b.m.1
6	38·70	42·9	32·8	29·790	46·8	N.W.2	N.W.2	N.W.1	b.m.2	o.	o. f.
7	35·40	38·9	32·8	29·813	43·1	c.	c.	c.	o. f.	r.	o. f.
8	36·10	39·9	32·8	29·822	43·1	c.	c.	c.	o. f. s.	o. f.	o. f.
9	35·70	39·9	30·6	29·769	46·0	W.1	c.	c.	f.	b.m.2	b.m.1
10	38·70	39·9	31·7	29·641	48·6	N.W.1	c.	c.	b.m.1	b.	b. f.
11	35·30	38·9	31·7	29·630	49·6	W.1	N.1	N.1	b.m.1	b.m.1	b.m.1
12	37·00	40·9	33·8	29·648	45·5	c.	c.	c.	o.	o.	o.
13	37·50	42·9	34·9	29·708	46·3	c.	c.	c.	b.m.2	o.	o.
14	40·90	51·9	34·9	29·770	46·4	c.	c.	c.	r.	o.	o.
15	36·81	39·4	32·7	29·642	42·2	c.	N.1	N.W.3	o.	o. s.	o.
16	35·90	36·9	33·7	29·578	41·9	N.1	c.	S.6	o.	b.m.2	o.
17	37·30	40·9	34·9	29·760	45·4	c.	c.	c.	b.m.2	b.m.2	o.
18	37·00	38·9	32·7	29·795	42·6	c.	c.	c.	b.m.2	b.m.2	o.
19	37·10	44·9	33·2	29·889	46·4	c.	c.	c.	o.	o.	o.
20	39·60	47·9	33·8	30·007	49·0	c.	N.W.1	N.W.1	b.m.2	b.	b.m.1
21	37·10	39·9	34·9	29·885	51·5	c.	c.	c.	o. r.	o. r.	o.
22	38·80	40·9	36·9	29·823	47·7	c.	c.	c.	b.	b.m.1	b.
23	43·81	50·9	40·9	29·768	50·6	c.	c.	W.1	b.	b.m.1	b.
24	42·70	46·9	38·9	29·840	45·9	c.	c.	c.	b.m.1	b.m.1	b.m.1
25	38·90	42·9	35·4	29·767	48·8	c.	c.	c.	o. r.	b.m.1	b.m.1
26	38·50	44·9	34·9	29·882	43·4	S.E.1	N.1	c.	o. r.	b.m.2	b.m.1
27	36·90	38·9	35·9	29·809	45·1	N.W.3	W.N.W.2	c.	b.m.2	b.m.2	o.
28	42·00	47·9	34·9	29·679	44·0	S.W.5	S.W.8	S.W.2	o.	b.m.2	o.
29	36·30	43·9	32·7	29·844	43·7	W.3	W.3	c.	b.m.1	b.m.1	b.m.1
30	36·50	40·9	32·7	29·632	46·5	W.2	N.W.3	N.W.1	b. f.	b.m.1	b.
31	33·40	36·9	27·6	29·719	.....	c.	c.	c.	b.m.1	b.m.1	o. r.
	+38·40	+53·9	+27·6	29·784	+46·67						

Date. Aug. 1854.	Mean Temp. of Air.	Maximum.	Minimum.	Mean Height of Barometer.	Attached Thermometer.	Wind: Direction and Force.			Weather.		
	°	°	°	inch.	°						
1	+36·10	+48·9	+27·8	29·644	+46·3	N.W.1	c.	c.	b.m.1	b.m.1	b. f.
2	34·80	42·9	28·5	29·583	43·4	c.	c.	c.	b.m.1	b.m.2	o.
3	34·20	36·9	30·6	29·730	41·1	c.	c.	c.	b.m.1	o.	b.m.1
4	36·70	39·9	32·7	29·849	41·8	c.	c.	c.	b.m.1	b.m.1	b.m.1
5	36·30	38·9	31·7	29·895	44·7	N.1	c.	c.	b.m.2	b.m.1	b.m.1
6	35·10	38·9	33·5	29·827	48·2	c.	c.	c.	b.	b.m.1	b.
7	34·90	43·9	29·5	29·820	46·5	c.	c.	c.	b.	b.	b.
8	36·50	41·9	31·1	29·946	46·9	c.	S.1	c.	b.	b.m.1	b.
9	36·50	40·9	32·7	30·047	43·0	c.	c.	S.1	b.m.1	b.	b.m.1
10	36·50	40·9	32·7	29·951	44·0	c.	S.1	c.	b.m.1	b.m.1	b.m.1
11	35·60	41·9	31·7	29·911	41·3	c.	W.1	S.1	b.	b. f.	b. f.
12	30·90	32·7	28·5	29·789	41·5	S.W.1	c.	S.E.1	b.m.1	b.m.1	b.m.1
13	28·60	33·8	26·6	29·604	35·7	N.2	N.W.2	c.	b.	o. f.	b. f.
14	30·80	35·9	27·6	29·339	35·4	S.E.1	W.4	N.W.3	o. f.	o. f.	o.
15	31·70	34·9	27·6	29·685	36·3	c.	N.W.1	c.	o. f.	o. s. f.	o. f.
16	32·10	37·9	24·3	29·722	39·0	c.	c.	c.	b.m.1	b.m.1	b.m.1
17	29·90	33·8	26·6	29·695	35·9	N.2	N.W.2	S.E.1	b.m.1	b.	b.m.1
18	31·60	34·9	27·6	29·726	39·0	W.2	N.W.2	N.W.3	b.m.1	b.m.1	b.m.1
19	30·40	33·8	26·6	29·664	34·6	N.1	S.E.1	N.1	b.m.2	o.	o. s.
20	30·60	33·8	26·8	29·662	35·0	N.W.1	W.2	N.W.1	o. s.	o.	b.m.2
21	28·10	30·6	25·7	29·708	34·2	W.1	c.	S.1	o. f.	b.m.1	o. f.
22	25·80	31·7	21·0	29·738	31·0	c.	c.	c.	o. f.	o. f.	o. f. s.
23	22·70	27·6	19·1	29·607	30·8	S.E.1	c.	c.	f.	b.	b.
24	26·40	31·7	19·1	29·721	32·6	S.1	S.1	N.W.3	b.	b.m.1	f.
25	27·70	31·1	23·4	29·719	31·8	c.	c.	S.W.2	o. f.	o. f.	o. f.
26	27·90	31·1	25·7	29·627	29·6	c.	S.E.1	c.	o. f.	o. f.	o. f.
27	27·80	30·6	24·7	29·708	32·0	S.E.1	S.1	c.	b.m.1	b.m.1	b.m.1
28	29·70	33·8	27·6	29·667	32·0	c.	c.	c.	o.	b.m.1	b.m.1
29	29·50	34·1	22·9	29·702	32·1	S.E.4	S.6	S.E.6	b.m.1	b.m.2	b.m.2
30	28·80	31·1	27·6	29·359	31·9	S.7	S.E.5	S.E.3	o.	o.	o.
31	27·80	32·2	20·1	29·400	29·9	S.2	c.	c.	b.m.2	o.	b.m.2
	+31·35	+48·9	+19·1	29·711	+37·66						

Date. Sept. 1854.	Mean Temp. of Air.	Maximum.	Minimum.	Mean Height of Barometer.	Attached Thermometer.	Wind: Direction and Force.			Weather.		
	°	°	°	inch.	°						
1	+22·30	+26·6	+17·2	29·485	+24·3	c.	c.	c.	b.m.1	b.m.1	b.m.1
2	+20·10	23·8	+15·3	29·331	23·8	c.	c.	c.	o. s.	o. s.	o.
3	+15·50	19·1	+ 8·4	29·429	18·9	c.	c.	c.	o. s.	o.	o.
4	+15·50	26·6	+ 4·3	30·006	19·3	c.	c.	c.	b.m.2	b.m.1	b.m.1
5	+ 9·80	17·2	+ 3·3	30·025	13·5	S.1	c.	S.1	b.m.1	b.m.1	b.m.1
6	+14·90	21·9	+ 7·9	29·940	19·0	c.	c.	c.	b.m.1	b.	b.
7	+10·60	17·2	+ 7·4	29·848	13·5	c.	c.	c.	b.m.1	b.m.1	b.m.1
8	+10·80	17·2	+ 7·9	29·867	13·7	c.	c.	c.	b.m.1	b.m.2	o.
9	+14·30	19·1	+ 6·4	29·925	16·6	c.	c.	c.	o.	b.m.2	b.m.2
10	+14·00	21·9	+ 6·4	29·761	18·4	c.	c.	c.	o. f. s.	b.m.1	b.m.1
11	+10·30	19·1	+ 2·3	29·772	24·7	c.	c.	c.	b.m.2	b.m.1	b.m.1
12	+ 5·47	12·4	— 0·8	29·882	44·4	c.	c.	c.	b.	b.m.1	b.
13	+ 5·60	9·5	— 4·8	29·892	42·2	N.W.1	c.	S.5	b.m.1	b.	b.
14	+ 9·60	14·3	+ 0·2	29·620	46·4	c.	S.W.2	S.1	b.m.1	o.	o.
15	+ 9·40	15·3	— 2·8	29·440	46·5	c.	N.2	c.	o. s.	o.	b.
16	+ 8·70	12·4	+ 3·3	29·657	58·0	c.	c.	c.	b.m.1	b.m.1	o.
17	+ 4·10	14·3	— 7·9	29·768	55·3	S.W.1	c.	N.1	o.	b.m.2	b.m.1
18	+ 3·90	9·5	— 2·3	29·806	52·9	S.E.4	c.	S.E.2	o.	o.	b.m.2
19	+ 1·60	9·5	— 8·9	29·782	54·6	S.E.2	c.	S.E.2	b.m.1	b.m.1	b.m.1
20	— 0·76	4·3	— 8·9	29·819	55·7	c.	c.	c.	b.m.1	b.m.1	b.m.1
21	+ 4·60	7·4	+ 1·2	29·633	58·3	c.	W.2	N.W.2	b.m.1	b.m.1	o.
22	+ 3·90	13·4	— 2·8	29·192	56·5	E.2	S.E.2	c.	o.	b.m.2	b.m.1
23	— 1·59	1·7	— 4·8	29·337	56·0	c.	c.	S.W.1	b.m.1	b.m.1	b.m.1
24	+ 9·40	15·3	— 2·8	29·254	61·2	W.1	E.1	c.	o.	o. s.	o. s.
25	+12·80	15·3	+10·5	29·232	60·2	c.	c.	S.3	o. s.	o. m.	o. s.
26	+14·40	17·2	+12·4	29·523	63·4	S.W.3	S.W.1	S.E.2	o. s.	o. s.	o. s.
27	+ 9·10	13·4	+ 4·3	29·838	59·0	S.W.3	S.W.4	S.W.5	o.	b.m.1	b.
28	+11·18	13·4	+ 4·3	29·776	57·6	S.W.2	S.W.3	S.W.5	b.m.2	b.m.1	b.m.1
29	+10·10	13·4	+ 6·4	29·737	62·2	S.4	S.W 2	S.5	o.	o. s.	o.
30	+14·60	17·2	— 1·3	29·880	52·8	S.W.7	S.W.7	S.E.3	b.m.2	b.m.2	o.
	+ 9·81	+26·6	— 8·9	29·682	+41·22						

Date. Oct. 1854.	Mean Temp. of Air.	Maximum.	Minimum.	Mean Height of Barometer.	Attached Thermometer.	Wind: Direction and Force.			Weather.		
	°	°	°	inch.	°						
1	+12·00	+15·3	+ 6·4	29·918	+53·7	S.1	c.	S.W.4	o.	o.	o.
2	+12·00	+17·2	+ 4·3	29·959	50·5	W.3	S.W.3	S.W.6	b.m.1	b.m.1	o.
3	+19·90	+22·9	+16·3	29·999	53·1	S.W.2	S.W.3	S.W.4	o.	o. s.	o. s.
4	+20·40	+22·9	+15·3	30·025	54·5	S.W.3	S.W.2	N.W.2	o.	o.	b.c.1
5	+18·50	+22·9	+13·4	30·087	57·0	S.W.1	c.	N.W.3	o.	o.	o.
6	+ 6·69	+14·8	— 1·8	29·611	62·8	......	......	......	...	...	...
7	— 2·23	+ 1·2	— 7·4	29·392	62·2	S.W.3	S.W.4	S.W.1	o.	b.m.1	o.
8	— 0·58	+ 4·8	— 8·9	29·197	61·2	S.1	c.	S.2	o.	b.m.2	o.
9	—15·64	— 7·9	—23·7	29·447	55·1	S.W.3	c.	c.	b.m.2	o.	b.m.2
10	—24·99	—22·8	—28·8	29·669	49·0	c.	c.	c.	b.m.2	b.m.1	b.m.1
11	—18·25	— 7·8	—29·8	29·515	51·1	c.	c.	W.2	o.	o.	o.
12	— 2·62	+ 2·8	— 6·9	29·171	49·7	S.W.1	S.E.1	c.	o.	o.	o.
13	— 8·77	— 1·8	—15·9	29·143	49·4	S.W.2	S.W.4	W.2	o.	b.m.2	o.
14	— 3·65	+ 2·3	— 9·9	29·097	54·1	N.W.1	N.W.3	S.3	o.	o.	o.
15	— 3·15	+11·5	—10·9	29·493	57·7	S.W.4	S.2	S.5	b.m.2	b.m.2	b.
16	—16·28	— 9·9	—21·8	29·957	53·6	S.1	c.	c.	b.	b.	b.
17	—17·67	—13·9	—21·8	29·809	50·1	c.	c.	c.	b.	b.m.1	b.
18	—14·21	— 9·9	—20·8	29·558	49·9	c.	c.	c.	b.	b.m.1	b.m.1
19	—10·56	— 5·9	—16·8	29·801	51·8	c.	c.	S.W.2	o.	b.m.1	b.m.1
20	—19·10	—11·9	—23·7	29·596	51·3	c.	c.	c.	b.m.1	b.	b.m.1
21	—21·60	—19·3	—23·9	29·654	48·3	c.	c.	c.	b.m.1	b.m.1	b.m.2
22	—13·95	—10·9	—21·8	29·896	49·9	S.E.1	c.	c.	b.m.1	b.m.1	b.m.1
23	—18·48	—13·9	—26·4	30·036	51·4	c.	c.	c.	b.m.1	b.	b.m.1
24	—10·62	— 5·9	—16·8	30·006	50·3	S.E.1	c.	S.E.1	b.m.2	o.	o.
25	—23·92	—18·8	—29·6	30·001	51·0	S.W.1	c.	S.E.2	b.	b.m.1	b.m.1
26	—26·96	—18·3	—35·1	30·125	48·5	c.	N.E.1	c.	b.	o.	b.m.2
27	—34·85	—31·0	—39·0	30·040	47·5	c.	c.	S.W.1	b.m.1	b.	b.
28	—28·70	—16·8	—41·0	29·911	44·8.	c.	S.2	c.	o.	o. f.	b.m.2
29	—27·27	—22·8	—32·2	29·845	45·1	c.	S.E.1	c.	o.	o.	b.m.2
30	—25·02	—20·8	—29·2	30·042	45·4	S.W.1	S.W.1	c.	o.	o.	b.m.2
31	—27·23	—20·8	—35·8	30·040	39·4	S.1	c.	c.	o.	o.	b.m.1
	—10·54	+22·9	—41·0	29·743	+51·60						

Date. Nov. 1854.	Mean Temp. of Air.	Maximum.	Minimum.	Mean Height of Barometer.	Attached Thermometer.	Wind: Direction and Force.			Weather.		
	°	°	°	inch.	°						
1	—29·16	—20·8	—39·0	30·029	+46·2	S.3	S.3	c.	b.m.2	b.m.2	b.
2	34·75	—26·9	41·2	29·869	45·0	c.	c.	c.	b.	b.	b.
3	31·92	—26·0	42·3	29·862	44·7	c.	c.	c.	b.m.1	b.	b.
4	......	...	...	......	...	......	......	......	...	...	...
5	......	...	...	......	...	......	......	......	...	...	...
6	......	...	...	......	...	......	......	......	...	...	...
7	......	...	...	......	...	......	......	......	...	...	...
8	......	...	...	......	...	......	......	......	...	...	...
9	......	...	...	......	...	......	......	......	...	...	...
10	......	...	...	......	...	......	......	......	...	...	...
11	21·55	—14·9	25·5	29·657	54·3	N.1	c.	c.	b.	b.	o.
12	20·50	—16·4	25·1	29·707	57·2	c.	c.	c.	o.	o.	b.
13	26·05	—21·8	31·0	29·743	56·9	c.	c.	c.	b.	b.	b.m.1
14	30·11	—25·1	35·6	29·835	52·4	S.W.1	c.	c.	b.	b.	b.
15	38·22	—33·3	42·3	29·988	52·7	c.	c.	c.	b.	b.	b.
16	38·39	—31·0	43·4	30·012	53·5	c.	c.	c.	b.	b.	b.
17	36·82	—26·4	45·1	30·084	53·2	c.	c.	c.	b.	b.	b.
18	16·16	— 4·9	35·6	30·272	48·0	S.E.3	S.1	E.1	o.	o.	o.
19	17·27	— 8·4	25·5	30·047	53·5	S.W.1	S.3	S.W.5	o. s.	o.	o.
20	5·82	— 0·8	12·9	30·321	53·8	S.W.8	S.W.2	S.W.3	o.	o.	b.m.1
21	20·30	—11·9	26·4	30·152	47·9	S.1	c.	N.1	b.	b.m.1	o.
22	12·63	— 8·9	18·8	29·561	51·1	c.	c.	c.	o. s.	o. s.	o.
23	3·41	+ 3·3	9·9	29·662	51·8	c.	N.E.2	S.W.2	b.	o.	o. s.
24	2·38	+ 4·3	6·9	29·632	55·9	S.2	c.	S.W.1	o. s.	o.	o.
25	10·15	— 2·8	18·8	29·835	56·4	S.W.2	E.3	S.W.2	b.m.1	b.m.2	o.
26	14·12	— 7·1	18·8	29·881	52·5	S.4	c.	S.3	b.m.2	b.m.2	b.
27	20·74	—13·3	24·6	29·601	54·3	W.1	c.	c.	b.m.2	o.	b.m.2
28	25·44	—19·3	29·8	29·199	52·6	S.W.2	c.	c.	b.m.1	b.	b.m.1
29	33·34	—21·3	49·9	29·753	50·0	c.	c.	c.	b.	b.	b.
30	40·36	—35·9	46·8	29·971	51·7	c.	c.	c.	b.	b.	b.
	—23·03	+ 4·3	—49·9	29·855	+51·98						

Date. Dec. 1854.	Mean Temp. of Air.	Maximum.	Minimum.	Mean Height of Barometer.	Attached Thermometer.	Wind: Direction and Force.			Weather.		
	°	°	°	inch.	°						
1	—36·62	—18·0	—45·7	29·829	+43·0	c.	c.	S.W.3	b.	b.	b.
2	35·34	23·7	44·6	29·793	44·4	c.	c.	c.	b.	b.	b.
3	26·80	16·8	36·7	29·756	50·2	S.W.1	S.W.3	S.W.1	b.	b.	b.
4	36·90	33·1	41·2	29·906	47·4	c.	c.	c.	b.	b.	b.m.1
5	35·60	30·1	45·6	30·134	42·8	c.	c.	c.	o.	o.	o.
6	44·90	40·1	56·8	29·815	47·0	c.	c.	c.	b.	b.	b.
7	42·95	35·6	47·4	29·407	47·8	S.W.3	S.1	c.	b.	b.	b.
8	41·57	29·8	47·2	29·854	41·1	c.	c.	c.	o.	o.	o.
9	43·54	39·6	45·8	29·399	47·2	S.1	c.	c.	b.	b.	b.
10	38·80	26·9	44·0	29·067	54·3	N.2	c.	S.4	b.m.1	b.m.2	b.m.2
11	39·23	26·6	57·8	29·543	48·3	S.E.2	c.	c.	b.	b.m.1	b.
12	35·73	27·9	51·8	29·430	50·5	S.W.1	S.W.3	c.	b.	b.m.2	b.m.2
13	42·78	35·9	54·3	29·487	56·0	c.	c.	c.	b.	b.	b.
14	49·37	42·8	54·7	29·816	54·1	c.	c.	c.	b.	b.	b.
15	48·15	41·2	53·1	29·648	52·5	c.	c.	c.	b.	b.	b.
16	45·98	38·4	52·2	29·858	50·0	c.	c.	c.	b.	b.	b.
17	42·60	26·4	49·5	29·903	50·4	c.	c.	c.	b.	b.	b.
18	23·70	8·4	42·4	29·596	50·0	c.	S.E.8	S.E.2	b.	b.	b.
19	23·69	11·9	31·0	29·842	55·3	S.E.2	c.	c.	b.	b.	b.
20	30·75	22·5	42·3	29·405	53·1	S.E.2	c.	c.	b.	b.m.1	b.
21	21·96	12·9	28·3	29·523	53·9	S.1	S.E.3	S.E.4	o.	o.	o.
22	38·34	19·3	47·4	29·834	52·8	c.	c.	c.	b.	b.	b.
23	52·10	48·5	56·6	29·820	47·3	c.	S.E.1	c.	b.	b.	b.
24	53·67	48·0	61·4	29·941	41·7	c.	S.W.1	c.	b.	b.	b.
25	40·06	29·6	55·6	29·939	51·5	S.W.2	S.2	c.	b.	b.	b.
26	45·84	39·5	49·6	30·022	45·1	c.	c.	c.	b.	b.	b.m.2
27	42·55	26·4	49·9	29·651	48·7	c.	c.	c.	o.	o.	o.
28	23·80	15·9	34·5	29·542	52·0	c.	S.W.5	c.	o.	b.m.2	b.
29	28·53	18·8	40·1	29·695	55·7	E.3	S.E.2	S.4	b.	b.	b.m.1
30	28·55	15·4	48·0	29·950	52·5	c.	c.	c.	o.	o.	b.
31	29·66	23·7	46·0	30·158	59·5	S.W.4	S.W.7	S.W.2	b.	b.	o.
	—37·74	— 8·4	—61·4	29·728	+49·98						

Date. Jan. 1855.	Mean Temp. of Air.	Maximum.	Minimum.	Mean Height of Barometer.	Attached Thermometer.	Wind: Direction and Force.			Weather.		
	°	°	°	inch.	°						
1	—34·54	—24·0	—47·3	30·379	+55·7	c.	c.	c.	o.	o.	b.
2	—45·02	—39·9	48·7	30·175	53·0	c.	c.	c.	b.	b.	o.
3	—39·43	—36·7	42·5	30·119	53·2	c.	N.1	c.	o.	o.	o.
4	—47·22	—40·6	52·7	29·797	52·8	c.	c.	c.	o.	o.	o.
5	—41·70	—33·1	50·5	29·967	49·5	c.	c.	S.E.2	o.	o.	o.
6	—50·09	—35·0	60·2	30·338	46·1	N.W.2	N.W.2	S.W.1	b.	b.m.1	b.
7	—56·00	—48·7	69·3	30·498	41·3	c.	c.	c.	b.	b.	b.
8	—59·09	—54·3	67·2	30·105	50·9	c.	c.	c.	b.	b.m.1	b.m.1
9	—54·81	—41·4	60·3	29·773	46·3	c.	c.	c.	b.	b.	b.m.1
10	—39·38	—35·6	44·6	29·824	47·1	c.	c.	c.	b.m.2	o.	o.
11	—36·67	—19·8	45·7	30·124	44·9	S.W.1	S.W.2	c.	b.	b.	b.
12	—44·23	—28·7	51·8	29·917	45·5	c.	S.E.1	c.	b.	o.	o.
13	—20·35	—11·9	28·3	29·708	47·0	S.W.2	S.W.6	S.E.9	o. s.	o. s.	o.
14	—24·76	—20·8	28·5	29·941	46·9	S.W.1	c.	c.	o.	o.	o.
15	—33·96	—30·1	38·4	29·731	47·6	W.2	W.4	S.3	o.	o.	o.
16	—35·23	—28·8	43·0	29·868	46·3	N.1	c.	c.	b.	b.m.2	b.m.2
17	—24·62	— 6·4	33·3	29·981	48·0	W.1	c.	c.	o.	o.	b.m.2
18	—21·51	—17·8	25·1	30·134	48·5	S.E.2	S.E.1	S.W.7	b.m.2	o.	b.
19	—24·89	—22·8	27·7	30·459	50·8	S.W.5	S.W.1	S.E.1	b.	b.	b.
20	—27·30	—19·8	30·1	30·797	48·4	S.E.1	c.	S.E.1	b.	b.m.2	b.m.2
*21	—31·21	—26·0	37·2	30·969	51·0	S.1	S.3	W.2	b.	b.	b.
22	—35·74	—27·4	43·0	30·565	50·1	c.	c.	c.	b.	b.	b.
23	—32·95	—27·9	35·8	30·518	50·8	c.	c.	c.	o.	b.	b.
24	—18·56	— 8·9	25·5	30·200	49·0	c.	c.	c.	o.	o.	o.
25	+13·28	+25·2	2·3	30·148	49·1	......	......	......	...	...	...
26	— 2·32	+ 9·5	12·9	30·445	50·7	......	......	......	...	...	...
27	+ 1·96	+10·5	2·3	30·499	52·5	......	......	......	...	...	...
28	+ 5·11	+12·4	0·8	30·482	52·3	......	......	......	...	...	...
29	+ 3·38	+13·4	2·8	29·964	52·8	......	......	S.E.2	...	...	b.
30	— 8·54	— 2·8	13·9	29·592	51·3	......	......	......	...	...	b.
31	—20·42	—16·8	21·8	29·360	49·1	W.2	c.	N.4	o. s.	o.	o.
	—28·61	+25·2	—69·3	30·141	+49·31						

* The highest stand of barometer recorded this morning was 31·02 inch. from 1h. to 4h. A.M.

Date. Feb. 1855.	Mean Temp. of Air.	Maximum.	Minimum.	Mean Height of Barometer.	Attached Ther-mometer.	Wind: Direction and Force.			Weather.		
	°	°	°	inch.	°						
1	—19·36	—18·8	—20·8	29·534	+53·9	N.1	N.W.1	c.	o.	o.	o.
2	—24·32	—17·8	—27·4	29·966	......	c.	N.W.1	c.	b.m.1	b.m.1	b.m.1
3	—22·34	—15·9	—29·6	29·968	49·5	c.	c.	c.	o.	o.	o.
4	—27·68	—19·8	—35·6	29·996	48·8	S.1	S.E.1	c.	o.	o.	o.
5	—18·15	—15·9	—22·8	29·878	48·9	c.	S.W.3	c.	b.	b.m.1	o.
6	—12·89	+ 4·3	—29·2	29·895	50·6	S.W.3	S.E.5	c.	o. s.	o.	b.m.1
7	— 2·56	+11·5	—11·9	29·451	52·2	S.W.2	c.	S.E.9	o.	o.	o. s.
8	—12·90	— 9·9	—14·9	29·971	53·1	S.8	S.E.2	c.	o.	o.	b.
9	—17·50	—12·9	—24·2	30·472	49·6	c.	S.1	c.	b.	b.	o.
10	—22·49	—10·9	—25·5	30·399	52·5	c.	c.	c.	b.m.1	o.	b.m.1
11	— 3·83	+11·0	—15·9	30·447	53·3	c.	S.E.2	S.E.5	o.	o. s.	b.m.1
12	— 7·72	+ 5·4	—15·1	30·475	50·5	c.	S.E.1	c.	o.	b.m.2	b.
13	+12·09	+19·1	+ 3·5	30·271	49·1	c.	S.E.1	S.E.3	o.	b.m.2	o.
14	+ 7·90	+19·6	— 8·9	29·918	50·5	N.W.1	S.E.8	S.E.6	o.	b.m.1	b.m.1
15	—17·21	+ 9·5	—27·4	29·919	50·1	c.	S.2	S.E.6	o.	o.	o.
16	—20·95	—11·9	—34·7	29·944	52·0	W.1	S.W.1	N.1	o.	o. s.	o. s.
17	—23·11	—16·8	—28·3	30·085	51·5	S.W.8	S.W.9	c.	o.	o.	o. s.
18	—30·64	—24·6	—36·9	30·096	48·1	c.	c.	c.	b.	o.	b.m.2
19	—26·00	—19·3	—39·0	30·306	49·9	S.W.3	S.W.7	S.W.5	o.	o.	o.
20	—23·86	—20·8	—27·4	30·333	48·4	c.	N.2	c.	o.	o.	b.m.2
21	—35·28	—26·0	—41·2	30·438	47·7	c.	c.	c.	b.	b.	b.
22	—21·72	—20·3	—23·0	30·435	47·0	c.	c.	c.	o.	o.	o.
23	—28·55	—25·3	—33·3	30·509	44·1	c.	c.	c.	b.	b.	b.
24	—28·24	—19·3	—37·8	30·367	52·3	c.	S.E.4	S.1	b.	b.	b.
25	—38·95	—37·8	—39·7	30·100	76·0	......	......	......	......	......	......
26	—36·74	—22·8	—46·0	30·188	50·0	c.	c.	S.2	b.	b.	b.
27	—40·97	—17·8	—48·5	29·652	57·9	c.	c.	c.	b.	b.	o.
28	—49·82	—46·3	—53·9	29·649	63·1	c.	c.	c.	b.	b.	b.m.1
	—21·21	+19·6	—53·9	30·095	+51·88						

Date. Mar. 1855.	Mean Temp. of Air.	Maximum.	Minimum.	Mean Height of Barometer.	Attached Ther-mometer.	Wind: Direction and Force.			Weather.		
	°	°	°	inch.	°						
1	—45·67	—39·0	—53·7	29·498	+52·0	c.	S.1	c.	b.	b.m.1	b.
2	39·99	—29·1	52·1	29·604	70·9	c.	c.	c.	b. h.	h.	b.
3	47·77	—45·7	51·8	29·650	68·2	S.W.1	c.	c.	b.	b.m.1	b.
4	48·53	—39·6	54·3	29·587	73·1	c.	c.	c.	b.m.1	b.	b.
5	51·22	—48·7	54·8	29·687	74·2	c.	c.	c.	b.	b.	b.
6	54·76	—53·4	56·2	29·751	68·9	c.	c.	c.	b.	b.	b.
7	51·41	—44·6	55·6	29·614	71·0	W.1	c.	c.	b.m.1	b.m.1	b.m.1
8	27·64	—17·8	40·1	29·578	73·5	c.	c.	c.	o.	b.m.1	b.
9	26·01	—22·3	40·1	29·821	71·4	S.W.4	c.	c.	b.	b.	b.
10	30·47	—24·6	34·5	30·015	70·0	S.W.3	S.E.2	c.	b.m.1	b.m.1	b.
11	41·45	—34·7	46·8	29·909	75·4	c.	c.	c.	b.	b.	b.
12	38·91	—30·6	44·6	30·037	70·6	......	......	......	......	......	......
13	44·90	—40·1	56·1	29·854	74·7	......	......	......	b.	......	......
14	43·08	—32·8	55·6	29·987	72·5	......	......	......	b.m.1	......	......
15	43·77	—35·0	55·6	29·968	72·1	S.W.1	......	......	b.	......	......
16	40·42	—32·2	49·9	30·174	73·2	......	......	......	......	......	......
17	32·40	—25·5	38·4	30·165	71·7	c.	......	......	b.	......	......
18	22·95	—10·9	35·6	30·198	72·4	c.	c.	......	b.	b.	......
19	21·16	—13·9	27·4	30·091	70·2	c.	S.W.2	......	b.	b.m.2	......
20	17·45	—12·9	23·7	29·995	69·3	c.	c.	c.	o.	o.	o.
21	16·21	— 8·4	27·4	30·060	73·2	W.1	c.	S.W.1	o.	o.	b.
22	17·84	— 5·9	26·4	30·016	59·4	S.1	c.	c.	b.	b.	b.
23	17·87	—15·7	19·8	29·985	61·1	c.	S.W.1	c.	b.m.1	b.	b.
24	8·84	+ 2·3	22·8	29·730	61·2	c.	c.	c.	o.	o. s.	o. s.
25	26·08	—17·8	38·4	29·808	57·4	c.	c.	c.	o.	b.	b.
26	30·51	—20·8	43·4	29·635	56·2	c.	S.W.3	c.	b.	b.	b.m.1
27	34·99	—21·8	48·0	29·634	57·1	S.E.1	c.	c.	b.m.1	b.	b.
28	40·02	—27·4	51·8	29·652	61·0	c.	c.	c.	b.	b.	b.
29	36·10	—25·5	49·3	29·397	59·5	S.1	c.	c.	b.	b.	b.
30	27·51	—22·8	41·7	29·207	60·3	c.	c.	c.	b.	b.	b.m.1
31	27·07	—17·8	43·4	29·341	60·5	S.E.4	c.	c.	o.	b.	b.
	—33·97	+ 2·3	—56·1	29·795	+67·17						

Date. April 1855.	Mean Temp. of Air.	Maximum.	Minimum.	Mean Height of Barometer.	Attached Thermometer.	Wind: Direction and Force.			Weather.		
	°	°	°	inch.	°						
1	—28·13	—20·8	—37·8	29·423	+60·7	......	......	......	......	......	......
2	—23·22	—16·8	31·8	29·892	60·3	E.2	c.	c.	o.	o.	o.
3	—24·09	—17·8	35·6	29·809	59·3	S.1	c.	S.1	o.	o.	o.
4	—21·53	— 8·9	36·7	29·586	59·2	S.E.1	c.	c.	b.	b.	b.m.1
5	—25·05	—10·9	33·9	29·641	59·8	W.1	S.W.1	c.	b.	b.	b.
6	—27·19	—10·9	33·9	29·651	56·0	c.	N.2	c.	b.	b.	b.
7	—12·52	— 5·9	42·3	29·830	62·2	S.E.6	S.E.5	S.E.5	o. s.	o.	o.
8	—21·33	—14·4	34·5	29·549	55·5	c.	c.	c.	b.	b.	b.
9	— 8·12	— 3·3	13·4	29·838	60·6	S.E.1	S.W.2	S.W.6	b.	b.	b.
10	— 4·92	+ 0·2	9·9	29·950	60·7	S.W.4	S.4	c.	o. s.	o.	o.
11	—16·82	—10·9	26·4	29·975	58·7	c.	c.	c.	b.	b.	b.
12	—10·98	— 3·3	22·8	30·022	60·6	S.4	S.4	S.6	b.	b.	b.m.1
13	— 4·57	+ 0·7	15·9	29·933	58·9	S.3	c.	S.2	o. s.	o.	o.
14	— 7·50	+ 7·4	13·5	29·950	58·7	c.	S.W.4	S.W.4	b.m.2	o.	o.
15	— 7·69	— 0·8	14·9	29·970	......	N.W.2	S.E.2	S.2	o. s.	o. s.	o. s.
16	— 7·00	— 3·8	17·8	30·167	......	S.W.2	c.	c.	o. s.	o. s.	o.
17	—17·01	—12·9	23·3	30·185	69·8	c.	c.	c.	b.	b.	b.
18	—19·12	—14·9	23·7	......	......	......	......	......	......	......	......
19	—24·35	—10·9	28·3	30·351	......	c.	c.	c.	b.	b.	b.
20	—17·30	—11·9	26·0	30·212	64·2	c.	N.1	c.	b.	b.	b.
21	—18·61	— 6·9	24·6	30·000	57·0	c.	c.	c.	b.	b.	b.
22	—14·61	— 6·9	21·8	30·040	57·0	N.1	N.2	c.	b.	b.	b.
23	—14·90	— 6·9	21·8	......	......	c.	c.	c.	b.	b.	b.
24	— 7·86	— 5·2	12·4	......	......	S.W.1	c.	c.	b.m.2	b.m.2	o.
25	— 8·11	— 2·8	15·4	......	......	c.	c.	c.	o.	b.	b.
26	—12·91	— 7·9	18·3	......	......	c.	N.1	c.	b.	b.	b.
27	— 8·40	— 3·8	18·3	......	......	N.W.1	S.W.2	S.4	b.	b.m.2	b.
28	— 5·04	+ 2·3	10·9	......	......	S.W.1	c.	N.W.1	b.	b.m.1	o.
29	— 2·58	+ 4·3	12·9	......	......	c.	c.	c.	b.	b.m.2	o. s.
30	+ 1·42	+ 8·9	4·3	......	......	c.	c.	N.W.1	o. s.	o.	o. s.
	—14·00	+ 8·9	—42·3	29·904	+59·93						

Synopsis of mean monthly readings of atmospheric temperature and pressure, and of observed maxima and minima temperatures.

Date.	Temperature of Air.			Barometer.	Attached Thermometer.
	Mean.	Maximum.	Minimum.		
	°	°	°	inch.	°
1853, June	+48·63	+70·0	+35·0	29·890	+55·73
July	+37·83	+51·0	+30·0	29·727	68·83
August	+33·41	+46·0	+25·0	29·661	68·92
September	+17·16	+32·0	— 2·2	29·678	55·86
October	+ 0·55	+17·8	—23·7	29·801	69·76
November	—23·01	+ 0·2	—43·2	29·726	34·35
December	—25·99	+15·8	—45·7	29·842	36·36
1854, January	—30·24	+11·0	—59·9	29·461	29·66
February	—33 60	—11·3	—68·0	29·642	24·69
March	—38·09	+ 0·9	—55·6	29·760	14·52
April	— 8·60	+14·3	—43·0	29·981	29·71
May	+12·89	+39·4	— 8·7	29·970	51·62
June	+29·23	+41·9	+17·7	29·780	53·98
July	+38·40	+53·9	+27·6	29·784	46·67
August	+31·35	+48·9	+19·1	29·711	37·66
September	+ 9·81	+26·6	— 8·9	29·682	41·22
October	—10·54	+22·9	—41·0	29·743	51·60
November	—23·03	+ 4·3	—49·9	29·855	51·98
December	—37·74	— 8·4	—61·4	29·728	49·98
1855, January	—28·61	+25·2	—69·3	30·141	49·31
February	—21·21	+19·6	—53·9	30·095	51·88
March	—33·97	+ 2·3	—56·1	29·795	67·17
April	—14·00	+ 8·9	—42·3	29·904	59·93
Autumn, (1853)	— 1·77	+32·0	—43·2	29·735	53·32
Winter, (1853–54)	—29·94	+15·8	—68·0	29·648	30·24
Spring, (1854)	—11·27	+39·4	—55·6	29·904	31,95
Summer, (1854)	+32·99	+53·9	+17·7	29·758	46·10
Autumn, (1854)	— 7·92	+26·6	—49·9	29·760	48·27
Winter, (1854–55)	—29·19	+25·2	—69·3	29·988	50·39

Difference, (Summer and Winter,) 62·93°
" warmest and coldest month, 76·49
" maximum and minimum 123·20

Mean of the year 1854.

Temp. of Air.	Barometer.	Attached Therm.
—5·01°	29·7581 inch.	+40·27°

The maximum of temperature was +53·9°, and occurred on the 4th of July, 1854.
The minimum in 1854 was —68·0°, and occurred on the 5th of February.
In 1855 it was —69·3° on the 7th of January.
From September, 1853, to April, 1855, (inclusive.) the observations were made at nearly the same place; hence the means of the same months in 1853, 1854, and 1855, would be combined for the mean annual temperature and the mean annual height of barometer given in the following table.

Lat. 78° 37′ N., lon. 70° 40′ W. from Greenwich.

Month.	Mean Temperature of Air.	Barometer.	Attached Thermometer.
	°	inch.	°
January	—29·42	29·801	+39·48
February	—27·40	29·868	38·29
March	—36·03	28·777	40·84
April	—11·30	29·942	44·82
May	+12·89	29·970	51·62
June	+29·23	29·780	53·98
July	+38·40	29·784	46·67
August	+31·35	29·711	37·66
September	+13·48	29·680	48·54
October	— 5·00	29·772	60·68
November	—23·02	29·790	43·16
December	—31·86	29·785	43·17
Year	— 3·22	29·805	+45·74
Spring	—11·48	29·896	45·76
Autumn	— 4·85	29·747	50·79
Summer	+32·99	29·758	46·10
Winter	—29·56	29·818	40·31

The preceding tables show that the mean temperature of the year 1854 was 1·79° colder than the mean temperature of the year as derived from twenty months' observations.

No. XIII.

Contribution to our knowledge of the Climate of the American Polar Regions, with an accompanying illustration, by CHARLES A. SCHOTT, ESQ., *United States Coast Survey.*

The relations of temperature, forming one of the most interesting features in the meteorology of Arctic America, demands equally, in preference to other studies, the attention of the navigator and physicist. Following the admirable thermal investigations of Dove, and making use of the peculiar advantages of a graphical representation, I have attempted, in the accompanying chart of mean monthly isothermal lines, to illustrate the changes of the atmospheric temperatures from month to month and season to season.

The several expeditions sent in search of Sir John Franklin have brought home a rich store of thermal material, but by far the greater part of which has not yet been made public; hence, the present map cannot pretend to give an elaborate and true picture of the observations on file, but should be received merely as an attempt to illustrate the temperature-relations or part of the climatology of the American Arctic archipelago. In its general outlines and conclusions no great change is anticipated from the addition of new facts.

In tracing the isothermal, or lines of equal average monthly temperature of the air, due allowance is to be made for the short period over which the observations extend at most of the places,—a circumstance of primary importance, not to be overlooked, since it is well known to what considerable changes the mean annual temperature at any given place is subject. Rink, in his valuable geographical description of North Greenland, gives several striking examples of this kind.

The isotherms are principally based upon observations made at the following places:—For the northern and western part of the map, Melville Island, Assistance Bay, Port Bowen, Boothia Felix, Igloolik, and Winterinsel; for the western coast of Greenland, Jacobshavn, Omeack, Upernavik, Wostenholm, and the northernmost station, Rensselaer Harbor. Some of the results are imperfect, on account of too limited a number of daily observations. Dove's curves, to which the necessary alterations and additions have been made, were used as a basis. The curves themselves were constructed by a graphical process, aided by some calculation when necessary, and require no correction to reduce them to the level of the sea.

Referring to the map, the seasons have been separated in accordance with the custom of meteorologists, which arrangement holds good in these high latitudes, except for one anomalous month, March, belonging decidedly to the winter season.

Examining first the winter months, December, January, and February, we recognise the meridian in the vicinity of 95° west of Greenwich as comparatively the coldest, a feature common to each of the three months. During February and March the curves, without any great change of form, have slowly descended to lower latitudes. During the same two months the temperature at Rensselaer Harbor is nearly the same as at Melville Island, although the latter place is nearly 4° farther south.

Spring opens with an anomalous and excessively cold month; yet it has, in common with the other two months, the preservation of the greatest cold at nearly the same meridian as noticed in the preceding season, this feature being well impressed upon every isotherm. While in March the mean temperature of Prince Patrick and Melville Islands has been considerably elevated, when compared with the previous month, it has as much been depressed at Rensselaer Harbor, where the atmosphere is found colder indeed than in any other month. A similar though less marked anomaly we find in the Wostenholm series, where the lowest temperature took place in February.

At the opening of summer the curves, before contracted longitudinally, widen, and a most rapid general increase of temperature takes place during this season. The summer months are characteristic for a decided circular bent in the isotherms, which in June was yet blended with the curvature of the previous month, but in July and August was apparently accommodating itself to the shore-line of Baffin's Bay. Affected by this alteration in the form of the isotherms, the meridian of comparatively greatest cold has shifted almost 20° to the eastward, it being now found during the summer months in longitude 75°. While the temperature in general was still rapidly on the increase from May to June, the curves have but slightly ascended to higher latitudes during July and August, nearly with the same velocity with which they had travelled in the opposite direction during the months of January and February. In September a rapid decrease of temperature is observed, and continues through October and November, but becoming less marked in December. While in September the meridian of greatest cold is still in the vicinity of Baffin's Bay, it shifts suddenly in the following month to Melville Island, and remains there during November.

The motion of this meridian of maximum cold is therefore slowly to the eastward from October through the succeeding months till September, when it suddenly recovers its westerly limit in a single month. The number of water-courses which separate the islands to the westward of Baffin's Bay, frozen over during the greater part of the year and cementing together these islands, form a large area which stands in the same relation to temperature as an Arctic continent, and may thus become one of the principal causes of the low temperatures observed; and this may explain the descent of the isotherms. The curves passing over Bank Land and Prince Patrick Island indicate by their curvature the presence of an open (not entirely frozen over) Polar sea. During the summer, the land absorbing heat more rapidly, we find the curves plainly pointing out the middle ice of Baffin's Bay; even the so-called North Water off Wostenholm appears to be indicated by the June isotherm of +32°. In September, the currents from the north and west (see my current-chart of Baffin's Bay, in Dr. Kane's narrative of the first Grinnell Expedition) also favor a low atmospheric temperature over Baffin's Bay. The above general climatic outlines cannot be extended to Greenland, whose interior is as yet a perfect terra incognita. Proceeding along its western coast to the northward, we find a regular decreasing temperature, which decrease appears to be accelerated as we approach the latitudes of Wostenholm and Rensselaer Harbors.

In the following it is proposed to give some comparative meteorological detail in support of, and further illustrating, the views presented in the above sketch.

C. A. S.

MEAN MONTHLY ISOTHERMAL LINES of BAFFIN BAY

projected by Charles A. Schott, Esq, U.S. Coast Survey from observations at Rensselaer Harbor and other places based upon H.W. Dove's isothermal charts.

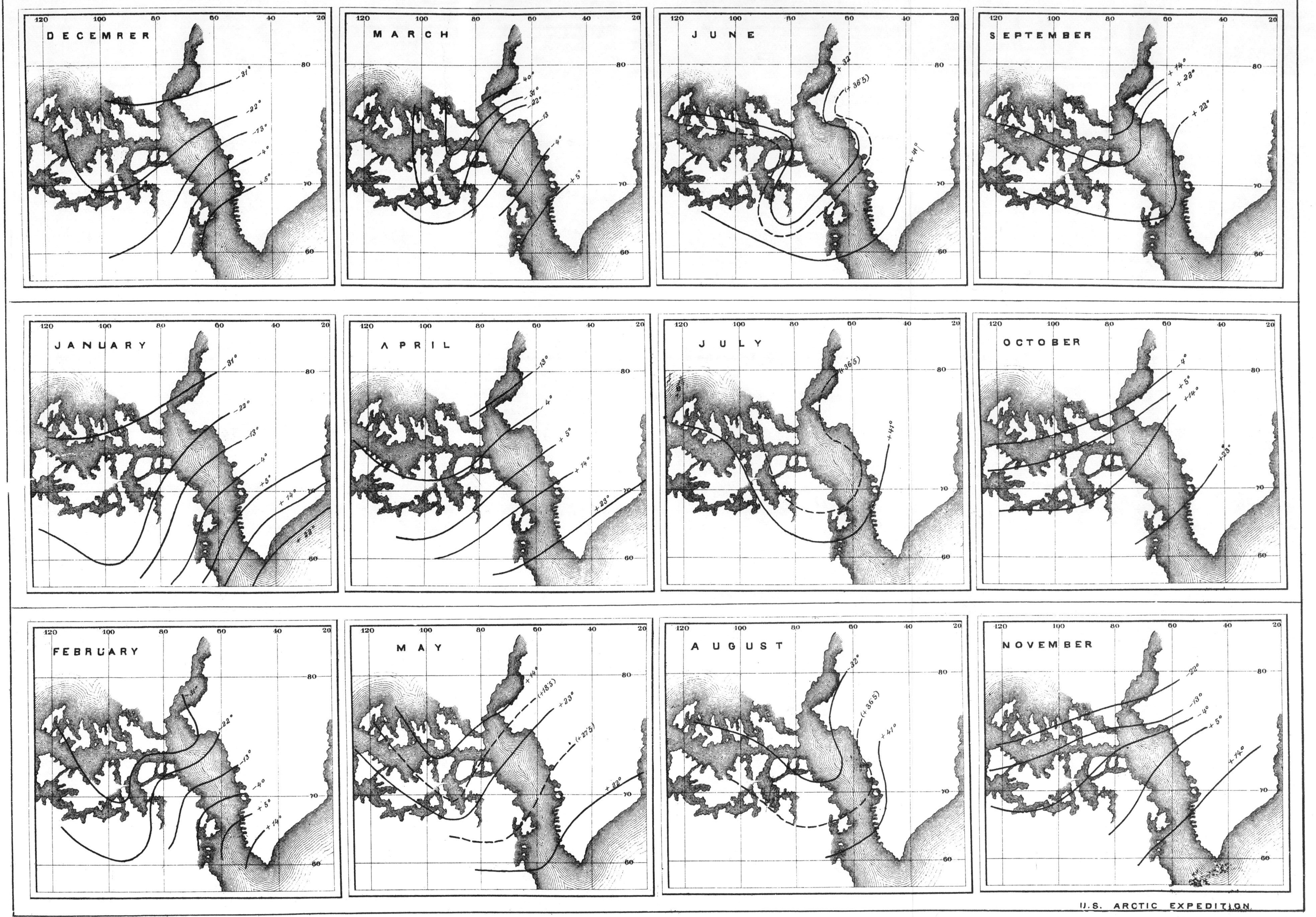

No. XIV.

Comparison of the Rensselaer climate with that at other Polar stations as depending on the difference of their respective mean Summer and Winter Temperatures.—By CHARLES A. SCHOTT.

The difference between the mean summer and winter temperatures of any given locality is an index to the nature of the climate, whether the same be continental, littoral, or insular. Great differences refer to the first, small differences to the latter. Small fluctuations in these figures indicate local disturbances; yet, upon the whole, they differ less among themselves than might have been anticipated, always bearing in mind that the conclusions depend on a small number of years of observations.

The stations have been arranged in three groups, in the order of their latitudes, and are either situated in or close to the Polar circle. The average temperature, in degrees of the Fahrenheit scale, during June, July, and August, is given in the column headed summer; and the average temperature during December, January, and February, follows in the next column.

STATION.	Latitude.	Summer Temperature.	Winter Temperature.	Difference.
1. *Siberian and Russian North American Stations.*				
	° ′	°	°	°
Yakoutzk	62 2	+58·3	—36·6	94·9
Yukon	66 0	+59·7	—23·9	83·6
2. *Stations on the West Coast of Greenland.*				
Rensselaer Harbor	78 37	+33·0	—29·6	62·6
Wostenholm	76 33	+38·0	—28·7	66·7
Upernavik	72 48	+35·2	—12·5	47·7
Omenak	70 41	+40·7	— 5·1	45·8
Jacobshavn	69 12	+42·4	+ 0·8	41·6
3. *Stations West of Baffin's Bay.*				
Melville Island	74 47	+37·1	—28·2	65·3
Assistance Bay	74 40	+35·9	—26·7	62·6
Port Bowen	73 14	+37·0	—25·1	62·1
Boothia Felix	69 59	+38·0	—27·7	65·7
Igloolik	69 21	+35·2	—21·3	56·5
Fort Hope	67 25	+39·7	—25·1	64·8
Winterinsel	66 11	+35·1	—20·5	55·6
Fort Franklin	65 12	+50·2	—17·0	67·2
				Mean, 62·3

The above table yields some interesting results; the principal one being the gradual approach, as we proceed to the northward along the western coast of Greenland, from an insular climate to the littoral climate of the western Polar archipelago, which latter, as we have seen, assumes itself a continental character. While the figure 90 may be taken as expressive of the Siberian continental climate, 62 is found for the North American Polar islands, and 45 for the western coast of South Greenland. This latter value is of course produced by the vicinity of the Atlantic Ocean. The high figures 62·6 and 66·7 for Rensselaer and Wostenholm, point most conclusively to either a considerable northern expanse of Grinnell Land on one side and an eastern extent of Washington Land on the other, or to a considerable elevation of the interior on both sides of the channel above its level. Both suppositions are supported by the highlands seen from the northernmost station reached, and by the location of a stupendous glacier, which, as is well known, requires extensive and elevated snow-areas as feeding-reservoirs. The above conclusion appears to be in opposition to the presence of water open to navigation; but the explanation offered can be reconciled with facts by supposing an unobstructed and broad connection of Kennedy Channel with the great Polar basin.

C. A. S.

No. XV.

Observations for Magnetic Dip and Intensity.

New York, May 18–20, 1853.

STATION, MR. RUTHERFORD'S OBSERVATORY.

	Magnetic Dip.		
1853, May 18	72° 54·2′	Needle No. 2.	2 sets.
" "	73 1·9	" " 2.	" "
" 20	72 59·6	" " 1.	" "
" "	72 54·5	" " 1.	" "
1853, May 19	72 57·55		8 sets.

1853, May 18. Lloyd Needle No. 2, Box A.

Dip + correction	73° 1·31′
Weight in end-hole, side B.	—26 37·43
	99 38·74

1853, May 18. Lloyd Needle No. 1, Box A.

Dip + correction	73° 13·18′
Weight in end-hole, side B.	—40 43·25
	113 56·43

1853, May 20. Lloyd Needle No. 1, Box A.

Dip + correction	73°	28·31′
Weight in end-hole, side B.	—40	28·31
	113	56·62

Fiskernaes. Lat. 63° 5·3′; long. 50° 34·4′.

STATION: FLAGSTAFF NEAR THE GOVERNOR'S HOUSE.

1853, June 29. Magnetic Dip, 80° 41·4′. Needle No. 2. 2 sets.

STATION: SMALL ISLAND ON THE NORTH SIDE OF THE HARBOR.

1853, June 30. Magnetic Dip, 80° 53·0′. Needle No. 2. 2 sets.

SAIKATLE, (ISLAND SOUTH FROM SUKKERTOPPEN.)

1853, July 9. Lloyd Needle No. 1, Box B.

	Magnetic Dip.	
Dip + correction	81°	32·7′
Weight in the middle hole	—29	52·3
	111	25·0

Sukkertoppen.

STATION: GARDEN NEAR THE GOVERNOR'S HOUSE.

1853, July 9. Magnetic dip, 80° 49·7′. Needle No. 2. 2 sets.

Force Bay. Lat. 78° 34′; long. 71° 33·6′.

1853, August 12. Magnetic dip, 85° 8·0′. Needle No. 2. 2 sets.

Marshall Bay. Lat. 78° 52′; long. 67° 1′.

1853, Sept. 4. Lloyd Needle No. 1, Box B.

Magnetic dip + correction	85°	26·1′
Weight in middle hole	—56	12·3
	141	38·4

Winter Harbor. Lat. 78° 37′; long. 70° 40′.

	Magnetic Dip.		
1854, January 26	84° 39·7′	Needle No. 2	2 sets.
February 16	84 52·7	" "	"
" 23	84 52·8	" "	"
March 2	84 49·0	" "	"
June 10	84 47·2	" "	"
" 10	84 51·0	" "	"
1855, April 24	84 48·73	" "	12 sets.
1855, May 20	84 35·60	" "	2 "

HORIZONTAL COMPONENT OF INTENSITY, OBSERVED WITH THE MAGNETOMETER.

Vibrations.

	Arc at beginning.	Arc at end.	Time of one vibr'n.	Temp.
1854, January 17	4° 36·5′	1° 26·9′	15·409s.	+50°
" 18	4 36·5	1 11·1	15·510	+68
February 21	5 47·6	3 22·2	15·5622	+79
" "	5 16·0	1 34·8	15·5129	+55

Deflections.

	Distance of magn.	Double arc of deflection.	Temp.
1854, January 31	13·00 inch	30° 46·75′	72·1°
February 13	9·75 "	78 39·75	60·5
" 27	13·00 "	30 49·75	57·5

1854, June 7.

Vibrations.

Arc at beginning.	Arc at end.	Time of one vibration.	Temp.
6° 3·4′	2° 45·9′	15·2881s.	+33°
6 3·4	2 45·9	15·3143	33
6 35·0	2 53·8	15·4079	35
7 22·4	3 9·6	15·4090	35
		15·3548	+34

Deflections.

Distance of magnets	Double arc of deflection.	Temp.
9 inch	107° 57·45′	36°
13 "	31 17·00	34·9

1854, June 8.

Vibrations.

Arc at beginning.	Arc at end.	Time of one vibration.	Temp.
5° 31·8′	3° 17·5′	15·5100s.	35°
6 3·4	3 9·6	15·5011	35
6 42·9	2 6·4	15·3820	35
6 50·8	3 17·5	15·3064	35
		15·4249	35

Deflections.

Distance of magnets.	Double arc of deflection.	Temp.
13 inch	31° 22′	36·9°
13 "	31 20	36
9 "	108 48·12	37
9 "	108 27·50	37·1

1854, June 19.

Vibrations.

Arc at beginning.	Arc at end.	Time of one vibration.	Temp.
7° 22·4′	3° 41·2′	15·4645s.	43°
6 50·8	3 57	15·4389	43
6 42·9	3 33·3	15·4417	42·4
6 58·7	3 25·4	15·4032	42·4
		15·4371	42·7

Deflections.

Distance of magnets.	Double arc of deflection.	Temp.
9 inch	106° 49′	41·1°
13 "	30 42·75	42·1
13 "	30 51·50	42·3
9 "	106 21	42·3

1854, June 24.

Vibrations.

Arc at beginning.	Arc at end.	Time of one vibration.	Temp
6° 11·3′	3° 17·5′	15·4382s	41.2°
5 47·6	3 17·5	15·3714	41·2
6 11·3	3 17·5	15·3774	41·2
6 42·9	3 17·5	15·4010	41·2
		15·3970	41·2

Deflections.

Distance of magnets.	Double angle of deflection.	Temp.
9 inch	105° 21′	38°
13 "	30 42·75	39·3
13 "	30 24·50	43
9 "	107 36	41·6

1855, May 16.

Vibrations.

Arc at beginning.	Arc at end.	Time of one vibration.	Temp
7° 22·4′	2° 22·2′	14·8965s	+17°
7 22·4	2 30·1	14·8319	19·3
7 22.4	2 30·1	14·7688	22
7 22·4	2 22·2	14·7422	19
		14·8097	+19·3

Deflections.

Distance of magnets.	Double angle of deflection.	Temp
13 inch	29° 14·25′	17°
9 "	101 41·50	17

1855, May 17.

Vibrations.

Arc at beginning.	Arc at end.	Time of one vibration.	Temp.
7° 22·4′	2° 45·9′	14·7874s	23°
6 13·4	2 0·6	14·7774	23
		14·7824	23

Deflections.

Distance of magnets.	Double angle of deflection.	Temp.
9 inch	99° 59·50′	23°
13 "	29 5.25	23

1855, May 18.

Vibrations.

Arc at beginning.	Arc at end.	Time of one vibration.	Temp
7° 22·4′	3° 9·6′	14·7661s	15°
7 22·4	3 25·4	14·7712	15
		14·7686	15

Deflections.

Distance of magnets.	Double angle of deflection.	Temp.
13 inch	28° 46·50′	27°
9 "	96 1·50	27

1855, May 19.

Vibrations.

Arc at beginning.	Arc at end.	Time of one vibration.	Temp.
7° 22·4′	3° 1·7′	14·8134s.	28°
7 22·4	3 1·7	14·8262	28·5
7 22·4	3 1·7	14·7917	28·
		14·8078	28·2

Deflections.

Distance of magnets.	Double angle of deflection.	Temp.
9 inch	98° 1·50′	27°
13 "	29 13·50	27

The time of one oscillation is always the mean of ten observed intervals between fifty oscillations of the magnet from the right to the left, and fifty from the left to the right.

By the observations of deflection, the two magnets are always under right angles upon another.

The magnet used for deflecting and oscillations was A 67.

Three observations, 1854, June 9, 14, and 26, gave the mean variation or magnetic declination, 1854, June 16, 108° 21·5′ W.

1855, June 21.

Hakluyt Island.

Vibrations.

Arc at beginning.	Arc at end.	Time of one vibration.	Temp.
7° 22·4′	5° 39·7′	14·0396s.	33·3°
7 22·4	5 39·7	14·0518	33·3
7 22·4	4 28·6	14·0660	33·8
		14·0525	33·5

1855, July 19.

Coast between Parker Snow's Point and Cape York. Lat. 76° 3′; long. 68° 0′.

Vibrations.

Arc at beginning.	Arc at end.	Time of one vibration.	Temp.
7° 22·4′	4° 44·4′	12·9504s.	40°
7 22·4	3 57·0	12·9784	41·5
7 22·4	4 36·5	13·0876	41·2
7 22·4	4 12·8	12·9482	39·5
		12·9911	40·5

The above observations were made with a unifilar magnetometer, kindly loaned by the United States Coast Survey, and a Barrow's dip-circle, received from Professor Henry, of the Smithsonian Institution, through the courtesy of Colonel Sabine. The observations were made by Mr. Sontag.

E. K. K.

No. XVI.

MAGNETIC OBSERVATIONS—*Continued.*

Tables of hourly readings of the changes of the magnetic declination at Rensselaer Harbor in 1854.

The following observations for diurnal inequality do not include the term-day observations, which are given elsewhere. The mean time refers to the meridian of our winter quarters,—viz.: 4h. 42m. W. of Greenwich, or 5h. 22m. W. of Göttingen. The scale readings commenced thirty minutes before and ended twenty-four minutes after the even hour, the observations being made every sixth minute; the scale readings in the second column of each table are therefore means of ten separate values. The third column contains the deviations from the mean direction, or the hourly changes in scale divisions.

The scale reading 280 corresponds to a magnetic declination of 108° 3′ west of north; greater readings correspond to a smaller westerly declination, and *vice versâ.* One scale division was found to equal 0·79′.

Hourly Changes of Magnetic Declination.

Mean Time.	January 10-11.		January 13-14.	
	Scale Readings.	Difference.	Scale Readings.	Difference.
h.				
5	296·80	—11·93	309·50	+ 8·51
6	292.38	— 7·51	319·31	— 1·29
7	287·42	— 2·55	331·20	—13·19
8	278·75	+ 6·12	342·30	—24·29
9	284·30	+ 0·57	359·40	—41·39
10	288·00	— 3·13	358·85	—40·84
11	295·35	—12·48	344·14	—26·13
12	299·70	—14·83	349·34	—31·33
13	307·90	—23·03	342·26	—24·25
14	309·38	—24·51	346·20	—28·19
15	308·18	—23·31	350·00	—31·99
16	305·83	—20·96	362·20	—44·29
17	298·30	—13·43	369·80	—51·79
18	291·60	— 6·73	339·50	—21·49
19	272·40	+12·47	317·80	+ 0·21
20	266·70	+18·17	278·93	+39·12
21	273·70	+11·17	268·07	+49·94
22	253·73	+31·14	279·93	+38·12
23	255·04	+29·83	267·15	+50·86
0	270·53	+14·34	264·50	+53·51
1	259·15	+25·72	243·20	+74·81
2	265·70	+19·17	277·50	+40·51
3	275·70	+ 9·17	296·18	+21·83
4	296·20	—11·33	305·05	+12·96
Mean	284·87		318·01	

Hourly Changes of Magnetic Declination—Continued.

Mean Time.	JANUARY 24–25.		JANUARY 27–28.		JANUARY 31–FEBRUARY 1.	
	Scale Readings.	Difference.	Scale Readings.	Difference.	Scale Readings.	Difference.
h.						
5	316·53	+20·31	314·00	+29·29	333·75	+28·31
6	345·75	— 8·89	306·50	+36·79	322·05	+40·01
7	358·25	—21·39	324·90	+18·39	350·45	+11·61
8	367·70	—30·84	324·00	+19·29	361·50	+ 0·56
9	361·20	—24·34	325·50	+17·79	371·05	— 8·99
10	362·10	—25·24	322·77	+20·52	372·30	—10·24
11	356·90	—20·04	324·28	+19·01	368·30	— 6·24
12	358·95	—22·09	330·08	+13·21	374·90	—12·84
13	354·15	—17·29	335·44	+ 7·85	374·50	—12·44
14	364·50	—27·64	333·24	+10·05	380·60	—18·54
15	357·38	—20·52	339·90	+ 3·39	381·90	—19·84
16	344·85	— 7·99	347·50	— 4·21	368·65	— 6·59
17	342·70	— 5·84	353·10	— 9·81	374·40	—12·33
18	338·80	— 1·94	383·80	—40·51	374·35	—12·29
19	345·90	— 9·04	382·40	—39·11	387·40	—12·34
20	348·30	—11·44	365·43	—22·14	387·88	—25·82
21	316·85	+20·01	362·20	—18·91	383·05	—20·99
22	296·95	+39·91	360·40	—17·11	327·30	—34·76
23	315·50	+21·36	363·30	—20·01	327·65	+34·41
0	311·70	+25·16	345·65	— 2·36	325·15	+36·91
1	291·90	+44·96	338·70	+ 4·59	336·75	+25·31
2	301·30	+35·56	356·70	—13·41	372·50	—10·44
3	312·65	+24·21	348·60	— 5·31	355·50	+ 6·56
4	313·91	+22·95	350·60	— 7·31	377·50	—15·44
Mean	333·86		343·29		362·06	

Mean Time.	FEBRUARY 3–4.		Mean Time.	FEBRUARY 7–8.		FEBRUARY 10–11.	
	Scale Readings.	Difference.		Scale Readings.	Difference.	Scale Readings.	Difference.
h.							
9	362·60	— 4·31	5	315·75	+17·01	286·90	+ 50·26
10	369·90	—11·61	6	321·30	+11·46	350·20	— 13·04
11	373·32	—15·03	7	340·90	— 8·14	362·35	— 25·19
12	396·30	—38·01	8	349·70	—16·94	379·00	— 41·84
13	405·90	—47·61	9	356·35	—23·59	392·42	— 55·28
14	431·10	—72·81	10	354·60	—21·84	384·00	— 46·84
15	412·50	—54·21	11	368·90	—36·14	378·10	— 40·94
16	395·25	—36·96	12	371·50	—38·74	382·60	— 45·44
17	401·70	—43·41	13	371·50	—38·74	390·20	— 53·04
18	381·40	—23·11	14	389·50	—36·74	402·50	— 65·34
19	360·55	— 2·26	15	381·10	—48·34	457·25	— 20·09
20	311·62	+46·67	16	348·60	—15·84	483·80	— 46·64
21	266·15	+92·14	17	335·90	— 3·14	392·40	— 55·24
22	293·90	+64·39	18	315·10	+17·66	363·70	— 26·54
23	345·90	+12·39	19	291·50	+41·26	321·85	+ 15·31
0	332·30	+25·99	20	277·70	+55·06	265·40	+ 71·76
1	336·50	+21·79	21	302·00	+30·76	271·20	+ 65·96
2	341·60	+16·69	22	303·40	+29·36	245·20	+ 91·96
3	313·70	+44·59	23	299·80	+32·96	205·10	+132·06
4	301·30	+56·99	0	321·30	+11·46	209·90	+127·26
5	353·80	+ 4·49	1	308·50	+24·26	202·80	+134·36
6	361·30	— 3·01	2	333·50	— 0·74	271·10	+ 66·06
7	375·10	—16·81	3	308·25	+24·51	331·30	+ 5·86
8	375·30	—17.01	4	319·60	+13·16	362·50	-- 25·44
Mean	358·29			332·76		337·16	

Hourly Changes of Magnetic Declination—Concluded.

Mean Time.	February 14–15.		February 17–18.		February 21–22.	
	Scale Readings.	Difference.	Scale Readings.	Difference.	Scale Readings.	Difference.
h.						
5	306·70	+ 54·76	181·80	+47·00	264·90	+ 6·18
6	345·80	+ 15·66	189·60	+37·20	254·70	+16·38
7	375·40	— 13·94	259·70	—32·90	265·40	+ 5·68
8	418·10	— 56·64	243·40	—16·60	281·00	— 9·92
9	421·50	— 60·04	246·00	—19·20	301·90	—30·82
10	469·40	—107·94	272·00	—45·20	289·00	—17·92
11	444·90	— 83·44	267·05	—40·25	277·60	— 6·52
12	479·50	—118·04	236·85	—10·05	293·40	—22 32
13	414·70	— 53·24	234·68	— 7·88	284·60	—13·52
14	451·90	— 90·44	247·90	—21·10	286·20	—15·12
15	457·50	— 96·04	238·35	—11·55	282·40	—11·32
16	489·90	—128·44	236·40	— 9·60	291·30	—20·22
17	454·90	— 93·44	242·90	—16·10	292·30	—21·22
18	409·30	— 47·84	229·30	— 2·50	272·50	— 1·42
19	380·00	— 18·54	233·70	— 6·90	258·50	+12·58
20	335·80	+ 25·64	197·00	+29·80	261·95	+ 9·13
21	344·30	+ 17·16	216·40	+10·40	231·50	+39·58
22	292·90	+ 68·56	222·80	+ 4·00	222·00	+49·08
23	249·70	+111·76	245·55	—18·75	256·20	+14·88
0	174·70	+186·76	234·95	— 8·15	260·90	+10·18
1	173·90	+187·56	226·00	+ 0·80	262·00	+ 9·08
2	245·80	+115·66	208·20	+18·60	259·00	+12·08
3	245·40	+116·04	154·95	+71·85	271·60	— 0·52
4	293·10	+ 68·36	177·60	+49·20	285·00	—13·92
Mean	361·46		226·80		271·08	

Mean Time.	February 28–March 1.		March 3–4.		March 7–8.	
	Scale Readings.	Difference.	Scale Readings.	Difference.	Scale Readings.	Difference.
h.						
5	200·6	+110·7	246·6	— 4·56	220·8	+53·13
6	189·5	+121·8	274·2	— 32·16	255·8	+18·13
7	217·4	+ 93·9	280·8	— 38·76	266·7	+ 7·23
8	260·2	+ 51·1	318·9	— 76·86	277·1	— 3·17
9	328·2	— 16·9	338·9	— 96·86	299·5	—25·57
10	360·6	— 49·3	276·8	— 34·76	292·6	—18·67
11	391·9	— 80·6	279·4	— 37·36	280·5	— 6·57
12	407·0	— 95·7	309·8	— 67·76	270·4	+ 3·53
13	443·1	—131·8	342·8	—100·76	285·4	—11·47
14	354·7	— 43·4	312·2	— 70·16	288·6	—14·67
15	337·9	— 26·6	287·1	— 45·06	287·7*	—13·77
16	323·8	— 12·5	280·0	— 37·96	286·8*	—12·87
17	343·7	— 32·4	258·5	— 16·46	285·8	—11·87
18	320·8	— 9·5	234·85	+ 7·19	291·7	—17·77
19	316·3	— 5·3	148·8	+ 93·24	262·3	+11·63
20	311·6	— ·3	199·1	+ 42·94	269·6	+ 4·33
21	302·1	+ 9·2	176·6	+ 65·44	271·4	+ 2·53
22	298·6	+ 12·7	185·9	+ 56·14	285·4	—11·47
23	279·4	+ 31·9	155·7	+ 86·34	273·4	+ ·53
0	331·3	— 20·0	156·3	+ 85·74	283·5	— 9·57
1	314·4	— 3·1	170·4	+ 71·64	249·7	+24·23
2	263·6	+ 47·7	175·9	+ 66·14	251·9	+22·03
3	269·1	+ 42·2	191·8	+ 50·24	271·7	+ 2·23
4	305·5	+ 5·8	207·7	+ 34·34	266·0	+ 7·93
Mean	311·3		242·04		273·93	

* These two numbers were supplied by interpolation.

Owing to the excessive cold and the difficulties of warming our observatory, it was not uncommon to have a temperature of 30° below zero at our feet, while other portions of the room ranged from +90° to —20°. Under these circumstances the task of observing was one of no common hardship.

It was not until the close of the winter that I was able to take my share in the preceding or the term-day observations; and I desire to express my obligations to Dr. Hayes and Mr. Bonsall, as well as to George Stephenson, for their zealous and intelligent co-operation with Mr. Sontag and myself. E. K. K.

No. XVII.

Magnetic Term-day Observations.

These observations were made at the following dates :—

1854, January 18–19,
February 24–25,
March 22–23,
April 19–20,
May 26–27,
June 21–22,

commencing at 5 P.M. local time, or 10 P.M. Göttingen time, and continued for twenty-four hours. The scale reading 280 corresponds to 108° 3′ west declination, and increasing scale readings denote a smaller westerly deviation. The value of one division equals 0·79′. The readings are in scale divisions.

January 18 *and* 19, 1854.

(The readings were taken 2m. 14s. earlier than indicated in the table.)

Göttingen Mean Time.	0m.	6m.	12m.	18m.	24m.	30m.	36m.	42m.	48m.	54m.	Rensselaer Mean Time.
10 P.M.	305	305	305	307	308	312	311·8	306·5	309·5	312·5	4h.37½m.P.M.
11	311·2	313	314	315·8	318·5	317	317	319·7	320·5	322·5	5 "
12	320	314·8	315	315·7	317·0	320·0	321	320	316	314	6 "
1	311	307	309	311	313	315	317	318	317	315	7 "
2	320	322	319	316	320	320	322	318	320	322	8 "
3	321	323	323·3	322·3	320	319	320	320	325	325	9 "
4	329	329	330	330	327	336	350	366	367	369	10 "
5	362	354	353	347	347	346	346	341	337	334	11 "
6	330	332	335	338	338	340	342	343·5	342	344	12 "
7	344	346·5	345	344	344	345	346	346·5	347	345	1 "
8	346	345	345·5	345	348	347·5	349	351·5	351·5	349·5	2 "
9	349	354	359	363·5	359·5	351	350	351	350·8	351	3 "
10	356	358	359	361·5	361	355	352·3	357·8	358	360·5	4 "
11	360·5	358	355	351·5	350	349	346	340	332	335	5 "
12	336	333	330·5	326	320	320	323	326	328	337	6 "
1	343	352	350	346	340	348	353	357	349	343	7 "
2	337	332	328	324	332	336	340	343	346	345	8 "
3	342	339	329	320	313	300	292	284	277·5	268	9 "
4	251	244·5	240·5	250	261	254	243	230	235	155	10 "
5	115	90	89	96	88	85	105	129	145	155	11 "
6	163	180	193	220	254	290	291	307	298	270	12 "
7	268	254	240	266	289	297	320	318	320	321	1 "
8	336	336	336	331	337	337	337	330	327	324	2 "
9	314	326	332	338	323	318	316	316	316	314	3 "
10	312	....	....	....	....	....	....	....	....	....	4 "

February 24 *and* 25, 1854.

(The readings were taken 2m. 15s. earlier than indicated by the table.)

Göttingen Mean Time.	0m.	6m.	12m.	18m.	24m.	30m.	36m.	42m.	48m.	54m.	Rensselaer Mean Time.
10 P.M.	312	322	329	338	341·5	319·5	342	359	377	407	4h.37½m.P.M.
11	408	411	405	418	437	445	445	447	441	439	5 "
12	438	438	440	432	460	482	477	471	480	494	6 "
1	490	493	506	520	516	509	519	531	530	527·5	7 "
2	541	558·5	532	527	518	511	521	532	538	535	8 "
3	532	529	527	528	530·5	542	526	521	516	513	9 "
4	510	508	506	504	493	483	446	470	503	495	10 "
5	490	493	496	498	500	502	500	500	501	503	11 "
6	503	502	502	502	503	500	494	490	492	494	12 "
7	496	495	495	492	488	499	506	498	492	501	1 "
8	514	509	502	506	509	501	491	490	492	498	2 "
9	504	509	517	516	514	512	511	512	512	517	3 "
10	521	529	535	536	529	508	510	516	514	510	4 "
11	511	507	490	491	489	489	488	488	486	485	5 "
12	502	499	496	489	496	500	499	500	484	475	6 "
1	456	448	440	435	442	447	451	457	456	449	7 "
2	445	440	425	412	427	438	449	445	440	417	8 "
3	370	312	384	289	268	298	326	332	360	375	9 "
4	390	400	415	403	405	405	392	396	401	401	10 "
5	404	408	390	375	370	372	....	393	403	402	11 "
6	402	407	390	374	370	358	355	370	381	380	12 "
7	376	377	379	380	382·5	365	370	373	380	375	1 "
8	381	385	372	386	398	406	435	437	438	439	2 "
9	438	438	437	442	446	444	455	448	446	443	3 "
10	450	....	....	....	....	....	....	....	....	....	4 "

March 22 *and* 23, 1854.

(The readings were taken 1m. 34s. earlier than indicated by the table.)

Göttingen Mean Time.	0m.	6m.	12m.	18m.	24m.	30m.	36m.	42m.	48m.	54m.	Rensselaer Mean Time.
10 P.M.	269	262	265	272	285	295	250	232	228	255	4h.37½m.P.M.
11	240	261	243	246	232	228	236	260	259	258	5 "
12	258	256	254	256	258	258	259	260	263	263	6 "
1	262	253	258	264	263	267	265	256	251	247	7 "
2	235	237	239	239	240	244	243	247	245	240	8 "
3	240	238	239	237	234	233	234	237	245	251	9 "
4	268	265	267	279	280	277	272	264	260	269	10 "
5	275	289	277	282	279	280	282	284	283	282	11 "
6	281	280	278	277	275	273	272	270	269	268	12 "
7	269	268	268	268	267	267	268	266·5	264	262	1 "
8	261	261	262	261	261	258	258	259	262	265	2 "
9	269	267	266	264	264·5	262	269	273	278	284	3 "
10	283	282	278·5	275	270·5	263	265	260	260	261	4 "
11	260	257	256	250	253	256	248	250	257	263	5 "
12	272	280	283	285	292	288	289	287	290	294	6 "
1	300	302	291	290	292	283	277	273	271	....	7 "
2	....	....	....	....	....	284	284	278	271	269	8 "
3	267	267	263	255	248	247	252	249	248	251	9 "
4	260	265	274	292	296	295	298	298	297	295	10 "
5	291	290	290	293	292	294·5	291	292	288	290	11 "
6	293	291	291	290	294	295	290	281	276	269	12 "
7	264	252	250	249	242	239	235	242	252	248·5	1 "
8	243	245	243	242	240	239	241	244	250	258	2 "
9	270	282	284	286·5	288	292	297	300	304	302	3 "
10	301	....	....	....	....	....	....	....	....	....	4 "

April 19 *and* 20, 1854.

(The readings were taken 2m. 14s. earlier than indicated by the table.)

Göttingen Mean Time.	0m.	6m.	12m.	18m.	24m.	30m.	36m.	42m.	48m.	54m.	Rensselaer Mean Time.
10 P.M.	....	....	....	....	....	....	....	....	....	....	4h.37½m.P.M.
11	....	....	....	....	....	....	....	....	....	....	5 "
12	....	....	....	....	....	....	....	....	....	....	6 "
1	....	....	....	....	....	....	....	....	....	....	7 "
2	....	....	....	....	....	....	....	....	....	....	8 "
3	....	....	....	....	....	....	....	....	....	....	9 "
4	....	....	....	272	271	275	273	272·5	278	282	10 "
5	289	299	298	312	310	305	301	296	299	262	11 "
6	271	287	294	290	289	286	280	268	254	230	12 "
7	236	250	245	242	239	234	229	230	242	256	1 "
8	265	262	260	256	252	247	243	236	231	228	2 "
9	225	224	230	236	229	226	231	233	230	227	3 "
10	226	222	218	215	213	189	187	183	190	187	4 "
11	184	182	194	220	221	223	218	220	222	225	5 "
12	231	236	242	236	238	240	235	224	215	203	6 "
1	194	190	187	184	181	180	178	178	168	164	7 "
2	175	208	236	242	212	205	202	190	190	193	8 "
3	196	196	199	200	210	192	180	175	164	152	9 "
4	140	137	139	148	147	160	164	152	140	121	10 "
5	107	113	116	136	145	132	130	120	90	63	11 "
6	62	43	30	32	....	....	—4	—7	+ 4	+ 8	12 "
7	+30	+23	+16	+12	+16	+11	+5	—2	+25	+58	1 "
8	+71	67	73	77	79	81	75	73	76	80	2 "
9	75	74	97	110	128	132	138	147	142	134	3 "
10	126	....	....	....	....	....	....	....	....	....	4 "

May 26 *and* 27, 1854.

(The readings were taken 1m. 34s. earlier than indicated by the table.)

Göttingen Mean Time.	0m.	6m.	12m.	18m.	24m.	30m.	36m.	42m.	48m.	54m.	Rensselaer Mean Time.
10 P.M.	244	243	258	262	278	280	279	276	292	304	4h.37½m.P.M.
11	330	345	357	365	372	369	365	360	364	368	5 "
12	360	355	345	342	350	348	341	333	330	338	6 "
1	349	356	364	359	354	351	355	360	381	395	7 "
2	403	413	411	408	400	389	395	400	407	410	8 "
3	414	423	428	436	442	443	442	438	436	433	9 "
4	435	434	440	450	476	490	520	555	570	575	10 "
5	593	600	575	548	533	523	516	506	498	492	11 "
6	485	482	479	477	477	476	475	475	477	480	12 "
7	483	487	493	495	488	495	527	552	568	587	1 "
8	595	612	624	630	633	631	625	620	612	604	2 "
9	599	603	609	612	615	626	633	635	644	650	3 "
10	663	667	665	661	658	659	653	646	640	637	4 "
11	639	641	632	618	595	590	583	572	559	541	5 "
12	543	545	546	546	544	540	537	536	535	537	6 "
1	538	525	523	537	527	520	515	513	480	479	7 "
2	487	493	498	503	506	509	509	533	562	571	8 "
3	573	553	537	517	495	489	486	488	496	510	9 "
4	512	510	507	513	514	512	511	506	497	487	10 "
5	486	485	483	484	480	477	476	476	477	463	11 "
6	449	443	442	440	441	443	447	454	463	470	12 "
7	478	483	487	489	488	483	471	459	457	446	1 "
8	435	447	460	468	475	490	487	478	485	491	2 "
9	493	513	525	530	533	535	534	515	500	....	3 "
10	....	....	....	....	....	....	....	....	....	....	4 "

June 21 *and* 22, 1854.

(The readings were taken 1m. 34s. earlier than indicated by the table.)

Göttingen Mean Time.	0m.	6m.	12m.	18m.	24m.	30m.	36m.	42m.	48m.	54m.	Rensselaer Mean Time.
10 P.M.	....	....	....	....	....	....	....	....	....	295	4h.37½m.P.M.
11	297	299	300	302	305	309	312	313	313	314	5 "
12	315	315	314	314	313	312	310	316	325	333	6 "
1	337	340	347	347	351	352	350	350	351	352	7 "
2	348	346	343	337	333	334	338	348	350	355	8 "
3	354	355	358	364	366	374	374	374	373	367	9 "
4	366	367	366	370	373	377	377	377	378	383	10 "
5	384	385	379	379	379	381	383	384	383	384	11 "
6	387	384	385	382	384	386	386	382	385	387	12 "
7	384	382	383	385	387	386	387	390	392	396	1 "
8	400	402	400	396	394	394	388	376	384	394	2 "
9	390	383	382	381	379	370	364	368	372	370	3 "
10	367	363	358	355	357	361	367	369	367	364	4 "
11	364	363	361	355	350	350	352	355	359	362	5 "
12	363	363	370	369	367	368	370	363	355	351	6 "
1	348	343	337	335	333	329	330	331	331	328	7 "
2	322	318	320	322	325	327	328	328	326	324	8 "
3	320	318	319	322	323	323	322	324	326	331	9 "
4	326	315	334	830	326	326	319	318	318	318	10 "
5	312	316	318	317	323	321	317	310	312	308	11 "
6	306	320	316	316	318	323	304	303	312	290	12 "
7	291	287	286	286	291	283	275	281	283	288	1 "
8	289	290	292	289	291	293	297	298	302	304	2 "
9	304	309	313	312	308	303	295	290	282	273	3 "
10	264	....	....	....	....	....	....	....	....	....	4 "

No. XVIII.

ENUMERATION OF PLANTS

Collected by Dr. E. K. Kane, U.S.N., in his first and second expeditions to the Polar Regions, with descriptions and remarks.

BY ELIAS DURAND.

I have brought together in the following enumeration all the plants collected by Dr. Kane at the stations of his two voyages, the whole belonging to the western coast of Greenland, and nearly to the same geographical zone.

These stations were, for the first voyage, (1850 and 1851,) Sukkertoppen, Holsteinburg, Egedesminde, Disco, Upernavik, and Wostenholm, between the 64th and 76th north parallels; and for the second, Fiske Fiord, Sukkertoppen, N. Proven, Upernavik and the different stations of Smith's Sound as far as 81° N. latitude.

The first collection was in pretty good order, but the second had suffered much from the peculiar hardships attending the last period of this eventful expedition, in which Dr. Kane's fortitude and devotion to science were so signally manifested. Surrounded with difficulties of every sort, and threatened by the impending danger of starvation and death, amid the drifts, disruptions and other impediments of a hyperborean climate, he did not hesitate sacrificing the useful articles of comfort and self-preservation, to make room in his luggage-boxes for as many of his scientific collections as he could pack in them.

Thus was the best portion of his botanical specimens preserved to science, after suffering much, as it may be imagined, from the inclemency of the weather and the hardships of a long and perilous voyage back to the United States. But for the zeal and self-denial of his comrades, and especially of his surgeon, Dr. I. I. Hayes, his co-laborer in the scientific field, Dr. Kane is pleased to acknowledge that he could never have undertaken their transportation.

Under these circumstances I have experienced great difficulty in determining several specimens,—difficulty arising not only from their damaged state, but also from their occasional incompleteness, some being just blooming, others in a fruiting condition, others again wanting some of the essential characters. To these disadvantages I must add the want, in several instances, of books of reference, and of authentic specimens for comparison.

When I attempted the task of determining these collections, I relied much, I confess, on the assistance of a learned and more experienced friend, Professor Asa Gray; but, owing to the pressure of his occupations, I have not been able to secure his valuable services to the extent of my anticipations. I am, however, greatly indebted to him for hints and remarks that have been very useful to me. I am under peculiar obligations to Professor Torrey for the determination of the *Gramineæ* and his assistance in some of the most perplexing genera; and also to my friend Thomas P. James, Esq., for the entire enumeration of mosses, Hepaticæ and Lichens. I am most happy to take this opportunity to render to these three gentlemen my sincere acknowledgments for their great kindness.

Laying aside the consideration of the lost packages, Dr. Kane's collections are yet among the richest and most interesting ever brought by Arctic and Polar explorers. They not only afford a considerable accession to our previous knowledge of the vegetation of Northern Greenland, but they develop facts of some importance in a physico-geographical point of view:—

First.—By exhibiting, throughout the range of coasts between the Arctic and Polar circles, no perceptible change in the number and identity of the species therein collected; thus establishing, as far at least as Greenland is concerned, that the third or Polar zone of Sir John Richardson* might as well begin at the 67th as at the 73d N. latitude.

Secondly.—By the reappearance, beyond the limits of Smith's Sound of *Hesperis Pallasii* and *Vesicaria arctica*, in a perfect fruiting state;—Two plants belonging rather to the milder regions of the Arctic zone, and which have never been found yet, I believe, in the higher intervening points. Both these plants belonged to a scanty collection of eight or ten specimens, made late in the season, on the newly-discovered lands of Washington and Humboldt, on the very verge of that mysterious Polar sea which Dr. Kane's expedition had the good fortune to espy and see free of ice as far as the eye could reach. Such a fact, indeed, although limited to two species, seems to indicate peculiar isothermal influences, depending either on warm currents, greater depth of water, or actual depression of our globe at its poles.

Another remarkable feature of Dr. Kane's collection is, that, dividing into two equal parts the whole extent of coasts visited by him, and each section presenting about the same number of stations at which herborizations were made, the northern section, from Upernavik to Washington Land, has yielded more dicotyledonous plants than the

* See Appendix to Searching Expedition, London, 1851, p. 319 and following.

southern, from Fiske Fiord to 73°; and Smith's Sound alone, only three degrees in length, has proved nearly as rich. (See Table No. 1.)

These unexpected results show that the Polar zone cannot properly be compared with the Alpine regions of the more temperate climates. The uninterrupted action of light and heat, during the whole period between the rising and setting of the sun, which marks the day or summer season of the poles,—a purer and damper atmosphere, aided, perhaps, by a greater accumulation of electric fluid, &c.—must necessarily and more promptly (in the lowest levels) actuate and perfect the vegetation, not only of plants inured to those climates, but also of those the seeds of which have been transported hither from milder regions by currents, migration of birds, or other causes. Unlike the snow-capped and barren summits of the Alpine regions, at all times destitute of verdure, it is probable that vegetation is permitted to extend to the very pole itself, wherever it meets with proper soil, favorable solar exposure, and protection from the blasts of winds.

The southern extremity of Greenland, from Cape Farewell to Sukkertoppen, has been well explored, and found to possess nearly the same climate as Labrador, with an almost identical vegetation. E. Meyer, in his *Plantæ Labradoricæ*, (1830,) enumerates 224 phænogamous species, the greater part of which are indigenous both to Labrador and to Greenland. Professor Giesecke, who resided several years in Greenland, for the express purpose of studying its Natural History, published in Brewster's Edinburgh Encyclopedia (1832) an enumeration of 171 phænogamous species, with a long list of Cryptogams, amounting to no less than 231 species, all indigenous to that island. From the two above works, and from all the other sources to which I have had access,—De Candolle, Torrey and Gray, Hooker, Brown, Richardson, Hornemann, Steudel,—for Cyperaceæ and Gramineæ, &c., I have compiled the following Table No. 2, which presents an amount of 264 phænogamous species, belonging to 109 genera and 36 families.

This apparent richness of the Greenland flora is, however, confined to the extreme southern point of the island; for, from Sukkertoppen to a few degrees higher, it is found to have lost already eight or ten families; and from Upernavik, 73°, to the outlet of Smith's Sound, it is reduced to twenty families, by the entire disappearance of *Violaceæ, Oxalidaceæ, Holorageæ, Umbellifereæ, Cornaceæ, Lentibulaceæ, Primulaceæ, Gentianaceæ, Boragineæ, Labiateæ, Plumbaginaceæ, Plantaginaceæ, Betulaceæ, Coniferæ, Orchidaceæ*, and *Melanthaceæ*.

Notwithstanding this prodigious decrease, the column headed North Greenland from 73°, in Sir John Richardson's Statistical Tables, will be found, by the accession of 27 other species from Dr. Kane's collections, now to be raised—from 49 phænogamous species allotted to that region by the eminent English botanist—to 76; which is a gain of fifty per cent.

The following species are to be added to Richardson's column of North Greenland from 73°:—

Ranunculus Sabinii?
Hesperis Pallasii.
Vesicaria arctica.
3 Draba.
Arenaria arctica.
Cerastium, N. Sp.
Dryas octopetala.
Alchemilla vulgaris.
Potentilla frigida.
Sedum rhodiola.
2 Saxifraga.
Gnaphalium sylvaticum.
Hieracium vulgatum.
Vaccinium uliginosum.
Pyrola chlorantha.
Diapensia Lapponica.
2 Pedicularis.
Empetrum nigrum.
1 Salix
2 Eriophorum.
Agrostis canina.
Festuca ovina.
27

Only two new species, *Pedicularis Kanei* and *Bryum lucidum*, have been found in the whole collections.

TABLE No. 1.

Enumeration of the Phænogamous plants collected by Dr. E. K. Kane, on the western coast of Greenland.

DICOTYLEDONOUS PLANTS.	From 64–73°.	From 73–80°.
1. *Ranunculaceæ.*		
1. Ranunculus aquatilis, var. Dur.	*	
2. " glacialis, L.........	*	
3. " nivalis, *a.* L.........		*
" " *β.* Br.......		*
4. " aff. sabinii?.........		*
2. *Papaveraceæ.*		
5. Papaver nudicaule, L...........	*	*
3. *Cruciferæ.*		
6. Arabis alpina, L..................	*	
7. Cardamine pratensis, var. H...	*	
8. Hesperis Pallasii, T. & Gr......		*
9. Vesicaria arctica, *a.* H...........		*
10. Draba alpina, *a.* H...............	*	
" " *β.* B...............		*
" " corymbosa........		*
" " micropetala........	*	*
" " var.................		*
11. " glacialis, *β.* H............	*	*
12. " rupestris, *a.* Br............		*
13. " nivalis, Willd............		*
14. " Lapponica, Willd........	*	
15. " hirta, L.....................		*
16. " incana, var. confusa, T. & Gr...	*	
17. Cochlearia fenestrata, Br... ...	*	*
18. " officinalis, L.........	*	
19. " Anglica..............	*	
4. *Caryophyllaceæ.*		
20. Arenaria Grœnlandica, Spr...	*	*
21. " arctica, var. H.......		*
22. Stellaria humifusa, Rottb......	*	
23. " longipes, var. *β.* minor H...	*	
" " *δ.* T. & Gr...		*
" " *ε.* T. & Gr...		*
24. Cerastium alpinum, *a.* L......	*	*
" " *β.* Fischerianum, T. & Gr...	*	
" " *δ.* uniflorum, D...	*	
" " var.........		*
25. Silene acaulis.....................	*	*
26. Lychnis apetala, *a.* L..........	*	*
" " *β*.............		*
27. " alpina, L..............	*	
5. *Rosaceæ.*		
28. Dryas octopetala, L............		*
29 " integrifolia, Vahl........	*	*
30. Alchemilla vulgaris, L.........		*
31. " alpina, L...........	*	
32. Potentilla pulchella, Br........		*
33. " nivea, *a.* fl. D.......	*	
" " *β.* H........	*	*
" " T. & G...		*
34. " frigida, Vill. A. Gr...		*

TABLE No. 1.—*Continued.*

DICOTYLEDONOUS PLANTS.	From 64–73°.	From 73–80°.
5. *Rosaceæ.*		
35. Potentilla aurea, β. D. C........	*	
36. " tridentata, Ait........	*	*
6. *Onagraceæ.*		
37. Epilobium angustifolium, L...	*	*
38. " latifolium, L.........	*	*
7. *Crassulaceæ.*		
39. Sedum rhodiola, D. C............	*	*
8. *Saxifragaceæ.*		
40. Saxifraga oppositifolia, L......	*	*
41. " flagellaris, Willd.....	*	*
42. " aizoides, Wahl.......		*
43. " tricuspidata, Retz...	*	*
44. " cœspitosa, *a.* L.......	*	
" " β. H......		*
45. " aizoon, Jacq..........	*	*
46. " nivalis, L. *a*...........		*
" " β...........		*
47. " foliolosa, Br...........		*
48. " cernua, L..............	*	*
49. " rivularis	*	
9. *Compositæ.*		
50. Gnaphalium sylvaticum, L.....		*
51. Hieracium vulgatum, Fries....	*	*
52. Arnica angustifolia, Vahl......		*
53. Taraxacum palustre, D. C.......	*	*
10. *Campanulaceæ.*		
54. Campanula linifolia, A. D......	*	
55. " uniflora, L.		*
11. *Ericaceæ.*		
56. Vaccinium uliginosum, L......	*	*
57. Cassiope tetragona, Don........	*	*
58. Phyllodoce taxifolia, Salisb...	*	
59. Rhododendron Lapponicum, Wahl...	*	
60. Loiseleuria procumbens, Desv.	*	
61. Ledum palustre, L...............	*	
62. Pyrola chlorantha, Sw..........	*	*
12. *Boragineæ.*		
63. Mertensia maritima, Don.......	*	
13. *Scrophulariaceæ.*		
64. Bartsia alpina, L.................	*	
65. Pedicularis arctica, Br.		*
66. " Kanei, D...........		*
67. " hirsuta, L............	*	*
14. *Labiatæ.*		
68. Thymus serpyllum, var.........	*	
15. *Diapensiaceæ.*		
69. Diapensia Lapponica, L........		*

DICOTYLEDONOUS PLANTS.	From 64–73°.	From 73–80°.
16. *Polygonaceæ.*		
70. Polygonum viviparum, L....	*	*
71. Oxyria digyna, Campd.......	*	*
17. *Empetraceæ.*		
72. Empetrum nigrum, L.........	*	*
18. *Betulaceæ.*		
73. Betula nana, L.................	*	
19. *Salicaceæ.*		
74. Salix desertorum, Rich......	*	
75. " uva-ursi, Pursh.........	*	
76. " arctica, Br..............	*	*
77. " herbacea, L.............	*	*
MONOCOTYLEDONOUS PLANTS.		
20. *Orchidaceæ.*		
78. Platanthera hyperborea, Lindl...	*	
21. *Melanthaceæ.*		
79. Tofieldia palustris, Huds....	*	
22. *Juncaceæ.*		
80. Luzula spicata, Desv..........	*	
81. " hyperborea, Br........		*
82. " arcuata, Mey..........		*
83. Juncus trifidus, Fl. Dan......	*	
84. " arcticus, L............	*	
23. *Cyperaceæ.*		
85. Carex rigida, Good............	*	*
86. " dioica, L................	*	
87. " aff. retroflexæ..........	*	
88. Scirpus cœspitosus, L.........	*	
89. Eriophorum capitatum, Host	*	*
90. " vaginatum, L...	*	
91. " polystachyon, L		*
24. *Gramineæ.*		
92. Alopecurus alpinus, Engl. Bt.	*	*
93. Phippsia algida, B...........	*	
94. Agrostis canina, B............		*
95. Calamagrostis Canadensis, Beauv...	*	
96. " stricta, Nutt..	*	
97. Glyceria arctica, H............	*	
98. Catabrosa aquatica, Beauv..	*	
99. Poa arctica......................	*	*
100. " alpina, L..................	*	*
101. Festuca ovina..................	*	*
102. " Richardsonii? H...	*	
103. Bromus Kalmii? Torr........	*	
104. Elymus arenarius, L.........	*	
105. Aira flexuosa, L..............	*	
106. Trisetum subspicatum, L....	*	*

TABLE No. 2.

GENERAL FLORA OF GREENLAND.			PRESENT FLORA OF NORTH GREENLAND, FROM 73°.			
Phænogamous Families.	Genera.	Species.	Phænogamous Families.	Genera.	Species.	Gain by the accession of the Kanean Plants.
1. Ranunculaceæ	4	12	1. Ranunculaceæ	1	2	1
2. Papaveraceæ	1	1	2. Papaveraceæ	1	1	
3. Cruciferæ	8	22	3. Cruciferæ	6	12	5
4. Violaceæ	1	2				
5. Caryophyllaceæ	6	21	4. Caryophyllaceæ	5	9	2
6. Oxalidaceæ	1	1				
7. Leguminosæ	4	4	5. Leguminosæ	1	1	
8. Rosaceæ	7	18	6. Rosaceæ	3	7	3
9. Onagraceæ	1	4	7. Onagraceæ	1	2	
10. Holorageæ	1	1				
11. Crassulaceæ	1	2	8. Crassulaceæ	1	1	1
12. Saxifragaceæ	1	18	9. Saxifragaceæ	1	9	2
13. Umbelliferæ	2	2				
14. Cornaceæ	1	1				
15. Compositæ	10	18	10. Compositæ	5	5	2
16. Campanulaceæ	1	3	11. Campanulaceæ	1	1	
17. Ericaceæ	10	19	12. Ericaceæ	3	3	2
18. Lentibulaceæ	1	2				
19. Primulaceæ	1	2				
20. Gentianaceæ	2	4				
21. Diapensiaceæ	1	1	13. Diapensiaceæ	1	1	1
22. Boraginaceæ	1	1				
23. Scrophulariaceæ	5	12	14. Scrophulariaceæ	1	3	2
24. Labiatæ	2	2				
25. Plumbaginaceæ	1	2				
26. Plantaginaceæ	1	1				
27. Polygonaceæ	4	7	15. Polygonaceæ	2	2	
28. Empetraceæ	1	1	16. Empetraceæ	1	1	1
29. Betulaceæ	2	3				
30. Salicaceæ	1	10	17. Salicaceæ	1	4	1
31. Coniferæ	1	1				
32. Orchidaceæ	2	3				
33. Melanthaceæ	2	3				
34. Juncaceæ	2	11	18. Juncaceæ	1	2	
35. Cyperaceæ	3	17	19. Cyperaceæ	2	3	2
36. Gramineæ	16	32	20. Gramineæ	6	7	2
36 Phæn. Families	109	264	20 Phæn. Families	44	76	27

ENUMERATION.—DICOTYLEDONOUS PLANTS.

RANUNCULACEÆ.

1. Ranunculus aquatilis, var. *arcticus*. *R. hederaceo proximus*, Giesecke. Foliis omnibus emersis, consimilibus, profunde tripartitis; partitionibus cuneatis, ad marginem dilatatis, crenatis; flore albo; sepalis ovalibus, concavis, petala fere æquantibus.

This form, of which I have only two specimens, is undoubtedly the *R. hederaceo proximus* of Giesecke. It has a great affinity with De Candolle's *R. aquatilis*, var. *hederaceus*, *R. hederaceus*, Lam., not of Linn. (vide Fl. Franç. vol. iv. p. 894.) The stems are fistulous repent, with small fascicles of radical fibres at each node below the scape. No capillaceo-multifid leaves; they are all suborbicular tripartite, on long vaginant petioles, 3–4 at the base of each peduncle; leaflets cuneate, with dilated crenate margins, each crenature having a blunt mucro. Scape thick, naked, one-flowered, 3–3½ inches high. Flower white, middle size, with five oval and concave sepals about the length of the petals.

Disco and adjacent coast, 70°.

2. R. GLACIALIS, Linn. sp. plant. p. 777. D. C. Prodr. 1, p. 30. Torr. and Gr. 1, p. 16.

North Proven, 72°.

3. R. NIVALIS, Linn. Fl. Lapp. p. 158—T. 8. D. C. Prodr. 1, p. 35. Hook, Fl. Bor. Am. 1, p. 17. Torr. and Gr. 1, p. 20.

a. R. nivalis Linn. Leaves glabrous, on long ciliate petioles, somewhat reniform, crenato-lobate, lobes obtuse, more or less deep, equal or narrower at base, with conspicuous divergent veins. Cauline leaves sessile, palmate. Flowers rather large, deep yellow; petal oval-rounded, about twice the length of the calyx, which, as well as the peduncle, is covered with a thick, brown toment. Root perpendicular, with numerous white and thick fibres, indicating a plant deeply rooted in mossy beds.

Stations of Smith's Sound, 78°–80°.

β. R. Br. in Parry's first voy. app. p. 264. *R. nivalis*, var. Vahl., Fl. Lapp, p. 157. *R. sulphureus*, Soland. in Phipps' Voy. p. 202. Leaves cuneate, palmately lobed, lobes generally narrower at base. Flower pale yellow.

Smith's Sound Stations, 78°–80°.

4. . . . . I have two very damaged specimens, closely allied, by the leaves, with the preceding variety, but widely different on other points, and which might be *R. sabinii*, R. Br., collected on the shores of Melville Island in Parry's first voyage. The radical leaves are cuneate, veined, ciliate, deeply 3-parted, with lateral partitions bifid, supported on long vaginant membranaceous petioles. Stem apparently two-flowered. Flowers pale yellow, smaller than the preceding. Sepals and peduncles covered with whitish hair. Petals partly destroyed, but seemingly narrower than in the above species.

Grows in dry levels at Bedevilled Reach, 79°.

PAPAVERACEÆ.

5. Papaver nudicaule, Linn. spec. pl. p. 725. Fl. Dan. T. 41. Pursh's Fl. p. 364, &c. The most hardy plant of the Polar regions, resisting the first frosts and remaining the last in flower. The leaves and especially the seeds, which are very oleaginous, are a great resort iu scorbutic affections, and agreeable to the taste.—Dr. Kane.

This plant was found at all the stations of the two voyages, and extends probably to the farthest limits of vegetation.

CRUCIFERÆ.

6. Arabis alpina, Linn. Fl. Dan. T. 62. Pursh's Fl. p. 427. Torr. and Gr. 1, p. 80.

North Proven, 72°.

7. Cardamine pratensis, *β. angustifolia,* Hook. Fl. Bor. Am. 1, p. 45.

Sukkertoppen, 64°; Disco, 70°.

8. Hesperis Pallasii, Torr. and Gr. suppl. p. 667. *H. minima,* Torr. and Gr. 1, p. 90. *H. pygmæa,* Hook. Fl. Bor. Am. 1, p, 60. *Cheiranthus Pallasii,* Pursh's Fl. p. 436. *C. pygmæus,* Adans. in D. C. prodr. 1, p. 137. Two fruiting specimens 4–6 inches high, scarcely to be mistaken from Dr. Hooker's fig. T. 19 of Fl. Bor. Am. Leaves only apparently narrower by drying. Found at the extreme north point of Dr. Kane's expedition, on Washington Land, 81° N. latitude. This plant was discovered by Pallas on the northwest coast of America, and never, I believe, in the Arctic Sea.

9. Vesicaria arctica, *a.* Hook. Fl. Bor. Am. 1, p. 48. Rich. in Frankl, 1st jour. ed. 2d, app. p. 20. *Alyssum arcticum,* Fl. Dan. T. 1526. Torr. and Gr. 1, p. 100.

Fruiting specimens found, August 27, at the junction of Humboldt and Washington Lands, 81° N. latitude.

10. Draba alpina, *a.* Hook. Fl. Bor. Am. 1, p. 50. *D. alpina,* Linn's Herb. ex R. Br. Torr. and Gr. 1, p. 103. Silicles glabrous; flowers yellow; leaves less hairy than var. *β.* Just flowering, and of smaller size than fig. in T. 56 in Fl. Dan

North Proven, 72°.

β. R. Br. Spitzb. pl. in Scoresby's Arct. Reg. Hook. Fl. Bor. Am. 1, p. 50. Torr. and Gr. 1, p. 103. Leaves, peduncles and silicles hairy. Flowers rather larger than the preceding, and of a deeper yellow color.

Rensselaer Harbor, 79°.

Var. *corymbosa.* Densely cespitose, and perhaps the same as the following. Scapes short, naked, almost glabrous, as well as the silicles. Flowers apparently white and quite corymbose. Style rather long; stigma emarginate. Perhaps var. δ. Hook., or *D. corymbosa,* R. Br. in Ross's Voy., but scarcely to be separated from *alpina.*

Bedevilled Reach, 78°.

Var. *micropetala.* Leaves larger than the preceding varieties, and retaining a lively green color in the dry state, ciliate, but scarcely hispid on the surface. Scape short, naked, pilose, as well as the calyx. Just blooming; flowers white, small, thickly corymbose, and almost capitate. Perhaps *D. micropetala,* Hook. in Parry's 2d voy. app. p. 385. Torr. and Gr. 1, p. 104, but scarcely any thing more than another form of *D. alpina.*

North Proven, 72°, and Rensselaer Harbor, 79°.

. . . . Another variety in the fruiting state, with scape naked, 3½ inches high; silicles corymbose, oval, much larger than in the other varieties, and conspicuously veined, very hairy, as well as the scape and pedicles. Style short, with a blunt stigma.

Rensselaer Harbor, 79°, August 27.

11. D. GLACIALIS, β. Hook. Fl. Bor. Am. 1, p. 51. Scapes and pedicles pubescent; silicles glabrous, with the habits of var. ε.

Disco and below Bedevilled Reach, 70° and 78°.

12. D. RUPESTRIS, α. R. Br. in Hort. Kew. 3, p. 91. D. C. Prodr. 1, p. 169. *D. hirta,* Engl. Bot. T. 1338. *D. hirta,* var. 4, Hook. in Parry's 2d voy. app. p. 386. Pubescent; scapes naked, or with a 3-cleft leaf about the middle.

Rensselaer Harbor, 79°, August 27.

13. D. NIVALIS, Willd. *D. rupestris,* β. Torr. and Gr. 1, p. 105. Leaves rosulate, scarcely linear-oblong, but otherwise according with Willdenow's description. Scapes 6–7 inches high, hirsute, with a small leaf below the middle. Silicles glabrous.

14. D. LAPPONICA? Willd. D. C. Prodr. 1, p. 169. R. Br. in Parry's 1st voy. app. p. 266. *D. hirta,* var. 3, in Parry's 2d voy. Torr. and Gr. 1, p. 105. Specimens in the fruiting state; scape naked, almost glabrous, as well as the lanceolate entire leaves.

Disco Island, 70°.

15. D. HIRTA, Linn. Scape and silicles puberulent-pilose. Radical leaves entire, oval-lanceolate; those of the scape toothed. Flowers rather large, white, racemose; silicles oval-oblong; style scarcely any.

Upernavik, 73°.

16. D. INCANA, var. *confusa,* Torr. and Gr. 1, p. 107. *D. incana,* var. Linn. *D. confusa,* Ehrh. in D. C. Prodr. 1, p. 170.

Fiske Fiord, 64°.

17. COCHLEARIA FENESTRATA, R. Br. in Ross' voy. ed. 2d, vol. ii. p. 193, and in Parry's 1st voy. app. p. 266. Torr. and Gr. 1, p. 109. A much smaller plant than the two following species, and agreeing with specimens collected in Capt. Franklin's voyage, in Herb. Torr. and Acad. of N. Sc.

Fiske Fiord, 64°, and as far north as Rensselaer Harbor, 79°.

18. C. OFFICINALIS, Linn. spec. pl. p. 903. Hook. Fl. Bor. Am. 1, p. 57. Silicles somewhat globose; root fleshy, fusiform.

Disco Island, 70°.

19. C. ANGLICA, Linn. spec. pl. p. 903. D. C. Prodr. 1, p. 354. Torr. and Gr. 1, p. 109. Silicles elliptical in a long raceme. Axis of the septum, in general, conspicuously fenestrate. Radical leaves wanting; those of the stem sessile, oblong-spathulate, with a few teeth. Root fibrous.

North Proven, 72°.

CARYOPHYLLACEÆ.

20. ARENARIA GRŒNLANDICA, Spreng. *Stellaria Grœnlandica*, Retz. Fl. Scand. D. C. Prodr. 1, p. 398. Fl. Dan. T. 1210. Torr. and Gr. 1, p. 180.

Sukkertoppen, 65°; Upernavik, 73°.

21. A. ARCTICA, var. *grandiflora*, Hook. Fl. Bor. Am. 1, p. 108, tab. 34, B. A beautiful pigmy species, not above one inch high, with comparatively very large flowers.

Upernavik, 73°.

22. STELLARIA HUMIFUSA, Rottb. Fl. Dan. T. 978. Hook. in Parry's 2d voy. app. p. 390, and Fl. Bor. Am. 1, p. 97. Torr. and Gr. 1, p. 184.

North Proven, 72°.

23. A. LONGIPES, *β. minor*, Hook. Fl. Bor. Am. 1, p. 95. Torr. and Gr. 1, p. 185. *S. stricta*, Rich. app. Frankl. Jour. ed. 2d, p. 15.

Sukkertoppen, 65°; Disco, 70°.

δ. Torr. and Gr. 1, p. 185. *S. læta*, Rich. app. Frankl. Jour. ed. 2d, p. 16. Hook. app. Parry's 2d voy., and Fl. Bor. Am. 1, p. 96.

Bedevilled Reach, 78°.

ε. Torr. and Gr. 1, p. 185. *S. Edwardsii*, R. Br. app. Parry's 1st voy. p. 271. Hook. Fl. Bor. Am. 1, p. 96. *S. nitida*, Hook. app. Scoresby's voy. p. 411. *S. ovalifolia*, Hook.

Rensselaer Harbor, 79°, August 27.

24. CERASTIUM ALPINUM, *a.* *C. alpinum*, Linn. Fl. Dan. T. 79.

R. Br. in Ross's Voy. Hook. app. Parry's 2d Voy. p. 390. Torr. and Gr. 1, p. 188.

Fiske Fiord, 65°; North Proven, 72°; Upernavik, 73°.

β. C. Fischerianum, Torr. and Gr. 1, p. 188. *C. Fischerianum*, Serr in D. C. Prodr. 1, p. 419. Cham. and Schl. in Linnæa, 1, p. 60. Hirsute, with stiff hairs and sub-viscose. Stems rigid, ascendent, elongated; flowers dichotomous or subumbellate.

Sukkertoppen, 65°.

δ. C. uniflorum. Perhaps a new species? The only specimen in the collection has a thread-like root about ten inches long, bearing marks of absent fibres, but, in the present state, perfectly naked. From the neck of this root project whitish, filiform, subterranean stems, simple or dichotomous, with short internodes, each provided with a pair of small scarious leaves; the external stems are furnished with a rosula of ovate and softly lanuginous leaves, and each stem has a solitary erect peduncle, with 2–3 pairs of remote and appressed hoary leaves, and a single erect flower, nodding in the fruiting stage. Stems very numerous.

North Proven, 72°.

Another form of *C. alpinum*, which may be the same as the preceding, is rather smaller, with fewer stems and shorter scapes. The flowers are very large, with sepals terminating in a very acute membranaceous point, and the petals deeply obcordate.

Sukkertoppen, 65°, and all the stations of Smith's Sound from 78°–80°.

25. SILENE ACAULIS, Linn. Pursh's Fl. p. 316. Hook. Fl. Bor. Am. 1, p. 87. Torr. and Gr. 1, p. 189.

Fiske Fork, 64°; Disco, 70°; N. Proven, 72° and 73°.

26. LYCHNIS APETALA, *a.* Linn. Spec. pl. p. 626, Fl. Dan. T. 806. Hook. Fl. Bor. Am. 1, p. 91. *L. uniflora*, Ledeb. Torr. and Gr. 1, p. 194.

At almost every station of both voyages, from 64° to 80°.

β. L. pauciflora, D. C. Prodr. 1, p. 386. Torr. and Gr. 194. *L. pauciflora*, Fisch.

Bedevilled Reach, and other stations of Smith's Sound.

27. L. ALPINA, Linn. Fl. Dan. T. 65. Pursh's Fl. p. 321. Torr. and Gr. 1, 194.

Fiske Fiord, 64°; Sukkertoppen, 65°; Holsteinborg, 68°.

ROSACEÆ.

28. DRYAS OCTOPETALA, Linn. Pursh's Fl. p. 350. D. C. Prodr. 2, p. 550. Hook. Fl. Bor. Am. 1, p. 174. Torr. and Gr. 1, p. 420.

Bedevilled Reach and Rensselaer Harbor, 78° and 79°.

29. D. INTEGRIFOLIA, Vahl. Fl. Dan. T. 1216. Hook. Fl. Bor. Am. 1, p. 174. Torr. and Gr. 1, p. 420.

Fiske Fiord, Holsteinborg, N. Proven, as far as the highest stations of Smith's Sound.

30. ALCHEMILLA VULGARIS, Linn. Fl. Dan. T. 693. Engl. Bot. T. 597. D. C. Prodr. 2, p. 589. Torr. and Gr. 1, p. 432. A plant indigenous to the north of Europe, but very seldom found in North America.

Upernavik, 73°.

31. A. ALPINA, Linn. Pursh's Fl. p. 321. Fl. Dan. T. 49. Torr. and Gr. 1, p. 194.

Fiske Fiord, Sukkertoppen, 64° and 65°.

32. POTENTILLA PULCHELLA, R. Br. Ross' Voy. and Parry's 1st Voy. suppl. p. 277. Hook. Parry's 2d Voy. and Fl. Bor. Am. 1, p. 191. *P. sericea,* Grev. Torr. and Gr. 1, p. 439. Stems 1–2 -flowered. Leaves silky tomentose on both surfaces in several of my specimens, pinnæ very acute; peduncles 2–3 inches long with 1–2 small leaves. Flower rather large, of a deep yellow color; petals obcordate, longer than the calyx.

Upernavik, 73°, and Rensselaer Harbor, 79°.

33. P. NIVEA, *a. discolor,* Fl. Dan. T. 1035. Pursh's Fl. p. 353. R. Br. in Parry's 1st Voy. app. p. 277. D. C. Prodr. 2, p. 572. Torr. and Gr. 1, p. 441.

Disco Island, 70°.

β. concolor, Hook. Parry's 2d Voy. app. p. 395. *P. frigida,* Grev. *P. Grœnlandica,* R. Br. in Ross' Voy. ed. 2d, p. 193. *P. verna,* Hook. Scoresby's Greenl. p. 431. Torr. and Gr. 1, p. 441. Leaves of the same color on both surfaces, sparsely villous; segments of the calyx very obtuse and shorter than the obcordate petals. Two flowerless specimens, with a woody perpendicular root of the size of a small quill and very long, dividing at top into several stems, is undoubtedly the state of this variety, which is described by Dr. Hooker in his note to *Potentilla nivea,* at p. 195 of Fl. Bor. Am. vol. i. The leaves are quinate, of a reddish hue, with obovate leaflets.

Fiske Fiord, Upernavik, Rensselaer Harbor.

γ. Torr. and Gr. 1, p. 441. *P. hirsuta,* Vahl. Fl. Dan. T. 1390. *P. Vahliana,* Lehm. *P. Jamesoniana,* Grev. A low species, resembling *P. nana,* with very hirsute leaves and brown toment underneath. Peduncles short, uniflorous; petals broadly obcordate, longer than the calyx.

Rensselaer Harbor, 79°.

34. P. FRIGIDA, Villars. in Lam. Dict. Encycl. A. Gray's Man. ed. 2d. D. C. Prodr. 2, p. 572.

Fog Inlet, 78°.

35. P. AUREA, β. D. C. Prodr. 2, p. 576. *P. salisburgensis*, Hænke, Torr. and Gr. 1, p. 441. A single specimen, with leafy and sparingly hirsute 2–3 -flowered stems. Radical leaves 3–5 foliolate, leaflets obovate, nearly glabrous, flowers on long filiform pedicels. Petals obcordate, deep yellow, nearly twice the size of the calyx. Resembling exactly the fig. of *P. aurea spontanea* of Halley's Synops. Potent. T. 8.

Fiske Fiord, 64°.

36. P. TRIDENTATA, Ait. Mich. Fl. Bor. Am. 1, p. 304. Hook. Fl. Bor. Am. 1, p. 195. Torr. and Gr. 1, p. 445.

Sukkertoppen, 65°; Holsteinborg, 68°; Rensselaer Harbor, 79°.

ONAGRACEÆ.

37. EPILOBIUM ANGUSTIFOLIUM, Linn. Hook. Fl. Bor. Am. 1, p. 205. *E. spicatum*, Lam. Dict. Bot. Torr. and Gr. 1, p. 487.

Fiske Fiord, Disco, Upernavik, 72°.

38. E. LATIFOLIUM, Linn. Fl. Dan. T. 365. Pursh's Fl. p. 259. Torr. and Gr. 1, p. 487.

Fiske Fiord, 64°; Upernavik, 73°.

CRASSULACEÆ.

39. SEDUM RHODIOLA, D. C. Prodr. 3, p. 401. *Rhodiola rosea*, Linn. *R. odorata*, Lam. Illustr. T. 1035. Torr. and Gr. 1, p. 558.

Holsteinborg, 68°; Upernavik, 73°.

SAXIFRAGACEÆ.

40. SAXIFRAGA OPPOSITIFOLIA, Linn. Fl. Lapp. T. 2. Pursh's Fl. p. 311. Hook. Fl. Bor. Am. 1, p. 243. Torr. and Gr. 1, p. 563.

At almost every station of the 1st and 2d Voyages.

This species varies very much in its forms. I have stems scarcely one inch high, densely cespitose, with leaves all imbricated in four rows and flowers almost sessile; others with numerous branches thickly set and spreading on the ground, leaves imbricated in the inferior part and opposite toward the top; others again with long sterile branches and leaves all opposite and remote. I have also the form *S. Eschscholtzii* of Sternb., with silvery-gray foliage, which cannot be separated from this species. From the large and beautiful purple flowers, apparently monopetalous, which are peculiar to this species, I have no doubt it is the plant mistaken for a gentian by Dr. Kane, in the narrative of his first expedition.

From N. Proven, 72°, to the most northern stations of Smith's Sound.

41. S. FLAGELLARIS, Willd. ex. Sternb. Rev. Saxifr. p. 25, T. 6. R. Br. Parry's 1st Voy. suppl. p. 273. *S. setigera,* Pursh's Fl. p. 312. Torr. and Gr. 1, p. 564.

Disco, 70°; Fog Inlet, 78°; Rensselaer Harbor, 79°, Aug. 27.

42. S. AIZOIDES, Wahl. Fl. Lapp. p. 115. Pursh's Fl. p. 312. Hook. Fl. Bor. Am. 1, p. 255. Torr. and Gr. 1, p. 565. *S. autumnalis,* Linn.

Upernavik, 73°.

43. S. TRICUSPIDATA, Retz. Prodr. Scand. Pursh's Fl. 1, 312. Hook. Fl. Bor. Am. 1, p. 254. Fl. Danica, T. 976. Torr. and Gr. 1, p. 565.

Holsteinborg, 68°; Fog Inlet, 78°; Rensselaer Harbor, 79°.

44. S. CŒSPITOSA, *α.* Hook. *S. cœspitosa,* Linn. Don. Saxifr. Pursh's Fl. 1, p. 311. Wahl. Fl. Lapp. p. 119. *S. Grœnlandica,* Linn. D. C. Prodr. 4, p. 27. Torr. and Gray 1, p. 565. Of this variety I have three different forms; one with cauline leaves all entire; the second with all the cauline leaves 3-cleft and cuneate; the third with both forms of leaves on the same stem.

Fiske Fiord, 64°; Disco, 70°; Proven, 72°, &c.

β. Hook. *S. uniflora,* R. Br. in Parry's 1st Voy. suppl. p. 274. *S. cœspitosa,* Engl. Bot. T. 764. *S. venosa,* Haw. Enum. Saxifr. p. 28. Torr. and Gr. 1, p. 565.

Upernavik to Rensselaer Harbor, 73–79°.

45. S. AIZOON, Jacq. Fl. Aust. 5, T. 438. Pursh's Fl. p. 310. Hook. Fl. Bor. Am. 1, p. 243. *Chondroza aizoon,* Haw. Enum. Saxifr. Torr. and Gr. 1, 566.

Fiske Fiord, Upernavik, 64–73°.

46. S. NIVALIS, *α.* *S. nivalis,* Linn. Pursh's Fl. p. 310. R. Br. Parry's 1st Voy. suppl. p. 275. D. C. Prodr. 4, p. 38. Torr. and Gr. 1, p. 571.

Fog Inlet, Bedevilled Reach, Rensselaer Harbor, 78–79°.

β. Hook. Fl. Bor. Am. 1, p. 248. Torr. and Gr. 1, p. 571. Heads loose and branched. It does not seem to differ from *S. reflexa,* Hook. Fl. Bor. Am. T. 85, otherwise than by the petals of the latter being bimaculate. In my specimens, which are rather advanced, the filaments of the stamina are purple.

Upernavik, 73°.

47. S. FOLIOLOSA, R. Br. in Parry's 1st Voy. suppl. p. 275. Hook.

in Parry's 2d Voy. suppl. p. 13, and Fl. Bor. Am. 1, p. 251. *S. stellaris, γ.* Linn. Fl. Lapp. *S. stellaris, β. comosa,* Willd. Torr. and Gr. 1, p. 570. Specimens not yet in bloom. Scapes 3–3½ inches high, naked at base and dividing at top into small branches, each crowned with a fascicle of small oval and concave leaves, in the centre of which a small oval flowering bud is just perceptible. Radical leaves cuneiform, with two minute lateral teeth on each side and terminating in an acute apex.

Fog Inlet, 78°.

48. S. CERNUA, Linn. Fl. Lapp. T. 2. R. Br. in Perry's 1st Voy. suppl. p. 275. Hook. Fl. Bor. Am. 1, p. 245. Torr. and Gr. Fl. 1, p. 575. Very remarkable by the upper leaves bearing in their axils little bulbs of abortive flowers.

Disco, 70°, and all the stations of Smith's Sound to 80° N. lat.

49. S. RIVULARIS, Linn. Fl. Lapp. T. 2. Pursh's Fl. p. 312. D. C. Prodr. 4, p. 36. Hook. Fl. Bor. Am. 1, p. 246. Torr. and Gr. 1, p. 574.

Fiske Fiord, 64°.

COMPOSITÆ.

50. GNAPHALIUM SYLVATICUM, Linn. Engl. Bot. T. 913. Pursh's Fl. p. 525. Hook. Fl. Bor. Am. 1, p. 319.

Upernavik, 73°.

51. HIERACIUM VULGATUM? Fries. *H. molle!* Pursh's Fl. p. 525. Hook. Fl. Bor. Am. 1, p. 299. Torr. and Gr. 2, p. 475. Stem 18–20 inches high, erect, naked above, with a corymb of 3–4 large flowers. Radical leaves petiolate, attenuate at both ends, with a few remote, obscure, and mucronate teeth from the base to the middle, entire upward. A few sessile cauline leaves to about the middle of the stem.

Fiske Fiord, 64°; and Upernavik, 73°.

52. ARNICA ANGUSTIFOLIA, Vahl. Fl. Dan. T. 1524. D. C. Prodr. 6, p. 317. *Arnica montana,* var. *alpina,* Linn. *A. alpina,* Wahl. *A. plantaginea* and *A. fulgens,* Pursh's Fl. p. 527. Torr. and Gr. 2, p. 449.

Near Smith's Sound, 78°.

53. TARAXACUM PALUSTRE, D. C. Fl. Fr. and Prodr. *Leontodon palustre,* Smith, Br. Fl. 2, p. 823. Hook. Fl. Bor. Am. 1, p. 296. *Leontodon taraxacum, β. salinum,* E. Mey. pl. Labr. p. 58. *Taraxacum montanum,* Nutt. in Torr. and Gr. 2, p. 494.

Wostenholm and below Bedevilled Reach, 76–78°.

CAMPANULACEÆ.

54. CAMPANULA LINIFOLIA, A. D. C. Camp. p. 179. *C. rotundifolia, β. linifolia,* Rich. in Frankl. 1st jour. ed. 2d, app. p. 61. The

only specimen I have is stripped of its radical leaves; the inferior cauline are petiolate, oval-lanceolate, the upper ones linear-lanceolate, entire or with a few teeth. Flowers only two, (there might have been three,) rather large, on filiform pedicels with two linear bracts at the base; teeth of the calyx very short and subulate; lobes of the corolla round-oval; stamina one-third the length of the style. Stigmata 5?

Holsteinborg, 68°.

55. C. UNIFLORA, Linn. Fl. Lapp. T. 9. Fl. Dan. T. 1512. Hook. Fl. Bor. Am. 2, p. 29. A form between the Linnean plant and β. *Gieseckiana* of D. C. Pr. 7, p. 482. Calyx invertedly conical, with divisions half the length of those of the corolla, but much shorter than in var. β. Otherwise corresponding with the Linnean description.

Upernavik, 73°.

ERICACEÆ.

56. VACCINUM ULIGINOSUM, Linn. Mich. Fl. Bor. Am. 2, p. 235. Pursh's Fl. p. 288. Rich. Frankl. 1st jour. ed. 2d, app. p. 22. Asa Gray, Man. ed. 1st, p. 261.

Fiske Fiord, Disco, Proven, Upernavik, Smith's Sound, 78°.

57. CASSIOPE TETRAGONA, Don. in D. C. Prodr. 7, p. 611. *Andromeda tetragona,* Linn. Fl. Dan. T. 1030. Pursh's Fl. p. 200. Hook. Bot. Mag. T. 3181, and Fl. Bor. Am. 2, p. 58. There are specimens among them very branching and more than a foot long.

Disco, Proven, Fog Inlet, Bedevilled Reach, from 70° to 80°.

58. PHYLLODOCE TAXIFOLIA, Salisb. A. Gray, Man. ed. 1, p. 267. *Menziesia cœrulea,* Sw. Eng. Bot. T. 2469. *Andromeda cœrulea,* Linn. Fl. Dan. T. 67. *A. taxifolia,* Pall.

Fiske Fiord, 64°; Disco, 70°.

59. RHODODENDRON LAPPONICUM, Wahl. Fl. Lapp. p. 104. Hook. Bot. Mag. T. 3106, Fl. Bor. Am. *Azalea Lapponica,* Linn. Fl. Lapp. p. 89, T. 6. Pallas's Fl. Ross, 2, p. 52. Asa Gray, Man. ed. 1, p. 269.

Holsteinborg, 68°.

60. LOISELEURIA PROCUMBENS, Desv. Asa Gray, Man. ed. 1, p. 270. *Azalea procumbens,* Linn. Pursh's Fl. p. 154. Hook. Fl. Bor. Am. 2, p. 44.

Egedesminde, 69°.

61. LEDUM PALUSTRE, Linn. Pursh's Fl. p. 301. Hook. Fl. Bor. Am. 1, p. 44.

Sukkertoppen, 65°; Holsteinborg, 68°.

62. PYROLA CHLORANTHA, Swartz. Hook. Fl. Bor. Am. 2, p. 46.

A. Gray, Man. ed. 1, p. 279. Rich. in Frankl. 1st jour. ed. 2, p. 13. Nutt. Gen. Am. 1, p. 273.

Disco, 70°; N. Proven, 72°; Smith's Sound Stations, 78°.

BORAGINEÆ.

63. MERTENSIA MARITIMA, Don. Gen. Syst. 4, p. 320. D. C. Prodr. 10, p. 88. *Pulmonaria maritima*, Linn. Fl. Dan. T. 25. *Lithospermum maritimum*, Lehm. Hook. Fl. Bor. Am. 2, p. 86. *Pulmonaria parviflora.* Mich.

Disco, 70°; N. Proven, 72°.

SCROPHULARIACEÆ.

64. BARTSIA ALPINA, Linn. Engl. Bot. T. 361. Fl. Dan. T. 43. D. C. Prodr. 10, p. 544.

Fiske Fiord, 64°.

65. PEDICULARIS ARCTICA, R. Br. in Parry's 1st Voy. app. p. 270. *P. Langsdorfii*, Fisch. MS. in Hook. Fl. Bor. Am. 2, p. 109. *P. purpurascens*, Spreng. *P. hirsuta*, Rich. app. Frankl. Voy. p. 25. D. C. Prodr. 10, p. 568. Stems short and few; cauline leaves with tomentose and conspicuously-dilated rachis. Bracts pinnate; flowers dark purple, with two small teeth at the helmet. Corolla and calyx of a tougher texture than in the following species, the former 3–4 times longer than the latter. Stigma emarginate; germ ovate.

Rensselaer Harbor, 79°.

66. P. KANEI, Nov. Spec. Caulibus compluribus; foliis linearibus glabris; pinnulis minutis, omnibus remotis, rachi petioloque vix dilatatis; corollâ roseâ, galeâ edentatâ.

Planta quâm præcedens robustior, radice carnosâ palmatim ramosâ. Caules complures, vix lanati; folia linearia, glabra, pinnatifida; pinnulæ minutæ, omnes remotæ, margine sursum fere integrâ, deorsum acute serratâ; petiolus foliorumque rachis vix dilatati; prior ad basin parce lanatus. Spica densa; bracteæ lanuginosæ angusto-lanceolatæ, fere integræ, ad apicem tantummodo obscurè pauci-dentatæ. Calyx 5–6 fidus, lanâ albâ densissimâ implexus; corolla rosea, texturâ tenerrimâ, calyce duplo longior; labium inferius tripartitum, suberoso-dentatum; lobus medianus subrotundus, (in præcedenti emarginatus,) galea minus incurva, angustior, edentata. Staminorum filamenta pilosa; stigma subrotundum, papillosum, integrum; germen subglobosum.

Pedicularis Kanei is easily distinguished from *P. arctica* by the delicacy of its pinnules, which are all remote, on a rachis scarcely dilated; by its bracts, perhaps more lanuginous, but almost entire; by its rose-colored flowers, its edentate helmet, and the thin texture of its corolla and calyx. The middle lobe of the inferior lip and stigma are not emarginate as in *P. arctica,* and the germ is of a more globose form. It is, moreover, a larger plant, with many more stems and a more fleshy root. Smith's Sound Stations.

67. P. HIRSUTA, Linn D. C. Prodr. 10, p. 578. Hook. Fl. Bor. Am. 2, p. 109. *P. lanata,* Willd. A larger plant than the two preceding, with erect, leafy and lanuginous stems. Leaves linear-lanceolate, pinnatifid with the rachis remarkably dilated; the lower pinnules very small, the other larger and dentate. Spike leafy and crowded; calyx half the length of the corolla, which is much smaller than in the two preceding species, and of a yellow color. An old stem in fruit, seven inches high and quite glabrous, with mucronate pods at least half an inch long, has the leaves bipinnate. Other imperfect specimens from N. Proven, not half the size of those from Smith's Sound, and with very small flowers, seem to belong to the same species, and are perhaps a variety *minor.*

Proven, 72°; Fog Inlet, 78°; Rensselaer Harbor, 79°.

LABIATÆ.

68. THYMUS SERPYLLUM, var. *arcticum.* Nov. var. Foliis pellucido-punctatis, ad basin ciliatis, 5-venosis, venis subtus valde prominentibus. Calycis dentibus corollæque lobis ciliatis.

This variety is probably the same as that collected by Vahl on the eastern coast of Greenland, and described by Professor Hornemann as var. *decumbens.* The stems are quite prostrate, as almost all the forms of *serpyllum;* the leaves are of a pale green color, with pellucid dots, ciliate at base, and with veins remarkably prominent and symmetrical. Flowers capitate among the upper leaves, which, as well as the calyces, are tinged with bright purple. Calycinal teeth and lobes of the corolla ciliate.

Fiske Fiord, 65°.

DIAPENSIACEÆ.

69. DIAPENSIA LAPPONICA, Linn. Asa Gray, Man. ed. 1, p. 346. I do not think this plant was ever found before in such high latitudes

Collected by Dr. Kane, on his return home, in latitude 73°.

POLYGONACEÆ.

70. POLYGONUM VIVIPARUM, Linn. Pursh's Fl. 271. Engl. Bot. T. 669. Rich. app. p. 43. Asa Gray, Man. ed. 1, p. 386.

Found at every station of both voyages.

71. OXYRIA DIGYNA, Campd. A. Gray, Man. ed. 1, p. 291. *O. reniformis,* Hook. *Rumex digynus,* Pursh's Fl. p. 248. Engl. Bot. T. 910.

With the preceding at almost all the stations from 64° to 80°.

EMPETRACEÆ.

72. EMPETRUM NIGRUM, Linn. Pursh's Fl. p. 93. Engl. Bot. T. 315. A. Gray, Man. ed. 1, p. 409. It is, in those regions, the ordinary food of deer and rabbits.—Dr. Kane.

Fiske Fiord, 64°; Disco, 70°; and on Smith's Sound.

BETULACEÆ.

73. BETULA NANA, Linn. Engl. Bot. T. 349. Pursh's Fl. p. 622. Fl. Dan. T. 91.

Holsteinborg, 68°.

SALICACEÆ.

74. SALIX DESERTORUM, Rich. app. p. 37. Hook. Fl. Bor. Am. 2, p. 151.

Fiske Fiord, 64°.

75. S. UVA-URSI, Pursh's Fl. p. 610. Hook. Fl. Bor. Am. 2, p. 152. A. Gray, Man. ed. 1, p. 429. *S. glauca,* Horn. app. Cap. Graah's Voy. and Dr. Kane. Stem erect, one foot high, or prostrate. Bark of branches greenish. Leaves elliptical or obovate, slightly toothed, glabrous and shining above, glaucous beneath. The specimens are all in a fruiting state, and larger than those of the White Mountains. Catkins long, cylindrical, rather loose; pods glabrous, shortly pedicellate, tapering into a beak, of an orange-color or turning black.

Fiske Fiord and Sukkertoppen, 64° and 65°.

76. S. ARCTICA, R. Br. Ross's Voy. ed. 2, vol. 2, p. 194, and in Melville Island Plants, p. 272, (not Pallas.) Hook. Fl. Bor. Am. 2, p. 152. *S. lanata!* Dr. K. Prostrate, with tortuous branches furnished with a light brown or yellow bark. Leaves entire and very variable, (lanceolate-acute, elliptic, oval or obovate, cuneate or spathulate,) strongly veined, subsericeous with long hairs, when young or even in the fruiting stage, generally very apt to turn black on drying. Fertile catkins long-pedunculate, cylindrical or ovoid-oblong; scales villous, broad-oval, of a brown or dusky color. Style elongated. Ovary thickly tomentose.

Sukkertoppen, 65°; Holsteinborg, 68°; as far as 76° N. latitude.

I have been somewhat perplexed with specimens collected by Dr.

Kane at the Smith's Sound Stations. They are comparatively smaller in all their parts, and have dried yellow, probably from some atmospheric causes, or the more advanced season. Some of these specimens, with leaves quite lanceolate and acute at both ends, and small ovoid catkins, resemble the figure of *S. Lapponum*, in Fl. Dan. T. 1050, except that their leaves are petiolate. They are, however, subject to all the same variations in leaves and catkins as *S. arctica* of the lower latitudes; and Dr. Torrey says they agree well with the Hookerian specimens of his herbarium.

77. S. HERBACEA, Linn. Hook. Fl. Bor. Am. 2, p. 153. A. Gray, Man. ed. 1, p. 43.

Holsteinborg, 68°; Upernavik, 73°.

MONOCOTYLEDONOUS PLANTS.

ORCHIDACEÆ.

78. PLATANTHERA HYPERBOREA, Lindl. Gen. Orch. p. 287. Hook. Fl. Bor. Am. 2, p. 198. *Habenaria hyperborea*, R. Br. and Rich. app. 2, p. 33. *Orchis hyperborea*, Pursh's Fl. p. 588.

Fiske Fiord, 65°.

MELANTHACEÆ.

79. TOFIELDIA PALUSTRIS, Huds. *T. borealis*, Wahl. *T. pusilla*, Pers. Pursh's Fl., p. 246. *Narthecium pusillum*, Mich. Fl. Bor. Am. 1, p. 219. Hook. Fl. Bor. Am. 2, p. 179.

Fiske Fiord, 64°.

JUNCACEÆ.

80. LUZULA SPICATA, Desv. A. Gray, Man. ed. 1, p. 505. *Juncus spicatus*, Linn. Engl. Bot. T. 1174.

Fiske Fiord and Sukkertoppen.

81. L. HYPERBOREA, R. Br. Melville Island Plants, p. 183. Hook. in Parry's 2d Voy. app. p. 405. *L. campestris*, R. Br. Spitzb. app. p. 75. *Juncus arcuatus*, Hook. Fl. Bor. Am. 2, p. 189.

Below Bedevilled Reach, 79°.

82. L. ARCUATA, Meyer. Asa Gray, Man. ed. 1, p. 505. Hook. Fl. Bor. Am. 2, p. 189.

Fog Inlet, 78°.

These two last species, which are of small stature and with black spikes, are easily distinguished from each other. *L. hyperborea* has the leaves flat, while *L. arcuata* has them channelled and linear.

83. Juncus trifidus, Fl. Dan. T. 107. Lam. Dict. Bot. Asa Gray's Man. ed. 1, p. 508.

Fiske Fiord, 64°.

84. J. arcticus, Linn. Fl. Lapp. p. 116. D. C. Fl. Fr. 3, p. 165. Scapes simple, rigid, naked, 8–10 inches high, furnished at base with long striated sheaths, springing up from matted horizontal rootstocks. Panicle few-flowered, apparently lateral from the spathe terminating in a long and acute point. Sepals dark brown.

Sukkertoppen, 65°; intermixed with *Luzula spicata.*

CYPERACEÆ.

85. Carex rigida, Good. *C. saxatilis,* Linn. Fl. Dan. &c.

Frequent at almost every station.

86. . . . . . . aff. *C. dioicæ.* A single specimen, with solitary staminate spikes of an ovoid form. Leaves all radical and flat. Culm apparently flat, (perhaps 3-angular,) 3 inches high and rather shorter than the leaves; scales obtuse, of a light brown color, stamina much exserted and whitish.

Fiske Fiord, 64°.

87. . . . . . . aff. *C. retroflexæ.* Too young to determine.

Fiske Fiord.

88. Scirpus cœspitosus, Linn. D. C. Fl. Fr. 3, p. 135. Asa Gray's Man. ed. 1, and Gram. and Cyper. Very small form, not three inches high.

Fiske Fiord and Sukkertoppen.

89. Eriophorum capitatum, Host. *E. scheuchzeri,* Hoppe. *E. vaginatum, β.* Sutt. Helv. p. 28. Lam. Dict. suppl. 3, p. 445. D. C. Fl. Fr. 3, p. 132. Culm cylindrical, 6–8 inches high, with smaller heads than the following, but hardly distinguished from it by other characters than being provided with a brown oval and persistent spathe instead of scales. Sheaths terminating in a short acumination, but sometimes quite leafy. Leaves channelled at base, flat above and terminating in a triangular blunt point, longer than the culm and more or less scabrous on the margin.

Fiske Fiord, 64°, and Rensselaer Harbor, 80°.

90. E. vaginatum, Linn. Engl. Bot. T. 873. D. C. Fl. Fr. 3, p 132. Asa Gray, Man. ed. 1, and Gram. and Cyper. No. 88. Hook. Fl. Bor. Am. 2, 231. Culm 7–8 inches high, with two sheaths at the base terminating in a short acumination. Leaves all radical, triangularly channelled, half the length of the culm. Spathe none; scales

numerous, ovate and acuminate, of a lead color; mature silky heads more than one inch in diameter, almost globular.

Sukkertoppen, 65°.

91. E. POLYSTACHYON, Linn. Spec. pl. p. 76. *E. latifolium*, Hoppe. Specimens from 4–15 inches high, not in fruit.

Stations of Smith's Sound to Rensselaer Harbor, 80°.

GRAMINEÆ.

92. ALOPECURUS ALPINUS, Engl. Bot. T. 1126. R. Br. in Parry's 1st Voy. p. 184. Rich. app. ed. 2, p. 3. Hook. in Parry's 2d Voy. app. p. 184.

Egedesminde, Bedevilled Reach, 79°; Aug. 11.

93. PHIPPSIA ALGIDA, R. Br. in Ross's Voy. ed. 2, p. 191, and in Parry's 1st Voy. app. p. 195. *Agrostis algida*, Soland. in Phipps's Voy. p. 200. *Trichodium algidum*, Swensk. Bot. p. 545.

North Proven, 72°.

94. AGROSTIS CANINA, *β. Melaleuca*, Bong. Veget. de Sitka, p. 20. Hooker, Fl. Bor. Am. 2, p. 240.

Two forms, one larger, 10–12 inches high, from Sukkertoppen; the other nearly half the size, from Smith's Sound.

95. CALAMAGROSTIS CANADENSIS, P. Beauv. *Arundo canina*, Mich. *Calamagrostis Mexicana*, Nutt.

Sukkertoppen, 65°.

96. C. STRICTA, Nutt. Torr. Rich. app. ed. 1, p. 3. *Arundo neglecta*, Ehrh.

Sukkertoppen, 65°.

97. GLYCERIA ARCTICA, Hook. Fl. Bor. Am. 2, p. 248. Dr. Torrey.

Holsteinborg, 68°.

98. CATABROSA AQUATICA, P. Beauv. Agrost. p. 97, T. 19, Fig. 8. Dr. Torrey. *Aira aquatica*, Linn.

Sukkertoppen, 65°.

99. POA ARCTICA, and var. R. Br. in Parry's 1st Voy. app. Hook. in Perry's 2d, 3d and 4th Voy., and in Bot. of Beech. Voy. p. 133. *P. laxa*, R. Br. Three different forms, a large one 15 inches, some middle forms 6–7 inches high, and a remarkably small one, with almost filiform leaves, which might prove a different species.

The largest from Sukkertoppen, the others from Smith's Sound.

100. P. ALPINA, Linn. Hook. Fl. Bor. Am. 3, p. 244. Dr. Torrey. Several forms.

Fiske Fiord, 65°; N. Proven, 72°; Rensselaer Harbor, 80°.

101. FESTUCA OVINA, Linn. Gray's Man. ed. 1, p. 599. Dr. Torrey. Two forms.

Sukkertoppen, 65°; Rensselaer Harbor, 80°. The latter not above 6 inches high.

102. F. RICHARDSONI? Hook. Fl. Bor. Am. 2, p. 250. Variety with smooth flowers. Dr. Torrey.

Fiske Fiord, 64°.

103. BROMUS KALMII? Dr. Torrey. A. Gray's Man. ed. 1, p. 600. *B. ciliata,* Muhl. *B. purgans,* Torr. Fl. N. S.

Sukkertoppen, 65°.

104. ELYMUS ARENARIUS, Linn. Engl. Bot. T. 1672. Hook. and Arn. Bot. of Beech. Voy. p. 119 and 132. Hook. Fl. Bor. Am. 2, p. 255.

Holsteinborg, 68°.

105. AIRA FLEXUOSA, Linn. A. Gray's Man. ed. 1, p. 605.

Sukkertoppen, 65°.

106. TRISETUM SUBSPICATUM, Linn. Hook. and Arn. Bot. of Beech. Voy. p. 119 and 132.

Fiske Fiord, 64°, and Bedevilled Reach, 79°.

CRYPTOGAMOUS PLANTS.

EQUISETÆ.

107. EQUISETUM ARVENSE, Linn. Barren fronds only.

Fiske Fiord, 64°; North Proven, 72°.

FILICES.

108. POLYPODIUM PHEGOPTERIS? Linn. Too young, and without fruit-dots.

Sukkertoppen, 65°.

109. WOODSIA ILVENSIS, R. Br. A. Gray's Man. ed. 1, p. 629. *Nephrodium rufidulum,* Mich.

Fiske Fiord, 64°; N. Proven, 72°.

110. CYSTOPTERIS FRAGILIS, Bernh. A. Gray's Man. ed. 1, p. 629. Large fruiting specimens 8–10 inches long, with stalks.

Disco, 70°; Wostenholm, 76°.

Another state (very young) of probably the same fern was collected at Rensselaer Harbor. It is scarcely more than 4 inches long, narrower and less divided, without fruit-dots. Perhaps var. *dentata,* Hook. A. Gray's Man. p. 629.

LYCOPODIACEÆ.

111. Lycopodium selago, Linn. Asa Gray's Man. ed. 1, p. 637.

112. L. annotinum, Linn. Asa Gray's Man. ed. 1, p. 637.

113. L. alpinum, Linn. Engl. Bot. T. 234.

All collected at Fiske Fiord, 64°.

MUSCI.

114. Sphagnum squarrosum, Pers.

Disco Island.

115. S. acutifolium, Ehrh.

Fiske Fiord.

116. S. recurvum, Brid.

Sukkertoppen.

117. Tetraplodon mnioides, Bruch and Schimper.

Disco Island.

118. Splachnum vasculosum, Linn.

Proven.

119. S. Wormskioldii, Horn.

Bedevilled Reach.

120. Bryum lucidum, James, Nova species.

Proven.

This species in all its characters resembles *Bryum crudum*, except the capsule, which is oval without a collum, and not pyriform, and of a dark brown color.

121. B. Muhlenbeckii, Bruch and Schimper.

Proven.

122. Aulacomnion turgidum, Schwæg.

Proven.

123. Polytrichum Juniperinum, Hedw.

Disco Island, Proven.

124. Dicranum scoparium, *β. orthophyllum*, Br. and Schimp.

Fiske Fiord.

125. D. elongatum, Schwæg.

Proven.

126. D. virens, Hedw.

Fiske Fiord.

β. Wahlenbergii, Br. and Schimp.

Disco Island.

Another variety.

Disco Island.

127. D. Richardsoni, Hook.

Fiske Fiord.

128. D. MUHLENBECKII, Br. and Schimp.
Fiske Fiord.

129. D. aff. FALCATUM, Hedw.
Fiske Fiord.

130. D. aff. STARKII, Weber and Mohr.
Fiske Fiord.

131. RACOMITRUM LANUGINOSUM, Brid.
Fiske Fiord.

132. WEISSIA CRISPULA, Hedw.
Proven.

133. HYPNUM RIPARIUM, Linn.
Bedevilled Reach.

134. H. UNCINATUM, Hedw.
Sukkertoppen, Fiske Fiord, Proven.

135. H. CORDIFOLIUM, Hedw.
Fiske Fiord.
H. cordifolium, var.
Fiske Fiord.

136. H. STRAMINEUM, Dickson.
Sukkertoppen and Fiske Fiord.

137. H. SARMENTOSUM, Vahl.
Fiske Fiord.

138. H. SCHREBERI, Willd.
Fiske Fiord.

HEPATICEÆ.

139. PTILIDIUM CILIARE, Nees.
Fiske Fiord.

140. SARCOCYPHUS EHRHARTI, Cord.
Proven.

141. JUNGERMANNIA DIVARICATA, Engl. Bot.
Fiske Fiord

142. J. SQUARROSA, Hook.
Fiske Fiord.

THALLOPHYTES.

143. CITRARIA ISLANDICA, Ack
Fiske Fiord.

144. PELTIGERA CANINA, Hoffm.
Fiske Fiord.

145. CLADONIA PYXIDATA, Fries.
Fiske Fiord.
146. C. RANGIFERA, Hoffm.
Fiske Fiord.
147. C. FURCATA, Floerk.
Fiske Fiord.
148. . . . . . . Another species in an imperfect state.
Fiske Fiord.

NOTE.—A full set of the above plants has been incorporated in the Herbarium Boreali-Americanum of the Philadelphia Academy of Natural Sciences.—E. D.

END OF VOL. II.

STEREOTYPED BY L. JOHNSON & CO.
PHILADELPHIA.

Physician Travelers

AN ARNO PRESS/NEW YORK TIMES COLLECTION

Abel, Clarke.
Narrative of a Journey in the Interior of China. 1818.

Bancroft, Edward.
An Essay on the Natural History of Guiana. 1769.

Bell, John.
Observations on Italy. 1825.

Brown, Edward.
Account of Some Travels. 1673-1677.

Granville, Augustus Bozzi.
St. Petersburgh: Travels to and From That Capital. 1828. (2 volumes)

Hamilton, Alexander.
Itinerarium. 1907.

Hodgkin, Thomas.
Narrative of a Journey to Morocco. 1866.

Holland, Henry.
Travels in the Ionian Isles, Albania, Thessaly, Macedonia, etc. 1815.

Holmes, Oliver Wendell.
Our Hundred Days in Europe. 1887.

Jeffries, John.
A Narrative of Two Aerial Voyages. 1786.

Kane, Elisha Kent.
Arctic Explorations in 1853, 1854, 1855. 1856. (2 volumes)

Linnaeus, Carl.
A Tour in Lapland. 1811.

Lister, Martin.
A Journey to Paris in 1698. 1698.

Park, Mungo.
Travels in the Interior Districts of Africa. 1799.

White, John.
Journal of a Voyage to New South Wales. 1790.

Wilde, William.
Lough Corrib: Its Shores and Islands. 1867.

Wittman, William.
Travels in Turkey, Asia Minor, Syria and Egypt. 1803.

Wurdeman, John G. F.
Notes on Cuba. 1844.